# 20 Retirement DECISIONS

## YOU NEED TO MAKE
## RIGHT NOW

### RAY E. LEVITRE

CERTIFIED FINANCIAL PLANNER™

sphinx
publishing

Published by Sphinx Publishing, an imprint of Sourcebooks, Inc.
P.O. Box 4410, Naperville, Illinois 60567-4410
(630) 961-3900
Fax: (630) 961-2168
www.sourcebooks.com

Library of Congress Cataloging-in-Publication data is on file with the publisher.

Printed and bound in the United States of America.
VP 10 9 8 7 6 5 4 3

To the awesome woman in my life–Erin

# CONTENTS

Warning from the Author . . . . . . . . . . . . . . . . . . . . . . . . . . . . . . . . . . . . . .vii

The 20 Financial Decisions You Must Make at Retirement . . . . . . . . xi

## SECTION 1: RETIREMENT PLANNING . . . . . . . . . . . . . . . . . . . . . . . .1

Chapter 1: Retiring Now! . . . . . . . . . . . . . . . . . . . . . . . . . . . . . . . . . . . .3

*Retirement Decision #1: Do I Have Enough Money to Retire Now?*

Chapter 2: Double Your Money . . . . . . . . . . . . . . . . . . . . . . . . . . . . . .20

*Retirement Decision #2: Is It Worthwhile to Develop a
Comprehensive Financial Plan if I'm Already Close to Retirement?*

Chapter 3: Fire Your Broker! . . . . . . . . . . . . . . . . . . . . . . . . . . . . . . . .27

*Retirement Decision #3: Who Should I Trust to Advise Me About
My Financial Future?*

Chapter 4: More Life than Money . . . . . . . . . . . . . . . . . . . . . . . . . . . .46

*Retirement Decision #4: How Much Can I Safely Withdraw from
My Portfolio?*

Chapter 5: Tapping Your IRA Early and Avoiding Penalties . . . . . . . .61

*Retirement Decision #5: If I Retire Early, Should I Withdraw
Funds from My IRA?*

## SECTION 2: SOURCES OF RETIREMENT INCOME . . . . . . . . . . . . . .73

Chapter 6: Maximize Your Social Security . . . . . . . . . . . . . . . . . . . . . .75

*Retirement Decision #6: When Should I Begin Taking
Social Security?*

Chapter 7: Maxing Your Pension . . . . . . . . . . . . . . . . . . . . . . . . . . . . .94

*Retirement Decision #7: Which Pension Payout Option Should I Choose?*

Chapter 8: Cash It, Roll It, Leave It, Roth It, Annuitize It, Stock It!  110

*Retirement Decision #8: Which Retirement Plan Distribution Option Should I Choose?*

Chapter 9: A Tax Loophole . . . . . . . . . . . . . . . . . . . . . . . . . . . . . . . 127

*Retirement Decision #8 (Continued): Which Retirement Plan Distribution Option Should I Choose–if I Have Company Stock in My 401(k)?*

## SECTION 3: DEVELOPING A SUCCESSFUL INVESTMENT STRATEGY 139

Chapter 10: Avoiding the Ten Most Common Investor Mistakes . . 141

*Retirement Decision #9: How Should I Manage My Personal Savings?*

Chapter 11: The Most Important Investment Decision You'll Make . . . . . . . . . . . . . . . . . . . . . . . . . . . . . . . . . . . . . 160

*Retirement Decision #10: How Much Should I Invest in Stocks, Bonds, and Cash?*

Chapter 12: Investment Consistency . . . . . . . . . . . . . . . . . . . . . . . . 172

*Retirement Decision #11: How Should I Diversify My Investment Portfolio?*

Chapter 13: Know Your Team . . . . . . . . . . . . . . . . . . . . . . . . . . . . . 181

*Retirement Decision #11 (Continued): How Should I Diversify My Investment Portfolio?*

Chapter 14: The Choice . . . . . . . . . . . . . . . . . . . . . . . . . . . . . . . . . . 208

*Retirement Decision #11 (Continued): How Should I Diversify My Investment Portfolio?*

Chapter 15: Divorce Your Stock . . . . . . . . . . . . . . . . . . . . . . . . . . . . 221

*Retirement Decision #12: What Should I Do if the Bulk of My Portfolio Is Invested in One or Two Stocks?*

Chapter 16: Ready…Set…Buy . . . . . . . . . . . . . . . . . . . . . . . . . . . . . 233

*Retirement Decision #13: What Criteria Should I Use to Identify the Best Investments?*

Chapter 17: Safer Ways to Own Stocks. . . . . . . . . . . . . . . . . . . . . . 252

*Retirement Decision #13 (Continued): What Criteria Should I Use
to Identify the Best Investments?*

Chapter 18: "No-Load" Means Lower Costs . . . . . . . . . . . . . . . . . . 267

*Retirement Decision #14: Should I Buy Load or No-Load Mutual
Funds, Annuities, and Life Insurance?*

Chapter 19: A Mission Statement for Your Money . . . . . . . . . . . . . . 278

*Retirement Decision #15: How Will I Manage My Portfolio
on an Ongoing Basis?*

Chapter 20: Routine Checkups. . . . . . . . . . . . . . . . . . . . . . . . . . . . . 284

*Retirement Decision #15 (Continued): How Will I Manage My
Portfolio on an Ongoing Basis?*

**SECTION 4: INSURANCE AND RETIREMENT** . . . . . . . . . . . . . . . . .297

Chapter 21: Heart Surgery Isn't Cheap . . . . . . . . . . . . . . . . . . . . . . 299

*Retirement Decision #16: How Will I Cover My Medical Expenses
During Retirement?*

Chapter 22: Toileting and Retirement. . . . . . . . . . . . . . . . . . . . . . . 313

*Retirement Decision #17: Should I Purchase Long-Term-Care
Insurance?*

Chapter 23: Please! No More Life Insurance Premiums . . . . . . . . . . 330

*Retirement Decision #18: Should I Cancel My Life Insurance
Policy Since I No Longer Need the Coverage?*

**SECTION 5: OTHER RETIREMENT CONSIDERATIONS** . . . . . . . . .337

Chapter 24: To Pay or Not to Pay . . . . . . . . . . . . . . . . . . . . . . . . . . 339

*Retirement Decision #19: Should I Pay Off My Mortgage
at Retirement?*

Chapter 25: You Can't Take It with You. . . . . . . . . . . . . . . . . . . . . . 347

*Retirement Decision #20: What Strategies Should I Use to Ensure
That My Estate Passes to My Heirs and Not to Uncle Sam?*

A Parting Thought . . . . . . . . . . . . . . . . . . . . . . . . . . . . . . . . . . . . . . 356

Notes. . . . . . . . . . . . . . . . . . . . . . . . . . . . . . . . . . . . . . . . . . . . 357

About the Author . . . . . . . . . . . . . . . . . . . . . . . . . . . . . . . . . . 370

# WARNING FROM THE AUTHOR

I f you are reading this book, you are likely retiring right now. So, congratulations are in order. CONGRATULATIONS! From now on every day is Saturday.

I have spent the past twenty years helping people successfully make the financial transition from the workforce into retirement. This book is a culmination of my experience with my clients.

During my time in the financial services industry, I have worked for some of the biggest and most well-known financial institutions in the United States. While I am grateful to each of these firms for the employment opportunities they provided, I think that their business models are severely flawed. They seem to be much more concerned with making money for themselves rather than making money for their clients. You should be aware of the conflicts of interest that exist in the financial services industry as you seek financial advice and buy financial products at retirement. Making a mistake now could negatively impact the way you live for the next thirty to forty years. Here are some words of warning and some advice to follow as you make the financial transition from the workforce into retirement.

## Warning #1: Hidden Agenda

Most people have the need for a financial advisor to help them make financial decisions at retirement. The problem with this is that most financial advisors work on commissions and have a hidden agenda to sell something. While most are well-meaning, keeping their jobs ultimately means they've got to make a commission. In their intense efforts to meet sales quotas and pay their mortgages, they wind up pitching loaded financial products (mutual funds, annuities, and life insurance) to make a quick buck. If this occurs, you will often wind up with investments and insurance that are best for your advisor and his/her firm and not necessarily what is best for you. Read Chapter 3, Fire Your Broker!, to see how to find an objective advisor who is more interested in your goals than in theirs.

## Warning #2: Expensive Products

The investment and insurance products sold by commissioned advisors are expensive. When you buy loaded (i.e., commissioned) financial products, the product sponsors simply build in additional up-front, back-end, and annual expenses so they can compensate your advisor. Since these fees are often hidden, most investors never really know what they are paying. You can read Chapter 18, "No-Load" Means Lower Costs, to learn how to avoid excessive fees.

## Warning #3: Poor Service

Because commissioned advisors are under such extreme pressure to make money for their firms, they have to keep finding new clients and selling more expensive products. This is a problem. When an advisor is focused on acquiring new clients, little time remains for existing clients. The bottom line is that most people receive poor to no service from their advisors. Unfortunately, this is accepted as the norm, thus advisors are not held to higher standards. As an investor you should know what you are paying in fees (both those seen and those hidden) and make sure your advisor is providing service equal to the fees you are paying.

## Advice

Due to the complexity of the financial world, I believe most people should hire a financial professional to help them develop a plan and make all the financial decisions outlined in this book. I also believe that investors need to be educated so they can monitor the advice they receive and hold their advisors to much higher standards. If you read this book, you'll have a good idea of the issues your advisor should be addressing, the way he/she is compensated, and the types of products and services they can offer. Armed with this information, you can make sure your advisors are working for you and not just pushing products to meet the pressures of corporate sales objectives.

To avoid the major problems in the financial services industry, I believe all investors should follow these four basic principles as they pursue financial success:

- Work with a fee-only CERTIFIED FINANCIAL PLANNER™ (CFP®) who has at least ten years of experience.
- Develop a written comprehensive financial plan, and review it with your advisor often.
- Create an investment policy statement to act as a framework for making investment decisions.
- Purchase only low-expense, no-load financial products (mutual funds, annuities, and life insurance).

The fact that you are reading this book says that you are serious about your retirement and making the right decisions with your money. Making the right decisions now will provide peace of mind and ensure financial success throughout retirement.

# THE 20 FINANCIAL DECISIONS YOU MUST MAKE AT RETIREMENT

A re you retiring now? If so, this book is for you. There are thousands of retirement planning books that focus on helping baby boomers manage their money in the years leading up to retirement. *20 Retirement Decisions You Need to Make Right Now* is the only book of its kind, written specifically for people who are retiring now.

If you are ready to leave the workforce and begin retirement, then the pressure is on to make the right choices with your retirement money. The decisions you make at this critical juncture, many of which are irrevocable, will profoundly affect your financial security and your lifestyle for the next thirty to forty years. There is much more to retiring than simply deciding what to do with the money in your 401(k). *20 Retirement Decisions You Need to Make Right Now* addresses the most significant financial decisions people must make as they transition from the workforce into retirement. Making all of these decisions is a big task, but one that is well worth it since the next thirty to forty years are riding on the decisions you make right now.

Every chapter deals with a decision you must make at retirement. My recommendation is to begin by reading Chapters 1, 2, and 3 on financial planning and choosing a financial advisor, then proceed through the rest of the chapters, reading about the topics that are the most pressing to you right now. Each chapter was written independent of the others, so it is not necessary to read the book in its chapter order. The 20 Decisions Checklist on page xiii will help you track your progress as you check off each decision you make and help ensure that nothing falls through the cracks.

## Do-It-Yourselfers and Delegators

If you are a do-it-yourselfer, you'll find all the resources necessary to develop and manage your financial plan on your own. However, I think you should seek a second opinion periodically from a financial professional who works on an hourly basis. If you are a delegator, then my advice is to use the book as you meet with your advisor to discuss each retirement decision. Being educated before you meet with your advisor will help you ask the right questions, address all the issues, and hold your advisor to higher standards.

## You Only Retire Once. Do It Right!

Each of the five sections of the book addresses various components of retirement planning. For instance, Section One: Retirement Planning will help you assess what your current retirement situation looks like and determine whether you are on track to meet your retirement goals. This section also outlines the importance of having a written, comprehensive financial plan, how to find objective financial advice, how to determine a safe portfolio withdrawal rate, and what to do if you plan to retire early.

In Section Two: Sources of Retirement Income, we'll explore the issues surrounding Social Security, teach you how to maximize your company pension benefits. This section also deals with the issues and choices facing people who, at retirement, take a distribution from an employer-sponsored retirement plan. Before making any decisions about your money, be sure to reference this section for a very detailed analysis of your retirement options.

Section Three: Developing a Successful Investment Strategy covers important investment planning techniques and will teach you how to avoid the most common investor mistakes so you can be sure not to sabotage your most important retirement income source—your investment portfolio. After all, reaching your retirement goals will depend largely on how successful you are as an investor. This section deals primarily with how to develop successful investment strategies, including asset allocation, proper portfolio diversification, choosing investments, ongoing portfolio management, how to protect principal while investing in the stock market, and how to handle company stock positions.

In Section Four: Insurance and Retirement, we'll discuss how to obtain health-care coverage during retirement, and whether you need long-term-care insurance. Without these safeguards in place, you could prematurely deplete all of your hard-earned assets. In addition, we'll figure out what to do with the life insurance policies on which you've been paying for so long. This section will teach you how to evaluate how much insurance you will need and when and how to purchase it.

Section Five: Other Retirement Considerations will help you determine what to do with your mortgage and also which estate planning documents you need to obtain.

*20 Retirement Decisions You Need to Make Right Now* explains, in basic terms, the highly complex financial concepts you need to understand to make the most critical retirement decisions. Use it as a comprehensive information source on retirement planning and successful money-management techniques. This book is an important resource that will help you build a financial strategy to guide you toward the retirement lifestyle you deserve. You only get to retire once. Do it right!

## The 20 Decisions Checklist

☐ **Decision #1:**  Do I have enough money to retire now?

☐ **Decision #2:**  Is it worthwhile to develop a comprehensive financial plan if I'm already close to retirement?

☐ **Decision #3:**  Who should I trust to advise me about my financial future?

☐ **Decision #4:**  How much can I safely withdraw from my portfolio?

☐ **Decision #5:**  If I retire early, should I withdraw funds from my IRA?

☐ **Decision #6:**  When should I begin taking Social Security?

☐ **Decision #7:**  Which pension payout option should I choose?

☐ **Decision #8:**  Which retirement plan distribution option should I choose?

☐ **Decision #9:**  How should I manage my personal savings?

☐ **Decision #10:**  How much should I invest in stocks, bonds, and cash?

☐ **Decision #11:**  How should I diversify my investment portfolio?

☐ **Decision #12:**  What should I do if the bulk of my portfolio is invested in one or two stocks?

☐ **Decision #13:**  What criteria should I use to identify the best investments?

☐ **Decision #14:**  Should I buy load or no-load mutual funds, annuities, and life insurance?

☐ **Decision #15:**  How will I manage my portfolio on an ongoing basis?

☐ **Decision #16:** How will I cover my medical expenses during retirement?

☐ **Decision #17:** Should I buy long-term-care insurance?

☐ **Decision #18:** Should I cancel my life insurance policy since I no longer need the coverage?

☐ **Decision #19:** Should I pay off my mortgage at retirement?

☐ **Decision #20:** What strategies should I use to ensure that my estate passes to my heirs and not to Uncle Sam?

# SECTION 1

## RETIREMENT PLANNING

# 1

# RETIRING NOW!

## RETIREMENT DECISION #1: DO I HAVE ENOUGH MONEY TO RETIRE NOW?

A re you ready for the time when every day is a Saturday? When it comes to retirement planning, too many people face a reality gap. Fifty-two percent of American retirees are confident that they will have enough money to live comfortably throughout retirement.[1] That same survey revealed that two out of three retirees have less than $50,000 total in savings and investments.[2] A $50,000

> America fails the Retirement IQ Test, with an average score of 33 percent.[3]

nest egg is barely enough to produce $200 income per month during retirement. Many studies indicate that middle-income baby boomers will need much more than $1 million in their investment accounts the day they retire.

Where do you stand? Are you overconfident that you will reach your retirement goals?

  Brokerage Accounts
+ IRA Accounts
+ 401(k)s
+ Insurance Cash Value
+ Annuities
+ Savings Bonds
+ Bank Accounts
+ Other Investments
_____

      ???

*figure 1.1*

When you add up all your financial assets on the first day of retirement (Figure 1.1), what will your portfolio need to total in order for you to reach your retirement goals? How far are you from that goal? You need to take a good hard look at your overall retirement situation to answer these questions and to ensure that your savings nest egg will generate enough retirement income to last for decades.

Of course, the amount needed at retirement differs for everyone and ultimately hinges on your answers to the following questions:

- When will you retire?
- What is your current income?
- What percentage of your current income will you need each year during retirement?
- How long do you estimate you will be in retirement?
- What will your income sources be during retirement?
- What will be the rate of return on your investment assets during retirement?
- What impact will inflation have on your retirement goals?

The best way to see if you're on track is to submit yourself to a retirement analysis. Don't worry, it's not that painful. I'll walk you through each step. To develop a retirement analysis, you will need to take the following nine-question quiz. Once you've completed the questions, I'll refer you to some online retirement calculators. We'll simply plug in some numbers and you'll see where you stand. Friends of mine, Ron and Linda Hansen, have already taken the quiz. To help spark your thinking as you evaluate your own situation, I've included the Hansens' answers as a case study. I'll also discuss each question to ensure you consider the right factors in your answer. Let's get started.

## 1. When do you plan on retiring?

If you are reading this book, you are probably planning to retire soon. The average American retires at age 62.[4]

The amount of money you will need to accumulate will depend on your age at retirement. An early retirement will require that you have a larger nest egg since you'll have to stretch your resources over more years. Pushing retirement back a few years will allow you to delay the time when you'll need to start withdrawing money from your investment portfolio. The longer you work, the longer your nest egg will likely last.

Question #1: When do you plan on retiring?
*Your Answer:* _____
*Case Study:* Ron and Linda Hansen, age 60, plan on retiring this year.

## 2. How much annual income will you need during retirement?

Financial planners suggest you'll need to have about 80 to 90 percent of your preretirement gross income to maintain your current standard of living. This, of course, can vary widely depending on your lifestyle. The average 55- to 64-year-old American has annual expenses of $55,486 while the average 65- to 74-year-old has $44,096 in annual expenses. This is a 20 percent decrease.[5]

During retirement you will pay less taxes, save less,

> Less than one-half of workers (44 percent) have tried to calculate how much money they need to accumulate for retirement.[6]

spend less on your children, and have less of a mortgage burden than you did while working. While many expenses will decrease during retirement, others will increase. Figure 1.2 outlines some of the most common changes in spending during retirement.

| Expenses Likely to Decrease | Expenses Likely to Increase |
|---|---|
| • Home Mortgage | • Health Care |
| • Savings | • Travel |
| • Income Taxes | • Second Home |
| • Work-Related Clothing | • Personal Education |
| • Life Insurance | • Hobbies/Recreation |
| • Commuting | |
| • Professional Education | |

figure 1.2

The way you decide to spend your retirement years will have an impact on how much income you will need. Have you thought about what you want to do during retirement? Figure 1.3 reflects the most common desires of retirees.

Moving to another city will also greatly affect your income needs. According to AARP, only one in ten Americans age 60 or older actually chooses to relocate during retirement.[7] However, if you do plan to move to another city, you must adjust your estimated retirement spending depending on the cost-of-living differences from region to region. A cost-of-living calculator is an easy way to see how your new home will affect your living expenses.

| What Americans Are Thinking About as They Prepare to Retire | |
|---|---|
| Staying healthy | 53% |
| Spending time with family | 40% |
| Traveling | 26% |
| Deciding where to live | 24% |
| Resting and relaxing | 24% |
| Pursuing hobbies | 21% |
| Doing meaningful work | 21% |
| Volunteering | 16% |
| Continuing education | 11% |

Source: Ameriprise, New Retirement Mindscape, 2012 City Pulse Index

figure 1.3

**Moving at Retirement: Cost-of-Living Calculator**

- Bankrate.com—www.bankrate.com /calculators/savings/moving-cost-of -living-calculator.aspx
- CNNMoney.com—http://cgi.money.cnn .com/tools/costofliving/costofliving.html

Use the worksheet in Figure 1.4 to help you get down to the nitty-gritty of your annual retirement costs. The more you detail your spending habits, the more accurate your retirement picture will be. Figure 1.4 shows a list of annual expenditures for the average American couple between the ages of 65 and 74. How your expenses match up to these average figures depends on your lifestyle.

In the column titled "Your Budget Now," estimate your current annual expenses. To make it easier, take your monthly expenses and multiply by 12. Then in the last column, "Your Budget at Retirement," estimate what these costs would be if you were to retire today. This figure is your yearly retirement income need.

Question #2: How much annual income will you need during retirement?
*Your Answer:* _____
*Case Study:* The Hansens have set their retirement income goal at $75,000 per year (in today's dollars).

| Annual Retirement Expenses | | | |
|---|---|---|---|
| | Average Budget for Couples 65 to 74 | Your Budget Now | Your Budget at Retirement |
| Housing | $11,323 | | |
| Transportation | $6,962 | | |
| Food | $5,804 | | |
| Health Care | $5,038 | | |
| Utilities | $3,782 | | |
| Taxes | $1,360 | | |
| Insurance | $2,957 | | |
| Contributions | $2,526 | | |
| Entertainment | $2,493 | | |
| Personal Care | $609 | | |
| Clothing | $1,195 | | |
| Miscellaneous | $1,535 | | |
| Total Spending | $45,584 | | |

*Source: Consumer Expenditure Survey, 2011*

figure 1.4

## 3. How many years will you spend in retirement?

Most financial planners assume people will live until about age 85. This assumption is based on average life expectancies (Figure 1.5). For example, a man who reaches age 65 can expect to live another seventeen years, or to age 82, while a 65-year-old woman can expect to reach 85.

In one aspect it is good news that we are living longer. Because of advances in science, medicine, and nutrition, we're aging slower. There are twice as many people over the age of 100 today–79,000–than there were just a decade ago. By 2055, it's estimated that more than 500,000 people in the United States will be older than 100.

On the other hand, longer life expectancies present a dilemma in developing your retirement plan. Let's assume you and your spouse are planning to retire at age 65. If you presume that you will live for thirty-five years, until 100, you may have to settle on a dramatically reduced level of income to make your nest egg stretch for so many years. However, if you assume you will live to age 85, as mortality tables suggest, and you or your spouse do live to age 100, you run the risk of outliving your money. In fact, some people will spend more years in retirement than they did in the

| Life Expectancy | | | |
|---|---|---|---|
| Male | | Female | |
| Age | Life Expectancy | Age | Life Expectancy |
| 50 | 29 | 50 | 33 |
| 55 | 25 | 55 | 28 |
| 60 | 21 | 60 | 24 |
| 65 | 17 | 65 | 20 |
| 70 | 14 | 70 | 16 |
| 75 | 11 | 75 | 13 |
| 80 | 8 | 80 | 10 |
| 85 | 6 | 85 | 7 |
| 90 | 4 | 90 | 5 |
| 95 | 3 | 95 | 3 |
| 100 | 2 | 100 | 2 |

Source: ssa.gov, Period Life Table, 2007

figure 1.5

labor force. Consider the example of Anne Scheiber. Anne retired from her $3,150-per-year IRS auditor job in 1943 at age 49 and passed away in 1995 at the age of 101. She spent more than fifty years in retirement.[8]

So how do you plan to optimize your chances of making your money last? Much like the investment decisions you have made, you must decide if you want to be a little more aggressive or a little more conservative in your planning. It is better to err on the conservative side. This can best be accomplished by adding at least five years to the life expectancy figures in Figure 1.5. For example, a married couple retiring this year, both age 65, should plan to be in retirement for twenty-five years (twenty years in the table, plus five) or until they reach age 90.

Question #3: How many years will you spend in retirement?
*Your Answer:* _____
*Case Study:* Ron and Linda, both age 60, have decided to be even more conservative. They're both in good shape and members in both of their families tend to live long. They are adding ten years to their life expectancy figures and are planning for thirty-two years in retirement.

## 4. How much income will you receive annually during retirement?

Now, we need to take an inventory of your retirement income sources. List your retirement income in Figure 1.6. Will any of your sources of income be adjusted each year for inflation? For example, Social Security has a cost-of-living adjustment (see Figure 6.9). Your company pension may or may not adjust annually for inflation. If you own rental property, most likely you will increase the rent periodically to keep pace with inflation. This is an important element to factor into your retirement planning. You may also have other forms of income such as payments being received due to selling your business or a loan being repaid to you, etc. For this exercise, exclude any income you'll earn from your investment portfolio (non-real-estate investments).

> More than half of American employees (70 percent) think they will be forced to work during retirement. In 2010, only 27 percent of retirees actually worked at some time.[9]

Question #4: How much income will you receive annually during retirement?
*Your Answer:* _____
(Complete the worksheet in Figure 1.6 to total your anticipated retirement income sources. Also estimate how much the income source will increase each year during retirement.)
*Case Study:* The Hansens are anticipating retirement income of $30,000 from Social Security and $5,000 from Ron's pension each year.

| Sources of Income Worksheet | | |
|---|---|---|
| **Annual Income Sources** | **$** | **Annual % Increase** |
| Your Social Security | | |
| Your spouse's Social Security | | |
| Your pension | | |
| Your spouse's pension | | |
| Rental income | | |
| Income from continued work | | |
| Other income | | |
| Other income | | |
| Total (excluding investments) | | |

*figure 1.6*

## 5. What inflation rate are you going to use in your planning?

Inflation is a measure of the annual increase in the costs of goods and services you buy. It's an unavoidable fact that the price of things you need in life will increase over time. During the past one hundred years, inflation has averaged about 3 percent per year, as it has since 1990 (Figure 1.7). However, during the past forty years, inflation has averaged a little over 4 percent. The U.S. economy experienced double-digit inflation during the period from 1977 to 1981, when inflation averaged a whopping 10 percent.[10]

If you fail to factor inflation into your retirement planning, you'll find prices rising while your income remains level, and eventually you'll be forced to lower your standard of living or deplete your assets. A fixed income in a rising-cost world is slow financial suicide. In Figure 1.8, you can see how the average costs of various products and services have increased over time and what they could cost in the future if they continue on the same inflationary course.

Of course, you don't know what the inflation rate will be during your retirement, so you must make assumptions. Here again, you have a choice between aggressive planning, in which you optimistically assume a lower inflation rate than the average, or more conservative planning, using a higher inflation rate assumption. Most financial planners assume a 3 to 4 percent rate in their planning.

| Inflation Since 1990 | | | |
|---|---|---|---|
| 1990 | 6.1% | 2002 | 2.4% |
| 1991 | 3.1% | 2003 | 1.9% |
| 1992 | 2.9% | 2004 | 3.3% |
| 1993 | 2.7% | 2005 | 3.4% |
| 1994 | 2.7% | 2006 | 2.5% |
| 1995 | 2.5% | 2007 | 4.1% |
| 1996 | 3.3% | 2008 | 0.1% |
| 1997 | 1.7% | 2009 | 2.7% |
| 1998 | 1.6% | 2010 | 1.5% |
| 1999 | 2.7% | 2011 | 3.0% |
| 2000 | 3.4% | 2012 | 1.8% |
| 2001 | 1.6% | Average | 2.7% |

Source: Consumer Price Index

figure 1.7

| Cost-of-Living Comparison (1900–2010) | | | | | | | |
|---|---|---|---|---|---|---|---|
| **Year** | **House** | **Car** | **Milk** | **Gas** | **Bread** | **Postage** | **Income** |
| 1900 | $4,000 | N/A | $0.30 | $0.05 | $0.03 | $0.02 | $637 |
| 1910 | $4,800 | N/A | $0.33 | $0.07 | $0.05 | $0.02 | $963 |
| 1920 | $6,396 | $500 | $0.58 | $0.10 | $0.11 | $0.02 | $1,179 |
| 1930 | $7,146 | $525 | $0.56 | $0.10 | $0.08 | $0.02 | $1,428 |
| 1940 | $6,558 | $810 | $0.51 | $0.15 | $0.08 | $0.03 | $1,231 |
| 1950 | $14,500 | $1,750 | $0.82 | $0.20 | $0.14 | $0.03 | $3,216 |
| 1960 | $30,000 | $2,275 | $1.04 | $0.25 | $0.20 | $0.04 | $5,199 |
| 1970 | $40,000 | $2,500 | $1.32 | $0.40 | $0.24 | $0.06 | $8,933 |
| 1980 | $86,159 | $5,412 | $1.60 | $1.03 | $0.51 | $0.15 | $11,321 |
| 1990 | $128,732 | $9,437 | $2.15 | $1.08 | $0.69 | $0.25 | $14,777 |
| 2000 | $205,000 | $17,700 | $3.35 | $1.51 | $0.93 | $0.34 | $21,950 |
| 2010 | $268,700 | $29,217 | $2.79 | $2.73 | $2.49 | $0.44 | $39,856 |
| **Average** | House | Car | Milk | Gas | Bread | Postage | Income |
| **Inflation** | 3.89% | 4.62% | 2.04% | 3.70% | 4.10% | 2.85% | 3.83% |
| *Where Prices Are Headed (if Past Inflation Repeats Itself)* | | | | | | | |
| **Year** | **House** | **Car** | **Milk** | **Gas** | **Bread** | **Postage** | **Income** |
| 2020 | $393,555 | $45,896 | $3.41 | $3.92 | $3.72 | $0.58 | $58,039 |
| 2030 | $576,425 | $72,099 | $4.18 | $5.56 | $5.56 | $0.77 | $84,518 |
| 2040 | $844,267 | $113,260 | $5.11 | $8.12 | $8.12 | $1.02 | $123,077 |

figure 1.8

If inflation remains at 3 percent during your retirement, you will need to increase your income by 3 percent each year to buy the same amount of goods and services you purchased the previous year to maintain your standard of living. Essentially, you should give yourself a 3 percent raise each year by withdrawing more money from your investments. For example, if you need $75,000 in the first year of retirement, you will need $77,250 the second year, $79,568 the third year, and so forth to maintain your purchasing power. At this rate, in the twentieth year of retirement, you will need $131,513 to purchase the same items that can be bought with $75,000 today. Figure 1.9 shows the impact of inflation during retirement.

Because of inflation, your investment portfolio must be structured to provide you with a rising income stream during retirement. This is especially critical if your pension or other sources of retirement income don't have built-in cost-of-living adjustments.

Question #5: What inflation rate are you going to use in your planning?
*Your Answer:* _____
*Case Study:* Ron and Linda are using a 3 percent rate.

| Equivalent of $75,000 Today (Assuming 3% Annual Inflation) | |
| --- | --- |
| Year | Amount Needed |
| 1 | $75,000 |
| 2 | $77,250 |
| 3 | $79,568 |
| 4 | $81,955 |
| 5 | $84,413 |
| 6 | $86,946 |
| 7 | $89,554 |
| 8 | $92,241 |
| 9 | $95,008 |
| 10 | $97,858 |
| 11 | $100,794 |
| 12 | $103,818 |
| 13 | $106,932 |
| 14 | $110,140 |
| 15 | $113,444 |
| 16 | $116,848 |
| 17 | $120,353 |
| 18 | $123,964 |
| 19 | $127,682 |
| 20 | $131,513 |

*figure 1.9*

## 6. How much money have you accumulated? Are you on track?

Do you currently have enough money set aside to be on track to reach your retirement goals? The chart in Figure 1.10 will tell you if you are in the ballpark. Simply multiply your current annual income by the factor that best represents your investment strategy.

For example, if you are a moderate investor making $100,000 per year and planning to retire in five years, you should have $773,000 already accumulated in your various investment accounts (7.73 multiplied by $100,000) to maintain your preretirement standard of living during retirement. This assumes you will spend twenty-five years in retirement, save 8 percent of your income each year prior to retirement, reduce your exposure to equities at retirement, experience 4 percent inflation, and exhaust all of your savings during retirement. (Figure 1.10 does not take Social Security or pensions into account.)

Alternatively, if you're an aggressive investor planning to retire in ten years and currently have a $50,000-per-year income, you would need to have accumulated $231,500 by now to be on track, using the same assumptions.

In Figure 1.10, the thing that determines whether you are an aggressive, moderate, or conservative investor is the amount of your portfolio invested in stocks and bonds. A portfolio consisting of 80 percent stocks and 20 percent bonds before retirement and 65 percent stocks and 35 percent bonds after retirement is considered aggressive. Moderate investors are those with 65 percent of their portfolios invested in stocks and 35 percent in bonds before retirement and 50 percent stocks and 50 percent bonds after retirement. Those investors who maintain a portfolio of 50 percent stocks and 50 percent bonds before retirement and only 35 percent stocks and 65 percent bonds after retirement are labeled conservative.

| Are You on Track? | | | |
|---|---|---|---|
| Years to Retirement | Aggressive Investor | Moderate Investor | Conservative Investor |
| 0 | 9.57 | 10.46 | 11.48 |
| 5 | 6.75 | 7.73 | 8.90 |
| 10 | 4.63 | 5.58 | 6.76 |
| 15 | 3.07 | 3.93 | 5.05 |
| 20 | 1.93 | 2.68 | 3.69 |
| 25 | 1.09 | 1.72 | 2.61 |
| 30 | 0.48 | 0.98 | 1.74 |
| 35 | 0.03 | 0.42 | 1.05 |

*Source: Wall Street Journal*

figure 1.10

If you are not on track, there is still hope; however, it may require you to make some sacrifices. Possible solutions include: saving more, living on less, and/or working longer. You could also add your home equity into your retirement nest egg. This would assume that you are willing to consume the equity in your home at some point during retirement. Typically you would tap home equity only if you completely run out of investment assets. Pulling the equity from your home could be accomplished by downsizing, using a home equity line, or obtaining a reverse mortgage.

Take an inventory of all your investments and complete the worksheet in Figure 1.11. (You'll also need this information for Question 7.) This will help you see how you are tracking toward reaching your retirement goals.

| My Portfolio Allocation | | |
|---|---|---|
| **Retirement Accounts: IRAs, 401(k)s, Profit-Sharing Plans, etc.** | | |
| Stocks or stock mutual funds | $ | |
| Bonds or bond mutual funds | $ | |
| Cash equivalents | $ | |
| **Non-Retirement Accounts** | | |
| Stocks or stock mutual funds | $ | |
| Bonds or bond mutual funds | $ | |
| Cash equivalents | $ | |
| **Total Investment Assets** | | |
| Stocks or stock mutual funds | $ | % |
| Bonds or bond mutual funds | $ | % |
| Cash equivalents | $ | % |
| Total | $ | 100 % |

figure 1.11

Question #6: How much money have you accumulated?
*Your Answer:* _____
(Use the chart in Figure 1.10 to see if you are on track to reach your retirement goals.)
*Case Study:* The Hansens earn $100,000 per year, are retiring this year, and are moderate investors. They are in the ballpark, having already accumulated $1.2 million in assets ($100,000 multiplied by 10.46 equals $1,046.000).

## 7. At what rate do you expect your investment portfolio to grow?

You now know how much your portfolio is worth and you've broken it down into asset classes. But how do you know if it's enough money to last you? To determine if you are on track to reach your retirement goal, we can forecast a reasonable rate of return you can expect to achieve between now and retirement, and your return once you are in retirement. In Chapter 13 we will examine, in more detail, the expected growth rates of various investment portfolios.

For our purposes here, let's keep it simple: since 1926, stocks have averaged a 9.84 percent rate of return; bonds, 5.70 percent; and Treasury bills (cash equivalents), 3.54 percent.

Figure 1.12 illustrates how different mixes of stocks, bonds, and cash performed, on average, from 1926 through 2012. Find the portfolio most resembling your own now. What is its expected rate of return?

What will your investment returns be during retirement? Most investors reposition some assets from stocks into bonds and cash during retirement to reduce their risk. This also reduces returns. I recommend that you remain conservative in your planning and assume a rate of return no higher than 6 percent per year during retirement.

| Asset Allocation Annual Returns 1926–2012 | |
| --- | --- |
| Stocks/Bonds/ Cash % | Average Annual Return |
| 100/0/0 | 9.84% |
| 90/0/10 | 9.40% |
| 80/10/10 | 9.17% |
| 70/20/10 | 8.88% |
| 60/30/10 | 8.54% |
| 50/40/10 | 8.15% |
| 40/50/10 | 7.72% |
| 30/60/10 | 7.24% |
| 20/70/10 | 6.71% |
| 10/80/10 | 6.14% |
| 0/100/0 | 5.70% |
| 0/0/100 | 3.54% |

*figure 1.12*

Question #7: At what rate do you expect your investment portfolio to grow?
*Your Answer:*
Before retirement: _____
After retirement: _____
*Case Study:* To be conservative, Ron and Linda expect their portfolio to grow at a rate of 6 percent during retirement.

## 8. What is your annual savings rate?

If you are still a year or two from retirement, you should be saving no less than 10 percent of your gross income; if married, you and your spouse should save 10 percent of your combined income. In most cases, you should work toward saving 15 percent. To accomplish this goal, work to control your expenses and strive to live within your means. The bestselling book *The Millionaire Next Door* outlines characteristics of America's millionaires. The book's authors, Thomas

The personal savings rate in 1984 was 11 percent. In 2005, the savings rate fell to 2 percent, its lowest point since the 1930s. Today, the rate hovers around 4 percent.[11]

Stanley and William Danko, conclude that the reason most millionaires accumulated so much wealth was due to their high savings rate and ability to live within their means.

To be a good saver, you need discipline and consistency. The best way to do this is to set up a systematic savings plan and have money drawn directly out of your bank account or paycheck and deposited into an investment account at least monthly.

Only 59 percent of American workers are saving money for their retirement.[12]

Here's a simple rule: If you can't get your hands on it, you won't spend it. That's why company-sponsored retirement plans work so well. The money is invested even before you receive your paycheck.

Question #8: What is your annual savings rate?
*Your Answer:* _____
*Case Study:* Ron and Linda have been consistently saving 10 percent of their income.

## 9. How much do you want to leave to family or charity?

It's natural to want to leave an estate to your heirs or to an organization or cause about which you care deeply. Be sure to incorporate this into your retirement planning. Determine how much you wish to leave; this is the amount of your financial portfolio you will not spend during retirement.

Question #9: How much do you want to leave to family or charity?
*Your Answer:* _____
*Case Study:* Ron and Linda have decided that their children will receive whatever is remaining in their estate at death. However, they are not planning to leave them a specific amount of money.

## Case Study Results: Are Ron and Linda Hansen on track to reach their retirement goals?

To answer this question, the Hansens visited www.fidelity.com, one of many places to find an online retirement calculator (page 18), and plugged in the following assumptions:

- Ron and Linda, both 60, are planning to retire this year.
- They need $75,000 per year of retirement income (in today's dollars).
- They will need this income until Linda reaches age 92 (thirty-two years of retirement).
- They are expecting income from various sources to provide them with $35,000 per year.
- They have accumulated a $1.2 million investment portfolio made up of 50 percent stocks, 50 percent bonds.
- They have been saving $10,000 per year (10 percent of their income).
- They've assumed an inflation rate of 3 percent per year and are anticipating their investments will experience a 6 percent growth rate during retirement.

Based on these figures and assumptions, Ron and Linda are on track to reach their goal of retiring this year. If they can obtain a 7 percent rate of return on their investment portfolio, they could increase their annual spending up to $80,000. The Hansens passed the retirement quiz with flying colors.

## *Your Results: Are you on track to reach your retirement goals?*

Question #1: When do you plan to retire?

Question #2: How much annual income will you need during retirement?

Question #3: How many years will you spend in retirement?

Question #4: How much income will you receive annually during retirement?

Question #5: What inflation rate are you going to use in your planning?

Question #6: How much money have you accumulated?

Question #7: At what rate do you expect your investment portfolio to grow?

Before retirement: _____%

After retirement: _____%

Question #8: What is your annual savings rate?

Question #9: How much do you want to leave to family or charity?

Now you have all the information you need to determine if you're on track to reach your retirement goals. There are a couple of ways to crunch the numbers.

The first involves simple linear equations in which you assume a constant rate of return on your investments during retirement (this was used in the Hansen case study). This approach is easy and works well, as long as you assume a conservative rate of return and you still have ten or more years until retirement. If you are investing for the long term, chances are you will enjoy a rate of return that is close to the long-term averages. Most web calculators use this approach.

> **Find It on the Web**
>
> - KJE Computer Solutions:
>   www.javacalc.com
> - American Funds:
>   www.americanfunds.com
> - MSN Money:
>   www.moneycentral.msn.com
> - Vanguard Funds:
>   www.vanguard.com
> - Yahoo Finance:
>   www.finance.yahoo.com

The second is a little more complex. It involves probability calculations to determine the chances of reaching your goals, given the fact that rates of return will fluctuate from year to year during retirement. This approach is referred to as Monte Carlo analysis (see Chapter 3). It is more helpful to those on the verge of retirement and those already retired. If you fall into this category, you do not have as many years to invest and your retirement savings would be devastated by an unexpected and extended market downturn. Monte Carlo analysis can account for the unexpected and will provide a more accurate view of whether you are on track to meet your retirement goals. Monte Carlo analysis will also help you determine how much you can withdraw from your investments during retirement without running the risk of depleting your assets.

Most financial advisors have access to planning tools and software that can take into account the many variables that will change during retirement. These factors can include a spouse who plans to work several years after you retire, changes in tax rates, the impact of inflation on some income sources, and different interest-rate assumptions for each of your investment assets.

If you have a large asset base or if your financial situation is more complex, it is highly recommended that you seek the counsel of a professional financial advisor to develop a retirement analysis. Otherwise, you can simply use one of the many retirement calculators on the Internet. Whether you decide to work with a financial advisor or develop a retirement plan on your own, you will need the answers to the questions asked in this chapter to complete your retirement analysis. Surprisingly, just a little under half of American workers have ever tried to figure out how much they need to save and accumulate for retirement.[13] Put yourself ahead of the crowd by visiting one of the websites listed in this chapter and determine if you are on track to reach your goal of never-ending Saturdays.

**Find It on the Web**

- Fidelity Investments: www.fidelity.com
- T. Rowe Price: www.troweprice.com

Now back to the burning question: Are you on track to reach your retirement goals? Hopefully, the answer is "Yes!" If not, don't panic. You just may need to save more money each year or adjust your investment portfolio to obtain better returns. If you have a lot of catching up to do, you might have to work longer before you can retire, or retire with less than you had originally planned. But at least you now know where you stand and you can plan accordingly.

If you are ahead of the game and don't need to seek a high rate of return, you may want to reposition your investments more conservatively. Why take additional and unnecessary risk if you are able to reach and exceed your goals without that risk?

Remember that retirement planning is not a one-time event. You should update and review your retirement analysis yearly at the least.

# 2

# DOUBLE YOUR MONEY

Want to double your money? Would you like a $1 million retirement portfolio instead of one with $500,000? What if I told you it's easy? Studies indicate that people with financial plans have more than twice as much money in savings and investments as those without plans. Imagine that: the mere act of developing a plan and updating it regularly could put more than twice as much money in your pocket.[1] Of course, developing a financial plan won't magically double your money overnight. A plan is nothing more than a road map that guides your financial decisions, motivates you to push a little harder to achieve your goals, and acts as a yardstick to measure your progress. Without a map, it can be very easy to start down the wrong path and never arrive at your desired destination.

> Only three out of ten families have a comprehensive financial plan.[2]

## Goal Setting

Financial planning is nothing more than goal setting. You determine where you are now and where you want to be in the future. You then spell out a specific course of action to get you from point A to point B. It's no secret that setting goals will increase your chances of accomplishing them. Committing your goals to writing will further increase your chances. Setting up a plan to reach your goals and reviewing your progress regularly will again boost the odds of success. By going a step further and regularly reviewing your goals with someone else (a coach, a trainer, a teacher, an advisor), your success is all but guaranteed. In the following example, who do you think is most likely to accomplish the goal of losing weight?

- The person who wants to lose weight (a goal)
- The person who wants to lose weight (goal) and writes down their goal (written goal)
- The person who wants to lose weight (goal), writes down their goal (written goal), and outlines a plan for achieving it (written goal with an action plan)
- The person who wants to lose weight (goal), writes down their goal (written goal), outlines a plan for achieving the goal (written goal with an action plan), and reviews it regularly (goal reviews)
- The person who wants to lose weight (goal), writes down their goal (written goal), hires a personal trainer to help outline a specific fitness and diet plan for achieving the goal (written goal with an action plan), and meets the personal trainer at the gym three days a week to weigh in and work out (goal reviews with accountability)

The answer is obvious. Which person most resembles your approach to accomplishing your financial goals? Needless to say, the last person is at least a hundred times more likely to accomplish the goal than the first.

These same rules apply to financial planning. According to a worldwide study released by HSBC, people (all ages) with financial plans reported having more than twice as much money in savings and investments as those without plans.[3] The study went on to show that people with financial plans who also receive financial advice from a financial advisor had four times as much money.

Another study of people in the United States over age 50 revealed similar results. It was discovered that the net worth of nonplanners was $122,000 while those with plans were worth $410,000, over three

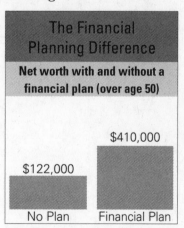

The Financial Planning Difference

**Net worth with and without a financial plan (over age 50)**

$410,000

$122,000

No Plan        Financial Plan

*Source: Financial Literacy: Implications for Retirement Security and the Financial Marketplace, January 2012*

figure 2.1

times more (Figure 2.1).[4] At least part of the explanation for why investors with plans have so much more money than those without has to do with the higher savings rate of those with plans. Fifty percent of those with plans report saving 10 percent or more of their gross income while only 27 percent of the nonplan group save 10 percent or more.[5]

To illustrate how a "map" can help you reach your destination, see how you do in the following exercise. The goal of this exercise is to spot as many numbers as you can in the allotted time. Take a look at the random numbers placed from 1 to 100 in Figure 2.2. Time yourself for thirty seconds and see how many numbers you can find in succession, beginning with the number 1, moving on to 2, then 3, and so on.

Start timing yourself now…and go!

```
        48              80          97      61
96          76      92      24  41      1       37      57
    28          20      68                  73      21  49
        64  4       44      56      13  33      5   69      85
    84          88      16              89          25
        12      8       36  81      53      17
    40      72      32          29          9       45      77
        52          100     60      65          93
        87          51              74          98
3           19  47      23          30      38  62      50
        99      75          31  54      2       14  86
    67      55      7   79          90      6           22
        27      59                          94
    43          11  15      35      18  58  10      66  46
71          39      83          42      26      34
        95      63      91          70      82      78
```

figure 2.2

How far did you get? Remember your score.

Now, we're going to try the exercise again, with a "map" to guide you to see if you can improve upon your first score. The strategy is simple: In Figure 2.3, a line has been placed down the center and across the middle of the chart, dividing it into four quadrants. The number 1 is located in the top right quadrant. The number 2 is in the bottom right quadrant. Number 3 is in the bottom left, and number 4 is in the top left. The numbers are sequentially located clockwise, moving from quadrant to quadrant.

Now, time yourself for another thirty seconds to see if you can beat your first score.

```
        48              80   |    97      61
96            76    92     24 | 41     1      37      57
    28            20    68    |            73      21 49
        64  4     44      56  | 13 33      5  69        85
    84            88    16    |            89         25
        12     8         36   | 81     53      17
    40        72     32       | 29          9      45      77
        52        100     60  | 65            93
-----------------------------------------------------------
        87        51         |        74         98
3            19 47     23    |     30       38 62      50
        99     75        31  | 54     2          14 86
    67        55     7  79    |     90       6            22
        27     59            |               94
    43           11 15    35 |     18 58 10      66 46
71           39     83       | 42       26      34
        95     63     91     |     70       82      78
```

figure 2.3

You improved, didn't you?

In many cases, people find they can double their score in the second exercise, and it's all because they have a map spelling out exactly how to get from point A to point B. In the same way, having a financial strategy will dramatically help you improve your financial situation.

Surprisingly, despite all the evidence, only one of four savers has a plan to guide his or her financial decisions. You would do well to be part of that savvy one-fourth.

# Developing a Plan: The Best Time to Start Is Now

Regardless of whether you are retiring soon, changing jobs, or simply look-ing toward your future, now is a good time to develop a comprehensive financial plan that addresses every component of your financial portfolio. These components include:

- Retirement
- Investments
- Taxes
- Liabilities
- Budgeting
- Insurance
- Asset Protection
- Estate Protection
- Children's Education
- Long-Term Care

A comprehensive financial plan will help you establish goals in each of these areas and outline strategies for accomplishing each of them.

To develop a financial plan, begin by taking inventory of your current financial portfolio. Include the details of all your assets and liabilities. Then think about your financial goals and write them down. You can purchase software or use web calculators that will provide you with some compo-nents of a comprehensive financial plan. Be aware, however, that these do-it-yourself programs, in most cases, will fall short of completely meeting your needs. While many programs will crunch the numbers for you and spit out endless pages of analysis, they often don't outline specific strategies, make specific recommendations, or help you implement your plan. These are the most important components of the planning process. For example, your plan may conclude that "You need to save an extra $200 per month to reach your retirement goals." While this recommendation is helpful, there is much more to it. A good financial advisor who understands all aspects of planning will prove invaluable when it comes to the specifics of imple-menting your strategy. For instance, a good advisor may add the following specifics to the recommendation to increase your retirement savings and provide you with the applications necessary to put it all in motion:

*Recommendations*

1.   Cut $200 out of your monthly dining and entertainment budget to squeeze out an extra $200 per month to meet your savings goal.
2.   Open a Roth IRA at a discount brokerage firm like Fidelity or Charles Schwab.
3.   Purchase the Vanguard 500 Index mutual fund in your Roth IRA.
4.   Link your bank account to your Roth IRA and have $200 automatically withdrawn each month to fund your Roth.
5.   After building a $3,000 position in the Vanguard 500 Index Fund, redirect your monthly investment into the Dreyfus Mid Cap Index Fund until the balance reaches $2,000. As time goes on, add a small-cap fund, an international fund, and a bond fund.

While a do-it-yourself software package is a good starting point for a less sophisticated financial situation, in most cases you should seek the assistance of an experienced financial advisor.

Most people will have more success in achieving their financial goals by hiring a financial planner to help them than by going it alone. As you'll find, setting your financial goals and developing a written plan for accomplishing them is the easy part. The hard part is having the discipline to stick to the plan, and this is where a good advisor will be a tremendous help.

But don't rush to hire the first financial planner who offers their services. Financial advisors love to talk about the importance of developing a comprehensive financial plan. Be careful: some advisors use financial plans for the sole purpose of pushing specific products (often insurance). In these cases, once the plan is complete, products sold, and the commission has been paid, clients are often neglected and the plan is never again reviewed. This type of "once-and-done" financial planning is a waste of your time and money. Financial planning is an ongoing process. If an advisor has no system in place to regularly review your finances and can't give objective advice because of the way he or she is compensated, *hire someone else!* To find a good financial advisor, follow the seven steps outlined in detail in Chapter 3.

> Fifty-three percent of consumers with a written plan used some type of financial professional for its preparation.[6]

Do you think the odds of accomplishing your goals would increase if you met with your financial advisor and did the following?

- Analyzed your current financial status.
- Outlined clear and precise short-term and long-term financial goals (set goals).
- Developed a written financial plan (written goals).
- Outlined a specific plan for accomplishing each goal (action plan).
- Implemented the plan by completing each action step (begin taking immediate action).
- Received a call from your advisor every six months to meet, update your plan, review your progress, and continue to check off items on the action plan (goal reviews with accountability).

While statistics make a compelling case for planning, I have found that the biggest reason to construct a comprehensive financial plan isn't monetary but rather psychological. After developing and reviewing hundreds of financial plans, I am convinced that the primary benefit is peace of mind. With an often-reviewed plan you'll be organized, motivated, and always know where you stand in relation to your financial goals. The bottom line is that, hopefully, you won't have to worry and stress about your money.

> Sixty-five percent of consumers who have a written financial plan review it at least annually.[7]

My personal experience is supported by a recent study that found that 52 percent of people with plans reported being very or extremely confident about their financial future as opposed to 32 percent for those without plans.[8] I believe that increased confidence translates into increased peace of mind.

Once you record your goals and objectives and map out a strategy to accomplish each goal, you will immediately and dramatically increase your chances of reaching them. If you would like to double your money, develop a written financial plan. You'll do much better financially with a plan than without one. You can't afford not to take this important step, especially if you're close to retirement.

# 3

# FIRE YOUR BROKER!

## RETIREMENT DECISION #3: WHO SHOULD I TRUST TO ADVISE ME ABOUT MY FINANCIAL FUTURE?

As you approach retirement, you will be hunted down by stockbrokers, insurance agents, bank investment representatives, and financial planners who would all like a piece of your nest egg. You may even get a sales letter like the one on the following page.

You may laugh at this advisor's brash but honest marketing approach. But if you read between the lines of the sales letters you receive from advisors (or the seminars you attend sponsored by advisors), they almost always say exactly what this letter says: "I don't have enough experience, I offer expensive products, I am under tremendous pressure to sell you something, and if given the choice *for myself*, I'd buy an investment or insurance product from another company before buying the one I am selling you."

After this bleak introduction to financial advisors, the question still remains. Should you hire an advisor? I believe that unless you have the tools, inclination, and experience to confidently address *every* topic in this book and then adhere strictly to the resulting financial strategy throughout retirement, you definitely need to hire a financial advisor.

## Advisors Put More Money in Your Pocket—but Be Careful

A recent study showed that investors who manage their investments with the aid of a financial advisor are more diversified, take less risk, and obtain better returns than self-directed investors.[1] Advisor-directed investors increased their returns by 2.92 percent per year after expenses.[2] Your odds

Dear Mr. or Mrs. Prospective Client,

I understand you will be retiring soon and have accumulated a ton of money in your company retirement plan. I would like a piece of it. I am under tremendous pressure to sell investments and insurance to hit the lofty sales quotas my firm requires me to reach. I need your help.

I work for a big firm and can offer you a lot of expensive financial products: mutual funds, annuities, life insurance, you name it. In fact, I've got a couple of investments in mind that will pay me a huge commission. Funny thing, most of the products I offer I wouldn't sell to my mom or buy myself, but if you don't know any better, I think you'll like them.

I don't have a whole lot of experience, but I would like to cut my teeth using your money. I call myself a financial planner, but I don't really do any planning; I'm really a salesman pushing my company's financial products. Although well-meaning, I really don't have the skills and training to give you the advice you need as you retire.

I am confident I can help you make me money. Could we meet soon? I have a mortgage payment coming due. I'll call you to arrange a time to meet.

Sincerely,
Joe Advisor
Financial Consultant

of increasing the size of your nest egg increases even further if your advisor develops a comprehensive financial plan for you, as we discussed in Chapter 2. People with advisor-directed financial plans have nest eggs that are over four times as large as those without plans and twice that of those with self-directed plans.[3]

But be careful: While good advice from a good advisor can mean the difference of hundreds of thousands of dollars during retirement, I wouldn't trust most advisors with my own money, and I don't think you should either.

## You're the Boss

Hiring a good advisor is similar to hiring a good employee. Consider, for instance, the steps Max Sontag took to find a new president to run his two-hundred-employee manufacturing company when he retired.

He started by listing the qualifications the new president would be required to have. He then advertised the job and began accepting resumes. Max sifted through the resumes and narrowed his search down to a few finalists. These people were called in for interviews. During these interviews, Max asked probing questions about their experience, background, and what kinds of things they would do to continue the success of his company. Of course, Max had to make sure he could trust and work with the person he would hire. After deciding on a new president, he drew up a contract to outline the salary he would pay and what expectations the new president was required to meet. Max also set up a schedule of meetings where he could give his input and the new president could report on the progress of the company. Max was careful to hire the right person to manage an asset he had worked his whole life to create.

*Essentially, you are the boss, and the financial advisor you hire is your employee.* You should undertake the job of finding an advisor with the same seriousness as Max did in his search for a president. Like Max, you will be trusting someone with an asset that has taken a lifetime to build.

**How Do People Choose Their Financial Advisor?**

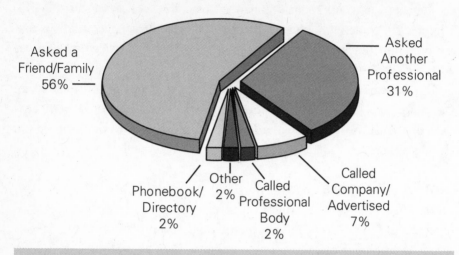

Asked a
Friend/Family
56%

Asked
Another
Professional
31%

Phonebook/
Directory
2%

Other
2%

Called
Professional
Body
2%

Called
Company/
Advertised
7%

*figure 3.1*

# Finding and Hiring a Financial Advisor:
# A Seven-Step Process

This chapter will help you know what to look for in an advisor, how to conduct an interview, how to spell out what is expected of your advisor over time, and how to outline what fees are involved. If you are already using an advisor, read this chapter to determine if your advisor can make the cut. If not, fire him or her, and find an advisor who can.

## *Step 1: Find an advisor with at least ten years of experience*

At retirement, Jack Rice attended a seminar taught by a young financial advisor who'd been working as an advisor for less than three years. The advisor was sharp, professional, and seemed to know his stuff. Jack was impressed. Since he knew no other advisors, he decided to hire this young rep for assistance in rolling over his $250,000 401(k) to an IRA. The advisor recommended Jack purchase an index annuity. Jack didn't know at the time that this annuity purchase made his advisor a 10 percent commission ($25,000).

One year later, Jack realized he had made a mistake. The problem was that he needed to withdraw more money from the annuity than he had originally planned, which would trigger a hefty 10 percent surrender charge. What Jack had missed in the glitzy sales presentation was that he was locked into the annuity for fifteen years before he could withdraw the balance of his investment without incurring penalties. Jack's inexperienced advisor was well-versed in just one product (annuities), didn't have any financial planning expertise, and wasn't knowledgeable about the many other investment options available. The advisor sold the one product he knew and made out like a bandit. As often occurs, the advisor had since left the firm. Jack was stuck holding the bag. In hindsight, Jack should have sought out an advisor who was not so wet behind the ears.

Let the young advisors cut their teeth on others' money, not yours. If you work with an advisor who is new to the financial services business, it is likely he or she won't be around five years from now. The turnover of financial advisors in their first few years in the business is extremely high. For example, brokerage firms retain only about 20 percent of their rookie advisors over the first four years.[4] This means that if you work with a rookie advisor, it's very likely you'll be working with a different advisor in four years. While the failure rate is high for brokerage firms, the insurance industry fares even worse. Only 12 percent of life insurance agents make it to the four-year mark.[5] To avoid hiring an advisor who will leave you behind for another career, consider advisors with at least ten years of experience or those who've spent the time and money to earn the CERTIFIED FINANCIAL PLANNER™ (CFP®) designation. Since the retention rate of a CFP® is 97 percent, the chances of your advisor leaving you behind is almost nonexistent.[6]

## Step 2: Find an advisor with a CFP® designation

Advisors come in all shapes and sizes. There are stockbrokers, life insurance agents, bank investment representatives, financial consultants, and financial planners, any of which use the title "financial advisor." The requirements for carrying that title, unfortunately, are minimal. While there are over 900,000 "financial advisors," fewer than one out of every ten has earned the CFP® mark. The CFP® title is awarded by the International Board of Standards and Practices for CERTIFIED FINANCIAL PLANNERs™. CERTIFIED FINANCIAL PLANNERs™ must undergo two years of intensive training followed by a rigorous two-day examination. A code of ethics must be adhered to and participation in a continuing-education program is required. CFPs® are trained in many aspects of the financial-services industry, including investment, insurance, retirement, tax, estate planning, and more.

*Step 3: Hire a fee-only advisor, not one who works on commission*
Can your advisor be objective? Objectivity largely depends on how he or
she is compensated. Financial advisors are paid by either fee, commission, or
a combination of the two. The advice and investment products you receive will depend on how your advisor is compensated.

| Financial Professionals: How Many Are There? |
| --- |
| 206,000 Personal Financial Advisors |
| 411,500 Insurance Agents |
| 312,200 Stock Brokers |
| 929,700 Total[7] |
| 67,323 Certified Financial Planners CFP® (7.2%) |
| 2,400 Fee-Only Financial Planners (0.3%) |

**Commissioned Advisors**
The majority of advisors are
paid via the commissions they
receive from the products
they sell to their clients. Most
advisors at brokerage firms,
insurance companies, and
banks (stockbrokers, insurance agents, and bank investment reps) fall into
this category. You won't have to pay a penny out of your pocket for their
services. The financial products you purchase from these advisors have
built-in investment and insurance expenses designed to compensate your
advisor. Although you will likely never see these fees, you are paying them
indirectly, and often paying too much. Because these fees are buried in the
pricing of the commissioned product, you'll have to read the prospectus
(funds) or contract (annuities) to understand what you are paying. Due
to the complexity of the pricing of these products, you may need a PhD
to figure out what you are actually paying. Unfortunately, commissioned
advisors are not required to disclose these expenses.

Figure 3.2 outlines common commissions paid out for different types
of financial products. Most products pay an up-front commission to the
advisor when you make your initial investment and a trailing, or ongoing,
commission each year thereafter. The commissions paid are generally split
by your advisor and his or her firm.

There is nothing wrong with working with a commissioned advisor as
long as you know exactly what you are paying, and you are getting an
equivalent amount of service. Discuss this with your advisor at the onset,
before investing any money.

| Commissions Earned from Financial Products ($500,000 Investment) | | | | |
|---|---|---|---|---|
| **Product Type** | **Up-Front Commission** | | **Annual Ongoing Commission** | |
| *Mutual Funds* | | | | |
| Class A Shares | 5.00% | $25,000 | 0.25% | $1,250 |
| Class B Shares | 4.00% | $20,000 | 0.25% | $1,250 |
| Class C Shares | 1.00% | $5,000 | 1.00% | $5,000 |
| *Variable Annuities* | | | | |
| Payout Option 1 | 5.00% | $25,000 | 0.25% | $1,250 |
| Payout Option 2 | 1.00% | $5,000 | 1.00% | $5,000 |
| *Index Annuities* | | | | |
| (Up-front commission from 5–10%) | 10.00% | $50,000 | 0.00% | $0 |
| *Life Insurance* | | | | |
| $7,000 Premium (variable universal life, 500k, 45 yr old) | 80.00% | $5,600 | 10.00% | $700 |

Note: Chart doesn't take into account possible mutual fund break-even points

figure 3.2

## Beware of Up-Front Commissions

It is usually not a good thing if your advisor receives an up-front commission when you purchase an investment. Not only could you be locked into paying penalties (back-end sales charges or surrender charges) if you sell the investment in the first five to ten years, but you also run the risk of getting poor service from your advisor for years to come. Here's why:

When an advisor receives a big up-front commission (Figure 3.2), he or she may be keen on servicing you initially while the big commission is still fresh. Five years from now, however, when your account is not generating any income for the advisor and the promises of great service are forgotten, your advisor may be less interested in managing your investments and financial plan.

Also, the more a fund company pays an advisor up front, often the longer you'll have to hold the fund before you can sell it without incurring the back-end sales charges and penalties. Then, to add insult to injury, many advisors persuade clients to sell an investment as soon as the back-end charges have expired. Clients then get pressured to buy another investment with a high up-front commission. This, of course, generates another commission for the advisor and extends the years of back-end charges.

Helping your advisor pay his or her mortgage every few years by buying a high-commission product is not often in your best interest. It is better that your advisor is paid something each year from the products you own, so there is continued incentive to service your accounts. My advice is to pay your advisor over time, not all at once. If your advisor sells you a financial product and receives an up-front commission, you have essentially prepaid for four to five years' worth of financial advice you may or may not receive. You wouldn't pay your dentist, doctor, CPA, or attorney for services you haven't yet received, and it's in your best interest not to pay your financial advisor this way either.

Commissions will skew your advisor's recommendations toward the financial products that pay the largest commissions, not necessarily those best suited for you. To show you what I mean, let's look at the products Wendy Forsgreen, a commissioned financial advisor, can offer her clients. She works for a large brokerage firm and often sells her clients loaded mutual funds and annuities. While she can make a lot of money selling you these products, you would never have to write her a check to pay for her advice. As we'll discuss in Chapter 18, each loaded financial product builds into its price an added expense to pay a commission to the advisor who sells it.

What advice do you think she would give you when you ask her how to invest the $100,000 in your IRA? Do you think the advice would be objective or slanted toward specific products? The only way to know is to see how she is compensated. Wendy receives a 4 percent ($4,000) commission on most funds she sells. However, if she sells you funds sponsored by her company, she will make 5 percent ($5,000). If she sells you a variable annuity, she will make 6 percent ($6,000). In addition, you should know that Wendy has to meet an annual production quota to keep her job, and her company has recently been pushing advisors to sell the funds and annuities they sponsor. Also, in any month she reaches $20,000 in commission, she qualifies for a trip to a nice resort. Knowing all of this, how objective do you think she can be?

If Wendy sold you a variable annuity and made $6,000 in commissions, wouldn't you like to know this? If you knew Wendy received $6,000, you would likely make sure she does $6,000 worth of work for you just like you would if you paid an attorney or CPA $6,000.

I believe commissioned advisors mean well and generally try to do the best they can for their clients given what they have to offer. However, even if they offer you the best of an inferior line of investment or insurance products, you will still end up with an inferior product. Unfortunately these advisors are crippled by a compensation model that forces them to put your interests second, at least some of the time.

## Fee-Only Advisors (Fiduciary)

Fee-only advisors get paid by the hour, the project, or as a percentage of the assets they manage for clients. These fees are negotiated and agreed upon in a contract. Unlike the fees that are buried into commissioned products that clients never see, the fees that fee-only advisors charge, by law, are fully disclosed and regularly reported to clients. Hourly fees range between $100 and $300 an hour. Projects, like preparing a financial plan, may cost between $500 and $5,000 depending on the complexity of the financial situation.

Figure 3.3 is a sample fee schedule outlining the annual fees advisors charge if they work for you for a percentage of the assets you invest with them (asset management fees). Many fee-only advisors also have account minimums of $100,000 or more.

Now consider the advice you could receive from Stephen Bryer, a fee-only financial advisor. Stephen will prepare a financial plan for you for a flat fee of $1,000 and, as part of that plan, recommend specific strategies to help you meet your goals. Once the strategies are outlined, he will recommend specific products and implement the plan for you. Since Stephen doesn't work on commissions, he is paid only what you agree to pay him. He uses only no-load (no-commission) products (i.e., mutual funds, annuities, life insurance, etc.) that have low

| Average Fees as a Percentage of Assets Being Managed ||
|---|---|
| **Account Size** | **Annual %** |
| $0–$249,999 | 1.20% |
| $250,000–$499,999 | 1.10% |
| $500,000–$999,999 | 1.00% |
| $1,000,000–$2,999,999 | 0.85% |
| $3,000,000+ | 0.75% |

*figure 3.3*

built-in expenses and no front- or back-end charges. He buys stocks and bonds for his clients through a discount brokerage firm to keep transaction costs down. Because the products you buy from Stephen don't pay him anything, he doesn't have a bias to sell you one product over another. After completing the plan, you can retain Stephen's services on an ongoing basis by paying him an annual retainer, which could be a flat fee or a fee based on a percentage of the assets he manages for you. It doesn't matter to Stephen's bottom line whether you buy an annuity or mutual funds or any other product since the only payment he will receive is from you.

Only 2,400 financial advisors are members of NAPFA, the nation's largest association of fee-only financial advisors. www.napfa.com

Fee-only advisors are fiduciaries. This means they are required by law to put your interests first. Commissioned-based advisors are not held to the same standard; in fact, they are required by law to act in the best interest of their employers.[8]

## Fee-Based Advisors

"Fee-based" is a way for commissioned advisors to say, "I do some fee-only business, but I may pull a commissioned product from my back pocket every once in a while so I can make a quick commission." "Fee-based" also says, "I will be objective sometimes." If you work with a "fee-based" advisor, find out what percentage of their income comes from fees and how much comes from commission. The average "fee-based" advisor derives 44 percent of his/her income from fees, 49 percent of their income from commissions, and 7% from other sources.[9] So, if you work with a "fee-based" advisor, there is about a 50 percent chance you'll be sold a commission-based product. Be careful: while "fee-based" sounds like "fee-only," they are definitely not the same thing.

## Commissions or Fees: Which Is Better?

Let's compare a $500,000 mutual fund investment made with a commissioned advisor and one made with a fee-only advisor. Let's assume the commissioned advisor receives a 1 percent commission and the fee-only advisor receives a 1 percent asset management fee. Both advisors will receive $5,000 annually from this investment. Although the total fee is the same, the fee-only advisor still may be your best bet for several reasons:

1. You may be able to negotiate a lower asset management fee. In addition, your fee may automatically be lowered as your portfolio grows larger. On the other hand, you can't negotiate the fees that are built into commissioned products, and these fees are not reduced as your portfolio grows.
2. The investment advisory fee you pay is often tax deductible; increased expenses built into mutual funds in order to pay the advisor a commission are not.
3. Fee-only advisors use no-load financial products, which do not carry back-end sales charges. With many commissioned funds, you could be slapped with a significant exit fee (deferred sales charge) if you sell within the first four to eight years of owning the fund.
4. Your fee-only advisor can be objective in his or her recommendations by not having to worry about meeting commission and product quotas.
5. Your fee-only advisor may be able to find funds with less costly expenses than commissioned funds.

Whatever you do, don't get "double dipped": do not pay both commissions *and* fees. Some advisors sell mutual funds that pay them big up-front commissions, and then add on an ongoing investment advisor fee of 1 percent or more of your assets each year.

The Federal Administration on Aging warns investors of the dilemma faced by commission-only advisors:

> *A financial planner who collects commissions is open to the criticism that he or she has an incentive to select or recommend investments partly on the basis of the commission offered–not solely on the quality of the investment... While competence and performance should be the primary considerations in selecting a planner, compensation should also be considered–especially in cases where commissions are involved.*[10]

This is not to say that you should not consider an advisor who works on commissions. The administration concludes, "The fact that commissions or other payments are made does not necessarily mean the investment is a bad one. Rather, it indicates that your planner may be faced with choosing between what is best for him or her and what is best for you."[11]

Fee-only advisors, who charge a flat fee, hourly rate, or a percentage of the assets they manage, work independent of brokerage firms, banks, and insurance companies. By not getting paid from the companies whose products they sell, they have put themselves in a better position to provide objective advice and have *your* best interests in mind.

> Fees you pay for investment advice may be tax deductible as a miscellaneous itemized deduction on Schedule A (Form 1040). Fees exceeding 2 percent of your adjusted gross income (AGI) are deductible. See IRS Publication 550.

## Step 4: Insist on a plan and a well-defined investment strategy

In Chapter 2 we discussed the importance of having a written financial game plan. You need a plan to provide you with a big-picture framework to make all of your financial decisions. Your advisor can't possibly give you advice in line with your goals without seeing the big picture. In the same way, you also need a well-defined investment strategy to spell out exactly how to allocate and diversify your money. As we'll discuss in Chapters 11–20, the investment strategy will also outline the type of investments you are going to buy and how you are going to evaluate and manage those investments. Both a carefully monitored plan and an investment strategy will help you stick to your financial game plan.

Research indicates that individual investors, left to their own devices, are fickle and rarely disciplined when it comes to sticking with an investment strategy. As Benjamin Graham, the legendary American investor, said, "The investor's chief problem—and even his worst enemy—is likely to be himself."[12]

Let's look at the evidence: Figure 3.4 illustrates the total returns of various market indexes compared with the total returns achieved by the average investor. If an investor had invested money in the S&P 500 Index and left it alone from 1992 to 2011, he or she would have earned an annualized return of 7.81 percent. Unfortunately, during this same period, the *average investor* purchasing stock mutual funds earned just 3.49 percent per year! Bond investors fared about the same. The average bond investor earned 0.94 percent per year while the overall bond market grew at a rate of 6.50 percent.[13]

Why did investors do so poorly during a period when the stock market did so well? One reason was the investors' inability to hold investments and adhere to a strategy over the long term. The average investor holds a stock fund for 3.29 years and a bond fund for 3.09 years.[14] People who use financial advisors hold their funds longer than those who don't. The job of your advisor is to provide needed encouragement and to help you stick steadfastly to an investment discipline, even when thundering market volatility and the media are tempting you to act out of panic.

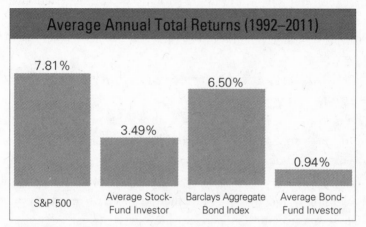

Source: DALBAR Quantitative Analysis of Investor Behavior Study, 2012

figure 3.4

Investors who do not seek advice are more likely to panic and sell when stocks dive. With the advice, knowledge, and experience of a financial consultant, investors are more likely to hold on to their investments for the long run.

An advisor can guide you through the turbulence of the financial markets and help you adhere to your strategy. By sticking to a fundamentally sound strategy, you will increase your chances of obtaining better investment performance. According to a study of 425,000 investors conducted by a large brokerage firm, investors who received financial advice from 2006–2010 enjoyed annual returns 2.92 percent better than investors who didn't obtain investment advice.[15] Based on this study, let's look at what an increase of 2.92 percent looks like. First, let's assume you opted to self-manage $100,000. If you achieved a 7 percent rate of return, your $100,000 would grow to $196,715 over ten years and to $386,968 over twenty years. If you tacked an additional 2.92 percent to the self-managed 7 percent (9.92

percent) rate of return, in this example, your $100,000 would be worth $257,494 after ten years and $663,032 after twenty years. Of course, there are no guarantees that using an advisor will make this much difference. However, the figures are compelling.

If your advisor doesn't develop a financial plan for you or fails to craft a well-defined investment strategy, you should hire someone who will. These documents are your financial constitution and will dictate what to do as the financial winds change direction over time.

## Step 5: Insist that your advisor has an action plan for servicing your account

You shouldn't have to call your advisor; your advisor should have a system in place to make sure you are consistently being contacted. Find out your advisor's plan of attack to monitor your financial plan and review your investments over time before you begin investing your money. If your advisor is not willing to meet with you semiannually to review and update your financial and investment plan, go elsewhere.

About half of all investors who work with advisors meet with their advisor less than once per year, and half of those people *never* meet with their advisor.[16] This means only half of all advisors are providing even a minimal level of customer service.

> Only half of all advisors meet with their clients more than once per year.

Outline the amount of service you expect to receive in writing before investing any money with your advisor.

## Step 6: Shop at the supermarket (avoid proprietary products)

One of the reasons stores like Walmart and Home Depot are so successful is that they offer an enormous number of products under one roof. Customers can compare many different brands of the same types of products before making a decision to purchase. Would you shop at these stores if they carried only one brand of the products you buy?

There are both narrow one-brand financial advisors and advisors who offer a Walmart-type mega selection of financial products. The more products and services your advisor can offer, the more likely it is you'll get a financial plan and products customized to specifically fit your needs. Make sure your advisor can provide the following products and services:

- A comprehensive financial plan
- A no-load mutual fund supermarket (at least 5,000 funds)
- No-load fixed and variable annuities from multiple companies
- Individual stocks and bonds with low commission rates
- Separate accounts from multiple managers
- No-load life insurance from multiple companies
- Online account access
- Banking features

Avoid advisors who primarily recommend proprietary products (products developed by your advisor's company). This one-brand approach will often leave you with mediocre investments. If, for example, the advisor puts together an investment proposal for you outlining seven or eight mutual funds that are proprietary, beware. What are the chances, when compared with the more than 29,176 funds available,[17] that all of the proprietary funds are among the best in each of their respective asset categories? Not very likely.

In fact, in 2012, I conducted a study of the fifty-two mutual funds offered by one of the nation's largest brokerage companies. I found that only *two* of the fifty-two funds the firm offers had a seasoned manager and performed better than its respective asset category average for the past one, three, five, and ten years.[18] If you bought a whole portfolio of funds from this company, you would end up with a bunch of below-average investments. In contrast, when I applied the same performance criterion to all 29,176 funds, I found 806 that made the cut.[19] In fairness, just because a product is proprietary doesn't necessarily mean it's bad. Just make sure that if you buy proprietary products, they can pass the performance test outlined in Chapter 16.

## Step 7: Investigate the advisor

Once you have narrowed your selection to a handful of individuals, be sure to undertake an in-depth investigation of each advisor's background and credentials. Remember, this is the person who will be handling your money and your future for potentially the next thirty years. The Forum for Investor Advice recommends, "Spend time to thoroughly check out your advisor's credentials, experience, investment philosophy, specialties, and client references to make sure you find someone whom you can trust and will give you valuable advice."

You can check the FINRA database, www.finra.org (Brokercheck), to examine your advisor's background and see if he/she has had any disciplinary actions filed against them.

### With What Type of Clients Does the Advisor Work?

Ask your prospective advisor the age of his or her average client. If most of the advisor's clients are between the ages of 55 and 70, the advisor has likely handled many retirement transitions like yours. Because you are retiring, ask your prospective advisor how many retirements he or she has handled during the past year. Ask for copies of financial plans the advisor has done for other people who have retired.

### Does Your Advisor Have Time for You?

How many clients does your advisor have? If your advisor has too many clients, he or she may be spread too thin and not be able to devote enough time to you. A large practice may also mean you end up working with your advisor's staff more than with your advisor. Let's look at this logically. If an advisor must devote ten hours each year to only you, then how many clients can the advisor service each year? We'll assume your advisor spends thirty-five hours per week working for clients and five hours per week doing administrative and marketing activities. If your advisor works 49 weeks per year, he or she could successfully work with a total of 171 clients (35 hours multiplied by 49 weeks, divided by 10 hours). As a general rule, you should not hire an advisor with more than 200 clients.

But don't automatically run to advisors with very small practices. They may be more interested in obtaining new clients rather than servicing the clients they already have.

### The Final Interview

Use the web resources at the end of this chapter to locate experienced advisors in your area. Then simply call the advisors you feel are the most qualified. You can explain your situation and get some initial feedback on what types of things they may suggest you do. If you like what you hear,

arrange for a face-to-face interview. The questionnaire below, provided by
the Forum for Investor Advice, will give you a sampling of questions you
can ask during this meeting.

*Qualifications:*

1. What is your educational background? College degree and area of
   study? Financial-planning education?
2. What financial planning certifications or designations do you hold?
3. What securities licenses do you hold?
4. What is your professional experience? How many years have you
   been a financial advisor?
5. How do you keep your financial knowledge base and planning
   skills current?

*Services:*

1. How would you prepare my financial plan? Do you recommend
   specific investments or investment products?
2. Can I see a sample financial plan? (Make sure that the plan is clear
   and comprehensive.)
3. What is your investment philosophy? What types of investments do
   you favor? Get a sense of the types of investment products (load or
   no-load, etc.) and methodology the advisor uses.
4. Do you have certain areas of expertise: insurance, estate planning,
   retirement planning, education planning, and tax issues?
5. Do you collaborate with professionals in accounting, law, and insurance to offer specialized services?

*Clientele:*

1. What is the minimum and maximum asset value of your clients?
   (Make sure your assets fall within this range.)
2. Do most of your clients have financial situations similar to mine?

*Accessibility:*

1. Describe how you and I will work together.
2. Will I be working with only you, or do you have an assistant?
3. How often will we meet or talk? Can I reach you by email? Can I view my accounts and research online? How often will I receive reports?
4. How do you help clients implement their financial plans? Do you only give advice or do you also make the transactions? Will you have discretionary power to buy and sell assets in my account?

*Compensation:*

1. What are your fees? Do you operate on a fee-only, fee-based, commission-only, or fee-plus-commission basis?
2. If fee-only, is the fee based on an hourly rate, a flat fee, or a percentage of assets?

*Other:*

1. Can you provide me with references from long-term clients and professional associates?
2. Is your business registered with the Securities and Exchange Commission (SEC)? With the state's securities office?

## Remember, you are the boss!

Interviewing candidates is the most important step in selecting your financial advisor. Keep in mind that *you're the boss*, so act as if you are interviewing a potential employee, an employee who will have a huge impact on your financial success or failure.

Choosing to work with a qualified financial advisor can dramatically increase your odds of success. Investors who employ the services of a good financial advisor are much more likely to reach their retirement goals and thus improve the long-term outlook of their retirement future. Set the bar high so you end up with an advisor who is ethical, competent, and reasonably priced. The information included in this chapter will help you select an advisor who can meet your needs. Don't forget, you're the boss and the advisor you hire is your employee. Be sure to hire a good employee to guide the assets you've worked a lifetime to accumulate.

## Find It on the Web

### Fee-Only Advisors
- National Association of Personal Financial Advisors: www.napfa.org
- Garrett Planning Network: www.garrettplanningnetwork.com
- Myfinancialadvice: www.myfinancialadvice.com

### CFPs® (Primarily Commissioned)
- Financial Planning Association: www.fpanet.org

### Commissioned Advisors
- WiserAdvisor.com: www.wiseradvisor.com

# 4

# MORE LIFE THAN MONEY

## RETIREMENT DECISION #4: HOW MUCH CAN I SAFELY WITHDRAW FROM MY PORTFOLIO?

There's a critical question you must answer by the first day of your retirement: How much can you withdraw from your retirement savings each year without incurring the risk of running out of money? A miscalculation could mean you outlive your assets and are forced to live on Social Security alone, which is the fate of one out of four Americans over age 65.[1] This chapter will review four withdrawal methods to help you choose a withdrawal rate that will be as safe as possible in the face of unknown life expectancies and ever-changing economic conditions.

People list outliving their savings as their greatest retirement concern.[2]

When calculating a safe withdrawal rate, you face two major obstacles. First, there is no way to know exactly how long you will live. Second, it is impossible to predict the exact rate of return your portfolio will generate during retirement. You must also consider the effect inflation and taxes will have on your withdrawals.

Bottom line? In most cases, you should withdraw no more than between 4 and 6 percent of your savings per year. Any more than this and you run the risk of running out of money.

For most of us to obtain the returns we need to maintain an acceptable income level, we must invest a portion of our retirement assets in stocks and bonds. A retiree expecting to be in retirement for thirty years will need more money invested in stocks than the retiree planning for only twenty years. Either way, investing in stocks and bonds brings unpredictability into the equation. But if we make conservative assumptions and err on the side of safety, we can calculate a cautious rate of withdrawal that will ensure our retirement savings last.

## The Withdrawal Myth

On the surface, it doesn't seem like it should be that difficult to determine a safe withdrawal rate. Since 1926, the annual rate of return of stocks is just about 10 percent. If you invest 100 percent of your retirement portfolio in stocks, it seems that you should be able to withdraw any amount less than 10 percent and never dip into your principal. It sounds so simple it must be effective, right? Well, as many inexperienced financial advisors and their clients have found, this approach can lead to disastrous results.

For example, if a $500,000 portfolio provides a constant 10 percent annual return and we withdraw just 7 percent of the principal each year, the results are astonishing (Figure 4.1). We don't even come close to touching our investment principal.

| Withdrawal Myth | |
|---|---|
| $500,000 portfolio growing 10% annually, with 7% ($35,000) annual withdrawals | |
| Year | Portfolio Value after Withdrawals |
| 1 | $515,000 |
| 5 | $770,255 |
| 10 | $1,261,871 |
| 15 | $2,053,624 |
| 20 | $3,328,750 |
| 25 | $5,382,353 |
| 30 | $8,689,701 |

figure 4.1

There's one problem with this simple scenario, however; stocks do not provide consistent returns. While stocks may average 10 percent growth over the long run, they often take investors on a very bumpy ride along the way.

For example, the annual investment results for the portfolio in Figure 4.2 would also provide a 10 percent *average* annual return over five- and ten-year periods. However, notice what happens to the $500,000 portfolio if the return varies from year to year and if the same 7 percent per year is withdrawn.

After only a couple of years, these annual withdrawals are already eroding the principal. In year eight, the nest egg that was supposed to last thirty years has been cut nearly in half. By year ten, the balance is $375,936, a far cry from the $1.2 million balance we projected in the fantasy world of Figure 4.1.

While it seems perfectly logical to base your withdrawal rate on average annual returns of stocks and bonds, these assumptions could lead to the total depletion of your investment assets. Actual returns, as opposed to average returns, vary from year to year. Taking this variance into account when deciding how much you can safely withdraw each year is crucial to your retirement planning.

| | Withdrawal Reality | | |
| --- | --- | --- | --- |
| | $500,000 portfolio growing at an average of 10% annually, with 7% ($35,000) annual withdrawals | | |
| Year | Portfolio Return | Annual Withdrawal | Portfolio Value at Year-End |
| 1 | –25% | $35,000 | $340,000 |
| 2 | 35% | $35,000 | $424,000 |
| 3 | –15% | $35,000 | $325,400 |
| 4 | 25% | $35,000 | $371,750 |
| 5 | 30% | $35,000 | $448,275 |
| 6 | –25% | $35,000 | $301,206 |
| 7 | 35% | $35,000 | $371,628 |
| 8 | –15% | $35,000 | $280,884 |
| 9 | 25% | $35,000 | $316,105 |
| 10 | 30% | $35,000 | $375,936 |

figure 4.2

There are all sorts of strategies and theories out there on how to determine a safe withdrawal rate. You've probably already heard some, especially if you've sought advice from financial planners. I've boiled them down to the four most common methods. To compare each of the four methods, we'll compare the experience of four couples who each retired in 1970. Review each, then choose the method that best fits your goals and objectives.

## Method 1: Too Fixed on Fixed-Rate

It's 1970, and David and Iris Meredith retire early at age 55 with a nice $500,000 nest egg. They think their portfolio is large enough that they can live solely off the interest and dividends it kicks off each year. This way, they'll never have to touch their principal.

David and Iris decide to put their retirement savings in ultraconservative six-month certificates of deposit (CDs). Their plan is simple: they'll continue to buy six-month CDs as each matures and withdraw the interest they earn each year. They'll be able to sleep well at night knowing that their principal is FDIC guaranteed.

As you can see in Figure 4.3, their plan worked great–for a while. In 1970, their CD earned 7.6 percent, kicking off a healthy $38,200 of interest.

| $500,000 6-Month CD (Withdraw Interest Only) | | | | | |
|---|---|---|---|---|---|
| Year | Year-End Balance | Year-End Withdrawal | Year | Year-End Balance | Year-End Withdrawal |
| 1970 | $500,000 | $38,200 | 1992 | $500,000 | $18,800 |
| 1971 | $500,000 | $26,050 | 1993 | $500,000 | $16,400 |
| 1972 | $500,000 | $25,050 | 1994 | $500,000 | $24,800 |
| 1973 | $500,000 | $45,250 | 1995 | $500,000 | $29,900 |
| 1974 | $500,000 | $50,100 | 1996 | $500,000 | $27,350 |
| 1975 | $500,000 | $34,500 | 1997 | $500,000 | $28,650 |
| 1976 | $500,000 | $28,150 | 1998 | $500,000 | $27,200 |
| 1977 | $500,000 | $29,550 | 1999 | $500,000 | $27,300 |
| 1978 | $500,000 | $43,000 | 2000 | $500,000 | $32,950 |
| 1979 | $500,000 | $57,100 | 2001 | $500,000 | $18,300 |
| 1980 | $500,000 | $64,700 | 2002 | $500,000 | $9,050 |
| 1981 | $500,000 | $78,950 | 2003 | $500,000 | $5,850 |
| 1982 | $500,000 | $62,850 | 2004 | $500,000 | $8,700 |
| 1983 | $500,000 | $46,400 | 2005 | $500,000 | $18,600 |
| 1984 | $500,000 | $53,550 | 2006 | $500,000 | $26,150 |
| 1985 | $500,000 | $41,200 | 2007 | $500,000 | $25,950 |
| 1986 | $500,000 | $32,500 | 2008 | $500,000 | $15,100 |
| 1987 | $500,000 | $35,050 | 2009 | $500,000 | $6,350 |
| 1988 | $500,000 | $39,550 | 2010 | $500,000 | $3,650 |
| 1989 | $500,000 | $45,400 | 2011 | $500,000 | $2,400 |
| 1990 | $500,000 | $40,850 | 2012 | $500,000 | $2,300 |
| 1991 | $500,000 | $29,550 | Total | | $1,323,150 |

figure 4.3

The strategy worked even better in 1981, with six-month CDs paying a whopping 15.79 percent. The Merediths withdrew the $78,950 of interest they earned. From then on, however, things went downhill. It turns out that interest rates were at their peak in the early 1980s. In 1993 their yearly income before taxes was just $16,400. By 2003, their CD was paying just 1.17 percent, earning them a scant $5,850. Having spent forty-three years in retirement, Iris turned 97 in 2012 and, sticking with her strategy, withdrew the meager $2,300 she earned in interest to help meet her living expenses.

Of course, the nice thing about this method is that David and Iris's $500,000 principal is still intact. The downside is severe, as many retirees like David and Iris have found out. Falling interest rates and falling incomes don't work for long in the world of rising costs. Over the long term, most fixed-rate investments just won't provide the income retirees need as costs increase.

To compare fixed-rate returns with your other options, see Figure 4.8 on page 58.

## Method 2: In Distributions We Trust

It's 1970, and Jeff and Marci Reynolds are also retiring with savings of $500,000. They want to maintain a fairly lavish lifestyle, so they'll need more income than David and Iris's short-term CDs can provide. They decide to invest their $500,000 into a mutual fund made up of 50 percent stocks and 50 percent bonds and cash. Their choice is a reputable, inexpensive mutual fund called the Dodge & Cox Balanced Fund. They plan to withdraw just the fund's distributions (dividends, interest, and capital gains distributions) at the end of each year. They know that their income will be volatile, but it will likely be much higher than the CD alternative. In addition, their $500,000 principal would have a chance to appreciate and keep up with inflation.

Jeff and Marci were prepared for a bumpy ride; they just didn't anticipate how extreme it would be (Figure 4.4). Their income in 1971 was $21,845 before taxes; in 1986, it hit $115,247. In 1992, it fell to $40,124 and shot up to $260,588 in 2000, before sliding back to $51,939 in 2003. Best of all, even after withdrawing all distributions from the fund since 1970, their $500,000 portfolio appreciated to a balance of $1.74 million by the end of 2012.

As Jeff and Marci discovered, retirees using this method are unlikely to deplete their portfolio. But few people have the luxury to be flexible enough to live on an ever-changing income level. For this approach to work, retirees must have the means to roll with the punches. Most do not.

To compare total-distribution withdrawals with your other options, see Figure 4.8 on page 58.

| $500,000 Balanced Mutual Fund (Withdraw Dividends and Capital Gains Distributions Only) | | | | | |
|---|---|---|---|---|---|
| Year | Year-End Balance | Year-End Withdrawal | Year | Year-End Balance | Year-End Withdrawal |
| 1970 | $479,938 | $32,099 | 1992 | $946,054 | $40,124 |
| 1971 | $510,031 | $21,845 | 1993 | $1,034,329 | $60,856 |
| 1972 | $545,921 | $21,176 | 1994 | $1,007,802 | $47,258 |
| 1973 | $460,544 | $32,544 | 1995 | $1,217,120 | $68,880 |
| 1974 | $348,417 | $25,189 | 1996 | $1,333,482 | $59,741 |
| 1975 | $429,113 | $20,731 | 1997 | $1,488,631 | $122,380 |
| 1976 | $514,044 | $22,291 | 1998 | $1,453,856 | $133,080 |
| 1977 | $472,358 | $24,966 | 1999 | $1,464,779 | $160,499 |
| 1978 | $468,569 | $31,208 | 2000 | $1,413,732 | $260,588 |
| 1979 | $498,217 | $32,768 | 2001 | $1,458,315 | $93,101 |
| 1980 | $562,416 | $38,341 | 2002 | $1,354,213 | $61,524 |
| 1981 | $491,306 | $57,957 | 2003 | $1,628,177 | $51,939 |
| 1982 | $561,748 | $48,371 | 2004 | $1,768,836 | $73,115 |
| 1983 | $609,229 | $45,251 | 2005 | $1,813,197 | $90,440 |
| 1984 | $577,798 | $57,066 | 2006 | $1,942,150 | $120,440 |
| 1985 | $711,770 | $46,142 | 2007 | $1,805,617 | $170,463 |
| 1986 | $727,151 | $115,247 | 2008 | $1,142,666 | $73,405 |
| 1987 | $684,797 | $97,413 | 2009 | $1,427,329 | $33,660 |
| 1988 | $715,337 | $47,703 | 2010 | $1,565,314 | $33,883 |
| 1989 | $821,444 | $55,060 | 2011 | $1,503,567 | $36,112 |
| 1990 | $780,874 | $47,703 | 2012 | $1,740,080 | $36,893 |
| 1991 | $893,669 | $45,697 | Total | | $2,795, 449 |

figure 4.4

# Method 3: Playing the Percentage

Jeff and Marci weren't the only retirees in 1970 to invest their savings in Dodge & Cox Balanced Fund; Jorge and Felicia Becerra likewise put their $500,000 nest egg in the fund at the exact same time. Jorge and Felicia, however, decided to use a different strategy to withdraw their money. They set a withdrawal rate at a level lower than what they expected the fund would annually produce. They figured the fund's annual total return would be about 8 percent. So they set their withdrawal rate at 6 percent. To determine how much money to deduct from their portfolio, they would simply take the balance of the portfolio at the end of each year and multiply it by 6 percent (Figure 4.5).

Jorge and Felicia's first-year withdrawal was $30,828 before taxes, leaving them with a portfolio worth $482,966. Because of a severe market downturn in 1973 and 1974, their 6 percent annual withdrawals produced a lot less cash. Their balance in the mutual fund at the end of 1974 dropped to $340,042, providing them with an income of a mere $21,705. The couple and their strategy continued to struggle during the 1970s as the market faltered. Then came the bull market in the 1980s. By the end of 1990, the portfolio topped $1 million and produced a withdrawal of $65,025; in 2006, it was worth more than $2.6 million and provided $170,258 in income. The 2008 market drop reduced their withdrawal to $95,608 (44 percent less than 2006) and their account balance to $1,593,460.

As Jorge and Felicia learned, retirees who use this constant-percentage strategy will earn a bigger paycheck when their investments do well and vice versa. In up markets, they will receive a larger income; in down markets, they will have to live on less. This method can also be effective in keeping pace with inflation. A fixed percentage of a rising dollar amount equals increased income.

The danger of this method is using too high of a withdrawal rate. Consistently withdrawing more than the portfolio is earning will slowly decrease income, and annual withdrawals won't keep pace with inflation.

This strategy provides a volatile income stream, but with the right investments and a conservative withdrawal rate, retirees should be able to keep their growth rate ahead of their withdrawal rate and see their income rise in most years.

To compare fixed-percentage withdrawals with your other options, see Figure 4.8 on page 58.

| $500,000 Balanced Mutual Fund (Withdraw a Constant 6% of Year-End Balance) | | | | | |
|---|---|---|---|---|---|
| Year | Year-End Balance | Year-End Withdrawal | Year | Year-End Balance | Year-End Withdrawal |
| 1970 | $482,966 | $30,828 | 1992 | $1,200,179 | $76,607 |
| 1971 | $503,684 | $32,150 | 1993 | $1,307,664 | $83,468 |
| 1972 | $527,465 | $33,668 | 1994 | $1,254,687 | $80,086 |
| 1973 | $447,494 | $28,563 | 1995 | $1,509,214 | $96,333 |
| 1974 | $340,042 | $21,705 | 1996 | $1,627,598 | $103,889 |
| 1975 | $413,601 | $26,400 | 1997 | $1,853,144 | $118,286 |
| 1976 | $487,030 | $31,087 | 1998 | $1,858,258 | $118,612 |
| 1977 | $442,835 | $28,266 | 1999 | $1,956,278 | $124,869 |
| 1978 | $441,360 | $28,172 | 2000 | $2,116,654 | $135,106 |
| 1979 | $470,811 | $30,052 | 2001 | $2,188,540 | $139,694 |
| 1980 | $538,564 | $34,376 | 2002 | $1,996,627 | $127,444 |
| 1981 | $493,818 | $31,520 | 2003 | $2,335,608 | $149,081 |
| 1982 | $584,845 | $37,330 | 2004 | $2,487,291 | $158,763 |
| 1983 | $642,231 | $40,993 | 2005 | $2,492,069 | $159,068 |
| 1984 | $632,177 | $40,352 | 2006 | $2,667,381 | $170,258 |
| 1985 | $786,657 | $50,212 | 2007 | $2,551,465 | $153,088 |
| 1986 | $878,803 | $56,094 | 2008 | $1,593,460 | $95,608 |
| 1987 | $885,752 | $56,537 | 2009 | $1,923,429 | $122,772 |
| 1988 | $928,850 | $59,288 | 2010 | $2,029,328 | $129,532 |
| 1989 | $1,073,339 | $68,511 | 2011 | $1,875,876 | $119,737 |
| 1990 | $1,018,727 | $65,025 | 2012 | $2,086,123 | $133,157 |
| 1991 | $1,154,773 | $73,709 | Total | | $3,516,172 |

figure 4.5

## Method 4: Playing It Safe with Monte Carlo

The first three methods all had serious drawbacks that will probably discourage you from using them. But what if there was a method in which you could earn predictable and increasing income while knowing that, regardless of market conditions, you aren't likely to run out of money? This type of retirement is possible, but it requires software to test your portfolio strategy and withdrawal rate using different rate-of-return possibilities. Here is a simple example. You may decide to withdraw $30,000 per year from your $500,000 portfolio, and over a three-year period you might average a 7 percent return. However, a 7 percent average return could be accomplished by receiving 20 percent in year one, 10 percent in year two, and –9 percent in year three and leave you with $513,270 after withdrawals. A 7 percent average return could also be achieved by receiving a –15 percent return in year one, 12 percent in year two, and 24 percent in year three, which by contrast would give you a $481,376 ending balance. Each of these return sequences produced a different end result. Using a Monte Carlo analysis, you can examine how thousands of rate-of-return combinations can impact your nest egg over long periods of time.

By using Monte Carlo, you will determine a withdrawal rate based on your initial investment balance that you are confident can be maintained through even the worst market conditions. Every year, you will simply withdraw that amount and give yourself a 3 percent raise to keep pace with inflation. Whether your investments are up or down in value, annually you will continue to take 3 percent more than the year before.

If you don't have access to a Monte Carlo calculator, you can utilize the results of an influential study to help you determine a safe withdrawal rate. In what is known as the Trinity Study, three Trinity University faculty members back-tested the effect of various withdrawal rates on five different portfolios of stocks and bonds over fifteen-, twenty-, twenty-five-, and thirty-year rolling time frames from 1926 to 2009.[3] This study is useful because it allows you to see the impact of different withdrawal rates through periods that included the worst-case scenario: the Great Depression. They used actual year-to-year returns of stocks and bonds rather than average returns. A success rate was calculated for each portfolio, time frame, and withdrawal rate. One hundred percent success was defined as having money remaining in the account at the conclusion of the specified withdrawal period. Figure 4.6 summarizes their research.

According to this research, a retiree starting with a $500,000 portfolio consisting of 50 percent stocks and 50 percent bonds who plans to be in retirement for twenty-five years should be 100 percent successful if he withdraws less than 4 percent, or $20,000, annually.

Using this method, what is your "safe" withdrawal rate? The table in

Figure 4.6 will help you answer that question. To use this table, first determine what percentage of your portfolio will be invested in stocks and bonds

| Portfolio Success Rates by Withdrawal Rate, Portfolio Composition, and Payout Period (1926–2009) | | | | | | | | | |
|---|---|---|---|---|---|---|---|---|---|
| **Portfolio Composition: 100% Stocks/0% Bonds** | | | | | | | | | |
| Payout Period | **Withdrawal Rate as a % of the Initial Portfolio Value** | | | | | | | | |
| | 3% | 4% | 5% | 6% | 7% | 8% | 9% | 10% | 11% | 12% |
| 15 Years | 100% | 100% | 100% | 94% | 86% | 76% | 71% | 64% | 51% | 46% |
| 20 Years | 100% | 100% | 92% | 80% | 72% | 65% | 52% | 45% | 38% | 25% |
| 25 Years | 100% | 100% | 88% | 75% | 63% | 50% | 42% | 33% | 27% | 17% |
| 30 Years | 100% | 98% | 80% | 62% | 55% | 44% | 33% | 27% | 15% | 5% |
| **Portfolio Composition: 75% Stocks/25% Bonds** | | | | | | | | | |
| Payout Period | **Withdrawal Rate as a % of the Initial Portfolio Value** | | | | | | | | |
| | 3% | 4% | 5% | 6% | 7% | 8% | 9% | 10% | 11% | 12% |
| 15 Years | 100% | 100% | 100% | 97% | 87% | 77% | 70% | 56% | 47% | 30% |
| 20 Years | 100% | 100% | 95% | 80% | 72% | 60% | 49% | 31% | 25% | 11% |
| 25 Years | 100% | 100% | 87% | 70% | 58% | 42% | 32% | 20% | 10% | 3% |
| 30 Years | 100% | 100% | 82% | 60% | 45% | 35% | 13% | 5% | 0% | 0% |
| **Portfolio Composition: 50% Stocks/50% Bonds** | | | | | | | | | |
| Payout Period | **Withdrawal Rate as a % of the Initial Portfolio Value** | | | | | | | | |
| | 3% | 4% | 5% | 6% | 7% | 8% | 9% | 10% | 11% | 12% |
| 15 Years | 100% | 100% | 100% | 99% | 84% | 71% | 61% | 44% | 34% | 21% |
| 20 Years | 100% | 100% | 94% | 80% | 63% | 43% | 31% | 23% | 8% | 6% |
| 25 Years | 100% | 100% | 83% | 60% | 42% | 23% | 13% | 8% | 7% | 2% |
| 30 Years | 100% | 96% | 67% | 31% | 22% | 9% | 0% | 0% | 0% | 0% |
| **Portfolio Composition: 25% Stocks/75% Bonds** | | | | | | | | | |
| Payout Period | **Withdrawal Rate as a % of the Initial Portfolio Value** | | | | | | | | |
| | 3% | 4% | 5% | 6% | 7% | 8% | 9% | 10% | 11% | 12% |
| 15 Years | 100% | 100% | 100% | 99% | 77% | 59% | 43% | 34% | 26% | 13% |
| 20 Years | 100% | 100% | 82% | 52% | 26% | 14% | 9% | 3% | 0% | 0% |
| 25 Years | 100% | 95% | 58% | 32% | 25% | 15% | 8% | 7% | 2% | 2% |
| 30 Years | 100% | 80% | 31% | 22% | 7% | 0% | 0% | 0% | 0% | 0% |

**Continued**

| Portfolio Composition: 0% Stocks/100% Bonds | | | | | | | | | |
|---|---|---|---|---|---|---|---|---|---|
| Payout Period | Withdrawal Rate as a % of the Initial Portfolio Value | | | | | | | | |
| | 3% | 4% | 5% | 6% | 7% | 8% | 9% | 10% | 11% | 12% |
| 15 Years | 100% | 100% | 100% | 81% | 54% | 37% | 34% | 27% | 19% | 10% |
| 20 Years | 100% | 97% | 65% | 37% | 29% | 28% | 17% | 8% | 2% | 2% |
| 25 Years | 100% | 62% | 33% | 23% | 18% | 8% | 8% | 2% | 2% | 0% |
| 30 Years | 84% | 35% | 22% | 11% | 2% | 0% | 0% | 0% | 0% | 0% |

Note: Stocks are represented by large-company U.S. stocks; bonds are represented by long-term, high-grade corporate bonds.

figure 4.6

during retirement. Second, estimate how many years you think you will be in retirement (payout period). Finally, choose a withdrawal schedule that has been successful at least 90 percent of the time. After examining the chart, you will notice that most of the portfolios could sustain a 3–5 percent withdrawal rate. Higher withdrawals will usually deplete the portfolio assets before your retirement period is over.

Notice what happens if you plan to be in retirement for thirty years and withdraw 9 percent each year. Even with a portfolio consisting of 100 percent stocks, your success rate is only 33 percent. Do you like those odds, running a 33 percent chance of completely running out of money?

Harvard University uses a similar strategy. In 1973, Harvard was interested in determining how much of its endowment portfolio could be withdrawn each year without depleting its principal. University researchers determined that a portfolio made up of 50 percent stocks and 50 percent bonds could safely support a 4 percent annual withdrawal rate, adjusted for inflation.[4] Since 1980 Harvard has withdrawn an average of 4.469 percent of its endowment each year from its $32 billion portfolio.[5]

Okay, now that we know a 4 percent withdrawal rate is considered safe, let's look at a real-world example. James and Arlene Reed retired in 1970 and invested $500,000 in Dodge & Cox Balanced Fund and lived into their late 90s. They decided to withdraw 4 percent ($20,000) at the end of each year, which as you'll notice is well below the amount withdrawn in our first three examples. They felt pretty confident they wouldn't run out of money because a portfolio of 50 percent stocks and 50 percent bonds has historically had a success rate of 96 percent. So, how'd they do? In the first year of their retirement, their income was $20,000, the second year $20,600, the third year $21,218, and so on, increasing their withdrawals by 3 percent each year for inflation. Forty-three years later, after enjoying a steady and increasing income, their annual withdrawal hit $69,213. This is an interesting period to measure since it shows the volatility of the stock

| \$500,000 Balanced Mutual Fund (Withdraw a Constant Dollar Amount: 4% of Initial Balance Inflated Annually) | | | | | |
|---|---|---|---|---|---|
| Year | Year-End Balance | Year-End Withdrawal | Year | Year-End Balance | Year-End Withdrawal |
| 1970 | $493,794 | $20,000 | 1992 | $2,190,024 | $38,322 |
| 1971 | $527,247 | $20,600 | 1993 | $2,498,993 | $39,472 |
| 1972 | $566,165 | $21,218 | 1994 | $2,510,146 | $40,656 |
| 1973 | $489,132 | $21,855 | 1995 | $3,170,204 | $41,876 |
| 1974 | $372,895 | $22,510 | 1996 | $3,593,972 | $43,132 |
| 1975 | $459,327 | $23,185 | 1997 | $4,308,777 | $44,426 |
| 1976 | $551,517 | $23,881 | 1998 | $4,550,697 | $45,759 |
| 1977 | $508,881 | $24,597 | 1999 | $5,049,399 | $47,131 |
| 1978 | $514,224 | $25,335 | 2000 | $5,763,528 | $48,545 |
| 1979 | $557,455 | $26,095 | 2001 | $6,289,648 | $50,002 |
| 1980 | $651,501 | $26,878 | 2002 | $6,052,869 | $51,502 |
| 1981 | $607,817 | $27,685 | 2003 | $7,479,405 | $53,047 |
| 1982 | $737,291 | $28,515 | 2004 | $8,418,923 | $54,638 |
| 1983 | $831,945 | $29,371 | 2005 | $8,917,229 | $56,277 |
| 1984 | $840,940 | $30,252 | 2006 | $10,095,795 | $57,966 |
| 1985 | $1,082,068 | $31,159 | 2007 | $10,213,771 | $59,705 |
| 1986 | $1,253,882 | $32,094 | 2008 | $6,724,440 | $61,495 |
| 1987 | $1,311,407 | $33,057 | 2009 | $8,571,679 | $63,341 |
| 1988 | $1,428,948 | $34,049 | 2010 | $9,555,624 | $65,241 |
| 1989 | $1,721,557 | $35,070 | 2011 | $9,329,669 | $67,198 |
| 1990 | $1,702,137 | $36,122 | 2012 | $10,968,373 | $69,213 |
| 1991 | $2,015,401 | $37,206 | Total | | $1,710,776 |

figure 4.7

## Four Withdrawal Methods ($500,000 Initial Investment)

| Year | 6-Month CD (Withdraw Interest Only) | | Balanced Mutual Fund (Withdraw Dividends and Capital Gains Only) | | Balanced Mutual Fund (Withdraw a Constant 6% of Year-End Balance) | | Balanced Mutual Fund (Withdraw 4% of Initial Investment, Inflated 3% Annually) | |
|---|---|---|---|---|---|---|---|---|
| | Year-End Balance | Year-End Withdrawal | Year-End Balance | Year-End Withdrawal | Year-End Balance | Year-End Withdrawal | Year-End Balance | Year-End Withdrawal |
| 1970 | $500,000 | $38,200 | $479,938 | $32,099 | $482,966 | $30,828 | $493,794 | $20,000 |
| 1971 | $500,000 | $26,050 | $510,031 | $21,845 | $503,684 | $32,150 | $527,247 | $20,600 |
| 1972 | $500,000 | $25,050 | $545,921 | $21,176 | $527,465 | $33,668 | $566,165 | $21,218 |
| 1973 | $500,000 | $45,250 | $460,544 | $32,544 | $447,494 | $28,563 | $489,132 | $21,855 |
| 1974 | $500,000 | $50,100 | $348,417 | $25,189 | $340,042 | $21,705 | $372,895 | $22,510 |
| 1975 | $500,000 | $34,500 | $429,113 | $20,731 | $413,601 | $26,400 | $459,327 | $23,185 |
| 1976 | $500,000 | $28,150 | $514,044 | $22,291 | $487,030 | $31,087 | $551,517 | $23,881 |
| 1977 | $500,000 | $29,550 | $472,358 | $24,966 | $442,835 | $28,266 | $508,881 | $24,597 |
| 1978 | $500,000 | $43,000 | $468,569 | $31,208 | $441,360 | $28,172 | $514,224 | $25,335 |
| 1979 | $500,000 | $57,100 | $498,217 | $32,768 | $470,811 | $30,052 | $557,455 | $26,095 |
| 1980 | $500,000 | $64,700 | $562,416 | $38,341 | $538,564 | $34,376 | $651,501 | $26,878 |
| 1981 | $500,000 | $78,950 | $491,306 | $57,957 | $493,818 | $31,520 | $607,817 | $27,685 |
| 1982 | $500,000 | $62,850 | $561,748 | $48,371 | $584,845 | $37,330 | $737,291 | $28,515 |
| 1983 | $500,000 | $46,400 | $609,229 | $45,251 | $642,231 | $40,993 | $831,945 | $29,371 |
| 1984 | $500,000 | $53,550 | $577,798 | $57,066 | $632,177 | $40,352 | $840,940 | $30,252 |
| 1985 | $500,000 | $41,200 | $711,770 | $46,142 | $786,657 | $50,212 | $1,082,068 | $31,159 |
| 1986 | $500,000 | $32,500 | $727,151 | $115,247 | $878,803 | $56,094 | $1,253,882 | $32,094 |
| 1987 | $500,000 | $35,050 | $684,797 | $97,413 | $885,752 | $56,537 | $1,311,407 | $33,057 |

| 1988 | $500,000 | $39,550 | $715,337 | $47,703 | $928,850 | $59,288 | $1,428,948 | $34,049 |
|------|----------|---------|----------|---------|----------|---------|------------|---------|
| 1989 | $500,000 | $45,400 | $821,444 | $55,060 | $1,073,339 | $68,511 | $1,721,557 | $35,070 |
| 1990 | $500,000 | $40,850 | $780,874 | $47,703 | $1,018,727 | $65,025 | $1,702,137 | $36,122 |
| 1991 | $500,000 | $29,550 | $893,669 | $45,697 | $1,154,773 | $73,709 | $2,015,401 | $37,206 |
| 1992 | $500,000 | $18,800 | $946,054 | $40,124 | $1,200,179 | $76,607 | $2,190,024 | $38,322 |
| 1993 | $500,000 | $16,400 | $1,034,329 | $60,856 | $1,307,664 | $83,468 | $2,498,993 | $39,472 |
| 1994 | $500,000 | $24,800 | $1,007,802 | $47,258 | $1,254,687 | $80,086 | $2,510,146 | $40,656 |
| 1995 | $500,000 | $29,900 | $1,217,120 | $68,880 | $1,509,214 | $96,333 | $3,170,204 | $41,876 |
| 1996 | $500,000 | $27,350 | $1,333,482 | $59,741 | $1,627,598 | $103,889 | $3,593,972 | $43,132 |
| 1997 | $500,000 | $28,650 | $1,488,631 | $122,380 | $1,853,144 | $118,286 | $4,308,777 | $44,426 |
| 1998 | $500,000 | $27,200 | $1,453,856 | $133,080 | $1,858,258 | $118,612 | $4,550,697 | $45,759 |
| 1999 | $500,000 | $27,300 | $1,464,779 | $160,499 | $1,956,278 | $124,869 | $5,049,399 | $47,131 |
| 2000 | $500,000 | $32,950 | $1,413,732 | $260,588 | $2,116,654 | $135,106 | $5,763,528 | $48,545 |
| 2001 | $500,000 | $18,300 | $1,458,315 | $93,101 | $2,188,540 | $139,694 | $6,289,648 | $50,002 |
| 2002 | $500,000 | $9,050 | $1,354,213 | $61,524 | $1,996,627 | $127,444 | $6,052,869 | $51,502 |
| 2003 | $500,000 | $5,850 | $1,628,177 | $51,939 | $2,335,608 | $149,081 | $7,479,405 | $53,047 |
| 2004 | $500,000 | $8,700 | $1,768,836 | $73,115 | $2,487,291 | $158,763 | $8,418,923 | $54,638 |
| 2005 | $500,000 | $18,600 | $1,813,197 | $90,440 | $2,492,069 | $159,068 | $8,917,229 | $56,277 |
| 2006 | $500,000 | $26,150 | $1,942,150 | $120,440 | $2,667,381 | $170,258 | $10,095,795 | $57,966 |
| 2007 | $500,000 | $25,950 | $1,805,617 | $170,463 | $2,551,465 | $153,088 | $10,213,771 | $59,705 |
| 2008 | $500,000 | $15,100 | $1,142,666 | $73,405 | $1,593,460 | $95,608 | $6,724,440 | $61,495 |
| 2009 | $500,000 | $4,150 | $1,427,329 | $33,660 | $1,923,429 | $122,772 | $8,571,679 | $63,341 |
| 2010 | $500,000 | $3,650 | $1,565,314 | $33,883 | $2,029,328 | $129,532 | $9,555,624 | $65,241 |
| 2011 | $500,000 | $2,400 | $1,503,567 | $36,112 | $1,875,876 | $119,737 | $9,329,669 | $67,198 |
| 2012 | $500,000 | $2,300 | $1,740,080 | $36,893 | $2,086,123 | $133,157 | $10,968,373 | $69,213 |

figure 4.8

and bond markets during several recessions, a couple of wars, terrorism, high inflation and interest rates, a stock market crash, and several different political administrations. In Figure 4.7 you can see that their fund balance at the end of 2007 reached an eye-popping $10 million. However, in 2008 their portfolio was reduced to just under $7 million. Even with the damage of the 2008 stock market, the fixed-amount withdrawal method ended with the highest balance of our four methods.

To compare the results of the four withdrawal methods, see Figure 4.8.

In summary, determining a safe withdrawal rate will help you avoid every retiree's worst nightmare–the premature exhaustion of portfolio assets during retirement. In this chapter, we have examined a number of ways to determine that rate in light of fluctuating personal and economic conditions. Regardless of the method you choose, be conservative.

# 5

# TAPPING YOUR IRA EARLY AND AVOIDING PENALTIES

## RETIREMENT DECISION #5: IF I RETIRE EARLY, SHOULD I WITHDRAW FUNDS FROM MY IRA?

Michael Henderson's company is experiencing some corporate down-sizing. At age 54, he is offered an early retirement package. The offer includes a one-time, $500,000 lump-sum distribution from the company's pension plan. With that money and the $500,000 balance he has accumulated in his 401(k) plan, he decides to retire and live off his $1 million portfolio.

It's easy street for Michael now, right? Well, hold on. Because he is not yet age 59½, distributions from his retirement plans will be subject to a 10 percent early-withdrawal penalty. Right out of the gate, Michael's retirement savings, which need to support him for thirty years, will take a big hit.

Fifty-one percent of retirees leave the workforce prior to age 60.[1]

All is not lost, I'm happy to report. If Michael follows the formula allowed by the IRS, he can *avoid* the penalty and still enjoy his riches far into retirement.

If, like Michael, you're fortunate enough to be able to retire before age 59½, a hearty congratulations to you! Early retirement, however, can throw some challenges your way for which you need to be prepared. This chapter will address those challenges and how to effectively deal with them without penalty.

## The Road to Penalty-Free Withdrawals: Section 72T

Gaining access to the investment assets you have locked up in qualified retirement accounts, such as IRAs, 401(k)s, and profit-sharing plans, is often the biggest issue to consider if you're planning to retire early. Each of these retirement plans carries a 10 percent penalty on withdrawals made before age 59½. This puts you, the early retiree, in a predicament: you've accumulated enough money to retire comfortably, but all, or at least a large part, of that money is invested in retirement plans that limit access to your money.

Don't worry. There's a way out of this problem. If you retire before age 59½, here's how to avoid early-withdrawal penalties.

There's a section in the Internal Revenue Code (IRC) called 72T. Follow it to a T, and your early withdrawals will be exempt from penalties. Anyone who has not yet reached age 59½ and who has an IRA is eligible for penalty-free distributions. Distributions can begin at any age and for any reason. The 72T distributions can even begin while you are still employed. In fact, many people trim their work hours back to part-time as they approach retirement. They then begin using 72T distributions to supplement their part-time income.

To qualify for 72T, roll your money to an IRA and then strictly adhere to the following rules:

1. The distributions must be a part of a "series of substantially equal payments" made regularly, at least annually.[2]
2. The amount withdrawn each year must be calculated using one of three IRS-approved distribution formulas: life expectancy, amortization, or annuitization.
3. Distributions must continue for five years or until the recipient is 59½, whichever is longer.[3]

This penalty-free withdrawal strategy also works with deferred annuities (nonqualified variable or fixed) as outlined in the IRC section 72Q.

## Taking the Distributions

The annual distribution amount you're allowed to withdraw is based largely on the size of your retirement account and your life expectancy (or, if married, your joint life expectancy, if you choose). Consequently, 72T distributions are typically better suited for those nearing retirement (between ages 50 and 59½) with large retirement balances. If you're younger than 50 or have a small account balance, your annual distribution amount will be much lower.

To determine how much you can withdraw annually from your IRA without penalty, you must choose one of three approved formulas: life expectancy, amortization, or annuitization. Each calculation will produce a different result.

The best way to determine which formula to use is to plug several combinations of variables into a 72T distribution calculator and compare the results side by side. You can google "72T calculator" or try the user-friendly calculator offered by KJE Computer Solutions at www.javacalc.com. Your tax or financial advisor also can perform these calculations for you.

## Method One: Life Expectancy–Required Minimum Distribution (RMD)

This formula will produce the lowest annual payment. To calculate the life expectancy distribution amount, simply take your previous year-end retirement account balance and divide it by your life expectancy or joint life expectancy. Life expectancy tables can be found on the IRS website: www.irs.gov (search for Publication 590). A 72T calculator will do this number crunching for you automatically. If you use this method, you must recalculate your distribution annually; thus, your yearly distributions will vary somewhat from year to year.

As you get older and your life expectancy decreases, your annual distribution will typically increase. This occurs, however, only if your IRA grows faster than the rate at which you are taking money out of your account.

## Method Two: Amortization

This formula provides a substantially higher distribution amount than the life expectancy method. This method amortizes your IRA balance over your life expectancy and assumes your account will grow at a reasonable interest rate. In addition, the annual withdrawal amount is determined in the first year before the first payment is made and remains fixed for the remaining distribution years. You cannot increase the amount to combat inflation or reduce it to offset the negative impact of a down year in the stock or bond market; doing either will trigger penalties.

## Method Three: Annuitization

The annuitization formula computes payments using a different life expectancy table and a reasonable assumed interest rate. With this method, the retirement account balance is divided by an annuity factor to determine the penalty-free distribution amount. As in the amortization method, the withdrawal amount is fixed in year one and does not change from year to year.

## Reasonable Interest Rate

What is a reasonable interest rate assumption? The IRS allows some flexibility in determining this. It approves using any rate under 120 percent of the federal midterm rate. For example, as of December 2012 the federal midterm rate was 0.95 percent (down from 5.51 percent in 2007); any interest rate under 1.14 percent, which is 120 percent of the midterm rate, would be acceptable. The midterm rate can be found at www.irs.gov (search for "federal midterm rate"). This is usually built into 72T calculators.

If you use an interest-rate assumption that is too high and deplete your IRA before completing your required withdrawals, there are severe penalties. These include both an interest penalty and the 10 percent early-withdrawal penalty you had tried to avoid. These penalties are retroactive on *all* previous 72T distributions.

# An Example of a 72T Distribution

Let's return to Michael Henderson. Remember, he's 54 and received an early retirement package that included $500,000 from the company's pension plan. He also has $500,000 in his 401(k) plan for a total of $1 million.

Because he is not yet age 59½, distributions from his retirement plans would normally be subject to a 10 percent early-withdrawal penalty. However, if Michael follows the formula outlined in Section 72T, he can avoid the penalty and begin taking withdrawals now.

Michael uses a 1.14 percent interest-rate assumption. After running the numbers using a 72T calculator, he discovers he could withdraw between $32,787 and $39,001 annually from his million-dollar portfolio without incurring penalties. Figure 5.1 outlines how much he could take out annually under each IRS-approved distribution formula.

As you manipulate the interest-rate assumptions, you can vary the annual distribution amounts. This flexibility is available only when you initially perform the calculations. Remember, when using the amortization and annuitization methods, you cannot change the amount once you begin receiving distributions.

| 72T Distribution ($1 Million, 1.14% Interest Rate Assumption) | | | |
| --- | --- | --- | --- |
| Age at Year End | Life Expectancy/ RMD Payout | Amortization Payout | Annuitization Payout |
| 54 | $32,787 | $39,001 | $38,664 |
| 55 | $32,962 | $39,001 | $38,664 |
| 56 | $33,139 | $39,001 | $38,664 |
| 57 | $33,318 | $39,001 | $38,664 |
| 58 | $33,498 | $39,001 | $38,664 |
| 59 | $33,679 | $39,001 | $38,664 |
| 60 | $33,861 | $39,001 | $38,664 |

figure 5.1

## Stick to Your Schedule

The method you choose to calculate your distributions isn't as important as adhering to your set schedule. To satisfy the "substantially equal payment" rule, you must choose one of the three methods discussed above and withdraw the calculated amount at least annually.

Failure to withdraw the calculated amount will result in a 10 percent early-withdrawal penalty tax, plus an interest penalty. The tax and penalty are imposed, retroactively, on all previous withdrawals received. Additionally, if you have been receiving payments and suddenly take a distribution amount that either exceeds or is below your annual distribution requirement, you will be penalized on every distribution you have received to date.

There is a single exception. In 2002 the IRS ruled that early retirees can change their distribution payout calculation one time from the annuitization or amortization methods to the life expectancy method. For example, if, due to market losses, your IRA is being depleted too quickly, this exception will allow you to change to an option that will reduce the amount you must withdraw each year.

Although the IRS's distribution structure is very rigid, it is very easy to automate your withdrawals by setting up a systematic withdrawal program from your IRA. Most financial institutions will allow you to establish automatic monthly, quarterly, or annual distributions from your IRA for a set number of years. By setting up a systematic withdrawal plan, you will not need to worry about breaking IRS rules by deviating from the required distribution amounts or how frequently you receive them.

Again, once you begin taking distributions, you must continue to do so for the next five years, or until you are 59½, *whichever is longer.* For example, if you begin taking distributions at age 52, you must continue for seven and a half years. If you begin taking distributions at age 57, you must continue for five years until you are 62. With this in mind, if you're 40, you would not be wise to begin taking distributions. Many changes could occur in your financial life in the years before reaching age 59½. For example, if you decide to go back to work and you no longer need the income generated from distributions, you cannot stop them without incurring the 10 percent early-withdrawal penalty. Of course, you could redirect your 72T distributions into a non-retirement investment account and simply earmark the funds for retirement.

Once you fulfill the five-year or age 59½ requirement (whichever is applicable to you), you can withdraw any amount without incurring penalties.

## Tax Considerations

The distributions from your IRA are penalty-free if you follow the guidelines outlined above. They are not, however, free from income tax. IRA distributions, regardless of when they are taken, are subject to income tax and will be taxed as ordinary income.

Each year after receiving distributions, you will receive a Form 1099R from your IRA provider indicating the amount of taxable withdrawals taken during the previous year. A distribution code 2 will be placed on the Form 1099R. This indicates that the distributions are part of early withdrawals with a known exception–"substantially equal payments." If the code 2 does not appear on your 1099R form, the IRS will view your distributions as premature and apply penalties. In situations where this occurs, don't be alarmed. Simply file a Form 5329 along with your 1040, indicating that you are taking a series of substantially equal payments according to the rules set forth in Section 72T of the IRS code. These forms and the instructions for completing them can be found at www.irs.gov.

Additionally, when you begin taking distributions from your IRA, you should, in most cases, request that taxes be withheld. Otherwise, you'll be facing a large tax bill when you file your taxes at year's end. Withholding taxes from your distribution is similar to the taxes withheld from your pay-roll check while working. Your IRA provider has a tax withholding form that allows you to specify the percentage of your distributions you want to withhold to pay federal and state income taxes. When determining your distribution amount, consider up front how much money you will need for taxes and living expenses.

## Future Flexibility: Splitting Your IRA

Before you begin taking distributions, consider the following important questions. First, do you anticipate needing to take withdrawals from your IRA in future years larger than your calculated 72T payments? And second, will your scheduled 72T distributions require you to continue taking with-drawals past age 59½ to satisfy the mandatory five-year withdrawal period? If the answer is "yes" to either of these questions, you may want to consider a more flexible strategy.

If you have a large enough portfolio balance, split your IRA into two separate IRA accounts before starting 72T distributions. Both accounts will be in your name but will have different account numbers. There are no limits to the number of IRA accounts you can open. In fact, you can have multiple IRA accounts at the same financial institution.

In the first IRA account, deposit only the amount necessary to provide you with the income you will need during the time you take 72T distri-butions. Using a 72T calculator, manipulate the account balance and the interest-rate assumption in the distribution formulas discussed above to determine the minimum amount to deposit into this IRA account. Be con-servative; deposit a little more than is needed to lessen the risk of depleting your IRA before completing your scheduled distributions.

Let's return to Michael Henderson again to see how this strategy works. Michael, who's retiring at age 54, figures he needs only $25,000 before taxes each year from his IRA to maintain his lifestyle until age 59½. If he deposits $650,000 of his $1 million portfolio into one IRA and uses a 1.14 percent interest rate assumption and the amortization method, he could receive distributions of up to $25,351 per year penalty-free. He could then deposit his remaining $350,000 into a second IRA and not take any withdrawals from this account until he's 59½ (Figure 5.2).

However, in the second year of his retirement (age 55), Michael decides he needs $10,000 more income annually. Because he set up a second IRA account, he can simply follow the same process above to tap into his second account penalty free. He has $350,000 in his second IRA but calculates he only needs $260,000 to generate the extra income he desires. He then directs the remaining $90,000 into a third IRA account, which is available for future needs.

| Splitting Your IRA ($1 Million) | | |
|---|---|---|
| | Year 1 | Year 2 |
| IRA #1 | Deposit: $650,000<br>Begin 72T Distributions: $10,000 | Continue 72T Distributions:<br>$25,351 |
| IRA #2 | Deposit: $350,000<br>No distributions | Transfer $90,000 to IRA #3<br>Begin 72T Distributions: $10,000 |
| IRA #3 | | Transfer from IRA #2: $90,000<br>No Distributions |

figure 5.2

Splitting his IRA before taking 72T distributions gave Michael income flexibility in the future. If Michael had kept all his money in one IRA account and had begun taking 72T distributions, he would not be able to make any changes until he turned 59½.

Splitting an IRA into two or more accounts also makes sense if you will turn 59½ during the mandatory five-year distribution period. Remember, normal IRA distributions can begin before age 59½ without penalty. Let's say you begin taking distributions at age 57; you must continue doing so until you reach age 62–the mandatory five-year period–to avoid the penalty. At age 60, three years after you start taking your 72T distribution, you decide to purchase a condo and need a lump sum of money. What can you do? With only one IRA, your options are limited because of the 72T rules. You can't take any additional withdrawals beyond the 72T distributions for two more years. Had you split your retirement money into two IRAs, the first account would have provided your 72T distributions and the second would be available after age 59½ for your condo, without penalty. Remember, you must split the IRA before beginning any 72T distributions.

If you die during the distribution period, your beneficiary is not required to continue receiving distributions. If the IRA beneficiary is your spouse, he or she has the option to roll the money into his/her own IRA account.

## More Penalty-Free Distribution Strategies

### *Lump-Sum Distributions for Those over Age 55 (or Age 50)*

If you are 55 or older and leave your company, you are eligible for a cash distribution from your employer-sponsored retirement plan without incurring the 10 percent early-withdrawal penalty. The age is reduced to 50 for qualified public safety retirees.[4]

This exception to the early-withdrawal penalty only applies to distributions taken directly from an employer-sponsored plan, not from an IRA. The employer must, however, withhold 20 percent of the distribution amount for taxes.

This distribution strategy works particularly well if you know you're going to need a large sum of money immediately upon leaving your company to do things such as launch your own business or buy resort property. In these cases, a penalty-free withdrawal can be especially useful.

Upon leaving your company, you can request to have all or part of the distribution sent directly to you free from penalty. Any portion not distributed directly to you can be rolled over into an IRA to avoid taxes and penalties on money you don't need immediately.

Be aware, however, that even though the early-withdrawal penalty is avoided, there are disadvantages to this distribution method. First, the amount you withdraw will be taxed as ordinary income, and a large distribution may launch you into a higher tax bracket. Second, your employer is required to withhold 20 percent of your distribution amount to pay taxes. If you owe more, you will be required to pay additional taxes when you file.

The biggest disadvantage, though, is the loss of tax deferral and future compounded interest on both the amount you withdraw and spend, as well as the portion of the distribution that goes to pay taxes. The severe impact of this approach is discussed in the Cash Distribution section of Chapter 8. A cash distribution early in retirement that greatly reduces the size of your retirement nest egg may hamper your ability to reach your long-term retirement goals. It is highly recommended that you seek professional advice before taking a cash distribution to make sure you have enough money to fund your retirement goals. Most investment advisors will recommend you take out as little as possible in the form of a lump sum, so you don't undermine your ability to enjoy your golden years.

## In-Service Withdrawals

To maintain company benefits, especially health insurance, many people work part-time as they ease their way into retirement. This move from full- to part-time employment usually means a significant drop in income. To compensate, many employees take "in-service withdrawals" from their company-sponsored retirement plans to supplement their income and maintain an acceptable standard of living.

As the name suggests, this distribution method allows an employee to take a withdrawal from the company's retirement plan while still an active plan participant. This distribution can initially be rolled over into an IRA to avoid taxes and penalties. Once in the IRA account, distributions can provide additional income. Remember, the usual taxes and penalties will apply to your IRA distributions. Consequently, if you are not yet age 59½, you should consider implementing a 72T distribution plan to avoid the 10 percent early-withdrawal penalty.

This is a sound strategy if a substantial portion of your retirement savings is invested in your company-sponsored retirement plan and you need additional income. You may also want to take an in-service distribution and roll the money into your IRA if your 401(k) plan offers limited or poor investment choices. In this situation, you could keep contributing to the 401(k) after the IRA rollover has taken place to continue taking advantage of the employer's matching contribution. In-service withdrawals are not permitted by all company-sponsored retirement plans. If, however, the plan allows in-service withdrawals, plan provisions will specify the portions of the plan available for distribution. Contact your retirement benefits administrator to determine if this withdrawal method is available and to determine the portion of your plan balance that can be withdrawn.

• • •

If you're thinking of retiring early, don't be intimidated by the penalties associated with withdrawals from retirement plans. By applying the strategies and tactics discussed in this chapter, you can avoid pitfalls that often harm early retirees. With foresight and savvy financial planning, you can develop a strategy to minimize the impact of penalties on your hard-earned nest egg.

# SECTION 2

## SOURCES OF RETIREMENT INCOME

Social Security
Company Pensions
Personal Savings

# 6

# MAXIMIZE YOUR
# SOCIAL SECURITY

## RETIREMENT DECISION #6: WHEN SHOULD
## I BEGIN TAKING SOCIAL SECURITY?

You've been paying Social Security taxes all of your working life. Now it's time for a tax refund. Those retiring want to know two things about their Social Security benefit: how much will their benefit be and when should they begin taking it so they receive the most money over their lifetime?

How much will Social Security really contribute to your income when it comes time to retire? Some people assume that because FICA taxes seem to take such a notable chunk out of their paychecks, they will be able to count on Social Security as their sole source of retirement income. Others

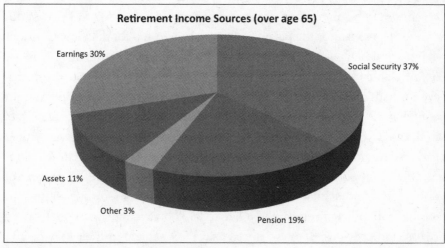

Source: Social Security Administration

figure 6.1

mistakenly suppose that Social Security benefits will be so insignificant that they will have almost no effect on their long-term retirement income. In truth, neither assumption is accurate.

Statistics show that 37 percent of the average American's income over age 65 is derived from Social Security, another 30 percent from continued work, 19 percent from pensions, and 11 percent comes from personal savings (IRAs, 401(k)s, brokerage accounts, annuities, certificates of deposit, checking and savings accounts, etc.) as illustrated in Figure 6.1.[1]

Social Security was never intended to be a reliable single source of retirement income. Still, it may be the biggest piece of your retirement income pie and is, therefore, worth taking the time to understand.

## Social Security Is a Good Investment

Let's think about Social Security in a different way. Let's look at it as we would an investment. By determining how much you've put in (tax) and how much you'll get out of it during retirement, we can see if it is a good investment. As it stands today, the Social Security program is a forced savings plan that works fairly well when you consider what it would take to mimic the program on your own. Of the 7.65 percent FICA tax *you* pay, 5.3 percent of it is earmarked for the Social Security trust fund. For example, if you turned 66 in 2012 and had paid the maximum FICA tax your entire forty-year career, you'd be responsible for depositing a total of $122,711 into the trust fund. If you choose to begin receiving benefits at 66, you'd receive $2,513 per month or $30,156 per year for the balance of your life adjusted for inflation. Consider what it would take for you to duplicate this program on your own. If at age 66 you plan to live twenty years, to age 86, you would need an investment account with a balance of $413,000 in order to withdraw $2,513 per month (assuming a 2 percent cost-of-living adjustment (COLA) and a 6 percent rate of return). If you live twenty-five years into retirement, to age 91, you would need a starting balance of $475,000. So, if this were an investment, would it have been a good one? Yes! You would have needed to save 5.3 percent of your income and achieve a 7.35 percent annual rate of return if you live to 86 or an 8.05 percent return if you live to 91. The average investor, as we've discussed in previous chapters, doesn't save 5.3 percent of their income and doesn't even come close to achieving a 7 percent annual rate of return. For those who receive Social Security, it is a great deal.

# Who Qualifies for Social Security?

If you think that simply being a U.S. citizen qualifies you for Social Security benefits, think again. As you work and pay FICA taxes, you earn Social Security credits. You must earn forty credits to be eligible for benefits. In 2012, you have to earn $1,130 in income during the year to obtain one credit. You can earn a maximum of four credits per year, earning them all in the first month or over twelve months. You must work at least ten years to be eligible for retirement benefits.

These credits simply qualify you to receive benefits. Most people will earn more credits than the minimum forty they need to be eligible for benefits. Extra credits will not increase the amount of benefits you receive; however, you won't receive any benefits if you don't have the minimum forty credits.

# How Much Have You Paid In?

If you earn $106,800 or less annually in 2012, you pay 7.65 percent FICA tax, which is paid into three different trust funds: 5.3 percent of your income is earmarked to pay Social Security retirement benefits (OASI: Old Age Survivors Insurance), 0.90 percent is set aside to pay disability benefits (DI: disability insurance), and 1.45 percent goes to Medicare to pay health benefits (HI: health insurance). Your employer pays an additional 7.65 percent of your salary into the funds. Any income over $110,100, however, is not taxed for Social Security (OASDI). Thus, the more you make above this level, the smaller the percentage of your annual income goes into the funds. The money in the trust funds is invested in government securities. In 2012, according to the Social Security Administration (SSA), the average interest rate paid by the government securities in the Social Security trust fund (OASI) was 3.83 percent.

# How Social Security Determines
# Your Benefit Amount

The average earnings over your working life determine how much your monthly Social Security benefits will be in retirement. The government uses the following elements to determine your benefit:

- Your earnings are adjusted to account for inflation. For example, if a 3 percent inflation rate is used, the $10,000 you earned in 1980 would be equivalent to a little more than $25,751 in 2012.

- Your total earnings during the thirty-five years in which you earned the most income are averaged to determine your average monthly "indexed" earnings. The maximum earnings used per year was $110,100 in 2012.
- A formula is applied to these earnings to arrive at your basic benefit or primary insurance amount (PIA). This is the amount you receive at your full retirement age. For most people preparing to retire in the near future, full retirement age is 66.

The benefit computation is complex, and there are no simple tables published by the SSA to show exactly how much you will receive. However, you can obtain a Social Security statement online at www.ssa.gov /mystatement/. The SSA does report the average and maximum benefits at various ages and in a range of circumstances (Figures 6.2 and 6.3).

**Find It on the Web**

You can request a Social Security statement via the Web by logging on to www.ssa.gov/mystatement.

| Maximum Social Security Benefit in 2012 | |
|---|---|
| Retirement Age | Monthly Benefit |
| 62 | $1,885 |
| 66 | $2,513 |
| 70 | $3,359 |

Source: Social Security Administration

figure 6.2

| Average Social Security Benefit | |
|---|---|
| Beneficiary | Monthly Benefit |
| All Retired Workers | $1,186 |
| Aged Couple | $1,925 |
| Widowed Mother & 2 Children | $2,455 |
| Aged Widow(er), No Children | $1,143 |
| All Disabled Workers | $1,072 |

Source: Social Security Administration, 2012

figure 6.3

# Full Retirement Age

Full retirement benefits are available when you reach full retirement age. The table in Figure 6.4 displays the SSA's definition of full retirement. Full retirement age is gradually being raised to reduce the strain on the Social Security system caused by increased life expectancy in the United States. As Americans continue living longer, it's reasonable to expect that the retirement age will continue to increase.

# When to Start Taking Social Security

Not everyone chooses to start receiving benefits at his or her full retirement age. Some people begin as early as age 62, while others postpone receiving benefits until reaching age 70. When should you begin taking your benefit? The answer depends primarily on two factors: how long you live and whether you are going to continue to work.

If you continue working after you begin receiving Social Security, your benefit may be reduced. If it is reduced, you likely should not take retirement early.

Let's look closer at each of these determining factors of when you should start taking Social Security.

| Full Retirement Age ||
| Year of Birth | Full Retirement Age |
| --- | --- |
| 1937 or earlier | 65 |
| 1938 | 65 + 2 Months |
| 1939 | 65 + 4 Months |
| 1940 | 65 + 6 Months |
| 1941 | 65 + 8 Months |
| 1942 | 65 + 10 Months |
| 1943–54 | 66 |
| 1955 | 66 + 2 Months |
| 1956 | 66 + 4 Months |
| 1957 | 66 + 6 Months |
| 1958 | 66 + 8 Months |
| 1959 | 66 + 10 Months |
| 1960 and later | 67 |

*Source: Social Security Administration*

*figure 6.4*

## *Life Expectancy*

If you knew exactly how long you were going to live, deciding when to begin taking Social Security would be an easy question to answer. You can begin receiving benefits as early as age 62, but your benefit will be less than what it would be if you waited until your full retirement age. Or you can delay receiving benefits until age 70 and receive a benefit greater than your full retirement age amount. The catch is that once you start, your benefit is locked for as long as you receive Social Security benefits (adjusted for inflation).

Let's assume you are trying to decide whether you should take your benefit at 62 or wait until your full retirement age of 66 or beyond. If your benefit is $10,000 per year at full retirement, it would be reduced to $7,500 if you begin at 62 (a 25 percent reduction). If you begin taking it at 62, the amount will stay the same for life; it won't adjust back up to $10,000 when you hit 66. (It will, however, adjust annually for inflation.)

So which option will put the most money in your pocket? Well, again it depends on how long you will live. The break-even point, when comparing the total benefits you'd receive at age 62 to those beginning at age 66, is about age 80 (Figure 6.5). If you don't make it to age 80, you would receive

| When Should I Start Taking Benefits? | | | |
|---|---|---|---|
| Annual Benefit at 62 | $7,500 | | |
| Annual Benefit at 66 | $10,000 | | |
| Annual Benefit at 70 | $13,200 | | |
| Cumulative Benefits (2% COLA) | | | |
| Age | | | |
| 62 | $7,500 | | |
| 63 | $15,150 | | |
| 64 | $22,953 | | |
| 65 | $30,912 | | |
| 66 | $39,030 | $10,000 | |
| 67 | $47,311 | $20,200 | |
| 68 | $55,757 | $30,604 | |
| 69 | $64,372 | $41,216 | |
| 70 | $73,160 | $52,040 | $13,200 |
| 71 | $82,123 | $63,081 | $26,664 |
| 72 | $91,265 | $74,343 | $40,397 |
| 73 | $100,591 | $85,830 | $54,405 |
| 74 | $110,102 | $97,546 | $68,693 |
| 75 | $119,805 | $109,497 | $83,267 |

**Continued**

| | | | |
|---|---|---|---|
| 76 | $129,701 | $121,687 | $98,133 |
| 77 | $139,795 | $134,121 | $113,295 |
| 78 | $150,091 | $146,803 | $128,761 |
| 79 | $160,592 | $159,739 | $144,536 |
| 80 | $171,304 | $172,934 | $160,627 |
| 81 | $182,230 | $186,393 | $177,040 |
| 82 | $193,375 | $200,121 | $193,780 |
| 83 | $204,742 | $214,123 | $210,856 |
| 84 | $216,337 | $228,406 | $228,273 |
| 85 | $228,164 | $242,974 | $246,039 |
| 86 | $240,227 | $257,833 | $264,159 |
| 87 | $252,532 | $272,990 | $282,643 |
| 88 | $265,082 | $288,450 | $301,495 |
| 89 | $277,884 | $304,219 | $320,725 |
| 90 | $290,942 | $320,303 | $340,340 |
| 91 | $304,261 | $336,709 | $360,347 |
| 92 | $317,846 | $353,443 | $380,754 |
| 93 | $331,703 | $370,512 | $401,569 |
| 94 | $345,837 | $387,922 | $422,800 |
| 95 | $360,254 | $405,681 | $444,456 |
| 96 | $374,959 | $423,794 | $466,545 |
| 97 | $389,958 | $442,270 | $489,076 |
| 98 | $405,257 | $461,116 | $512,057 |
| 99 | $420,862 | $480,338 | $535,499 |
| 100 | $436,779 | $499,945 | $559,409 |

figure 6.5

more money by starting your benefit at age 62. If you live past age 80, you would receive more total benefits if you wait until age 66, your full retirement age, to begin receiving Social Security. If, however, you live past age 85, you would receive the most money by delaying the start of your benefit until age 70.

To make an educated guess at your life expectancy, review Figure 1.5 from Chapter 1 on page 8. Also, consider your current health and future health based on your family medical history.

## Receiving Benefits Prior to Your Full Retirement Age

As we saw above, if you choose to receive benefits before reaching your full retirement age, your benefits will be reduced (Figure 6.6); waiting beyond your full retirement age will increase your benefits (Figure 6.7).

Let's consider the choices facing Edwin, age 62, who would like to retire now before he is eligible for full retirement benefits. Edwin has determined that he will need at least $700 monthly in Social Security benefits to supplement his other retirement income to maintain his desired standard of living. At his full retirement age, 66, his Social Security monthly benefit would be $1,000. Will Edwin's Social Security benefits amount to $700 if he retires at age 62, forty-eight months before full retirement?

Using the information in Figure 6.6, we can determine that Edwin will meet his goal: his full retirement benefit would be reduced by 25 percent if he were to retire now (0.52 multiplied by 48 months equals 25 percent).

| Social Security Reduction for Early Benefits (Age 62) | | | | |
|---|---|---|---|---|
| Year of Birth | Full Retirement Age | Months Short | Monthly Reduction | Total Reduction |
| 1937 or earlier | 65 | 36 | 0.555% | 20.00% |
| 1938 | 65 + 2 months | 38 | 0.548% | 20.83% |
| 1939 | 65 + 4 months | 40 | 0.541% | 21.67% |
| 1940 | 65 + 6 months | 42 | 0.535% | 22.50% |
| 1941 | 65 + 8 months | 44 | 0.530% | 23.33% |
| 1942 | 65 + 10 months | 46 | 0.525% | 24.17% |
| 1943–1954 | 66 | 48 | 0.520% | 25.00% |
| 1955 | 66 + 2 months | 50 | 0.516% | 25.84% |
| 1956 | 66 + 4 months | 52 | 0.512% | 26.66% |
| 1957 | 66 + 6 months | 54 | 0.509% | 27.50% |
| 1958 | 66 + 8 months | 56 | 0.505% | 28.33% |
| 1959 | 66 + 10 months | 58 | 0.502% | 29.17% |
| 1960 and later | 67 | 60 | 0.500% | 30.00% |

*Source: Social Security Administration*

figure 6.6

Consequently, his benefit would drop from $1,000 to $750 per month. If he decided to wait to receive benefits until age 65, his benefits would be reduced by only 6 percent (0.52 multiplied by 12 months equals 6 percent). In this case, his monthly benefit would be reduced by only $60 to equal $940 per month.

The SSA's website, www.ssa.gov, offers the following guideline:

> *If your full retirement age is 67, the reduction for starting your benefits at 62 is about 30 percent; at age 63, it's about 25 percent; at age 64, about 20 percent; at age 65, about 13⅓ percent; and at age 66, about 6⅔ percent.*

Every person approaching retirement age should keep in mind one very important point: if you choose to receive Social Security before your full retirement age, your benefit is *permanently* reduced. So do the math before making your final decision.

## Delaying Social Security Benefits

Depending on your circumstances, it may be beneficial to delay receiving Social Security until after your full retirement age. The longer you wait to begin receiving benefits, up to age 70, the larger your benefit will be. Figure 6.7 outlines the rate of increase for delaying your retirement benefits.

Let's take the example of Alice Treynor, a 66-year-old who enjoys her job as a sales manager for a pharmaceutical company. Because she likes working and has a comfortable income from her employer, she has decided to delay Social Security benefits until age 68. What will her benefit amount be at 68 if, at her full retirement age, 66, her benefit is $1,000 per month?

In Alice's case, the benefit increase is 8 percent per year. Delaying benefits two years will increase the amount Alice receives

| Social Security Increase for Each Month/Year Delayed Benefits | | |
|---|---|---|
| Year of Birth | Monthly Increase | Yearly Increase |
| 1933–1934 | 0.458% | 5.5% |
| 1935–1936 | 0.500% | 6.0% |
| 1937–1938 | 0.542% | 6.5% |
| 1939–1940 | 0.583% | 7.0% |
| 1941–1942 | 0.625% | 7.5% |
| 1943 and later | 0.667% | 8.0% |

*Source: Social Security Administration*

figure 6.7

by a total of 16 percent. As a result, her benefit at age 68 will be permanently increased by $160, to $1,160 per month.

The SSA issues the following advice to those who delay retirement. "If you decide to delay your retirement, be sure to sign up for Medicare at age 65. In some circumstances, medical insurance costs more if you delay applying for it."

## Spousal Benefits

Your spouse's Social Security benefits will be calculated in the same manner as your own—by using the number of years he or she has worked and the amount he or she has earned. Your spouse will receive his or her earned benefit or one-half the amount of your benefit, whichever is greater. (This rule also applies to nonworking spouses who haven't qualified for their own benefit.) The same rules apply for early or delayed retirement. Additionally, your spouse can qualify for Medicare on your record at age 65, if he or she has not already qualified.

### Divorced Spouse

Your divorced spouse (even if you have remarried) may qualify for benefits based on your record, if you are 62 or older, even if you are not receiving benefits yet. There are three main requirements for your former spouse to qualify for benefits based on your record:

- The marriage must have lasted at least 10 years.
- Your former spouse must be at least 62 years old.
- Your former spouse must currently be unmarried.

The amount of benefits your former spouse will receive does not affect your benefits nor those of your current spouse.

## Working and Receiving Benefits

Like Alice, many people simply enjoy working and choose to continue doing so well past their Social Security retirement age. Others continue to work because they need or want extra income. In either case, the good news is that if you work and are at full retirement age, you can keep all your Social Security benefits no matter how much you earn. However, if you retire early and continue working, there are limits on the amount you can earn. Exceeding those limits will reduce your benefit. The annual earning limitations are posted at www.ssa.gov.

Using 2012 limits, if you are working and collecting benefits between age 62 and your full retirement age, your benefit will be reduced $1 for every $2 you earn over $14,640. In the year you reach your full retirement age, you will lose $1 for every $3 you earn over $38,880 until the month you reach full retirement age. If you plan to continue working after age 62, these reductions will dictate whether you should begin taking your benefits.

For example, in 2012, Ken Ashton qualified to receive the maximum $22,620 per year Social Security benefit available to those age 62. He earned $59,880 in salary in 2012. He wants to know how much his benefit will be reduced if he continues to work and earn the same amount in 2013. His $59,880 income is $45,240 over the $14,640 earnings limit. His benefit will be reduced by $1 for every $2 he earns over $14,640 (divide $45,240 by 2). Consequently, in 2013 Ken's benefit will be reduced by $22,620, wiping out his entire benefit. Obviously, Ken should not begin taking his benefit at age 62. It should be noted that if you retire and begin receiving benefits early, the income your spouse earns will not adversely affect your benefit.

Diane Jamison, 62, also qualifies for the $22,620 per year maximum benefit. She earns $37,260 per year but decides she needs a little extra money. Her $37,260 salary is $22,620 over the $14,640 earnings limit. Her benefit will be reduced by $11,310 to equal $11,310 per year. By earning $37,260,

> One out of three people over age 65 continue to work.[2]

her $22,620 benefit will be cut in half. Even though adding her income ($37,260) and the reduced Social Security benefit ($11,310) would provide 30 percent more money each year, Diane should wait to start receiving her benefits.

Don't forget, in the month you reach full retirement age your earnings will not affect your Social Security benefit. You can earn as much as you want.

## Advanced Social Security Strategies

If you are married, in addition to deciding whether to begin taking your benefits before or after your full retirement age, you should also look at a couple of additional strategies. The first is called "file and suspend" benefits, and the second is referred to as "restricting" benefits. There are a couple of important things to note as we consider these options. First of all, these options are only available to those who wait until their full retirement age to begin taking benefits. Secondly, your spouse cannot begin receiving a spousal benefit until you begin taking your Social Security benefit. Here is how the strategies work. Let's look at Bart and Janene Saunders, who both just turned age 66. At Bart's full retirement age of 66, he filed to begin receiving his $2,000/month benefit. However, he immediately suspended his benefit so no checks were sent to him. Since he suspended the receipt of his benefit, he qualifies for the delayed retirement credit of 8 percent per year. His plan is to wait until age 70 to begin receiving his benefits. By delaying his benefit he will receive $2,640 per month at age 70 instead of the $2,000 per month at age 66 (a 32 percent increase). Because Bart filed for benefits, Janene can now begin receiving a spousal benefit on Bart's record. Rather than receiving the $750/month benefit she earned on her own record, she will receive a $1,000 per month spousal benefit, or one-half of her husband's benefit.

To look at the second strategy, let's assume that Janene's full retirement benefit is $1,500/month instead of $750/month. If this were the case, she could file and then restrict her $1,500 benefit and begin receiving the $1,000 spousal benefit. Since she is delaying the receipt of her earned benefit, $1,500/month, it will qualify for the 8 percent per year delayed retirement credit. So, Janene will receive a $1,000 spousal benefit until age 70, at which point she will stop the spousal benefit and begin taking her own benefit, which will be increased 32 percent from $1,500/month to $1,980/month.

Filing for and then suspending your benefits allows your spouse to begin receiving a spousal benefit (one-half of your benefit). Restricting your benefit allows you to delay the receipt of your benefits while at the same time receiving a spousal benefit.

## Investing Your Benefits

So far we've talked about taking your benefit early and receiving a reduced amount, delaying the receipt of your benefit and receiving an increased benefit, filing and suspending benefits, and also filing and restricting benefits. Now let's add another variable. If you don't need your Social Security benefit to cover your living expenses and you expect to live a long time, is there any reason to start receiving reduced benefits at age 62 as opposed to increased benefits at age 70? The answer depends on what you'll do with the money if you begin receiving it at age 62. If you invest your benefit and obtain a decent return, you may just receive more money over your lifetime. Keith Alexander opted to take his $1,500 per month benefit at age 62 and invest the money into a balanced stock and bond portfolio. He had the option of waiting and receiving $2,000 per month at age 66, his full retirement age, or $2,640 at age 70. Did he make a good decision?

If he delays receiving benefits until age 70 ($2,640) and lives to age 85, he'll receive a total of $628,626 in cumulative benefits (assumes a 2 percent COLA). If, however, he takes the $1,500 at age 62, invests it, and receives an 8 percent annual return, he will receive cumulative benefits of $1,379,814 over his lifetime. At a 6 percent return, his lifetime benefits would be $1,063,301. Is it possible to obtain a 6 to 8 percent return on your investments? As we'll discuss in upcoming chapters, the answer is yes, it is possible, if you have a good strategy and discipline. For example, had you invested in the Dodge & Cox Balanced Fund over the past twenty years, your annual return would have been 9.4 percent.

If taking your Social Security benefit allows you to stop taking portfolio withdrawals, so the money can stay invested, then it's really the same as if you were investing your Social Security benefit. For example, at age 62, I could take a $1,500 withdrawal from my investment portfolio to cover my living expenses and delay receiving my Social Security benefit, or I could receive my $1,500 Social Security benefit and use it to cover living expenses and delay taking any withdrawals.

Since there are so many options, I recommend you use Social Security optimizer software to look at each option side by side to determine which one will put the most money in your pocket over your lifetime. A sample Social Security optimizer is located at the end of this chapter (Figure 6.11).

## Applying for Benefits

Deciding when to start taking Social Security benefits can be a difficult decision to make. By now, however, armed with the information in these pages, you are far more knowledgeable on Social Security than the average person. Still, even if you've decided when to start taking benefits, meet with a Social Security representative or professional financial advisor one year before you plan to retire. The rules governing Social Security are complicated, and according to the SSA, "It may be to your advantage to start your retirement benefits before you actually stop working."

When you're ready, you can apply for your benefits in one of three ways:

- Apply online at www.socialsecurity.gov/applyonline.
- Call toll-free: (800) 772-1213. Hearing impaired: TTY at (800) 325-0778.
- Apply in person at your local Social Security office.

## Taxation of Your Social Security

Whether your Social Security benefits are taxed depends on the level of your income during retirement. If your income is between $25,000 and $34,000 for individual filers, or between $32,000 and $44,000 for joint filers, 50 percent of your Social Security benefit is subject to income tax. If your income is greater than $34,000 for a single filer and $44,000 for joint filers, up to 85 percent of your Social Security benefits are subject to income tax.

Income is calculated by combining all of your wages, earned interest, taxable dividends, tax-free interest, and retirement plan distributions, and then adding half of your Social Security benefit.

At the beginning of each year, the SSA issues a Social Security Benefit Statement (Form SSA-1099), which shows the total amount of benefits you received during the previous year. Use this statement when you complete your federal income tax return.

| Taxation of Social Security Benefits | |
|---|---|
| **Individual Filing Status** | |
| **Yearly Income** | **% of Benefit Taxable** |
| $25,000–$34,000 | 50% |
| $34,000+ | 85% |
| **Joint Filing Status** | |
| **Yearly Income** | **% of Benefit Taxable** |
| $32,000–$44,000 | 50% |
| $44,000+ | 85% |

Source: Social Security Administration

figure 6.8

## Strategies for Reducing Taxes on Social Security Benefits

One item that may be pushing your income above the threshold listed in Figure 6.8 is interest and dividends derived from stocks, bonds, mutual funds, bank accounts, money market accounts, municipal bonds, and other interest-bearing investments. If you are not spending the interest or principal from these investment vehicles and are just reinvesting all of your earnings, you may want to consider repositioning the money into a no-load fixed or variable annuity.

Annuities provide tax-deferred growth. Therefore, your investment earnings are not reported each year for tax purposes and aren't added to your income. If you are not using the money right now, it does not make sense to have the investment earnings increase your income and, thus, the amount of tax you pay on your Social Security benefits.

# Cost-of-Living Adjustments

As you can see in Figure 6.9, in most years Social Security adjusts upward to help retirees keep pace with inflation. Since 1975, benefits have increased an average of about 4 percent per year. However, since 1990 the pace has slowed, averaging an increase of a little under 3 percent per year.

# The Status of the Social Security Trust Fund

Many people are wondering these days, and understandably so, whether Social Security benefits will be available when they are eligible to receive them. Even the SSA acknowledges that the program is on dangerous ground. In the 2012 Annual Report, the SSA reported that unless lawmakers make changes the trust fund will be depleted in 2033, after which point the taxes we pay into Social Security would be enough to pay about three-fourths of scheduled benefits through 2086.

The main thing that contributes to the depletion of Social Security is Americans' increased life expectancy. We're healthier today than ever before, and life expectancies continue climbing. When the Social Security program first began paying benefits in 1940, the average life expectancy for men and women reaching age 65 was 77 and 78, respectively. Today, life expectancy has increased six years for men, to age 83, and seven years for women, to age 85.

In addition, we face a shift in demographics as the baby-boomer

| Social Security Cost-of-Living Adjustments | | | |
|---|---|---|---|
| Year | COLA | Year | COLA |
| 1975 | 8.0% | 1995 | 2.6% |
| 1976 | 6.4% | 1996 | 2.9% |
| 1977 | 5.9% | 1997 | 2.1% |
| 1978 | 6.5% | 1998 | 1.3% |
| 1979 | 9.9% | 1999 | 2.5% |
| 1980 | 14.3% | 2000 | 3.5% |
| 1981 | 11.2% | 2001 | 2.6% |
| 1982 | 7.4% | 2002 | 1.4% |
| 1983 | 3.5% | 2003 | 2.1% |
| 1984 | 3.5% | 2004 | 2.7% |
| 1985 | 3.1% | 2005 | 4.1% |
| 1986 | 1.3% | 2006 | 3.3% |
| 1987 | 4.2% | 2007 | 2.3% |
| 1988 | 4.0% | 2008 | 5.8% |
| 1989 | 4.7% | 2009 | 0.0% |
| 1990 | 5.4% | 2010 | 0.0% |
| 1991 | 3.7% | 2011 | 3.6% |
| 1992 | 3.0% | 2012 | 1.7% |
| 1993 | 2.6% | 2013 | 1.7% |
| 1994 | 2.8% | | |

figure 6.9

generation moves toward retirement. In the future, there will be fewer workers to support each retiree. The ratio of workers to retirees has plummeted and will continue to fall (Figure 6.10).

There is considerable debate today over what the government should do to ensure that Social Security is around for future generations. Several options are currently being discussed. Now more than ever, with the program's future less certain, you should devote significant attention to other sources of retirement income, such as pensions and personal savings.

Despite Social Security's uncertainty, it currently comprises more than one-third of most retirees' income. Therefore, it requires that you under-stand how the program works and how to incorporate Social Security into your retirement plan. Using the information presented in this chapter, you should now be better informed about the issues surrounding Social Security and how you can best take advantage of it. Figure 6.11 compares each option we've discussed side-by-side.

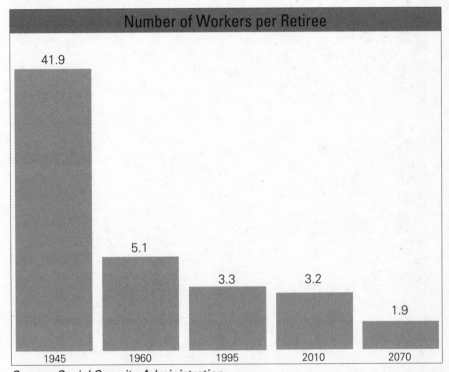

Source: Social Security Administration

figure 6.10

## Maximize Your Social Security Benefits

| Strategy (John/Kathy) | How Strategy Works | Cumulative Lifetime Benefits | Cumulative Lifetime Benefits Invested at 6% |
|---|---|---|---|
| 62/62 | John files for worker benefits at age 62 for 75% of his PIA. Kathy files for worker benefits at age 62 for 75% of her PIA. | $1,273,007 | $3,388,237 |
| 62/66 | John files for worker benefits at age 62 for 75% of his PIA. Kathy files for worker benefits at age 66 for 100% of her PIA. | $1,316,339 | $3,379,871 |
| 62/70 + Spouse Spousal benefit | John files for worker benefits at age 62 for 75% of his PIA. Kathy files at age 66 for 100.00% of her Spousal Benefit. Kathy files for worker benefits at age 70 for 132% of her PIA. | $1,419,791 | $3,581,387 |
| 66/62 | Kathy files for worker benefits at age 62 for 75% of her PIA. John files for worker benefits at age 66 for 100% of his PIA. | $1,424,027 | $3,452,048 |
| 66/66 | John files for worker benefits at age 66 for 100% of his PIA. Kathy files for worker benefits at age 66 for 100% of her PIA. | $1,466,472 | $3,443,677 |
| 66/70 + Spouse Spousal | John files for worker benefits at age 66 for 100% of his PIA. Kathy files for worker benefits at age 70 for 132% of her PIA. | $1,554,144 | $3,623,808 |
| 70/62 | Kathy files for worker benefits at age 62 for 75% of her PIA. John files for worker benefits at age 70 for 132% of his PIA. | $1,592,963 | $3,504,341 |

| | | | |
|---|---|---|---|
| 70/62 + Primary Spousal benefit | Kathy files for worker benefits at age 62 for 75% of her PIA.<br>John files at age 66 for 100.00% of Spousal Benefit.<br>John files for worker benefits at age 70 for 132% of his PIA. | $1,632,239 | $3,668,187 |
| 70/66 | Kathy files for worker benefits at age 66 for 100% of her PIA.<br>John files for worker benefits at age 70 for 132% of his PIA. | $1,635,408 | $3,495,970 |
| 70/66 + Primary Spousal benefit | Kathy files for worker benefits at age 66 for 100% of her PIA.<br>John files at age 68 for 100.00% of Spousal Benefit.<br>John files for worker benefits at age 70 for 132% of his PIA. | $1,655,424 | $3,574,698 |
| 70/70 | John files for worker benefits at age 70 for 132% of his PIA.<br>Kathy files for worker benefits at age 70 for 132% of her PIA. | $1,654,908 | $3,423,001 |
| 70/70 + Primary Spousal benefit | Kathy claims and suspends benefits at age 66.<br>John files for a 'restricted application' at age 68 for 100% of Spousal Benefit.<br>John files for worker benefits at age 70 for 132% of his PIA.<br>Kathy files for worker benefits at age 70 for 132% of her PIA. | $1,674,924 | $3,501,729 |
| 70/70 + Spouse Spousal benefit | John claims and suspends benefits at age 66.<br>Kathy files for a 'restricted application' at age 66 for 100% of Spousal Benefit.<br>Kathy files for worker benefits at age 70 for 132% of her PIA.<br>John files for worker benefits at age 70 for 132% of his PIA. | $1,723,080 | $3,676,102 |

*figure 6.11*

# 7

# MAXING YOUR PENSION

## RETIREMENT DECISION #7: WHICH PENSION PAYOUT OPTION SHOULD I CHOOSE?

There was a time, not long ago, when most full-time employees could count on their companies to provide a generous pension plan at retirement, allowing employees to retire and essentially continue receiving a check for life. But today, the traditional company pension plan is fast becoming an endangered species. More and more U.S. corporations are discontinuing their pension plans to cut costs and are shifting the responsibility of retirement saving to their employees through employee savings programs such as 401(k)s and other types of qualified plans. For example,

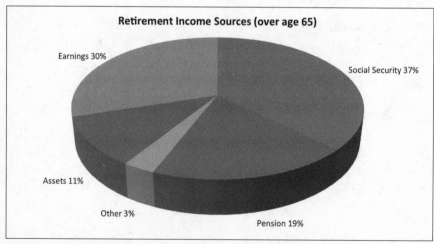

Source: Social Security Administration

figure 7.1

in 1985 nearly 90 percent of Fortune 100 companies offered pension plans to new employees. By 2012 that number had dropped to only 11 percent.[1]

Despite this move away from traditional pension plans, thirty-five million Americans are still covered by these plans.[2] If you are fortunate enough to work for a company that can still afford to offer one and you qualify for benefits at retirement, you will receive a monthly pension check for the rest of your life. This benefit can be an important piece of your retirement income, because statistics show that company pensions currently account for 19 percent of the average retiree's income (Figure 7.1).[3]

Understanding pensions and their payment options will be important to the overall success of your retirement planning. This chapter is intended to help you better understand these options and to help you learn simple, effective strategies to maximize your pension and ultimately put more money in your pocket during retirement.

## How Big Will Your Pension Payment Be?

The formula that determines the size of your pension payments is usually based on your level of income and the length of service with your employer. When you retire, you will be given a statement outlining several pension payout options (Figure 7.2). Some employers will even provide you with the option of taking a one-time, lump-sum distribution rather than monthly payments. It's important to realize that the decision you make at this time

| Pension Payout Options (Sample) | | |
| --- | --- | --- |
| | Monthly Benefit | Monthly Benefit to Spouse upon Death |
| Single Life Annuity | $1,000 | $0 |
| Joint and 100% Survivor Annuity | $850 | $850 |
| Joint and 75% Survivor Annuity | $880 | $660 |
| Joint and 50% Survivor Annuity | $920 | $460 |
| Life and 10-Year Period Certain | $950 | $950* |
| * For the first 10 years after retirement | | |
| One-Time Lump Sum (not offered by all plans) | $150,000 | |

figure 7.2

is irrevocable. Thus, you should fully understand your options and make a choice that will help you accomplish your retirement goals.

In addition, make sure you don't retire just before your pension benefit is going to be bumped up. All it takes is a quick call to your human resources benefits coordinator to find out when your benefits are scheduled to increase and at what point your benefits level out. This will help you set your exact retirement date.

## Common Pension Payment Options

Figure 7.2 outlines the most common pension payout options and an example of what each may pay in relation to the other options.

Which should you choose? This is an important decision you will be required to make at retirement. Study your options carefully because once you make your choice, you can't change it.

- **Single Life Annuity:** This option provides you with the most money each year during retirement. However, benefits cease upon your death, so your surviving spouse and heirs will not continue receiving any income. If you pass away only weeks after signing the final pension paperwork, all payments will immediately cease.
- **Joint & 100% Survivor Annuity:** At retirement, this annuity pays a pension for your lifetime and continues to pay your surviving spouse the same amount after you die. Benefits will not be paid to your heirs upon your spouse's death. Defined benefit pension plans are required to provide this annuity as an option. If you decide to choose an option other than this one, you must obtain your spouse's consent.
- **Joint & 75% Survivor Annuity:** This option allows you to receive a higher benefit than the Joint & 100% Survivor option. However, your surviving spouse receives only 75 percent of the benefit amount upon your death.
- **Joint & 50% Survivor Annuity:** This option provides you with an even higher benefit than the Joint & 100% and 75% Survivor options. As the name suggests, however, your surviving spouse receives only 50 percent of the monthly benefit amount upon your death.
- **Life Only with 10-Year Period Certain:** This annuity provides benefits to you for your lifetime. However, if you die within the

period certain (ten years from the time payments commence), payments will continue to your beneficiary (spouse or others) for the remainder of the ten-year period. (Some plans will provide fifteen- and twenty-year period certain payment options, but the longer the period certain, the lower your annuity benefits will be.) If you die after the period certain time frame, benefits will be discontinued.

- **Lump-Sum Distribution (not offered by all plans):** At retirement, the pension will make a one-time distribution. This money can be rolled into an IRA, avoiding taxes and penalties. If you choose this payout option, you must be ready to make your own investment decisions. These include where to invest the money and how much you can take out each year without completely depleting your assets during retirement.

## Pension Plan Advantages

The biggest advantage of receiving a pension plan payout is the peace of mind that comes with receiving a consistent paycheck for the rest of your life, regardless of how the financial markets or economy perform. Your employer hires a team of professional money managers to handle the portfolio of investments in the pension plan for you, lifting the management burden from your shoulders.

> The maximum benefit paid by the PBGC to participants of defunct company pension plans is $57,477 per year (sixty-five year old in 2013).[4]

In addition, the Pension Benefit Guaranty Corp. (PBGC) insures most defined benefit pension plans. If your plan does not have sufficient money to pay all of your promised benefits, the PBGC will step in and keep your benefits flowing. Your benefits could be reduced, however, if this occurs.

## Pension Plan Disadvantages

Even though pension plans have many perks, there are some disadvantages. First, many pensions do not have a cost-of-living adjustment. This means inflation will take its toll on your pension. You will receive the same amount of money every year, even though the prices of goods and services will increase dramatically during your retirement. Historically, prices double every twenty to twenty-two years. For example, the $35,000 annual pension payment you receive today may be more than adequate to meet your current income needs. However, in twenty years you will likely need $70,000 to buy the same amount of goods and services you're purchasing today. You can overcome this disadvantage with additional income from other retirement investments.

Also, the fact that your choice of an annuity option is irrevocable can be problematic. Let's assume, for example, you choose the Joint & 100% Survivor Annuity option (Figure 7.2) and you receive an $850 monthly pension. You would be choosing a lower monthly check than the $1,000 you could have received with the Single Life Annuity. By accepting the reduced amount, you are ensuring that upon your death, your spouse will continue to receive $850 per month during his or her lifetime. What if your spouse passes away first? You will continue to receive the reduced $850 amount for your lifetime and can't change it to reflect your new circumstances. Additionally, if you choose this option and both of you die during the first year, no further benefits will be paid to your heirs.

## Pension Maximization Strategy

Selecting the best pension payout option can be difficult. Should you choose the option with the highest monthly payment that will provide a benefit for your lifetime only? Or do you select the option with the largest payout to your surviving spouse?

Believe it or not, there is a way to have your proverbial cake and eat it, too. You can obtain the highest annuity payment and still provide for your spouse upon your death by "maxing" your pension. Before pursuing this strategy, there are a couple of points you need to consider. The younger you are, the better this strategy will work. Most advisors will suggest you implement this strategy

| Pension Comparison | | |
|---|---|---|
| | Yearly Benefit | Yearly Benefit to Spouse upon Death |
| Single Life Annuity | $45,000 | $0 |
| Joint and 100% Survivor Annuity | $35,000 | $35,000 |

figure 7.3

well before retirement; although, if you're in good health, it may be worth considering at the time you retire..

Here's how it works: At age 60, Nate Strong is considering retiring and taking a Joint & 100% Survivor Annuity to ensure that his wife, Sheila, will be provided for upon his death. Instead of $45,000 a year he could get with a Single Life Annuity, Nate will receive $35,000 per year, and, after his death, Sheila will continue to collect $35,000 annually (Figure 7.3).

To make sure Sheila is financially protected, Nate is essentially forfeiting $10,000 per year—the difference between the highest-paying Single Life Annuity and the Joint & 100% Survivor Annuity. Nate doesn't realize it, but by choosing the survivorship annuity he is really buying the equivalent of life insurance. Like most people, Nate would love to have the best of both options: the higher single life annual payout and the greatest yearly payment to Sheila for the rest of her life at his death. Such an option is possible if Nate can find a cheaper way of providing Sheila with $35,000 a year after his death. Read on.

First, Nate needs to ask himself this question: "How much money would I need in a separate interest-bearing account to produce $35,000 of income per year for Sheila until she reaches age 85?" If Nate had an investment portfolio (in addition to his current investment assets) earning 6 percent per year, he would need $615,000 to produce $35,000 of annual income for twenty-five years (assuming 3 percent inflation). A portfolio growing at 8 percent would require a total of about $500,000 to produce the required income.

If Nate had a separate portfolio from which Sheila could draw $35,000 of income each year after his death, he could then opt for the Single Life Annuity and obtain $10,000 more in income per year and enjoy the best of both worlds.

This is possible, but the strategy requires the use of life insurance. Like most people who are nearing retirement, the idea of purchasing more life insurance isn't too appealing. However, taking the survivorship option is like buying a life insurance policy large enough to provide Sheila with $35,000 per year upon his death. The premium for this insurance policy is $10,000 per year. Is that a good deal? Perhaps not.

If Nate could purchase a $500,000 life insurance policy for less than $10,000 per year, then he could opt for the higher $45,000 pension payout of the Single Life Annuity and still protect Sheila. If, for example, the premium for a $500,000 insurance policy is only $5,000 per year, Nate could use some of the additional $10,000 he receives each year to pay his life insurance premiums and still be ahead of the Joint & 100% Survivor Annuity by $5,000. When Nate dies, his Single Life Annuity will cease, but Sheila will receive $500,000 tax-free from the life insurance policy. She can use that money to buy a portfolio of investments that will provide her with income to replace the pension. In addition, while Nate is alive, he has access to the cash value of the policy as needed.

In hindsight, knowing that he would be receiving a pension in the future, Nate should have purchased the insurance at age 40 or 50 to lock in much lower premiums. Fortunately, he is in good health and can still qualify for a policy at age 60.

If Nate's health was poor and consequently the $500,000 life insurance policy cost him $13,000 each year, then choosing the 100 percent survivorship option would have been a better choice.

## Type of Policy

It's important to realize that the sole purpose of the insurance policy is to replace some or all of Nate's pension income at his death. If he dies at age 60 just one day after choosing the Single Life Annuity, then Sheila would need a full twenty-five years or more of income. As they get older, however, there are fewer years of income they will need to replace. For instance, at age 70 Sheila would probably only need income for fifteen more years. Consequently, they can reduce their life insurance coverage over time or buy a policy that does this automatically. Buying a policy that automatically reduces the coverage will drop the annual premiums. Universal or variable universal life can provide this flexibility.

The critical question for Nate is determining how much $500,000 of life insurance will actually cost. Age and health are the biggest determinants. Figure 7.4 illustrates annual universal life insurance price ranges at different ages and compares load (commission) policies to no-load (no-commission) policies. Based on these premium levels, the pension maximization strategy would work well for Nate whether he purchased $500,000 or $600,000 of coverage. Remember, all he needs is an annual premium less than $10,000. If he is comfortable with a little more risk, he could purchase a variable universal life policy and invest the cash value he accumulates in subaccounts (like mutual funds).

You may be wondering why Nate doesn't just buy term insurance, which usually costs much less than cash-value policies (i.e., whole life and universal life). You are right, in that term insurance is typically much cheaper; however, with term insurance he runs the risk of picking a term that Sheila outlives. In addition, it may be difficult for Nate to find an affordable policy that has a twenty-five- to thirty-year term (coverage until Sheila is at least 85 or 90). At age 60 a twenty-five-year term insurance policy will cost him about $6,000 per year. If he only wanted enough insurance to cover Sheila for twenty years, he could likely find a term insurance policy for $4,000 to $5,000 per year. It makes sense to compare both term and cash-value life insurance before making a decision.

*Warning:* Do not purchase a life insurance policy from a commissioned agent without comparing the cost to a no-load policy. No-load life insurance often has premiums that are 50 percent to 70 percent lower, which can make

## What Will Life Insurance Cost?

### $500,000 Universal Life Insurance

| Age | Load Premium | Load Cash Value* | No-Load Premium | No-Load Cash Value* |
|-----|--------------|------------------|-----------------|---------------------|
| 40 | $2,720 | $0 | $1,615 | $975 |
| 45 | $3,620 | $0 | $2,195 | $1,345 |
| 50 | $5,315 | $0 | $3,150 | $1,991 |
| 55 | $6,540 | $0 | $3,910 | $2,372 |
| 60 | $7,780 | $0 | $4,715 | $2,847 |
| 65 | $10,010 | $0 | $6,255 | $3,564 |

### $600,000 Universal Life Insurance

| Age | Load Premium | Load Cash Value* | No-Load Premium | No-Load Cash Value* |
|-----|--------------|------------------|-----------------|---------------------|
| 40 | $3,264 | $0 | $1,938 | $1,170 |
| 45 | $4,344 | $0 | $2,634 | $1,614 |
| 50 | $6,378 | $0 | $3,780 | $2,390 |
| 55 | $7,848 | $0 | $4,692 | $2,847 |
| 60 | $9,336 | $0 | $5,658 | $3,417 |
| 65 | $12,012 | $0 | $7,506 | $4,276 |

*End-of-first-year cash surrender value

figure 7.4

buying a policy at retirement much easier to stomach. In addition to lower premiums, no-load policies carry no surrender charges, so your cash value is available immediately. Loaded commission policies carry surrender charges that often last ten to fifteen years and will penalize you for withdrawing any money during this period. (See Chapter 18, No-Load Means Lower Costs.)

## How Much Insurance Will You Need to Make This Strategy Work?

Nate figured he needed a $500,000 policy to make his strategy work. How much will you need? The amount of insurance you need depends on four factors: (1) the amount of annual income your surviving spouse will need, (2) the length of time the income is needed, (3) the rate-of-return assumption, and (4) inflation.

Figures 7.5, 7.6, and 7.7 contain tables to help you determine how much life insurance you will need to purchase. Once you know the amount, obtain some no-load life insurance quotes to determine how much it will cost. Figure 18.5 in Chapter 18 for a list of insurance companies offering no-load life insurance.

The return-rate assumption you choose will determine which chart you use. For example, Figure 7.5 assumes when the proceeds of your insurance policy are paid out to your surviving spouse, he or she will invest the money in a portfolio earning 6 percent annually. Figure 7.6 uses 8 percent, and Figure 7.7 uses 10 percent. Each chart has a built-in inflation adjustment and assumes your surviving spouse will need 3 percent more income than the previous year. If you are working with an insurance agent, make sure inflation is factored in. Otherwise, your insurance need will be skewed lower and may be insufficient for your spouse.

Here's how to use the charts: Assume you would like to provide your spouse with $35,000 of annual inflation-adjusted income for twenty-five years after your death. First, choose the chart that most closely reflects the rate of return (6 percent, 8 percent, 10 percent) you believe your surviving spouse could achieve if required to invest your insurance proceeds upon your death. I recommend selecting the most conservative percentage, 6 percent. Next, go to the row that says $35,000 and the column under 25 years. The intersecting number, $615,437, is the amount of insurance you should consider purchasing to make your strategy work.[5]

## Pension Maximization

*How much insurance do you need?*
*6% Rate of Return*

| Annual Income Needed | Number of Years Income Is Needed | | | | | |
|---|---|---|---|---|---|---|
| | 10 | 15 | 20 | 25 | 30 | 35 |
| $10,000 | $85,684 | $120,137 | $149,984 | $175,839 | $198,237 | $217,640 |
| $15,000 | $128,526 | $180,206 | $224,976 | $263,759 | $297,355 | $326,459 |
| $20,000 | $171,367 | $240,275 | $299,968 | $351,678 | $396,474 | $435,279 |
| $25,000 | $214,209 | $300,343 | $374,959 | $439,598 | $495,592 | $544,099 |
| $30,000 | $257,051 | $360,412 | $449,951 | $527,517 | $594,711 | $652,919 |
| $35,000 | $299,893 | $420,481 | $524,943 | $615,437 | $693,829 | $761,739 |
| $40,000 | $342,735 | $480,549 | $599,935 | $703,356 | $792,948 | $870,558 |
| $45,000 | $385,577 | $540,618 | $674,927 | $791,276 | $892,066 | $979,378 |
| $50,000 | $428,418 | $600,687 | $749,919 | $879,195 | $991,184 | $1,088,198 |
| $55,000 | $471,260 | $660,755 | $824,911 | $967,115 | $1,090,303 | $1,197,018 |
| $60,000 | $514,102 | $720,824 | $899,903 | $1,055,034 | $1,189,421 | $1,305,838 |
| $65,000 | $556,944 | $780,893 | $974,895 | $1,142,954 | $1,288,540 | $1,414,658 |
| $70,000 | $599,786 | $840,961 | $1,049,887 | $1,230,873 | $1,387,658 | $1,523,477 |
| $75,000 | $642,628 | $901,030 | $1,124,878 | $1,318,793 | $1,486,777 | $1,632,297 |
| $80,000 | $685,469 | $961,099 | $1,199,870 | $1,406,713 | $1,585,895 | $1,741,117 |
| $85,000 | $728,311 | $1,021,168 | $1,274,862 | $1,494,632 | $1,685,014 | $1,849,937 |
| $90,000 | $771,153 | $1,081,236 | $1,349,854 | $1,582,552 | $1,784,132 | $1,958,757 |
| $95,000 | $813,995 | $1,141,305 | $1,424,846 | $1,670,471 | $1,883,250 | $2,067,576 |
| $100,000 | $856,837 | $1,201,374 | $1,499,838 | $1,758,391 | $1,982,369 | $2,176,396 |

figure 7.5

## Pension Maximization

*How much insurance do you need?*
*8% Rate of Return*

| Annual Income Needed | Number of Years Income Is Needed | | | | | |
|---|---|---|---|---|---|---|
| | 10 | 15 | 20 | 25 | 30 | 35 |
| $10,000 | $77,766 | $104,826 | $126,175 | $143,020 | $156,310 | $166,795 |
| $15,000 | $116,650 | $157,239 | $189,263 | $214,530 | $234,465 | $250,193 |
| $20,000 | $155,533 | $209,652 | $252,351 | $286,040 | $312,619 | $333,591 |
| $25,000 | $194,416 | $262,065 | $315,439 | $357,550 | $390,774 | $416,988 |
| $30,000 | $233,299 | $314,478 | $378,526 | $429,059 | $468,929 | $500,386 |
| $35,000 | $272,182 | $366,891 | $441,614 | $500,569 | $547,084 | $583,783 |
| $40,000 | $311,066 | $419,304 | $504,702 | $572,079 | $625,239 | $667,181 |
| $45,000 | $349,949 | $471,717 | $567,789 | $643,589 | $703,394 | $750,579 |
| $50,000 | $388,832 | $524,130 | $630,877 | $715,099 | $781,549 | $833,976 |
| $55,000 | $427,715 | $576,543 | $693,965 | $786,609 | $859,704 | $917,374 |
| $60,000 | $466,598 | $628,956 | $757,053 | $858,119 | $937,858 | $1,000,772 |
| $65,000 | $505,481 | $681,368 | $820,140 | $929,629 | $1,016,013 | $1,084,169 |
| $70,000 | $544,365 | $733,781 | $883,228 | $1,001,139 | $1,094,168 | $1,167,567 |
| $75,000 | $583,248 | $786,194 | $946,316 | $1,072,649 | $1,172,323 | $1,250,964 |
| $80,000 | $622,131 | $838,607 | $1,009,403 | $1,144,158 | $1,250,478 | $1,334,362 |
| $85,000 | $661,014 | $891,020 | $1,072,491 | $1,215,668 | $1,328,633 | $1,417,760 |
| $90,000 | $699,897 | $943,433 | $1,135,579 | $1,287,178 | $1,406,788 | $1,501,157 |
| $95,000 | $738,781 | $995,846 | $1,198,667 | $1,358,668 | $1,484,942 | $1,584,555 |
| $100,000 | $777,664 | $1,048,259 | $1,261,754 | $1,430,198 | $1,563,097 | $1,667,953 |

*figure 7.6*

## Pension Maximization

*How much insurance do you need?*
*10% Rate of Return*

| Annual Income Needed | Number of Years Income Is Needed | | | | | |
|---|---|---|---|---|---|---|
| | 10 | 15 | 20 | 25 | 30 | 35 |
| $10,000 | $70,903 | $92,264 | $107,640 | $118,708 | $126,675 | $132,410 |
| $15,000 | $106,354 | $138,396 | $161,460 | $178,062 | $190,012 | $198,614 |
| $20,000 | $141,805 | $184,527 | $215,280 | $237,416 | $253,350 | $264,819 |
| $25,000 | $177,256 | $230,659 | $269,100 | $296,770 | $316,687 | $331,024 |
| $30,000 | $212,708 | $276,791 | $322,920 | $356,124 | $380,025 | $397,229 |
| $35,000 | $248,159 | $322,923 | $376,740 | $415,478 | $443,362 | $463,434 |
| $40,000 | $283,610 | $369,055 | $430,559 | $474,832 | $506,699 | $529,638 |
| $45,000 | $319,062 | $415,187 | $484,379 | $534,186 | $570,037 | $595,843 |
| $50,000 | $354,513 | $461,319 | $538,199 | $593,539 | $633,374 | $662,048 |
| $55,000 | $389,964 | $507,450 | $592,019 | $652,893 | $696,712 | $728,253 |
| $60,000 | $425,415 | $553,582 | $645,839 | $712,247 | $760,049 | $794,458 |
| $65,000 | $460,867 | $599,714 | $699,659 | $771,601 | $823,387 | $860,663 |
| $70,000 | $496,318 | $645,846 | $753,479 | $830,955 | $886,724 | $926,867 |
| $75,000 | $531,769 | $691,978 | $807,299 | $890,309 | $950,061 | $993,072 |
| $80,000 | $567,220 | $738,110 | $861,119 | $949,663 | $1,013,399 | $1,059,277 |
| $85,000 | $602,672 | $784,242 | $914,939 | $1,009,017 | $1,076,736 | $1,125,482 |
| $90,000 | $638,123 | $830,373 | $968,759 | $1,068,371 | $1,140,074 | $1,191,687 |
| $95,000 | $673,574 | $876,505 | $1,022,579 | $1,127,725 | $1,203,411 | $1,257,891 |
| $100,000 | $709,026 | $922,637 | $1,076,399 | $1,187,079 | $1,266,749 | $1,324,096 |

*figure 7.7*

If your insurance premiums will be less than the difference between the Life Only Annuity and the Joint & 100% Survivor Annuity you are planning to take, then the pension maximization strategy may work well for you. It is definitely worth obtaining an insurance quote before locking yourself into a lifetime pension payment. It may mean thousands of extra dollars each year during retirement.

## Taking a One-Time Lump-Sum Distribution

What if your company offers you the chance to take a one-time lump-sum distribution instead of a yearly pension? Take it. If you choose the pension over the lump sum, you are betting that your company and the PBGC will have the financial strength to meet the pension obligation to you and your spouse for the next thirty to forty years. Are you willing to make that bet? If not, choose the lump sum.

This recently happened to Craig Lennar, who, at age 60, was given the following choices at retirement: (1) an annual pension payment of $25,000 per year for the rest of his and his wife's life without a cost-of-living adjustment, or (2) a one-time lump-sum distribution of $500,000. What should he do? Is it better to take the lump sum or receive a lifetime of annuity payments?

### Lump-Sum Advantages

If Craig takes the lump-sum money and transfers it into an IRA, he can gain tremendous flexibility and avoid taxes and penalties in the process. Once in the IRA, he can begin taking withdrawals to obtain the income he and his wife, Linda, need. Craig could withdraw $25,000 each year from his IRA and in essence create his own pension payout. He can even give himself a "raise" by withdrawing a little bit more each year to compensate for inflation—a benefit not available with his pension. Whether he chooses to take the monthly pension payout or distributions from his IRA, the tax treatment of both will be the same.

He can also withdraw principal at any point in time if he ever needs a large cash infusion to buy real estate, for example, or pay for his daughter's wedding. Because the money is in an IRA, he can develop and manage an investment strategy on his own or with the aid of a financial advisor instead of relying on his former employer to do it for him.

Any assets left in his IRA at death can be transferred into Linda's IRA without taxes or penalties and continue to grow tax-deferred. Linda can continue managing the money and taking out income as needed. Upon her death, the remaining balance in the portfolio will pass on to their children or whomever they name as beneficiaries. (Read more about IRA rollovers in Chapter 8.)

## Lump-Sum Disadvantages

If Craig and Linda invest their IRA money in stocks or bonds (or stock or bond mutual funds), there are no guarantees that they'll obtain the rate of return they need. If they are unsuccessful in managing their portfolio, they could be in danger of depleting their IRA assets prematurely. This risk won't exist if they choose the pension option with the guaranteed monthly payments.

## Lump Sum vs. Annual Pension

Before making a final decision, Craig and Linda should run some numbers and review the advantages and disadvantages of each option (Figure 7.8). Let's go back in time and say Craig received this same offer in 1983. A $25,000 annual pension for the rest of their lives would have sounded pretty good then. Of course, walking away with $500,000 wouldn't have been too bad either. Which turned out to be the best deal? Let's break it down.

An annual payment of $25,000 seemed like a substantial income in 1983. That's $60,000 in today's dollars. But what seemed plush in 1983 is barely cutting it today. A $500,000 lump-sum distribution invested into an IRA, however, would only need to grow 3 percent per year to outperform the pension, assuming they'll be in retirement for thirty years. Let's assume they rolled the lump sum into their IRA and bought a balanced mutual fund consisting of about 50 percent stocks and 50 percent bonds–essentially meaning that half of their money is in relatively conservative investments, while the other half is at risk in the stock market.

To make this a fair comparison, let's say they withdrew only $25,000 annually–the same amount they would have received from their pension–from their IRA every year from 1983 to 2012, with no cost-of-living adjustment. How much would be left in their IRA account thirty years later?

Brace yourself. The answer is a whopping $7 million. Craig and Linda would have had that much money left over even after withdrawing $25,000 per year ($750,000 in total withdrawals). Their balanced portfolio would have enjoyed an average annual return of 11.34 percent. Even if they had given themselves a 3 percent raise each and every year to keep up with rising prices, increasing their annual income from $25,000 per year in 1983 to $58,914 in 2012, their portfolio would still contain a very substantial $6 million at the end of 2012.[6] Had they chosen the annual pension payment, all they could look forward to was their measly annual benefit of $25,000.

| Pension or Lump Sum? | |
|---|---|
| **Lifetime Pension Payouts** | **Lump Sum** |
| Choice of annuity payout option is irrevocable | Flexible and changeable payout schedule |
| Income is guaranteed | Income is not guaranteed |
| Recipient does not manage an investment portfolio | Recipient must manage an investment portfolio |
| Access to investment principal is not available | Investment principal is available at any time |
| Payouts do not pass to heirs upon death | Any money not spent during retirement passes to heirs |

figure 7.8

Although these numbers look very convincing, it should be noted that this balanced fund would have followed the natural ups and downs of the stock and bond markets. Their success, then, would depend on their ability to tolerate the rough economic circumstances of the early 1980s, the 1987 stock market crash, negative markets in 1990 and 1994, and the 2000–2002 and 2008 recessions, without deviating from their balanced investment strategy. Some people simply do not have the ability to weather this kind of volatility.

The lesson to learn here, however, is that if you have the choice between a lump sum and a pension, it's not a choice you should make lightly. Look at both options very carefully, work through the different scenarios you could pursue, and then make the decision that will best help you reach your retirement objectives. Who knows, with results like these you may just end up with a large amount of money in your portfolio after thirty years of retirement.

● ● ●

After reading this chapter you should be more familiar with the various pension payment options and the risks and benefits associated with each. With a more firm understanding of the way your pension will be paid out, you can now use the maximization strategies outlined in this chapter to help you make the most of those payments at retirement.

**Pension Tips from AARP**

1. Make sure you get credit for the last year you work. You may need to work a certain number of hours during the year or continue working until a specified date. Quitting at the wrong time could mean being credited for only nineteen years instead of twenty. This would severely affect your total lifetime benefit.

2. Find out if your plan uses "Social Security Integration" to calculate your benefits. If it does, your pension may be reduced by up to 50 percent when you start receiving Social Security benefits.

3. Calculate your own benefit. Mistakes are made. Find out how your benefit is calculated and double-check your company's math.

4. Determine if any of your past employers had pensions. If so, you may be entitled to a benefit. If you don't have a record of a pension benefit from a former employer, call the Pension Benefit Guaranty Corporation's Pension Search Program at (800) 400-7242 or visit www .pbgc.gov.

# 8

# CASH IT, ROLL IT, LEAVE IT, ROTH IT, ANNUITIZE IT, STOCK IT!

## RETIREMENT DECISION #8: WHICH RETIREMENT PLAN DISTRIBUTION OPTION SHOULD I CHOOSE?

In 2012, Bruce Richardson, an engineer, retired at age 59. One of the first decisions he faced was what to do with the $625,000 in his 401(k) plan. Without fully understanding his distribution choices, Bruce quickly took the advice of fellow employees, who suggested he just "roll it to an IRA." For most people, rolling to an IRA is the best decision.

Unfortunately for Bruce, his quick decision will end up costing him thousands of dollars in unnecessary taxes during retirement. At first glance it looks as if he made the right choice. However, because the bulk of his 401(k) money is invested in company stock, there is a better option. As you will see, had he spent just a little time comparing and evaluating his choices, he would be in a much better position to handle his thirty-year retirement.

> 401(k) plan assets have soared to more than $3.5 trillion.[1]

How are you going to take a distribution from your 401(k) at retirement? Your answer to this question will have a serious impact on whether your retirement plan is a success or failure. In this chapter, we'll discuss your six distribution options. The information in this chapter and Chapter 9 will prepare you to make the right distribution decision and avoid costly mistakes. You'll understand how to get the most out of the money you have worked so hard to accumulate during your working years.

> Forty percent of workers participate in a retirement savings plans through their employers.[2]

Each distribution option has its own set of advantages and disadvantages. There's not one option that's best for all retirees. Your choice of distribution will depend on when you retire, your current and future tax brackets, the type of retirement accounts you own, how much you have saved, and how much income you will need during retirement. You will need to carefully consider each of these distribution methods to make the smartest choice. Remember, the name of the game is to maximize your retirement nest egg and to avoid paying unnecessary taxes and penalties. At retirement, your distribution options are:

1. Taking a lump-sum cash distribution
2. Rolling the money into an IRA
3. Leaving the money in your former company's retirement plan
4. Rolling the money into a traditional IRA, then converting it to a Roth IRA
5. Receiving an annuity payout
6. Withdrawing company stock and rolling money into an IRA

## Option 1: Cash It

Quick cash has its appeal. If you choose a lump-sum cash distribution of your 401(k) funds, your employer will simply send you a check for the vested balance in your plan (minus tax withholding).

> Cash distributions account for 14 percent of retirement plan distributions.[3]

Think of what you could do with all that money. You could purchase a new house, a luxury car, a boat, or an exotic vacation. Doesn't sound too bad, does it?

For most retirees, taking a cash distribution can be a grave mistake. Although having cash in hand may be an appropriate option in some limited circumstances, such as emergencies, choosing this option is usually shortsighted because it opens you up to penalties and severe tax consequences. Right off the bat, your employer is required by law to withhold 20 percent of

> Consider a lump-sum cash distribution only when:
> - You are faced with a financial emergency and have absolutely no other source of money.
> - You own highly appreciated company stock (we'll discuss this in Chapter 9).

the amount distributed to you as a prepayment of taxes. The government anticipates that you will owe this amount as a result of the distribution. You could get some of this refunded if you owe less tax than the amount withheld. If, however, you owe more tax, Uncle Sam will require you to pay additional taxes when you file a return.

(Note: The 20 percent withholding does not apply to company stock distributed to you in shares. In this case, the company will send you a stock certificate, often referred to as an "in-kind" distribution. All other cash and securities you own in your plan upon distribution are subject to the 20 percent tax withholding.)

In addition, the entire withdrawal is considered ordinary income for the year in which you take the distribution. When you add the distribution amount to your earned income for the year, you may find yourself thrust into a much higher federal income tax bracket (Figure 8.1). If your state imposes local taxes, you will be required to pay those, too. And if you are not yet age 59½, you will be subject to an additional 10 percent penalty for taking a premature distribution.

When you add up penalties and taxes, depending on your bracket, you could lose almost half of your retirement savings by taking a cash distribution–and surprisingly that's not even the worst aspect of this distribution method. You'll feel sick years later when you realize how large your retirement plan could have grown with years of compound interest and tax deferral.

### 2013 Federal Personal Income Tax Rates

| Tax Rate | Single | Married (filing jointly) |
|---|---|---|
| 10% | up to $8,925 | up to $17,850 |
| 15% | $8,926– $36,250 | $17,851– $72,500 |
| 25% | $36,251– $87,850 | $72,501– $146,400 |
| 28% | $87,851– $183,250 | $146,401– $223,050 |
| 33% | $183,251– $398,350 | $223,051– $398,350 |
| 35% | $398,351– $400,000 | $398,351– $450,000 |
| 39.6% | $400,001 and above | $450,001 and above |

figure 8.1

Still not convinced that taking a cash distribution is a bad mistake? Let's peer into the world of Clark Whittaker. Clark, 50, has a 401(k) balance of

$500,000. He just changed jobs and now has the option to take a cash distribution from his 401(k). He'd like to use the money to pay off his mortgage, buy a new car, and take a trip to Hawaii. Since a cash distribution is treated as regular income, this withdrawal would be added to his earned income for the year and would vault Clark into the highest tax bracket. He'd have to pay $125,000 in federal taxes (nominal tax rate 25 percent) and $25,000 in state income taxes. In addition, because he's not yet 59½, he'd take a $50,000 hit for the 10 percent early-withdrawal penalty. Instantly, he'd turn 40 percent, or $200,000, of his hard-earned retirement savings over to the federal and state government, leaving him only $300,000 (Figure 8.2).

| Cash Distribution | |
|---|---|
| **$500,000 cash distribution** | |
| *Taxes and Penalties* | |
| $125,000 | 25% federal taxes |
| $25,000 | 5% state and local taxes |
| $50,000 | 10% early-withdrawal penalty |
| ($200,000) | **Total taxes and penalties** |
| $300,000 | **Cash distribution after taxes and penalties** |

*figure 8.2*

Taxes would be bad enough, but it would get worse for Clark when we consider his nest egg's future growth that would be lost if he cashed out. If the $200,000 he'd have to "donate" to the government to pay taxes remained invested and grew tax-deferred at 8 percent, it would be worth $431,784 in ten years when he hits age 60 and almost $1 million in twenty years. The leftover $300,000 he wants to use to pay off his home, buy the new car, and take a trip would grow to $647,677 and almost $1.4 million, respectively, over the same periods (Figure 8.3). That's a lot of money Clark would have had to meet his retirement needs over the next thirty years. In fact, choosing a cash distribution would make it impossible for him to reach his retirement goals. Even if he were over 59½ and beyond any early-withdrawal penalties, he would still be better off to withdraw from his retirement accounts over time, not all at once. That way he would be able to control his tax burden and keep the power of tax deferral working to his advantage as long as possible. Clark, like most people, *should not* take a cash distribution.

Remember, one of the reasons you made pretax contributions to your retirement account was to obtain much-needed tax advantages. In most cases, by making these contributions, you avoided paying taxes while earning income in a high tax bracket in hopes of being in a low tax bracket when you stop working and begin taking withdrawals during retirement. If you can control when you pay taxes, it makes sense to pay them at a time when your tax bracket is the lowest. Would anyone in their right mind defer paying taxes now so they can pay even higher taxes in the future? If you take a lump-sum cash distribution and wind up in a higher tax bracket, you would do just that. As long as your funds remain in a retirement plan, the money grows tax-deferred. This privileged status ends as soon as the money is withdrawn from the plan. You should preserve this tax shelter as long as possible.

| Loss of Future Growth | |
| --- | --- |
| *20 years at 8% growth* | |
| Taxes and Penalties | Remaining Cash |
| $200,000 | $300,000 |
| ↓ | ↓ |
| $932,191 | $1,398,287 |
| Total $2,330,478 | |

figure 8.3

## Are There Any Good Reasons to Take a Cash Distribution?

Some people take cash distributions if they lose their jobs, choose to buy or start a business, want to get rid of unwanted debt, or want to pay off their homes. In each of these cases, dipping into retirement funds is still a bad idea. It would usually be better to obtain a loan, home equity or otherwise, rather than tap into retirement funds for a purpose other than retirement. This holds true even for emergencies.

If you absolutely must take a cash distribution, there are ways to control and, in some cases, minimize some taxes.

If you roll over 100 percent of your vested plan balance to an IRA, no taxes or penalties will be withheld upon this transfer. Once your money is deposited into the IRA, you can take multiple distributions over a period of years to spread out your tax burden. In addition, when you pull money from an IRA, the financial institution that holds your money is not required to withhold 20 percent as your employer would. When you pull money out, you can request that taxes be withheld or not be withheld from your distribution. Keep in mind that if no taxes are withheld you will still have to pay all of the taxes you owe on the IRA distribution when you file your 1040 at year's end. Once in an IRA, you can also opt to use 72T distribution rules to avoid paying early-withdrawal penalties (see Chapter 5).

# Option 2: Roll It

In most cases, rolling your money to an IRA makes the most sense. IRAs are tax-deferred retirement programs designed by the federal government to encourage retirement savings. An IRA is a type of account; it is not an investment. Think of an IRA as a personal storage unit for your retirement money. It's a place where you store your

> Seventy-five percent of all retirement plan distributions are rolled over to IRAs.[4]

money, tax-deferred, while investing it in virtually any legitimate investment you choose. In many IRAs, you can buy stocks, bonds, mutual funds, annuities, certificates of deposit, and money market mutual funds. The rate of return your IRA produces is determined by the investments you select.

## *Types of IRAs*

You can open an IRA at a bank, a brokerage firm, a mutual fund, or an annuity company. The firm you choose to hold your IRA money will determine what investments are available to you. An IRA held at a brokerage firm will allow virtually unlimited investment options. By contrast, if you open an IRA at a bank, you are essentially limiting yourself to one investment option: a fixed-

> Consider rolling money to an IRA if:
> • You would like to increase the investment options available to you.
> • You would like to further diversify your portfolio.
> • You would like more control and flexibility.

interest-rate account. The rates for most bank IRAs are comparable to the rates for one- to five-year certificates of deposit (CDs). There are better places to invest long-term retirement money than in low-fixed-rate bank IRAs.

It's true that a bank IRA offers FDIC insurance, which protects your principal up to $250,000. However, it doesn't protect you from one of the most serious retirement risks: inflation. Investing long-term retirement money in short-term, low-interest accounts can be a costly mistake. If you keep your funds from growing, it may be difficult to reach your retirement goals.

By contrast, an IRA held at a brokerage firm, a mutual fund company, or an insurance company offers a panorama of investment choices, giving you better ability to diversify your holdings to reduce risk. In these IRAs, you can choose from thousands of stocks, bonds, and mutual funds, hundreds of fixed or variable annuity contracts, and more. With additional investment options, you can uncover better investments than those available in a bank IRA or in your former company's retirement plan.

The flexibility of an IRA allows you to control how much money you want to withdraw from your IRA and how frequently you make withdrawals. You can take a distribution from your IRA at any time you choose, in any amount, and for any purpose. The same early-withdrawal penalty applies to distributions taken before age 59½, unless the distribution qualifies for an exception to this penalty. Withdrawal flexibility will prove essential if you decide to take early withdrawals (before age 59½) from your IRA under the penalty exception of Section 72T of the IRS Code (see Chapter 5).

If you own company stock in your plan, you can roll it into a brokerage IRA without having to sell it. This is called an "in-kind" transfer. Your company will issue a stock certificate for the number of shares you own and send it directly to the institution handling your IRA, presuming the institution can hold individual securities. Once in the IRA, you can sell the stock anytime.

The ability to sell company stock when you wish is an important element of IRA flexibility. Many companies place restrictions on selling company stock in employer-sponsored retirement plans. For example, if you sell company stock while it's being held inside your company's plan, you will usually receive the closing price of the stock on that trading day, not the price at the time you requested the stock be sold. This could result in costly losses to you if the stock drops dramatically between the time you call and the end of the trading day.

In a brokerage IRA, you can use limit orders to ensure that a stock is sold before it goes into free fall and seriously erodes your retirement savings. This mechanism is invaluable in protecting your hard-earned nest egg. For example, you may want to protect your stock from loss by entering a stop-loss order and having your stock sold automatically if it falls below a price you specify. In addition, you may want to enter a limit order to have your stock automatically sold when it appreciates to a certain target price. Specifying a price to sell usually cannot be done in a company-sponsored retirement plan.

If you are ever unhappy with your IRA provider, simply transfer your account to another firm. You can do this as often as you like, as long as you have the money transferred directly from one institution to another without it ever touching your hands along the way. You are limited to one transfer per year if you physically receive the IRA money and then redeposit it in a new IRA at another institution. This is called a sixty-day rollover. As the name suggests, you have sixty days to deposit the money into another IRA before you will be taxed and penalized (if applicable).

## Opening a New IRA Account

Although there is a limit on the amount of new money you can contribute annually to an IRA, these limits do not apply to rollovers or transfers. Any amount can be rolled over from a qualified retirement plan or from another IRA. If you leave your company, you can have the entire balance of your retirement plan rolled into an IRA. Your money will continue to grow tax-deferred without incurring any taxes or penalties.

Once you open an IRA account, you can add to that account each year you have earned income. However, there are limits on the amount you can add. Recent tax law changes have upped this contribution amount (Figure 8.4). To contribute to an IRA, you must have earned income or have a spouse who has earned income. If you participate in a company-sponsored retirement plan, your IRA contribution may or may not be deductible, depending on your income level.

| IRAs/Roth IRAs | | |
| --- | --- | --- |
| Year | Contribution Limit (under age 50) | Contribution Limit (over age 50) |
| 2013 | $5,500 | $6,500 |

figure 8.4

## 401(k) to IRA: Rollover Methods

There are two ways to take a distribution from your employer's plan and roll the money into an IRA account. Method 1 is cumbersome, Method 2 is easy.

### Method 1: Lump-Sum Cash Distribution and Sixty-Day Rollover

To initiate this method, you must request that your plan balance be sent directly to you just as if you were taking a lump-sum cash distribution.

Upon receiving the money, you have sixty days to deposit it into an IRA to avoid penalties. Be advised, however, that there is a major hitch to this method. Distribution rules mandate that your employer withhold 20 percent of all cash distributions—the prepayment of income taxes that may be owed if the money doesn't get rolled into an IRA. Since the IRS has no idea whether your retirement plan money is going to be rolled over or spent, the withholding is applied to every cash distribution.

This presents a huge problem. How can you roll the full distribution amount to an IRA if 20 percent is taken off the top and sent to the IRS before you even receive the distribution? You know the IRS is not going to be able to refund that money to you within sixty days. Let's do the math: Say you decide to take a $100,000 cash distribution from your company's 401(k) and opt to roll it over into an IRA within sixty days. Your company will send you a check for $80,000 and withhold $20,000. You then have sixty days to deposit the full $100,000 into an IRA to avoid taxes and penalties. This means you will have to withdraw $20,000 from your savings account or elsewhere to make up the difference. (When you file your income taxes at year's end, you will get back the $20,000 initially withheld.)

As you can see, the whole process is fairly complicated and an inefficient way to move money from your company's retirement plan to an IRA. Using a direct rollover will enable you to reach the same result with fewer headaches.

### Method 2: Direct Rollover

To avoid the problems that come with taking direct receipt of your retirement money, instruct your employer to transfer the entire vested balance of your plan to a previously established IRA. This way, you will not receive a check made payable to you for the balance of your plan, and the tax-withholding problem never arises. Because the check is made payable to your IRA institution, the IRS knows the money was transferred directly to an IRA account–no taxes are withheld in the process.

Some plans will mail the rollover check to your IRA provider, and others will mail the check to you. In either case, it will be made payable to your IRA provider for and on behalf of you. In cases where the check is mailed to you, don't be alarmed. Simply forward it to your IRA provider to deposit in your account.

At year's end, you will receive a 1099R form from your former employer showing that a distribution was made. You will also receive a statement from your IRA provider showing the money was deposited into your IRA. As long as these transfer balances match, there will be no tax consequences or penalties.

## Steps for Initiating an IRA Rollover

The direct rollover process is very simple. First, open an IRA account at the financial institution of your choice. After completing the necessary paperwork, you will be assigned an IRA account number. You will need your IRA account number and the IRA provider's address to complete the rollover.

Company-sponsored retirement plans usually process distributions in one of two ways. Some will provide you with retirement distribution forms. If this is the case, complete these forms and return them to your employer. The second method processes the rollover via the telephone. When phone distributions are available, simply call your 401(k) provider (usually a mutual fund company or brokerage firm) and request your money be rolled into an IRA account. Distributions processed by phone usually speed up the process. In either case, you will likely be asked for the following:

1. Your Social Security number (and Personal Identification Number [PIN], if processing the transaction over the phone).
2. Your IRA account number and the address of your IRA provider.
3. Whether you would like to sell your company stock or transfer it to your IRA in-kind. (If you transfer stock to your IRA, you will have more control of the price at which it is eventually sold, but you will probably have to pay some commission fees to do so. If you request that your employer sell the stock for you, you will usually receive the

closing price on the day of your request and you won't pay any trade commissions. Before making a final decision about your company stock, read Chapter 9 on Net Unrealized Appreciation. You may be able to obtain favorable tax treatment upon selling your stock if you own highly appreciated shares.)

4.   Whether you would like taxes withheld; indicate that you do not.
5.   If you have received and read the Special Tax Notice explaining the tax considerations associated with each retirement plan distribution option. If you haven't read this notice, your rollover request will not be processed.

Allow two to four weeks for the distribution to be sent to your IRA.

When you request an IRA rollover, the investments in your employer's plan will be liquidated and a check for the balance will be sent to your IRA provider. New investments will need to be purchased in the IRA. The process for developing a successful investment strategy is discussed in Chapters 10 through 20.

## Other Rollover Considerations

Have you borrowed any money from your retirement plan? If you have an outstanding loan balance at the time you retire, you should repay it before taking a distribution. Plan loans must typically be repaid within thirty to sixty days from the time you leave the company. If the loan is not repaid and you leave money in your former employer's plan, or choose to roll over money to an IRA without repaying it, the loan amount will be treated like a cash distribution and be subject to taxes and penalties.

If you have stock in your company's retirement plan, you can choose to have the shares sent directly to you and roll the balance of the plan into an IRA. This combination distribution method is used in the Net Unrealized Appreciation strategy (see Chapter 9) and may allow you to qualify for favorable tax treatment.

You may have some after-tax contributions in your retirement plan. If so, this money can also be rolled into your IRA; however, be sure to keep track of the amount of the after-tax rollover. This is easily done when you report your after-tax rollover on IRS form 8606. If you don't track it, you could wind up paying taxes on this money twice: when contributed and when withdrawn. When you begin taking withdrawals from your IRA, you won't have to pay taxes on money contributed on an after-tax basis. Unfortunately, you can't withdraw all the after-tax money out of the IRA first and then begin pulling out the taxable money. If your IRA contains after-tax contributions, withdrawals are made on a pro-rata basis. Part of your withdrawal is considered taxable and part is not taxable.

There are other considerations you should keep in mind. If you are over age 55, once your money transfers into an IRA, you are no longer eligible to take a penalty-free, lump-sum distribution (see Chapter 5). In addition, depending on your IRA provider, you may be required to pay an IRA custodial fee and commissions to purchase investments in your IRA. While invested in your company's retirement plan, your employer pays these fees.

# Option 3: Leave It

Deferring distribution and leaving your money in your former company's retirement plan is the simplest thing to do because you don't have to do anything. There are no forms to fill out and no additional investment decisions to make. Because you are not taking a distribution, there are no taxes or penalties to pay, and your money will continue to grow tax-deferred. In addition, there are no fees or commissions. Although the mutual funds you own in your 401(k) charge annual management fees, you don't actually pay anything out-of-pocket. Many employers cover account and transaction-related costs and will continue to do so if you defer your distribution.

## *The Downside*

Leaving money in your former employer's plan does have its downside. Most company-sponsored retirement plans have limitations, primarily concerning the number and quality of the investment choices offered. This inhibits your ability to properly diversify. The average retirement plan only offers nineteen investment choices.[5] Although nineteen investment options could easily provide an acceptable level of diversification, many retirement plans lack important components of a well-balanced portfolio, such as a combination of both growth and value stocks, mid-cap and small-cap stocks, and international positions.

In addition to diversification limitations, it is unlikely that each of the nineteen investments offered is among the best available, compared with the thousands accessible outside the plan. If your plan offers only one large-company growth stock fund, for example, and it's not among the best funds in its category, you'll be stuck with it if you want exposure to large-company growth stocks. In an IRA, you could choose from over one thousand large-company growth stock funds and hand-pick the best one.

Leaving your money in place also costs you some control and flexibility. Once you're off the company payroll, you can no longer make contributions, and you cannot obtain a loan from the plan. Some plans may limit how often you can make changes to your investments. Also, you may be unable to set up a systematic withdrawal program, like you could from an IRA, to supplement your other retirement income.

> Consider deferring your distribution if your former employer's plan:
>
> • Offers numerous investment choices.
> • Offers investment choices that are above average.
> • Offers flexibility of investment changes.

In some plans, leaving your money in the plan may not even be an option. Not all employers allow former employees to keep money invested in the retirement plan and may mandate that you take a distribution from the plan by a certain date. This is almost always the case for accounts with balances of $5,000 or less.

If the limitations presented by leaving your money in your former employer's plan concern you, your choice is clear. You'll want to look at other choices. If the limitations are insignificant and the plan offers plenty of good investment choices, consider deferring distribution and leaving your money in place.

## Option 4: Roth It

A Roth IRA is very similar to a traditional IRA when it comes to annual contribution limits, investment choices, and flexibility. It differs, however, when it comes to the way taxes are applied.

Money contributed to a Roth IRA is done so on an after-tax basis. By contrast, traditional IRAs and most company-sponsored plans consist of pretax contributions. Money invested in Roth IRAs grows *tax-free*, not *tax-deferred* like traditional IRAs/401(k)s. This means that you can pull money out of your Roth IRA tax-free, whereas money in traditional IRAs/401(k)s is taxed when withdrawn. For many Americans, it makes sense to take advantage of these tax differences by converting to a Roth IRA.

In order to deposit your pretax 401(k) retirement plan money into a Roth IRA, you must initially transfer it to a traditional IRA and then convert the IRA to a Roth. There is no cap on the amount you can convert. Prior to 2010, this conversion option was only available to those with modified adjusted gross incomes under $100,000. However, the income limit was removed in 2010, making conversions available at all income levels.

> Consider converting your IRA to a Roth IRA if:
>
> - You are in a low tax bracket now and anticipate being in a higher tax bracket.
> - You would like to withdraw some retirement funds before age 59½ without penalty (applies to principal only).
> - You would like to be "tax diversified" at retirement.

Does tax-free growth coupled with tax-free withdrawals sound too good to be true? You think there has to be a catch?

## The Catch

In a sense, there is a catch. You will be required to pay federal and state income taxes on any amount converted from a traditional IRA to a Roth IRA (see tax brackets in Figure 8.1). The entire amount converted will be added to your taxable income in the year of the conversion; you pay taxes now to avoid paying taxes later.

You can control the way you make this transfer. Because taxes are due in the year of conversion, you may want to convert money from your traditional IRA to a Roth IRA a little at a time to avoid having your tax bracket ratcheted higher. The strategy many retirees use is to review their income in December and then convert only an amount that will keep them from moving into a higher tax bracket. You can convert any amount from an IRA to a Roth IRA and do so as often as you choose; the 10 percent early-withdrawal penalty does not apply when making a conversion from an IRA to a Roth.

## Pay Now or Later

Should you convert your IRA to a Roth? To find the answer, you need only ask yourself one question: Do I want to pay my taxes now or later?

Determining whether to convert depends on your current tax bracket and your future bracket, and when you begin withdrawing the funds. For example, if you are in the highest tax bracket now, 39.6 (2013) percent, and you anticipate being in a lower bracket, say 15 percent, during retirement, converting to a Roth IRA wouldn't make much sense—you would pay high taxes now to avoid paying lower taxes later.

On the other hand, if you are in a 15 percent tax bracket now and anticipate being in a higher bracket during retirement, then it makes perfect sense to convert your IRA to a Roth.

This was the case with Gary Kruger, a 60-year-old executive who retired in 2008 from a large bank. His plan was to withdraw money he'd accumulated in his non-retirement bank and brokerage accounts during the early years of retirement and then tap into his IRA later. In 2009, Gary had no earned income, which dropped him from the 35 percent tax bracket to the lowest bracket. In several years, his non-retirement accounts will be drained, and he will be forced to withdraw large sums from his IRA to meet his living expenses. The money he will pull from his IRA will be taxable, and his tax bracket will get bumped up from 15 to 25 percent. Anticipating these tax-bracket changes, Gary began converting portions of his IRA to his Roth IRA in 2009. He decided to pay taxes on some of his IRA money while in a lower tax bracket so he can avoid paying taxes later when his tax bracket goes back up.

If your tax bracket doesn't change between now and retirement, both options will yield the same result.

## Become Tax Diversified

If you are in a tax bracket that is neither very high nor very low, there is a middle ground you can pursue. Convert some of your IRA to a Roth IRA. This will make you "tax diversified." Some of your money will be invested in before-tax accounts, while your Roth IRA money will have already been taxed. If tax rates are higher at some point during retirement, you can take money out of your Roth IRA and not pay any taxes. If tax rates are lower, you can take money from your traditional IRA. This diversified approach makes sense for people who are in the midrange tax brackets.

Another benefit of the Roth IRA is liquidity. Unlike a traditional IRA, you can withdraw your principal without penalty or taxes prior to age

59½. However, withdrawals cannot take place for five years after the Roth conversion. For those retiring prior to age 59½, the ability to tap some retirement funds without penalty may be very helpful.

## *Roth IRA Conversion Process*

The process for rolling your money to an IRA and then converting to a Roth is identical to that for rolling your company retirement plan over to an IRA except for one additional step. Once your retirement plan money has been rolled over into a traditional IRA, your financial institution will provide you with an IRA/Roth Conversion Form, on which you indicate the amount of your IRA you would like converted to a Roth. At year's end, you will receive a 1099R form from your IRA provider indicating the taxable conversion amount.

# Option 5: Annuitize It

When you choose to take annuity payments, your vested account balance is used to buy an immediate annuity. Annuity payments will be made to you for your entire lifetime and possibly your spouse's as well, depending upon the payout option you choose.

> Only 12 percent of plan distributions are taken as annuity payments.[6]

With annuity payments, you do not have to worry about the management of the balance in your plan or the stock market's ups and downs. Although the annuity payout is generally lower than what could be produced by an investment portfolio moderately invested, the freedom of not having to manage the money or worry about market downturns makes this option a nice fit for some.

> Consider annuity payments if:
> - You don't want to be involved in the management of your own portfolio.
> - You want to guarantee your income for life.

The various annuity payout options are usually identical to those offered to people receiving company pensions. Examples of these annuity options are outlined in detail in Chapter 7.

The downside of annuity payments, in addition to a possible lower payout rate, is the inability to reverse your decision. Once the decision is made to annuitize, it is irrevocable. You are guaranteed a lifetime income; however, you can never again tap into your total retirement plan balance.

## Option 6: Stock It

Investors in high tax brackets who own low-tax-basis shares of company stock in their 401(k)s can save thousands in taxes by using a little-known strategy called Net Unrealized Appreciation (NUA). Bruce Richardson, the retiree mentioned at the beginning of this chapter who without thinking rolled his 401(k) money to an IRA, could have saved a lot of money using this strategy.

To initiate the NUA strategy, all Bruce would have had to do is request that his $600,000 of company stock be transferred into a non-retirement account and that the remaining $25,000 balance of his 401(k) be rolled to an IRA. Once in the non-retirement account, Bruce could sell the company stock at some point and pay *capital gains* taxes (15 percent) on the gains instead of income taxes on the entire balance, which in his case would be much higher. Unfortunately, because he rolled his money to an IRA, his withdrawals will be taxed at income tax rates. The NUA strategy would have allowed Bruce to pay fewer taxes on his retirement nest egg. In addition, had he initiated the NUA strategy and never sold the company stock, no taxes would be due during his lifetime. Due to the complexity of this strategy, Chapter 9 has been dedicated entirely to outlining how it works. If you own company stock in your 401(k) plan, you may be able to save thousands of dollars using the NUA strategy.

> Consider the NUA strategy if:
>
> • You're in a high tax bracket.
> • You own company stock in your 401(k).
> • You would rather pay taxes at capital gains rates instead of income taxes.

## Making a Final Distribution Decision

Which distribution option should you choose? It's not a decision to take lightly because of the impact it will have on your retirement years. Before choosing, look at your options side by side, comparing the long-term effects of each. By making educated decisions about your money during job changes and at retirement, you can ensure that one of your largest and most critical assets is managed properly.

# 9

# A TAX LOOPHOLE

At retirement, Grace Vincent had accumulated more than $450,000 in her 401(k). Of that amount, $300,000 was invested in highly appreciated company stock. She wondered whether she should roll it all to an IRA or if there was a better strategy.

To fully maximize her nest egg, Grace decided to use a little-known distribution tax strategy referred to as Net Unrealized Appreciation (NUA). Using NUA, she'll be able to lower the taxes she'll be required to pay on withdrawals from her investment portfolio during retirement. To make this strategy work, she simply rolled the money invested in mutual funds in her 401(k) to an IRA. She then transferred the company stock into a non-retirement brokerage account. With money in both accounts, Grace has a choice where to withdraw the money she needs to meet retirement expenses. If she pulls money from the IRA, she'll have to pay income taxes at her 28 percent tax rate. If she sells stock and pulls money from the brokerage account, she'll only have to pay capital gains taxes of 15 percent on her stock's appreciation.

Let's see: would you rather pay taxes at 28 percent or 15 percent? Grace opted for the tax savings and is pulling money from her brokerage account to meet her living expenses.

Upon withdrawal, the money you've invested in mutual funds in a 401(k) and other types of employer-sponsored retirement plans must be liquidated. Most people choose to roll this money into IRAs. As we saw in Chapter 8, rolling money into an IRA is often the best distribution method for money invested in mutual funds. It may not, however, be your best choice for the portion of your plan that is invested in company stock.

According to research, 401(k) participants invest 8 percent of their retirement savings in their company's stock.[1] In fact, at the largest U.S. companies, company stock represents more than 12 percent of total plan balances.[2] Often you'll find this overconcentration in plans where employers provide matching contributions in their own stock. If you own company stock in your employer-sponsored retirement plan, you may be able to save thousands of dollars upon distribution by using this rarely considered IRS tax strategy.

NUA works best in situations where an investor is in a high tax bracket, has low-cost-basis stock in his or her plan, and desires to hold on to the stock for many years after distribution. It also works extremely well in combination with the IRA rollover distribution method covered in Chapter 8.

It's inevitable that the money in your retirement plan is going to get taxed at some point. The NUA strategy allows you some control over how it is taxed. If you sell your company stock while in the 401(k) plan or after rolling it into an IRA, you will be required to pay income taxes on the entire balance when you withdraw the proceeds, whether that occurs immediately or later in retirement. The NUA strategy allows your company stock gains to be taxed at capital gains tax rates, which, depending on your tax bracket, are generally lower than income tax rates.

Compare your income tax rate with the capital gains rates in Figures 9.1 and 9.2. You will probably see a significant difference.

What is NUA? It is the value of company stock upon distribution from the plan minus the value of the stock when you bought it or it was

## 2013 Federal Personal Income Tax Rates

| Tax Rate | Single | Married (filing jointly) |
| --- | --- | --- |
| 10% | up to $8,925 | up to $17,850 |
| 15% | $8,926–$36,250 | $17,851–$72,500 |
| 25% | $36,251–$87,850 | $72,501–$146,400 |
| 28% | $87,851–$183,250 | $146,401–$223,050 |
| 33% | $183,251–$398,350 | $223,051–$398,350 |
| 35% | $398,351–$400,000 | $398,351–$450,000 |
| 39.6% | $400,001 and above | $450,001 and above |

figure 9.1

given to you (the cost basis). For example, let's say, while working at your company you invested a total of $10,000 into your company's stock (this is the cost basis), and it is now worth $60,000–you have NUA of $50,000. When you retire from your company, you must decide what to do with the company stock held in your retirement plan. You have four options, as listed below. Three of these options were covered in Chapter 8.

1. Sell the stock in the plan and take a cash distribution. Income taxes are due immediately as well as applicable early-withdrawal penalties.
2. Sell the stock and roll over the cash balance into an IRA. Income taxes are due when you eventually take a withdrawal from your IRA.
3. Don't sell the stock, but roll it over "in-kind" into an IRA. Again, you must pay income taxes when you eventually sell and take a withdrawal.
4. Don't sell the stock, take a stock distribution in-kind, and deposit the shares into a non-retirement account (NUA). Capital gains taxes are due when you eventually sell shares.

| Capital Gains Tax Rates | | |
| --- | --- | --- |
| **Long-Term Capital Gains** (Holding period longer than one year) | **2012** | **2013** |
| 10-15% tax brackets | 0% | 0% |
| 25-35% tax brackets | 15% | 15% |
| 39.6% tax bracket | 15% | 20% |
| **Short-Term Capital Gains** (Holding period less than one year) | **2012** | **2013** |
| All tax brackets | Income Tax Rates | Income Tax Rates |
| **Medicare Surtax on Capital Gains** | **2012** | **2013** |
| The Medicare surtax on net investment income applies to those with adjusted gross income (AGI) exceeding $200,000 for singles and $250,000 for married couples. | 0% | 3.8% |

figure 9.2

The last option is the NUA strategy. A quick comparison of each of these options shows the value of the NUA strategy. Option 1 triggers immediate income taxation upon distribution. In options 2 and 3, income taxes must be paid when withdrawals are taken in retirement. But the fourth option, the NUA strategy, allows you to pay capital gains taxes upon selling your company stock, rather than pay income taxes. Using the NUA strategy defers taxation on the appreciation of the stock until it is eventually sold, at which point capital gains taxes are imposed only upon the appreciation.

## How the NUA Strategy Works

To initiate this strategy, you must request a lump-sum distribution and have the "qualifying" company stock in your plan sent directly to you in-kind. Qualifying shares are those contributed to your plan by your employer and those pretax shares purchased by you (to the extent that they are both part of a lump-sum distribution from your plan).[3] Deductible shares purchased by you do not qualify for this favorable tax treatment.[4] A lump-sum distribution is defined as a payment of your entire plan balance occurring in one taxable year that takes place after a "qualifying event," such as separation from service (including retirement), attaining age 59½, or death.

After you make the request, your stock shares will be sent to you in certificate form. These shares can then be deposited into a taxable brokerage account (a non-retirement account). Retirement plan money that is not invested in your company's stock can be rolled into an IRA. Mutual fund shares, for example, will be liquidated and distributed to you in cash; the cash portion of the distribution can subsequently be rolled into an IRA.

Some plans will allow you to split your plan distribution. If this is the case, your eligible stock shares will be sent to you in-kind while the remaining balance of your account can be directly rolled to an IRA.

Sound complicated? It is. Therefore, I recommend that you talk to your financial advisor or a tax advisor before you take a distribution of your employer's stock.

The distribution of the stock is subject to immediate taxation because you are moving money from a retirement account to a non-retirement account. This may set off some alarms in your mind, but don't worry, you're going to save money in the long run.

Upon taking a stock distribution, you will be required to pay taxes (at income tax rates) on only the cost basis of the stock–the average value of the shares at the time they were initially purchased in the plan–*not* the stock's total current value. Your employer will not withhold any tax upon distribution of stock shares. The 20 percent mandatory withholding tax we discussed in Chapter 8 applies only to cash distributions. If you are not yet age 55, you will also be required to pay a 10 percent early-withdrawal penalty. Again, though, this penalty is imposed only on a cost basis, not the entire value of the stock distribution. Having to pay taxes immediately is a sticky point for many people who are simply unwilling or unable to pay taxes now, even if it will save them money in the long run. However, if your cost basis is very low, the tax and penalty will not be a heavy burden.

You are not required to pay any tax on the appreciation of the stock (its NUA) until you sell it. At that time, any appreciation is subject only to capital gains taxes, not income tax. This means you have a built-in 20 percent capital gains ceiling, a far cry cheaper than the maximum income tax bracket of 39.6 percent.

## Who Should Consider the NUA Strategy?

If you have low-basis stock, are in a high tax bracket (usually over 28 percent), and would like to sell your stock upon distribution and spend the proceeds, it's generally advantageous to use the NUA strategy. As a general rule, the current value of the stock should be at least double, and probably three or four times the cost basis, for the strategy to make sense.

Let's look at an example: Robert Stewart accumulated 5,000 shares of company stock in his 401(k) plan. The average purchase price was $5 per share for a total of $25,000 (his cost basis). When he retires in the near future, he is planning to sell the stock and use the proceeds to buy a retirement home in Palm Springs. He is trying to decide between a stock distribution to a taxable account (NUA strategy) or a rollover to his IRA. Which should he choose?

If he requests a stock distribution and deposits the shares into a taxable nonretirement account, he will owe income tax on the cost basis ($25,000). In Robert's 28 percent tax bracket, that amounts to $7,000. Robert is over age 59½, so there are no early-withdrawal penalties applied to his distribution. He plans to sell his stock shares at $60 per share. Multiplying that price by his 5,000 shares will give Robert $300,000. His NUA is $55 per share, or $275,000. (This is calculated by subtracting the $25,000 cost basis from the total value of the stock.)

When he sells those shares, he will owe capital gains tax (15 percent) on the $275,000 of appreciation, for a total of $41,250 in taxes. This $41,250 is due in the year he sells the stock. If he never sells the stock, he will never have to pay the tax. Assuming he does sell, however, his total tax bill will equal $48,250 ($7,000 of income tax on the cost basis, plus $41,250 in capital gains taxes when the stock is sold). After taxes, Robert is left with $251,750 to buy the property. Remember this number.

Now let's say Robert chose to roll his stock shares directly into an IRA account, realized the same appreciation, sold the shares at the same time, and then took a distribution from his IRA to buy the property. In this case, the $300,000 distribution would vault him into the 33 percent marginal tax bracket (25 percent nominal) and he would owe $75,000 in federal income taxes and possibly some additional state income taxes, leaving him with just $225,000.

Robert could maintain his tax bracket at 28 percent if he chooses simply to take IRA distributions over a period of years rather than all at once. This won't help him, however, if he needs a large sum of money now to buy a property in Palm Springs. In this scenario, the NUA strategy actually saved Robert $26,750.

Saving this amount of money makes the effort to transfer the shares into a separate taxable account worthwhile. The higher the tax bracket and the greater the NUA, the more valuable the NUA tax break becomes. See Figure 9.3 for a summary of this example.

## Who Should NOT Consider the NUA Strategy?

If you are planning to sell your stock immediately upon distribution to reinvest and diversify the proceeds into other investments, the tax advantages are lessened. Also, the NUA strategy will not yield as many benefits if you own high-basis stock in your plan or are currently in a low tax bracket.

When you sell stock immediately to buy a diversified portfolio, you will have to pay income taxes on the cost basis of the stock and capital gains taxes on the appreciation. The money left over can be reinvested; however, in a taxable account, some of your portfolio growth will be lost to taxes

| Low-Basis Stock | NUA | IRA Rollover |
|---|---|---|
| **NUA vs. IRA Rollover** | | |
| *Sell stock immediately and spend the proceeds* | | |
| Total value of shares at time of distribution | $300,000 | $300,000 |
| Cost basis of shares | $25,000 | N/A |
| Net unrealized appreciation of shares at time of distribution | $275,000 | N/A |
| Income tax on cost basis of shares at time of distribution (28%) | $7,000 | N/A |
| Capital gains tax on stock when sold (15%) | $41,250 | N/A |
| Income tax on IRA distribution (25% nominal) | N/A | $75,000 |
| Total taxes | $48,250 | $75,000 |
| Total after taxes are paid | $251,750 | $225,000 |
| **NUA strategy yields $26,750 more** | | |

Assumption: employee is over age 59½ (no early-withdrawal penalty upon distribution)

figure 9.3

each year. If your objective is to diversify your stock position, it is generally wiser to sell the stock in a retirement account and let the proceeds continue to grow tax-deferred.

Let's look at another example. William Atkinson is age 59 and about to retire. His primary objective is to sell his 5,000 shares of company stock ($5 per share cost basis) and reinvest the proceeds into a more diversified portfolio. He doesn't plan on spending any of this money for twenty years. Which strategy should he choose?

Following the NUA strategy, he would transfer 5,000 shares of low-basis stock into a taxable brokerage account. If he sells the stock at $60 per share ($300,000) and pays the $48,250 in taxes (income and capital gains), he would have $251,750 after taxes to reinvest in a diversified portfolio. William is considering what his portfolio will be worth if he averages a 10 percent growth rate. Now that his money is in a taxable account, some of that growth (interest, dividends, and capital gains) is subject to taxes each year. Assuming that 15 percent of his return goes to pay the taxes, he will average just 8.5 percent growth after taxes have been paid.

Because William's objective is to diversify and invest for the long term, it

would make far more sense for him to roll over his money to an IRA. This
will allow his growth to take place in a tax-deferred account (Figure 9.4).
Most people do not withdraw money from their IRAs all at once. If, for
instance, money is withdrawn over a twenty-year period during retirement,
the tax rate may be reduced even further. This makes the IRA rollover
strategy even more advantageous.

### NUA vs. IRA Rollover

*Sell stock immediately and diversify into other investments*

| Low-Basis Stock | NUA | IRA Rollover |
|---|---|---|
| Total value of shares at time of distribution | $300,000 | $300,000 |
| Cost basis of shares | $25,000 | N/A |
| Net unrealized appreciation of shares at time of distribution | $275,000 | N/A |
| Income tax on cost basis of shares (paid immediately; 28%) | $7,000 | N/A |
| Capital gains tax on stock (paid immediately; 15%) | $41,250 | N/A |
| Balance to invest | $251,750 | $300,000 |
| Balance of portfolio in 20 years (after-tax) | $1,286,957 | N/A |
| Balance of IRA in 20 years (before-tax) | N/A | $2,018,250 |
| Income tax on portfolio upon withdrawal (28%) | N/A | $565,110 |
| Ending balance after taxes | $1,286,957 | $1,453,140 |

**IRA Rollover strategy yields $166,183 more**

Assumptions: Capital gains rate 15%; pretax growth rate for diversified portfolio 10%,
after-tax rate 8.5%; employee over age 59½ (no early-withdrawal penalty upon distribution);
tax rate applied to IRA distribution 28% (the rate would be higher if the investor took the
distribution all in one year rather than spreading it out)

*figure 9.4*

If you own high-cost-basis stock, it is usually better to keep the stock in a
retirement account. In this case, if you did use the NUA strategy, you would
pay income tax on most of the value of the stock due to its high cost basis.
Capital gains tax would only be applied to a small portion of the stock's
value (the amount above the cost basis).

In addition, the NUA strategy may not be as effective if you are not yet age 55. In this case you will be required to pay a 10 percent early-with-drawal penalty on the original cost basis of the stock. Again, this is money that won't be compounding toward your retirement. The good news is that no penalties are owed on your stock appreciation.

## NUA and "Stepped-Up" Cost Basis for Heirs

If you roll your stock into an IRA, you not only face paying income taxes whenever you take a withdrawal, but income taxes must also be paid upon your death.

When you pass away, your spouse can transfer your IRA balance to his or her IRA and avoid taxation. However, upon your spouse's death, your heirs must pay ordinary income tax on the entire amount distributed from the IRA.

Let's go back to the case of Robert Stewart. Assume that when he and his wife pass away, the stock is worth $100 per share and has a total value of $500,000. Their heirs would be required to pay income taxes on the entire $500,000 if it was distributed from an IRA. This would inevitably place Robert's estate in the highest tax bracket (39.6 percent marginal and 29 percent nominal) when computing the final income tax owed. Before his heirs received anything, the government would take $145,000.

If, however, he had used the NUA strategy and transferred his 5,000 shares of company stock into a non-retirement account, his heirs would enjoy some big tax advantages. They would be required to pay capital gains tax on the NUA of the shares while they were in the employer-sponsored retirement plan. This is referred to as "income in respect of the decedent." In Robert's case, he had $275,000 of NUA at the time he took an in-kind distribution from the plan. However, any appreciation that occurred after the stock was distributed from the plan will receive a "stepped-up basis" and will be tax-free after death.

If Robert dies when his stock is selling at $100 per share ($500,000), the $100 price would become the new cost basis for the heirs. The appreciation from $60 (value of stock at the time of distribution from the plan) to $100 (the value of the stock upon death) is tax-free. In Robert's case, this amounts to $200,000. If the heirs subsequently decide to sell the stock, they will pay capital gains tax on the difference between $100, the new stepped-up basis, and the price at the time they sell. If, for example, they sold the shares for $105, they would pay capital gains tax only on the appreciation since Robert's death: $5 per share.

## No Mandatory Distributions

If you own an IRA, you must begin taking mandatory distributions at age 70½, whether you need the money to live on or not. Mandatory distribution is synonymous with mandatory taxation. If you opt for the NUA strategy and deposit your company stock in a taxable account, you are not required to take any distributions at any age. Having funds in different types of accounts (both retirement and non-retirement) can help you stretch your nest egg and provide more money to your heirs.

## What Is the Process for Initiating the NUA Strategy?

Your first step should be determining the cost basis of your employer's stock. This will help you determine its increase in price (the NUA) since being purchased in your retirement plan and whether it makes sense to pursue this strategy.

Next, determine if your company stock shares are eligible for the NUA strategy. It may take several phone calls or letters to acquire this information. You'll need to contact your benefits department or the company that administers your employer's retirement plan. Because this information is sometimes difficult to obtain, you should start requesting it at least six months before you expect to retire or separate from service. Due to the technicalities involved, it may be advantageous to hire a tax professional. IRS Tax Code Section 402(e)(4) may also be helpful.

You will need to complete the distribution paperwork. If you are going to take advantage of the NUA strategy, you must request a lump-sum distribution and have the stock shares sent directly to you. If your employer allows split distributions, you can roll the remaining balance of your plan directly into an IRA. If it does not allow for split distributions, you will receive your stock shares and a check for the balance of your plan. Of course, your company must withhold 20 percent from the money distributed that was not invested in stock. You will have sixty days, upon receiving the check, to roll it into an IRA to avoid taxes and penalties. (See sixty-day rollover section in Chapter 8.) At year's end after distributing the stock, your employer will provide you with a copy of Form 1099R and will report the transaction to the IRS.

Before deciding what to do with your company stock, obtain a retirement plan distribution analysis, so you can compare each of your six distribution options side by side. Depending on your goals and objectives, you may be able to save a lot of money in taxes by using the NUA strategy.

# SECTION 3

---

# DEVELOPING A SUCCESSFUL INVESTMENT STRATEGY

Asset Allocation

Diversification

Buying the Best Investments

Ongoing Portfolio Management

# 10

# AVOIDING THE TEN MOST COMMON INVESTOR MISTAKES

## RETIREMENT DECISION #9: HOW SHOULD I MANAGE MY PERSONAL SAVINGS?

M ax Haley has been investing in the stock market for the past twenty years. In 1993, at age 40, he started with $50,000. Since then, he has invested in a number of individual stocks and stock mutual funds. Max prides himself on his "investment expertise." To determine what stocks and funds to buy, when to buy, and when to sell, he reads *Money Magazine*, subscribes to the *Wall Street Journal*, frequently visits investment websites, and tunes in to CNBC several times each day to obtain stock prices and reports.

So how's he doing? By the end of 2012, his investment had grown to $109,556. Max's annual return was a meager 4 percent. Had Max simply invested his $50,000 into a good balanced stock and bond mutual fund and never looked at it again for the twenty years, he would have almost tripled his low-return investment portfolio and ended with $299,576.

If Max retires and wants his nest egg to last thirty years, he can only withdraw $6,336 each year. If he had simply invested in the balanced fund, assuming returns similar to those the fund produced in the past, he could pull out over $20,000 each year. What's really surprising about his performance is that Max's 4 percent annual return was better than what the average U.S. stock investor earned during this same period!

After applying so much effort, why did Max do so poorly? Max, like most individual investors, was guilty of making ten mistakes. Had he read and applied the lessons you'll learn in this chapter when he started in 1993, he likely would be sitting on a much larger nest egg today.

## Mistakes Will Cost You

And no doubt about it: You will need a large nest egg to retire on. Social Security is under pressure as more and more baby boomers start tapping into the system. Companies are eliminating traditional pension plans. More than ever before people need solid returns from their own investment portfolios in order to produce a livable retirement income. Plain and simple, your success as an investor may well dictate whether you reach your retirement goals. The message here is that retirement in the future is going to look a lot different than it does today. As time goes on, your retirement success is going to rely more and more on you, your savings habits, and your investment results than on your company and the government.

In the future, your assets (savings and investments) will take on an even greater importance and will become a bigger slice of the retirement income pie (Figure 10.1).[1] This is a huge problem for most retirees. Why? Because most people–hopefully not you–simply don't invest very well.

A twenty-year investor study dramatically illustrates the grim lack of success many investors have experienced. According to the study, the average stock-fund investor achieved returns of only 3.49 percent a year from 1992 through 2011 while the average bond-fund investor obtained an annual return of only 0.94 percent. Had these same investors simply invested their money in the S&P 500 Index (composed of large U.S. company stocks) or the Barclays Aggregate Bond Index (U.S. bond market) and forgotten all about

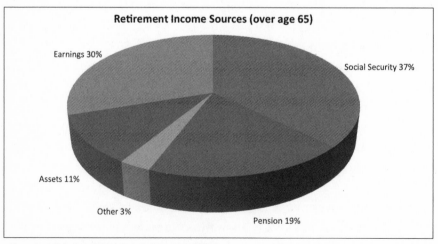

Source: Social Security Administration

figure 10.1

| $100,000 Invested at Different Growth Rates | | | | |
|---|---|---|---|---|
| | Average Bond Fund Investor | Barclays Aggregate Bond Index | Average Stock Fund Investor | S&P 500 Index |
| *Annual Rate of Return* | 0.94% | 6.50% | 3.49% | 7.81% |
| 10-Years | $109,808 | $187,714 | $140,924 | $212,124 |
| 20-Years | $120,577 | $352,365 | $198,595 | $449,967 |
| 30-Years | $132,403 | $661,437 | $279,867 | $954,490 |

*figure 10.2*

it, they would have earned an annual return of 7.81 percent and 6.50 percent respectively.[2] The stock market provided results double those experienced by millions of stock mutual fund investors! It should have been easy for even the average investor to make substantial sums of money over this period of time.

Consider for a moment the difference between an investor earning an average annual return of 3.49 or 0.94 percent as opposed to an investor earning a 7.81 or 6.50 percent return. Compare the results in Figure 10.2.

Over the long run, even during bull markets, most investors struggle to obtain performance better than low-yielding investments, like money markets and certificates of deposit, because they make common investor mistakes. How is it that investors do so poorly at times when investments are doing so well? No single mistake explains this poor performance. Rather, there are a combination of errors repeated over and over–mistakes that can be overcome by simply implementing and adhering to a disciplined investment strategy. (Developing a strategy is discussed in the following chapters.)

In this chapter, you will learn that it's possible to obtain good long-term returns by avoiding the obstacles that plague so many investors. By avoiding common mistakes, you will be in a better position to reach your retirement goals. Here are the ten most common investor mistakes.

## Mistake #1: Excessive Buying and Selling

Like the amateur chef who continually seasons food until it's inedible, investors who are overactive in their trading undermine their goals.

A study of more than 66,000 households with investment accounts at a well-known brokerage firm found that investors who traded most frequently underperformed those who traded the least. For the study, the investors were split into five groups based on their trading activity. The returns achieved by the 20 percent of investors who traded the most lagged behind the least active group of investors by 5.5 percentage points annually.[3]

Another study showed that men trade 45 percent more actively than women, and consequently, women outperformed men.[4]

Many investors make the mistake of thinking that the more often they trade, the better their returns will be. The advertisements aired by many discount brokerage firms promoting active trading want you to believe this is true. However, the evidence suggests exactly the opposite. So sit back and relax!

From 1992 to 2011 the average stock fund investor held his or her positions for a short 3.29 years, while bond fund investors held their positions for 3.09 years.[5]

Does this hold true for professionals too? Do mutual funds with lower portfolio turnover (less buying and selling) do better than funds with higher turnover? The answer is yes, but by a much smaller margin than individual investors. The average U.S. stock fund has a 77 percent turnover rate, meaning they sell 77 percent of their portfolio each year. The lowest turnover funds beat their high-turnover peers by 1.94 percent per year for five years, 0.66 percent for ten years, and 1.20 percent for fifteen years.[6]

## Mistake #2: Information Overload

Too much information can be dangerous to your wealth.

Not long ago, at the beginning of an investment seminar, I offered a $20 bill to the smartest investor in the room. I then asked the audience how many knew the previous day's closing level of the Dow Jones Industrial Average. Many hands went up, and these "smart" investors had no difficulty citing the index's closing value.

Then I asked who in the audience didn't have a clue where the market had closed. Timidly, a woman with very little investment experience raised her hand. The crowd was surprised as I handed her the $20 bill. I explained that investors who rarely check the market and the value of their investments keep more of their money invested in stocks, thus, they often obtain better long-term results. Those who monitor the market too closely have a tendency to undermine their portfolios with self-destructive behavior.

What role should information play in your investment decisions? University of Chicago Professor Richard Thaler, the father of behavioral economics, conducted an experiment to see how much investors would allocate to stocks and bonds based on how often they reviewed their investment performance. Three simulations were developed, each representing a different frequency of investors reviewing their portfolio performance over a twenty-five-year period.

Those participating in the study were assigned to participate in one of three simulation groups. Group A was bombarded with investment performance information. Their test simulated the experience an investor would have if they looked at the performance of their investment portfolio every month for a twenty-five-year period. Group B received performance information replicating the scenario of looking at their investments just once each year. Group C received investment updates only once every five years. Which group do you think did the best?

The investors who received the most performance information allocated the smallest amount of their portfolios—about 40 percent—to stocks (Figure 10.3). They not only maintained the lowest equity exposure but tended also to sell stocks immediately after a loss. The group that only received updates every year devoted 70 percent of their portfolios to stocks, while those who received performance information every five years invested 66 percent of their portfolios in stocks.[7] And, as we all know, based on the history of the market, investors with greater exposure to the equity markets have enjoyed far better long-term performance than those with lesser exposure.

The bottom line: The more closely investors follow the market, the more tentative they become about investing in stocks, which ultimately hurts their returns.

| Information Overload | | | |
|---|---|---|---|
| | **Group A** | **Group B** | **Group C** |
| Total Reports | 200 | 40 | 5 |
| Report Frequency | Monthly | Annually | Every 5 Years |
| Stock Allocation | 41% | 70% | 66% |

*figure 10.3*

The solution? Develop a fundamentally sound investment strategy and maintain your stock allocation through up and down markets. Stay away from financial sites on the Internet, turn off CNBC, consider canceling the *Wall Street Journal*, and quit worrying about your investments every day. Professor Thaler said it best: "My advice to you is to invest in equities, and then don't open the mail."[8]

## Mistake #3: Market Timing

History has shown that the stock market rises about 70 percent of the time. The danger, when investing, is in finding yourself out of the market during the 70 percent of the time it's going up, all because you're trying to avoid the 30 percent of the time the market is falling.

Market timing is different than excessive trading. Market timers attempt to be invested in stocks while they are going up and out of stocks when they drop. Excessive trading doesn't make you a market timer. You could make one hundred trades each year buying and selling only stocks. When you sell one stock, you turn around and buy another one. In this scenario you'd always be 100 percent invested in stocks. Market timers move money from stocks to bonds or cash and then back to stocks.

Trying to choose the right times to jump in and out of the market is an impossible task. Too many investors make the mistake of thinking they can do it. Investors attempting to time the ebbs and flows of the market tend to jump in too late, missing major upswings, and jump out after the market has fallen. Consequently, many investors end up buying high and selling low, yielding poor results that often lead to the kind of frustration that keeps investors out of the stock market altogether.

If you had invested in the Dow Jones Industrial Average Index from 1997 to 2011, covering 3,768 trading days, you would have enjoyed a 6.63 percent annualized return and a $10,000 initial investment would have grown to $26,176. If you had missed the market's forty best days in this fifteen-year period, your annualized return would have been cut to –5.75 percent! There's a dramatic difference between an investor who spent 3,728 days invested in the stock market and another who stayed invested all 3,768 days (Figure 10.4).[9] There is a huge price to pay if you mistime the market.

Market timing is typically driven by emotion. Investors are notorious

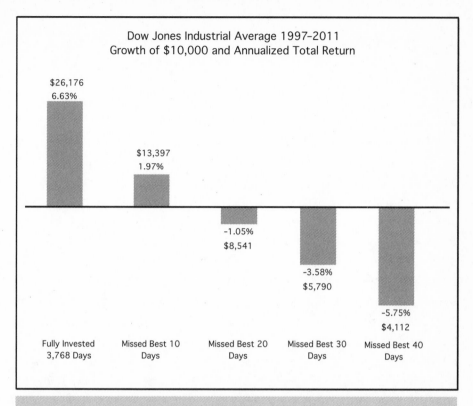

Dow Jones Industrial Average 1997–2011
Growth of $10,000 and Annualized Total Return

| | | | | |
|---|---|---|---|---|
| $26,176 6.63% | $13,397 1.97% | -1.05% $8,541 | -3.58% $5,790 | -5.75% $4,112 |
| Fully Invested 3,768 Days | Missed Best 10 Days | Missed Best 20 Days | Missed Best 30 Days | Missed Best 40 Days |

figure 10.4

for buying stocks when they feel good and selling when they feel bad. Think about this: You feel good once the market has run up 20 percent or more, and you feel bad when your portfolio is down 20 percent. With the "feel good/bad" investment strategy, you will always buy after the market has gone up and sell when the market has taken a big fall. The biggest days in the stock market normally occur early in a recovery. So if you pull your money out of the market when it's down and hope that you will be smart enough to get back in the day it hits the bottom and starts to climb, the odds are stacked against you. And if you are late, you will likely miss the best days. Following the "feel good" strategy will lead you to poor returns.

Individual investors are awful market timers. How about professional market timers? Can anyone successfully call the market? I'll let you be the judge. Reviewing the performance of market timing newsletters will answer this question. For the past three years, 44 percent of newsletters that focus on U.S. stocks beat the market (S&P 500 Index), and for the past five years, 40 percent beat the market. Over a longer time period, market timing newsletters fare a little better. Over the past ten years, 48 percent of the newsletters provided better than market performance, and for the past fifteen years, 63 percent beat the market.[10] The difference between an individual and a professional trying to time the market is emotion. Market timing newsletters follow well-defined investment strategies and make logical investment decisions as opposed to individuals who are often driven by their emotions.

## Mistake #4: Chasing Returns

Individual investors are famous for buying last year's winners. Guess which mutual funds attract the most new money each year? You got it; money flows into mutual funds that have just enjoyed the greatest performance in the *previous* year. 2007 is a great example since it was followed by a year where the market dropped big. Investors poured more than $208 billion into international funds, the asset class with the greatest performance in 2006. The returns of the three international funds that brought in the most assets in 2007 provided returns 10 percent higher than the U.S. stock market in 2006. In 2008, however, these same three funds on average lost 43.04 percent. International funds were the worst major equity asset class in 2008.[11] In other words, investors who chased market-beating returns in 2008 got soundly beaten by the market (Figure 10.5).

It shouldn't be surprising that chasing returns is a very common investor mistake. There's an entire financial media industry built around one simple theme: "Don't Miss Out on the Ten Hottest Stocks," or some variation of it. For many investors, the lure of phenomenal past returns is just too tempting to pass up. This allure leads to critical mistakes.

For example, in 1999, just before the tech bubble burst, the Nicholas-Applegate Global Tech I Fund posted an unbelievable 494 percent return, and investors saw instant riches parading before their eyes. An individual investing in this fund at the start of 2000, however, experienced the following returns: -36.37 percent in 2000, -49.26 percent in 2001, and -44.96 percent in 2002.[13] At the end of three years, a $10,000 investment was worth

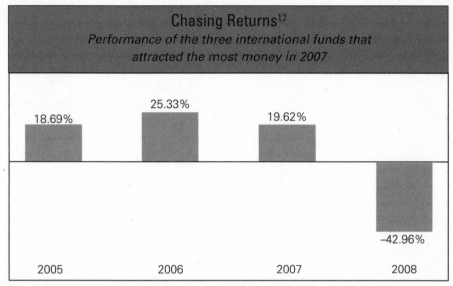

**Chasing Returns**[12]
*Performance of the three international funds that attracted the most money in 2007*

18.69%   25.33%   19.62%

−42.96%

2005      2006      2007      2008

Source: *Average performance of the Dodge & Cox International Stock, American Europacific, and Thornburg International Value Funds*

figure 10.5

just $1,777. Investors who buy last year's winners are essentially saying, "I believe last year's phenomenal returns will repeat this year and I don't mind buying high." When the fine print says, "Past performance is no guarantee of future returns," believe it!

# Mistake #5: Believing Persuasive Advertising Messages

Many brokerage firms advertise in order to convince you how easy, fun, and inexpensive it is to delve into the stock market and make big money. In fact, the brokerage industry spends hundreds of millions of dollars each year on TV commercials convincing us that it's easy to be a success in the market.

The most classic example is the series of Stewart commercials run for a large brokerage firm that was touting its online trading system. You may remember Stewart? He was that red-headed punk rocker who taught us and his boss how easy it is to make money in the stock market. Stewart advised that all you had to do was open an online account, start trading, and watch the money roll in. As Stewart said in the commercial:

*"I don't want to beat the market. I wanna grab it, sock it in the gut a couple of times, turn it upside down, hold it by the pants, and shake it till all those pockets empty out the spare change."*[14]

Although the Stewart commercials, like many ads for the investment houses in the late '90s, were hilarious, they did more damage than good. In fact, the commercial is even funnier in hindsight. In one of the commercials Stewart recommends that his boss buy one hundred shares of Kmart stock. In 2002 Kmart filed for bankruptcy and the value of the stock subsequently went to zero. We don't see Stewart talking about investing anymore, probably because he lost his shirt in the 2000–2002 recession. He learned the hard way that there is more to developing a solid investment strategy than merely opening an online brokerage account and trading.

No question about it, buying and selling stocks can be exhilarating. Many investors roll up their sleeves and play with their money, checking stock prices and market values throughout each day. While this may be a great form of entertainment, most discover it's also a successful formula for losing money.

Rarely a day passes when a brokerage firm isn't telling Americans that they can trade stocks for as little as $5 to $8 per transaction. Think about it. By offering such cheap trades, these firms have to make up for it by dealing in quantity. Their goal is to have you trade as often as possible without concern for cost. What they don't tell you is what it's *really* costing you. As we've seen, hyperactive trading equals poor performance.

## Mistake #6: Poor Diversification

Investors tend to be concentrated in one or two companies or sectors of the market, which often occurs when employees are offered company stock in their retirement plans. Overconcentration can hurt a portfolio whether the market is performing well or poorly. Poor diversification leads to excessive volatility, and excessive volatility causes investors to make hasty, poor decisions.

Suppose in 2008 you had invested the bulk of your portfolio in a big company like Lehman Brothers (–99.18 percent), AIG (–96.24 percent), General Motors (–86.86 percent), or Citigroup (–73.40 percent). That year, you would have watched your portfolio head into an unrecoverable tailspin. Many Lehman employees invested a large portion of their retirement plan money in their company stock. You are probably thinking, "Who would invest the majority of their nest egg in just one company?" Surprisingly it is fairly common. A little over one out of every ten people who have the option of buying shares of their company stock in their retirement plan have invested at least 60 percent of their money in their company stock.[15] People who had concentrated the bulk of their portfolios in these four companies saw values drop to almost zero. Many were left with no other option but to start from scratch and begin rebuilding an entirely new portfolio.

You would think we'd learn. Many investors who got caught up in the technology craze of the late 1990s suffered a similar fate. Staggering amounts of money poured into technology mutual funds as investors bulked up their investments in this single market sector. This lack of diversification proved fatal for technology investors when the average tech fund fell 30.7 percent in 2000, another 35.2 percent in 2001, and another 42.73 in 2002.[16] By comparison, a well-diversified growth portfolio consisting of 80 percent stocks and 20 percent bonds would have fallen just 4 percent in 2000, 8 percent in 2001, and 13 percent in 2002.[17] When volatility is controlled, it's easier for investors to maintain a long-term investing outlook.

Another lesson from history shows that poor diversification even takes its toll during rising bull markets. In 1999, the S&P 500 Index recorded a 21 percent return. However, just eight of the 500 stocks in the index accounted for half of its 21 percent gain. The odds were stacked against the investor who bought just a few S&P stocks during 1999. The chances of an investor successfully choosing those eight big winners out of 500 would be a little better than winning the lottery.[18] Most investors would have been far more successful by simply buying an S&P 500 Index fund, and owning stakes in all 500 companies.

## Mistake #7: Lack of Patience

Most mutual fund investors hold their funds for only two or three years before impatience gets the best of them. Individual stock investors are even less patient. The average holding period for a stock in the 1960s was a little over eight years, from 2000–2009 it was a little over one year,[19] and today, the average holding period is three months. You simply can't realize good returns from the stock market if you only invest for weeks, months, or even a couple of years. When investing in stocks or stock funds, investors must learn to set their investment sights on five- and ten-year periods.

Investors would do well to study the example of the Amana Trust Growth fund, which has one of the best fifteen-year track records for the period ending December 31, 2012, as measured against all large-company U.S. stock funds. During this time, this stock fund provided investors with an annual return of 9.39 percent. A $10,000 investment in the Amana Trust Growth fund would have grown to $38,434 during this period. Most investors, it's safe to say, would be very happy with this performance. However, it didn't deliver huge returns every single year. In fact, during that fifteen-year period, two years were pretty rough, losing 25.17 and 29.67 percent.[20] An investor would have had to endure these two negative years (years when an FDIC bank account would have done much better) to gain the 9.39 percent long-term average annual return. Patient investors were rewarded.

Anne Scheiber is a model of patience whom all investors should emulate. She retired from her $3,150-per-year IRS auditor job in 1943. At that time, she invested $5,000–a little over one year's salary–into a portfolio of stocks. Over the years, she bought and held mostly blue-chip U.S. stocks and some municipal bonds. She didn't worry about daily market fluctuations and rode out the difficult market periods. When Anne died in 1995, at age 101, her $5,000 had grown to more than $22 million, which she donated to a Jewish university. Patience was at the core of Anne's stunning investment success.[21]

## Mistake #8: Not Understanding the Downside

Many investors are just convinced that their investment portfolios should always go up. When returns don't meet these unrealistic expectations, they tend to throw in the towel and give up. It's a mistake to sell *good* investments just because they are having a sluggish year or struggling through a bear market. You need to invest with your eyes wide open, knowing beforehand what to expect from your investments in both bull and bear markets. In most cases, when your investments take near-term dips or fluctuate with the market, you should stay invested and hold on.

Most investors ask only one question before buying a portfolio of investments: "What will my return be?" Usually, they answer this by looking at recently posted one-year returns. Stopping at this question will likely leave you disappointed at some point during your investment journey.

In addition to knowing what the returns of your investments have been recently, be sure to ask the following:

- What has the portfolio returned on average over the past one, three, five, and ten years?
- What was the *best and worst* three-month period during the past ten years?
- What was the *best and worst* one-year period during the past ten years?
- What was the *best and worst* three-year period during the past ten years?
- How has the investment performed during past wars, bear markets, terrorist attacks, and elections?

Once you know the answers to these questions, you can then ask yourself an even more significant question: "If I want the long-term returns this investment or portfolio can produce, can I withstand the volatility?" Without understanding this risk from the onset, volatility will likely get the best of you somewhere down the road. See the asset-allocation chart in Chapter 11 (Figure 11.6) to examine the ups and downs of various mixes of stocks, bonds, and cash.

Let's investigate the market's ups and downs during different periods. Figure 10.6 shows the worst one-year results for different segments of the stock and bond markets from 1970 to 2012. You need to take downturns in context. For example, during the 1973–1974 recession, large-company stocks fell 37 percent. An investor would have been shortsighted to sell a portfolio of large-company stocks after this poor-performing year. In the following two years (1975–1976), large-company stocks provided patient investors with 37 percent and 24 percent returns, respectively. A $10,000 investment into an S&P 500 stock index fund starting in January 1970 would have grown to $586,904 by December 2012, a return of 9.93 percent per year. Figures 10.7 through 10.10 review the stock market's performance during various bear markets, wars, acts of terrorism, and elections.

Despite all the recessions, wars, terrorist attacks, and market crashes, the stock market has been an excellent investment over the long term. The key is to stay invested through thick and thin. When you invest in a portfolio of

| Risk and Return of the Stock and Bond Markets 1970–2012 | | |
| --- | --- | --- |
| Asset Class | Annual Rate of Return | Worst Year |
| Large-Company U.S. Stocks | 10% | –37% |
| Small-Company U.S. Stocks | 12% | –38% |
| International Stocks | 10% | –43% |
| Long-Term Corporate Bonds | 9% | –7% |
| Long-Term Government Bonds | 10% | –12% |
| U.S. Treasury Bills | 5% | 3% |

figure 10.6

stocks and bonds, be aware of the potential upside *and* downside associated with your investments. If you don't understand the risks at the outset, you are more likely to react poorly during periodic market setbacks and get scared out of the market.

When you buy an investment, you should plan on worst-case scenarios occurring when you invest. If you understand the risk from the outset, you are more likely to stay invested for the long term and realize solid long-term gains. It is true that past performance isn't guaranteed to repeat, but it does give us an indication of what to expect.

## Mistake #9: Focusing on Individual Investment Holdings Rather than Your Portfolio as a Whole

In 2008, I had a client, Marcus Ramsey, who each time we met to review his investments was convinced that he was going to go bankrupt due to the market's tumble. Why was Marcus so concerned? One of his brokerage accounts was invested in some fairly aggressive individual stocks that were routinely getting hammered. He watched the value of this account drop 50 percent. Because of this one account, he was ready to sell every stock investment he owned and move to money markets and CDs. However, when we evaluated his overall portfolio, including the money he had in his bank, 401(k), IRA, brokerage accounts, and an annuity, we discovered just how well he was weathering the bear-market storm.

When we viewed Marcus's total investment portfolio, we saw that only 30 percent of it was invested in stocks and stock funds; 40 percent of his

| Bear Markets | | | | | |
| --- | --- | --- | --- | --- | --- |
| *S&P 500 Index* | | | | | |
| Bear Market Begin | End | Total Months | Total Return S&P 500 | Total Return One Year Later | Months to Break Even |
| Jul '48 | May '49 | 11 | −9.8% | 42.4% | 4 |
| Jan '53 | Aug '53 | 8 | −8.7% | 35.0% | 5 |
| Aug '57 | Dec '57 | 5 | −14.9% | 43.6% | 7 |
| Jan '60 | Oct '60 | 10 | −8.4% | 32.6% | 2 |
| Jan '62 | Sep '62 | 9 | −19.4% | 31.7% | 7 |
| Feb '66 | Sep '66 | 8 | −15.6% | 30.6% | 6 |
| Dec '68 | Jun '70 | 19 | −29.2% | 41.9% | 9 |
| Jan '73 | Sep '74 | 21 | −42.9% | 38.1% | 21 |
| Jan '77 | Feb '78 | 14 | −14.1% | 16.6% | 5 |
| Dec '80 | Jul '82 | 20 | −16.9% | 59.4% | 3 |
| Sep '87 | Nov '87 | 3 | −29.5% | 23.2% | 18 |
| Jul '90 | Sep '90 | 3 | −14.7% | 33.5% | 3 |
| Feb '94 | Jul '94 | 5 | −8.0% | 26.0% | 3 |
| Mar '00 | Oct '02 | 30 | −47.6% | 29.4% | 48 |
| Oct '07 | Mar '09 | 17 | −56.5% | 68.6% | 57 |
| Average | | 12 | −22.4% | 36.8% | 13 |

figure 10.7

| War | | | | |
|-----|-------|-----|--------------|---------------|
| Dow Jones Industrial Average (DJIA) | | | | |
| War | Begin | End | Total Months | Change in DJIA |
| World War I | Apr '17 | Nov '18 | 20 | -19% |
| World War II | Dec '41 | Aug '45 | 45 | 41% |
| Korean War | Jun '50 | Jul '53 | 37 | 20% |
| Vietnam War | Aug '64 | Jan '73 | 102 | 21% |
| Gulf War | Jan '91 | Feb '91 | 2 | 15% |
| Iraq War | Mar '03 | Dec '11 | 105 | 43% |
| Average | | | 52 | 20% |

figure 10.8

| Terrorism on U.S. Soil | | |
|------------------------|------------------|----------------------|
| S&P 500 | | |
| Attacks of September 11, 2001 | Days after Attack | Total Return S&P 500 |
| Initial Market Reaction<br>September 17, 2001 | 7 | –4.9% |
| Market Bottom after Attack<br>September 21, 2001 | 11 | –11.6% |
| One Month after Attack<br>October 11, 2001 | 30 | 0.4% |
| Two Months after Attack<br>November 10, 2001 | 60 | 2.5% |
| Three Months after Attack<br>December 10, 2001 | 90 | 4.3% |

figure 10.9

| Election-Year Returns |||
| S&P 500 |||
| Year | S&P 500 | President Elected |
| --- | --- | --- |
| 1960 | –3.0% | John F. Kennedy |
| 1964 | 13.0% | Lyndon B. Johnson |
| 1968 | 7.7% | Richard Nixon |
| 1972 | 15.6% | Richard Nixon |
| 1976 | 19.1% | Jimmy Carter |
| 1980 | 25.8% | Ronald Reagan |
| 1984 | 1.4% | Ronald Reagan |
| 1988 | 12.4% | George H. W. Bush |
| 1992 | 4.5% | Bill Clinton |
| 1996 | 20.3% | Bill Clinton |
| 2000 | –9.1% | George W. Bush |
| 2004 | 10.9% | George W. Bush |
| 2008 | –37.0% | Barack Obama |
| 2012 | 16.0% | Barack Obama |

*figure 10.10*

money was invested in municipal bonds; and 30 percent was in money markets and CDs. The single aggressive account that caused him so much heartburn (and nearly persuaded him to give up on the stock market entirely) represented less than 1 percent of his overall portfolio.

So how did Marcus do? In 2008, when the stock market, as measured by the S&P 500, was down 37 percent, and the NASDAQ dropped a whopping 41 percent, Marcus lost 7 percent. While everyone else was losing sleep because of their stock losses, Marcus realized he could relax and his money anxiety went away.

If you are properly diversified, I can guarantee you that each year some of your investments will lag behind others in your investment portfolio. If you look at investments in isolation rather than in context of your overall portfolio, you will be tempted to make poor decisions. You may get yourself into trouble by getting rid of investments when they're low in value and replacing them with those that just experienced success (buying high and selling low). This is often a mistake made by investors who gauge their entire portfolio by the performance of just one account or one investment.

So remember, evaluate your portfolio as a whole rather than by its individual pieces.

## Mistake #10: Lack of a Clearly Defined Investment Strategy

Let's imagine for a moment that you are in charge of investing the $100 million in your state's retirement pension plan. The money will be used to provide pension incomes and other benefits to thousands of employees who have diligently worked for the state. These employees are counting on you to make good investment decisions to help secure their financial futures. What steps would you take to make sure this money is managed properly?

Most likely you would begin by developing an investment strategy that outlines your objectives and the parameters you will follow as you make investment decisions and manage the money. Then you would use the services of institutional money managers to handle the day-to-day buying and selling of stocks and bonds. You would likely interview many financial professionals, hire the best ones, and then monitor their performance very closely.

Picture yourself in one of these interviews. You would no doubt ask lots of specific questions about each manager's investment strategy and how successfully they have managed money. How much confidence would you have in a candidate who answered your questions with this statement?

*"Well, our investment management company doesn't really have a strategy. We usually read* Money Magazine *and look for hot tips. We always watch CNBC and often get good investment ideas there. Sometimes we even look on the Internet for investment ideas. On occasion, I talk to my doctor or father-in-law to get their thoughts and ideas. We buy a little here and a little there and hope the investments work well and complement each other. Once we purchase the portfolio of investments, we go to the Internet to obtain stock quotes several times each day. When it feels right, we sell. It's kind of a gut feeling we get. I think you will be happy with our investment management services."*

How much of your state's $100 million are you going to trust with this money manager candidate? It's safe to say you would usher him out of your office as quickly as possible.

You are the money manager of your own money. Now, put yourself in the hot seat. How would you respond if asked, "What strategy do you follow in managing your own portfolio?" All too often, investors respond the same way the money manager did in our previous example. If your investment strategy consists of hot tips from television, the web, and the guy next door, how successful will it be? Can you effectively manage your own money? Not without a well-defined and disciplined investment strategy.

Just as you wouldn't hire a money manager lacking a clearly defined investment strategy to oversee your state's pension, you shouldn't manage your own money without developing a similarly disciplined strategy. A strategy doesn't work unless it has structure and is carried out with discipline. Investors who do not follow a disciplined investment strategy continue to repeat the same costly mistakes mentioned in this chapter.

Now, more than ever, the size of your retirement nest egg will heavily depend on your ability to turn yourself into a good investor. By following the steps that will be outlined in the subsequent chapters, you will significantly magnify your chances of attaining sound returns and living a secure retirement!

# 11

# THE MOST IMPORTANT INVESTMENT DECISION YOU'LL MAKE

## RETIREMENT DECISION #10: HOW MUCH SHOULD I INVEST IN STOCKS, BONDS, AND CASH?

While playing high school basketball, I developed a bad habit of throwing showy, "behind-the-back" passes to my teammates. This made my coach crazy, especially considering the number of times I threw the ball out-of-bounds or to the other team. My coach insisted I stop my unpredictable passing habits and focus on the fundamentals, or join him on the bench.

Many investors take a "behind-the-back" pass approach to investing. They skip the fundamentals and focus on gimmicky or speculative investing. The volatility often associated with this approach to investing lands many retirees on the bench, or in the case of investing, on the sidelines in a money market or certificate of deposit (CD) paying 1 or 2 percent. Sitting on the bench earning little to no return will reduce your chances of reaching your retirement goals.

A fundamentally sound investment portfolio can control unwanted volatility. It can help keep you in the game earning good rates of return, so your money will last throughout retirement. Retirees would do well to follow a four-step process that will ensure their investment strategy focuses on the fundamentals: asset allocation, diversification, prudent investment selection, and strategic ongoing management. Leave the "behind-the-back" passes of investing to those who still have time to earn back big losses.

Rarely do investors call their brokers or financial advisors and ask first about the fundamentals–what percentage of their money should be invested in stocks, bonds, and cash. In most cases, the first question an investor asks is, "What stock or fund is hot?" The second is, "When should I buy?" Most investors are concentrating on security selection and market timing, the two variables that are the most fun to talk about but that matter least in investment success.

## Asset-Allocation Methods

Figure 11.1 outlines the annualized investment performance of stocks, bonds, and cash (U.S. Treasury bills) from 1926 to 2012. Stocks provided the highest returns but, of course, also carried the greatest risks. What percentage of your portfolio should be invested in each of these asset classes? There is not a "one size fits all" answer to this question. You must factor in your time frame, age, income requirements, level of risk tolerance, and desired rates of return. Let's examine several asset-allocation methods based on each of these variables, and then depending on your priorities, determine your personal asset-allocation policy.

| Stocks, Bonds, and Cash | |
| --- | --- |
| **Annualized Returns 1926–2012** | |
| Stocks | 10% |
| Bonds | 6% |
| Cash | 4% |

figure 11.1

### *Age-Based Allocation Method*

An age-based approach is a conservative one, and the way it works is simple. Take the number 110 and subtract your age. The result is the percentage of your investment portfolio you should invest in stocks or stock mutual funds. For example, if you're 60, 50 percent of your money should be invested in stocks and the rest in bonds and cash. An 80-year-old, by this formula, should invest 30 percent of his or her portfolio in stocks. Why at age 80 would you continue to invest money in securities with a higher risk factor? Is there a chance an 80-year-old could live another twenty years? Yes, there is, and due to this possibility, a portion of the portfolio needs to be growing at a higher rate to provide a hedge against inflation.

If you follow this formula and adjust your portfolio each year, your investment strategy will slowly become more conservative as you get older. Although this formula is a good general guideline, there are additional variables to consider in addition to your age.

| Age-Based Asset Allocation | | | | |
|---|---|---|---|---|
| **Age** | **Stocks %** | **Bonds %** | **Cash %** | **Average Return\*** |
| 20 | 90% | 10% | 0% | 9.65% |
| 30 | 80% | 20% | 0% | 9.41% |
| 40 | 70% | 30% | 0% | 9.11% |
| 50 | 60% | 40% | 0% | 9.76% |
| 60 | 50% | 40% | 10% | 8.15% |
| 70 | 40% | 50% | 10% | 7.72% |
| 80 | 30% | 60% | 10% | 7.24% |
| 90 | 20% | 70% | 10% | 6.71% |

\* 1926–2012; Cash = 3-Month Treasury Bills; Bonds = Long-Term Govt. Bonds; Stocks = Large Company U.S. Stocks

figure 11.2

The chart in Figure 11.2, using the age-based formula, outlines asset-allocation mixes at different ages with their corresponding historical returns.

## Income-Needs Allocation Method

This formula can be more aggressive than the age-based formula. With this method, you simply allocate your money based on when you are planning to spend it.

Picture three buckets in front of you. The first bucket contains money you plan on spending during the next one through three years. The second bucket contains money you will need to generate income from year four to year nine, and in the third bucket, you place money you don't plan on spending for more than ten years (Figure 11.3).

The money in Bucket 1 is invested in cash-type investments that protect your principal (CDs, money markets, Treasury bills, bank savings accounts). This is your short-term money and is not put at risk by being invested in the stock or bond markets.

In Bucket 2, intermediate-term money is invested in bonds and or bond funds (corporate, government, municipal, international). You can structure your bond portfolio by purchasing bonds that mature each year from year four through year nine. This is known as a "bond ladder." As each bond

Cash | Bonds | Stocks

**Short-Term**
**1-3 year money**

**Intermediate-Term**
**4-9 year money**

**Long-Term**
**10+ year money**

*figure 11.3*

matures, money is available to provide income during the upcoming year. Bonds are guaranteed by the bond issuer and typically pay a higher rate of interest than cash-type investments. Although bonds will fluctuate in value, the volatility is usually far less than that of stocks.

Your long-term money in Bucket 3 is invested in stocks (individual stocks or stock mutual funds). This money won't be spent for at least ten years. This is the growth portion of your portfolio and will naturally increase or decrease with the fluctuations in the stock market.

When handled properly, the pieces of this strategy fit together perfectly to ensure you a steady flow of retirement income. As you spend and deplete the money in your cash accounts, a bond will mature to replenish your cash reserves and provide the income needed during the upcoming year. To maintain your allocation, you will occasionally need to sell some stock positions to replenish your bond portfolio as bonds mature. If the stock market has a poor year, you can wait to transfer money from stocks to bonds, so you're not selling stocks in a down market.

At any point, you are ensured to have income for nine years (three years via cash and six years via bonds). Consequently, you don't need to worry excessively about a down year in the stock market because you're not going to be spending any of your stock investments for at least ten years. In that lengthy time span, your stock portfolio has plenty of opportunity to regain any losses from a down year or two.

Let's consider Catherine Dalton, a 60-year-old retiree who has accumulated $500,000 and has an income need of $25,000 per year. Following the income-needs allocation method, she has decided to invest $75,000 in secure cash investments to provide income during her first three years of retirement, $150,000 in bonds to provide income in years four through nine, and the remaining $275,000 in stocks to help meet her long-term retirement goals (Figure 11.4).

**Bucket 1 Income needs (during years one through three)**

Year One: Money Market
Year Two: One-Year CD
Year Three: Two-Year CD

**Bucket 2 Income needs (during years four through nine)**

Year Four: Bond maturing in year four
Year Five: Bond maturing in year five
Year Six: Bond maturing in year six
Year Seven: Bond maturing in year seven
Year Eight: Bond maturing in year eight
Year Nine: Bond maturing in year nine

**Bucket 3 Income needs (during years ten plus)**

Year Ten Plus: Diversified portfolio
                      of stock funds

figure 11.4

Investing $275,000, or 55 percent, of her money in stocks may be too aggressive for Catherine. If this is the case, she can adjust her portfolio very easily, making it more conservative by simply reducing her stock exposure and adding a little more money to bonds.

Now, let's look at the case of Darin Zimmerman, age 30, who plans to retire at age 60. So far, he has accumulated $50,000 in his company's 401(k) plan. Because retirement is far into the future, his primary goal is to see his money grow. He has a regular paycheck and doesn't require any income from his investment portfolio. Choosing to use the income-needs allocation approach, he allocates his portfolio as shown in Figure 11.5.

### Bucket 1 Income needs (during years one through three)

Year One: Money Market
Year Two: One-Year CD
Year Three: Two-Year CD

### Bucket 2 Income needs (during years four through nine)

Year Four: Bond maturing in year four
Year Five: Bond maturing in year five
Year Six: Bond maturing in year six
Year Seven: Bond maturing in year seven
Year Eight: Bond maturing in year eight
Year Nine: Bond maturing in year nine

### Bucket 3 Income needs (during years ten plus)

Year Ten Plus: Diversified portfolio
of stock funds

figure 11.5

As you can see, Darin has allocated 100 percent of his portfolio to stocks. This approach is much more aggressive than the age-based strategy, which would have allocated just 80 percent of Darin's money to the stock market.

Darin eschews the age-based approach because his priority is growth rather than income.

## Risk-Tolerance Allocation Method

How much volatility can you endure? That's the central question in the risk-tolerance allocation method.

Many investors are overconfident and choose an investment mix because they like the high potential rate of return. They often fail to consider, however, the potential downside. When the markets go south, these investors frequently run for the hills, selling their most volatile investments at the worst possible time, losing sight of their long-term objectives. Obviously, selling is not a wise option when investments are down in value. By simply examining the potential downside of your asset-allocation mix *before* initiating your investment strategy, you can avoid unfortunate decisions down the line.

The average rate of return for different mixes of stocks, bonds, and cash from 1926 through 2012 is illustrated in Figure 11.6. The chart also outlines how often each portfolio lost money and the magnitude of the average loss. Most importantly, it shows the worst-case scenario for each mix.

Determining your asset allocation using this method is simple and involves a question only you can answer: "What is my breaking point?" Determine how far your portfolio can drop before you decide you want out. If your portfolio starts at $100,000 and market losses take it down to $90,000, $80,000, or even $70,000, at what point do you begin losing sleep at night?

Locate the Largest Annual Loss column in Figure 11.6, and review the worst-case scenarios for the different asset-allocation models. How much downside can you tolerate? For example, if you could handle a 25 percent loss in the worst-case scenario—without modifying your investment strategy— then a mix of 50 percent stocks would be suitable for you. Although you may never see the worst-case scenario occur, this method of asset-allocation prepares you in advance for the downturns that may occur in the markets.

## Target-Rate-of-Return Allocation Method

What annual rate of return is required for you to reach your retirement goals? Once you've determined that rate by developing a retirement plan,

| Asset Allocation: Risk & Reward | | | | | |
|---|---|---|---|---|---|
| Annual Returns 1926–2012 | | | | | |
| Portfolio | Average Return | Largest Annual Gain | Largest Annual Loss | Positive Years | Negative Years |
| 100% Stocks 0% Bonds 0% Cash | 9.84% | 54% | –43% | 63 | 24 |
| 90% Stocks 5% Bonds 5% Cash | 9.53% | 49% | –39% | 63 | 24 |
| 80% Stocks 10% Bonds 10% Cash | 9.17% | 43% | –35% | 64 | 23 |
| 70% Stocks 20% Bonds 10% Cash | 8.88% | 38% | –31% | 65 | 22 |
| 60% Stocks 30% Bonds 10% Cash | 8.54% | 34% | –27% | 68 | 19 |
| 50% Stocks 40% Bonds 10% Cash | 8.15% | 32% | –24% | 68 | 19 |
| 40% Stocks 50% Bonds 10% Cash | 7.72% | 31% | –20% | 71 | 16 |
| 30% Stocks 60% Bonds 10% Cash | 7.24% | 32% | –16% | 74 | 13 |
| 20% Stocks 70% Bonds 10% Cash | 6.71% | 34% | –12% | 71 | 16 |
| 10% Stocks 80% Bonds 10% Cash | 6.14% | 35% | –8% | 70 | 17 |
| 0% Stocks 90% Bonds 10% Cash | 5.52% | 37% | –11% | 67 | 20 |

**Cash:** 3-Month Treasury Bill

**Bonds:** Long-Term Government Bonds

**Stocks:** Large Company U.S. Stocks

*Sources: SBBI and Morningstar*

*figure 11.6*

you can also use Figure 11.6 to determine an appropriate asset-allocation mix. This will help you create a portfolio that has historically produced the rate of return you've targeted. If, for example, you've determined that you need an 8 percent annual return on your investments, then your portfolio should consist of at least 50 percent stocks, 40 percent bonds, and 10 percent cash according to historical market returns from 1926 to 2012 (see the Average Return column in Figure 11.6).

## Combining All Four Allocation Methods

Each of these asset-allocation methodologies—age, income needs, risk tolerance, and target rate of return—is useful. In your allocation strategy you can follow one of these methods alone, or blend them together. One way to blend the allocation methods together is to complete an investment questionnaire like the one that follows.

These questions are a sampling of those that most financial advisors will ask their clients before making asset-allocation recommendations. Your answers will help you select the most appropriate asset-allocation model for your goals and circumstances. Corresponding points are listed next to each question. After you finish the questionnaire, you'll total the points of the answers you selected to determine which mix of stocks, bonds, and cash fits you.

## Asset-Allocation Questionnaire

**Investment Objective**

1. What is your primary purpose for investing?
   A. Preserve investment capital (2)
   B. Emphasis on current income (4)
   C. Emphasis on income with some growth (6)
   D. Emphasis on growth with some income (8)
   E. Maximum growth (10)

**Time Horizon**

2. When do you plan on spending the money you are investing?
   A. 0–2 Years (2)
   B. 3–7 Years (4)
   C. 8–15 Years (6)
   D. 16+ Years (10)

**Risk Tolerance**

3. Which statement best describes your feelings about risk?
   A. I am willing to take a lot of risk to obtain maximum growth. (8)
   B. I am willing to take some risk to obtain moderate growth. (6)
   C. I am willing to take a little risk, realizing that my potential for growth will be less. (4)
   D. I am not willing to risk my investment principal. (2)

4. I can endure periods of principal erosion and volatility if my portfolio has potential for high returns.
   A. Strongly Agree (10)
   B. Agree (8)
   C. Somewhat Agree (6)
   D. Somewhat Disagree (4)
   E. Disagree (2)

5. Review the risk and returns of the following hypothetical investment portfolios. Choose the portfolio that most accurately reflects your long-term return requirements and risk tolerance.

|  | Average | Worst Year | Best Year | |
|---|---|---|---|---|
| Portfolio A | 12% | –27% | 53% | (10) |
| Portfolio B | 10% | –17% | 36% | (8) |
| Portfolio C | 9% | –11% | 26% | (6) |
| Portfolio D | 7% | –3% | 25% | (4) |
| Portfolio E | 6% | –2% | 12% | (2) |

6. What would your reaction be to a 15 percent drop in the value of your investment portfolio?

    A.  I would consider this an opportunity to buy more investments at lower prices. (8)

    B.  I am investing for the long term. I would not alter my strategy if the market fell 15 percent. (6)

    C.  This would make me very anxious. I would consider repositioning my portfolio more conservatively in attempts to cut any further losses. (4)

    D.  I would sell my volatile investments. (2)

## Scoring

After answering each of these six questions, add up the numbers found at the end of each of your answers. Then find the portfolio below that corresponds with your score.

| Scoring Point Range | Portfolio | Percent of Portfolio to Invest in Stocks |
|:---:|:---|:---:|
| 12 to 21 | Conservative | 0–25% |
| 22 to 30 | Conservative to Moderate | 25–50% |
| 31 to 40 | Moderate | 50–70% |
| 41 to 50 | Moderate to Aggressive | 70–85% |
| 51 to 56 | Aggressive | 85–100% |

Review Figure 11.6 again, and locate the portfolio that consists of stock exposure that most closely fits your score. Figure 11.6 will also help set your expectations for your target portfolio.

# Don't Forget Emergency Reserves

In addition to investing to cover your long-term income needs, you also need to allocate some of your money to an emergency fund. When you need a new furnace, the roof begins to leak, or your car breaks down, you'll need sufficient money to cope with the problem without having to disrupt your long-term investment strategy. As a general guideline, you should have three to six months' worth of living expenses set aside. For example, if you need $5,000 each month to cover your expenses, your reserve fund should contain between $15,000 and $30,000.

Most of your reserves should be placed in cash investments, so you can withdraw the money immediately. Depending on how comfortable you are with risk, a portion could also be invested in stocks and bonds in a non-retirement investment account. Stocks and bonds can be sold and turned into cash within three business days. As a general guideline, the older you are, the more money you want to have in cash and bonds and the less in stocks.

# Conclusion

Step 1 of the investment process, as outlined in this chapter, was designed to help you see the importance of having a wise asset-allocation policy; the different methods of asset allocation discussed here will help you determine how much of your money should be allocated to stocks, bonds, and cash. Allocating your portfolio properly can help you develop a successful investment strategy that will aid in the overall strength of your retirement plan. Don't bypass the most important step of the investment planning process.

Step 2 of the investment process, which is covered over the next three chapters, will help you understand the reasons for diversifying your portfolio within each asset class, the various components of a diversified portfolio, and how various portfolios have performed in the past.

# 12

# INVESTMENT CONSISTENCY

## RETIREMENT DECISION #11: HOW SHOULD I DIVERSIFY MY INVESTMENT PORTFOLIO?

E ven the most casual baseball fan knows that a winning team doesn't put all nine of its players in the same position. How good would the New York Yankees be if most of the players stood in left field (Figure 12.1)?

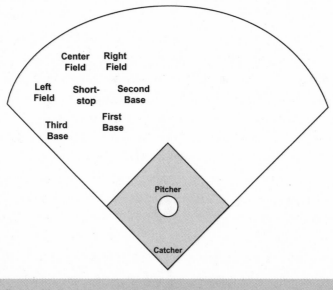

figure 12.1

There's an obvious reason why coaches position their players all over the field: they have no way of knowing where the batter will hit the ball. With some players in the infield and some in the outfield, there is a good chance, as shown in Figure 12.2, of having someone in the right place to field the ball.

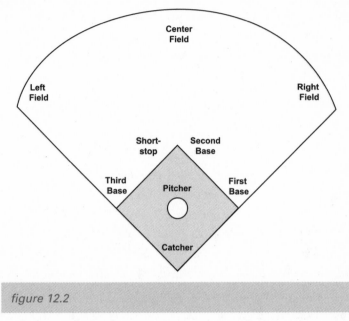

figure 12.2

Step 2 of the investment process is determining how to diversify your portfolio. The stock and bond markets are much like a batter in a baseball game. When the "market" steps up to the plate, nobody knows exactly where the ball is going to fly. Will the markets go up or down? Will interest rates rise or fall? Will the economy see expansion or recession? Will there be tax reforms? Will the nation experience a change in leadership? Will there be inflation? What will foreign economies do?

There is no way of knowing the answers to these questions with absolute certainty. You can try to project the future, but you can't guarantee an accurate prediction. However, if you have properly covered the field with your investments, you will be able to take advantage of market conditions, whatever they may be. It is crucial that you are properly diversified so that no matter what occurs in the market, some of your investments do well.

Did this hold true even during the bear markets of 2000–2002 and 2008? Did some investments actually do well? If your portfolio was properly diversified, then yes, you would have seen growth in some of your investments even during some of the worst stock market conditions (see Chapter 13, Figure 13.22).

For example, during the 2000–2002 bear market, large-company U.S. stocks, as measured by the S&P 500 Index, were down 9 percent in 2000, 12 percent in 2001, and 22 percent in 2002, respectively. More aggressive companies, as measured by the NASDAQ Index, fell 39 percent, 21 percent, and 32 percent, respectively. In 2008 the S&P 500 Index fell 37 percent while the NASDAQ dropped 41 percent.

If you owned a well-diversified portfolio of stocks and bonds during these difficult years, you may have made money when everyone else was losing money. For example, mid-cap value stocks rose 25 percent in 2000.[1] In 2001, small-company value stocks gained 19 percent,[2] and in 2002, while most sectors of the stock market lost money, international bonds made 22 percent,[3] and long-term government bonds rose 17 percent.[4] In 2008, long-term government bonds gained 21 percent[5] and international bonds climbed 10 percent.[6] It's true that if you were diversified, some pieces of your portfolio really struggled during these periods. If you were properly diversified, however, many of your investments did well and greatly softened the blow of some of the worst years in the stock market.

Although baseball managers would never consider the thought of positioning all their players in left field, many investors make this very mistake. Too often, investment portfolios are positioned like the team in Figure 12.1. This is best illustrated by looking at 2000 and 2001. Many investors accumulated a long list of hot-performing investments in 1998 and 1999, only to find out that every investment they owned was concentrated in one or two asset classes, typically large and midsize company growth stocks. Many technology stocks fell into these categories. This strategy worked fine in 1998 and 1999, when the market routinely enjoyed good performance, whacking the ball to these two areas of the growth market. However, in 2000 and 2001, the market changed directions and hit the ball the other way, to value stocks and bonds. Investors who didn't own value stocks and bonds experienced dramatic losses.

Many investors get confused about what it means to be properly diversified, falsely believing that diversification can be achieved by owning ten different stocks or mutual funds. This, however, doesn't guarantee true diversification. For example, it is possible to own ten mutual funds and still end up with a portfolio that looks like the baseball team in Figure 12.1. How? If each of your funds buys high-tech growth stocks, you are not diversified. If high tech does well, you'll feel like you hit a home run; if it does poorly, your portfolio strikes out. Many technology-fund investors were ecstatic in 1999 when the average technology fund rose 128 percent. A $10,000 investment made on January 1, 1999, in the average tech fund grew to more than $22,800 by year's end; that would definitely be considered a grand slam. However, in 2000, 2001, and 2002, this sector of the market plummeted back to earth, losing 32 percent, 36 percent, and 43 percent, respectively.[7] The portfolio that grew so quickly to $22,800 nosedived below the original amount invested, finishing at $5,656. This inconsistent performance and high volatility often lead investors to make frequent portfolio changes and ultimately earn poor returns.

There are three major reasons why diversification is so important to successful long-term investing.

1. Diversification lowers portfolio risk by reducing volatility.
2. Diversification protects the overall portfolio from one or two poorly performing investments.
3. Diversification provides investors with more consistent returns and helps them stay invested for the long term.

Diversification allows investors to purchase investments that alone may be very volatile, but when combined with other investments actually reduce the volatility of the portfolio as a whole. *In essence, diversification is a way of covering the entire field to make sure all of those hits get caught.*

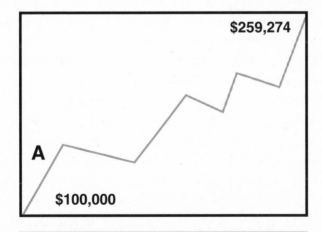

figure 12.3

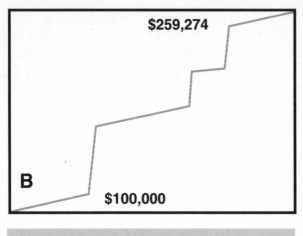

figure 12.4

## Lowering Portfolio Risk by Reducing Volatility

Compare the two hypothetical investments in Figures 12.3 and 12.4. Assuming the two investments experience the ups and downs depicted in the charts, and over time, both provide an average annual return of 10 percent, which would you choose? As you can see, regardless which investment you select, an investment of $100,000 would grow to $259,274. Notice that although the average return for each investment is identical over the long run, Investment A and Investment B experienced ups and downs at different times.

Now let's say that you split your $100,000 investment equally between Investment A and B (Figure 12.5). Your $100,000 would still grow to $259,274 in ten years. However, from year to year, your performance would be much more consistent. In fact, in this example, your portfolio would never encounter a down year. In years when one investment does poorly, the other picks up the slack. In other words, when one investment is "zigging," the other is "zagging." The key to developing a portfolio that reduces volatility is to buy investments that complement each other as Investment A and B do in Figure 12.5. Proper diversification will reduce portfolio volatility.

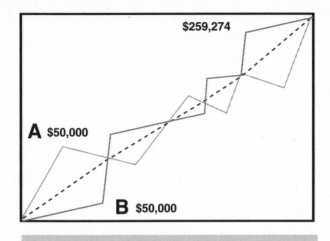

figure 12.5

## Protecting Your Portfolio from the Risk of a Bad Investment Choice

Have you ever made a really bad investment? One or two bad investment decisions could dramatically reduce the returns of your overall portfolio. Diversification will protect you from this possibility.

Twenty years ago, Edward Brantley rolled $100,000 into his IRA and decided to diversify into five investments equally. Unfortunately, Edward made a couple of poor investment choices. Figure 12.6 shows his results.

Although Edward's team didn't have a perfect game, they still won. His portfolio still produced a respectable 8.74 percent annual return, even though three of the five investments performed very poorly.

| Five $20,000 Investments | |
| Value after 20 Years | |
| --- | --- |
| Investment 1: $20,000 lost 100% | $0 |
| Investment 2: $20,000 broke even | $20,000 |
| Investment 3: $20,000 gained 5% per year | $53,066 |
| Investment 4: $20,000 gained 10% per year | $134,550 |
| Investment 5: $20,000 gained 15% per year | $327,330 |
| Total Initial Investment | $100,000 |
| Total after 20 Years | $534,946 |
| Compounded Annual Rate of Return | 8.74% |

figure 12.6

Edward could have taken a big chance, invested all of his money in just one or two of these investments, and hoped for great returns. If he guessed right, he'd have ended up with an average annual return of 10 to 15 percent; if he guessed wrong, however, he would have been stuck with a meager growth rate of 5 percent or less.

Diversification protected Edward from the risk of having a majority of his assets in losing investments. If he had placed all his money in the poorest-performing investment, his portfolio at retirement, instead of being valued at $534,946, could have been worthless.

Poor diversification often occurs with investors who have their money invested too heavily in their employer's stock. There are far too many examples of people losing their nest egg because they bet everything on their company's stock. (Handling company stock will be discussed in Chapter 15.) Diversification can protect your nest egg from this disastrous possibility.

Let's take a look at an example. Linda Monson at age 59 retired from Citigroup in January of 2007. At retirement, she had more than $1 million invested in Citigroup stock. In the past, the stock had generated huge profits, growing at 18 percent annually since the time Linda began buying the stock in her retirement plan. In fact, her company stock was the very reason she could retire much earlier than she had expected. At retirement she had a very difficult decision to make: She had to choose between keeping the shares, which she felt confident would continue to rise at a similar pace, or selling some or all of the shares, into some investments that hadn't done as well as Citigroup, in order to diversify her portfolio. She finally made the decision to break the emotional ties to her company and sell the stock and diversify. She realized that a drop in her employer's stock could keep her from accomplishing her retirement goals.

Linda's decision was a good one. Shortly after retirement, the market went south and her company's stock dropped severely from $54 per share when she retired to $2.97 per share on June 30, 2009, a price drop of 95 percent.[8] Had she stayed invested in Citigroup, her $1 million nest egg would have fallen to $59,243. Although it's true that the diversified portfolio of stock and bond mutual funds she chose to replace her company stock suffered a 15 percent drop during this same period, leaving her with $846,891, she can recover from this loss and still reach her retirement goals. A 95 percent loss, however, would require growth of an impossible 1,588 percent for her to break even.

If your portfolio loses 20 percent of its value, how much does it need to earn to get back to even? It seems logical that 20 percent of growth would offset a 20 percent loss; this is not the case. If a $100,000 portfolio dropped 20 percent to $80,000, it would require a 25 percent gain to get back to $100,000. If the same portfolio dropped 50 percent to $50,000, it would require a 100 percent return to climb back up to $100,000.

# Importance of Performance Consistency

How important is performance consistency? We can best determine that by studying the examples of Grant Wilson and Ann Schilling, two people who each have $100,000 to invest. After reviewing the returns each achieved in Figures 12.7 and 12.8, who do you believe will accumulate the most money over the five-year period?

## *Profile of Investor One: Grant*

Grant is an aggressive investor whose goal is to take advantage of the big moves in the market. All of Grant's money is concentrated in one sector of the stock market. Consequently, he experiences very high "highs" and very low "lows." Figure 12.7 illustrates his results over the past five years.

| Performance Results for Grant | |
|---|---|
| Year 1 | 20% |
| Year 2 | 40% |
| Year 3 | 20% |
| Year 4 | –50% |
| Year 5 | 40% |
| Five-Year Average Annual Return | 14% |

figure 12.7

## *Profile of Investor Two: Ann*

Ann is a moderate investor whose goal is to obtain good, consistent returns. She has split her money into two different investments. Each investment moves in a typical cycle of ups and downs. The two investments, however, have a zigzag relationship. When one is zigging, the other is zagging. The result is consistent performance. Her diversified portfolio does not produce returns as high as Grant's, but it doesn't drop as low as his does either. Figure 12.8 illustrates Ann's results.

Who experienced better performance, Grant or Ann? Whose results

| Performance Results for Ann | |
|---|---|
| Year 1 | 9% |
| Year 2 | 9% |
| Year 3 | 9% |
| Year 4 | 9% |
| Year 5 | 9% |
| Five-Year Average Annual Return | 9% |

figure 12.8

would you rather have? Not only did Ann's portfolio perform much better (see the results in Figure 12.9), but her portfolio was also far less volatile than Grant's. One also can't help but wonder how many bad decisions Grant made due to the additional volatility in his quest to capture the big moves. Higher returns coupled with lower risk are the magic combination that every investor should seek. This can often be accomplished with proper diversification. Remember, consistency is the key.

It is also interesting that Grant's average annual return was 14 percent, compared to Ann's 9 percent (add up the returns for each year and divide by 5). Ann's actual *compounded* annual rate of return was 2 percentage points higher than Grant's. Be careful not to be misled by *average* annual rates of return.

| Initial Investment of $100,000 | | | | |
|---|---|---|---|---|
| | Ann | | Grant | |
| Year | % Change | Investment Value | % Change | Investment Value |
| 1 | 9% | $109,000 | 20% | $120,000 |
| 2 | 9% | $118,810 | 40% | $168,000 |
| 3 | 9% | $129,503 | 20% | $201,600 |
| 4 | 9% | $141,158 | –50% | $100,800 |
| 5 | 9% | $153,862 | 40% | $141,120 |

figure 12.9

In this chapter, we have discussed the vital importance of having a properly diversified portfolio. The goal is to invest so that no matter what occurs in the market, some of your investments will perform well. As we continue our discussion of Step 2 of the investment process in the following chapter, the various components of a well-diversified portfolio will be outlined.

# 13

# KNOW YOUR TEAM

## RETIREMENT DECISION #11 (CONTINUED): HOW SHOULD I DIVERSIFY MY INVESTMENT PORTFOLIO?

M any years ago, I played Little League baseball. We practiced every day and our coach became very familiar with our individual talents and abilities. Because my coach knew his players well and knew what to expect from each of us, he was able to position each player on the field according to his talents, giving us the best chance at winning games.

By the end of this chapter, you will know how to manage your retirement portfolio in the same manner my Little League coach ran our team. To build a sound retirement portfolio (your team of investments), you need to properly diversify. It is important to understand each asset class and how each has performed historically in relation to the others. Once you understand each investment's pluses and minuses, you will be better equipped to position them to your portfolio's advantage.

Figure 13.1 illustrates the components of a well-diversified investment portfolio. Remember that, like the fielders on a baseball team, each asset class covers a different part of the market field. You want to be in position to take advantage of favorable market conditions wherever they may be. Therefore, some of your money should be invested in ten to twelve asset classes.

However, what do we mean when we say "small and mid-cap growth," "large-cap value," or "government bonds"? What attributes do these stock and bond asset classes have? How has each asset class traditionally performed during bull and bear markets? How will rising interest rates affect bond funds? Learning the answers to these types of questions will make you better equipped to manage your retirement portfolio. Let's begin by talking about stocks; then we'll cover bonds and cash.

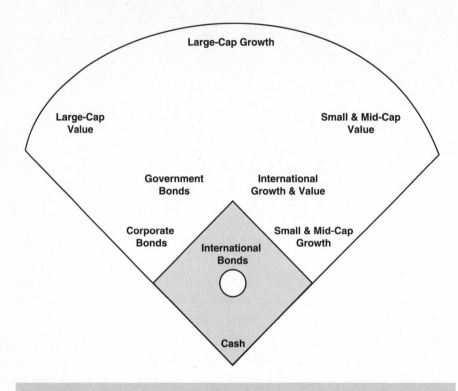

figure 13.1

# Stocks

## *Size*

Stocks are categorized as large, midsize, or small based on their market capitalization. Market capitalization is simply the price of a stock multiplied by
the number of outstanding shares. For example, a stock that is priced at $50
per share with 100 million shares outstanding has a market capitalization of
$5 billion, which makes it a mid-cap stock. Here's what you should know
about each stock size.

### Large U.S. Stocks

Large-cap U.S. stocks are usually defined as companies with market capitalizations of more than $10 billion. The market capitalization for the average
large-cap U.S. stock mutual fund is $37 billion.[1] Some of the largest U.S.
company stocks with their respective market capitalizations are listed in
Figure 13.2.

| Large-Cap U.S. Company Stocks<br>*December 31, 2012* | | | |
|---|---|---|---|
| **Company Name** | **Ticker** | **Industry** | **Market Cap** |
| Apple | AAPL | Computer Systems | $500 Billion |
| Exxon Mobil | XOM | Oil & Gas | $394 Billion |
| Google | GOOG | Internet | $232 Billion |
| Wal-Mart | WMT | Discount Stores | $228 Billion |
| General Electric | GE | Diversified Industrial | $220 Billion |
| IBM | IBM | Computer Systems | $216 Billion |
| Chevron | CVX | Oil & Gas | $212 Billion |
| Johnson & Johnson | JNJ | Drugs | $194 Billion |
| AT&T | T | Telecom Services | $191 Billion |
| Procter & Gamble | PG | Personal Products | $186 Billion |

figure 13.2

## Mid-Cap U.S. Stocks

Mid-cap U.S. stocks are defined as companies with market capitalizations usually between $2 billion and $10 billion. The market capitalization for the average mid-cap U.S. stock fund is $6 billion.[2] Examples of mid-cap U.S. stocks with their respective market caps are listed in Figure 13.3.

| Mid-Cap U.S. Company Stocks<br>*December 31, 2012* | | | |
|---|---|---|---|
| **Company Name** | **Ticker** | **Industry** | **Market Cap** |
| Alcoa | AA | Aluminum | $9.3 Billion |
| Dr Pepper, Snapple | DPS | Beverages | $9.2 Billion |
| TDAmeritrade | AMTD | Capital Markets | $9.1 Billion |
| Xerox | XRX | Leisure | $8.6 Billion |
| CarMax | KMX | Auto | $8.6 Billion |
| Staples | SPLS | Retail | $7.7 Billion |
| Hertz | HTZ | Rental | $6.8 Billion |
| Hyatt Hotels | H | Lodging | $6.3 Billion |
| Unum | UNM | Insurance | $5.7 Billion |
| Netflix | NFLX | Retail | $5.1 Billion |

figure 13.3

| Small-Cap U.S. Company Stocks |||| 
| December 31, 2012 |||| 
| Company Name | Ticker | Industry | Market Cap |
| --- | --- | --- | --- |
| Wendy's | WEN | Restaurants | $1.8 Billion |
| Cheesecake Factory | CAKE | Restaurants | $1.7 Billion |
| Advanced Micro Devices | AMD | Semiconductor | $1.7 Billion |
| JetBlue | JBLU | Airlines | $1.6 Billion |
| Janus Capital | JNS | Asset Management | $1.6 Billion |
| Men's Warehouse | MW | Apparel | $1.6 Billion |
| Bankrate.com | RATE | Internet | $1.2 Billion |
| Rite Aid | RAD | Pharmaceutical Retail | $1.2 Billion |
| Aeropostale | ARO | Apparel | $1.0 Billion |
| Office Depot | ODP | Retail | $0.9 Billion |

figure 13.4

## Small U.S. Stocks

Small-cap U.S. stocks are defined as companies with market capitalizations below $2 billion. The market capitalization for the average small-cap U.S. stock fund is $1.4 billion.[3] Examples of small-cap U.S. company stocks with their respective market caps are shown in Figure 13.4.

Which market cap has provided the best returns? Over the long run, small- and mid-cap stocks have outperformed large-cap stocks. From 1926 through 2012, small-company stocks had an average annual return of 11.9 percent, while large-company stocks returned 9.8 percent.[4] Large companies tend to hold up better in market downturns because of their financial strength and stability. Although small and midsize company stocks offer more potential growth, they also possess more potential for loss—thus, to obtain higher returns, you must be willing to endure more risk.

Figure 13.5 shows the performance of large-, mid-, and small-cap stocks from 2007–2012. While smaller stocks have provided higher returns than larger stocks over the long term, don't be fooled into thinking this is a consistent rule. During some periods, large caps have outperformed their small- and mid-cap counterparts. The main point here is that there are no hard and fast rules to indicate which size will perform best in the future. Therefore, it is important to diversify your portfolio and own an array of large-, mid-, and small-cap stocks.

Half of all U.S. households own stocks either directly or indirectly through mutual funds.[5]

| Stock Index Returns 2007–2012 | | | | | | |
|---|---|---|---|---|---|---|
| Asset Class | 2007 Return | 2008 Return | 2009 Return | 2010 Return | 2011 Return | 2012 Return |
| Large-Cap U.S. Stocks (S&P 500 Index) | 5.5% | –37.0% | 26.5% | 15.1% | 2.1% | 16.0% |
| Mid-Cap U.S. Stocks (S&P MidCap 400 Index) | 8.0% | –36.2% | 37.4% | 26.6% | –1.7% | 17.9% |
| Small-Cap U.S. Stocks (S&P SmallCap 600 Index) | –0.3% | –31.1% | 25.6% | 26.3% | 1.0% | 16.3% |

*figure 13.5*

## Investment Styles—Growth and Value

A stock's market-cap size is an important tool to use when determining how diversified your portfolio is, but you need to drill down deeper. After all, not all large-company stocks perform exactly the same way. We can further categorize stocks, whether they are large, midsize, or small, based on their investment "style," or how fast the companies that issue the stocks are growing. A stock can be classified as either growth or value. This is an important distinction because growth and value stocks have a lead and lag relationship over time (Figure 13.6). If your portfolio contains both types of stocks, you can reduce your overall portfolio risk and volatility.

> According to a financial literacy survey by the National Association of Securities Dealers (NASD), only 14 percent of Americans can tell the difference between a growth and a value stock, while 63 percent of Americans know the difference between a halfback and a quarterback.[6]

### Growth Stocks

Buying a growth stock is similar to shopping at a trendy store and purchasing fashions that are in *vogue*. Because these items are in such high demand, you will be required to "pay up" for them—maybe even more than they are worth.

Growth stocks are typically in high demand due to their high earnings-growth rates and their tendency to outperform the market when the economy is strong and robust. Because of investor demand, prices of growth stocks are often bid up to astronomical levels, as occurred in 1998 and 1999. Growth investors buy high in hopes that the company's earnings momentum will carry the price even higher. When the stock market falters, growth stocks tend to fall harder than their value stock equivalents. For example, from 2000 to 2002, the Dow Jones Large-Cap Growth Index posted a –52 percent return. By comparison, the Dow Jones Large-Cap Value Index recorded a –29 percent return during this period. percent.[7] Another thing to know about growth stocks is that they typically pay no, or low, dividends.

## Value Stocks

Like buying growth stocks, buying value stocks is similar to shopping at your favorite store. In this case, though, instead of buying the high-priced, trendy items, you're sifting through the discount racks and purchasing only items that are marked down. Value companies are considered "on sale" in the stock market because they have temporarily fallen out of favor and sell for less than their true value. Their prices are low because of their relative standing in categories like earnings, book values, and sales. These companies are often located in industries that have fallen out of favor or have profitability or management problems. Investors who buy value stocks buy low, patiently wait, and hope the company rebounds. Because value stocks are already trading at low prices, there is less room to fall if the stock market turns sour. Also, value companies usually pay dividends.

## Distinguishing between the Two

There are many technical measurements to help investors distinguish between growth and value stocks, the most common being the price-to-earnings ratio (P/E). A company's P/E ratio is determined by dividing its stock price (the "P") by the previous twelve months' earnings per share (the "E"). The P/E ratio measures how much investors are willing to pay for each dollar of the company's profit.

Other characteristics to look for are price-to-sales ratios and price-to-book ratios. The higher these ratios, the more growth-oriented a stock is. You can also use these ratios when comparing mutual funds. Funds list their portfolio's average P/E, price-to-sales, and price-to-book ratios. These figures are used to categorize a fund as growth or value. The average large-company growth and large-company value mutual funds had the following

| Growth and Value 1980–2012 | | | | | | | |
|---|---|---|---|---|---|---|---|
| *Dow Jones Large-Cap Growth and Value Indexes* | | | | | | | |
| Year | Growth | Value | Winner | Year | Growth | Value | Winner |
| 1980 | 35.6% | 29.3% | Growth | 1997 | 34.7% | 24.2% | Growth |
| 1981 | –9.1% | –3.4% | Value | 1998 | 47.6% | 16.7% | Growth |
| 1982 | 18.6% | 18.9% | Value | 1999 | 29.9% | 13.3% | Growth |
| 1983 | 14.8% | 25.1% | Value | 2000 | –22.3% | –2.4% | Value |
| 1984 | 23.1% | 11.9% | Growth | 2001 | –19.7% | –8.4% | Value |
| 1985 | 34.8% | 30.0% | Growth | 2002 | –23.8% | –20.3% | Value |
| 1986 | 15.7% | 20.4% | Value | 2003 | 24.8% | 29.8% | Value |
| 1987 | 5.8% | 3.0% | Growth | 2004 | 6.6% | 13.4% | Value |
| 1988 | 12.2% | 20.2% | Value | 2005 | 2.0% | 12.3% | Value |
| 1989 | 32.8% | 31.6% | Growth | 2006 | 9.2% | 21.9% | Value |
| 1990 | 3.2% | –8.4% | Growth | 2007 | 10.9% | 1.8% | Growth |
| 1991 | 41.4% | 21.8% | Growth | 2008 | –37.5% | –36.6% | Value |
| 1992 | 4.7% | 10.1% | Value | 2009 | 37.4% | 17.2% | Growth |
| 1993 | 4.3% | 17.0% | Value | 2010 | 17.0% | 15.2% | Growth |
| 1994 | 3.3% | –0.9% | Growth | 2011 | –0.6% | 3.8% | Value |
| 1995 | 38.3% | 39.4% | Value | 2012 | 17.2% | 15.2% | Growth |
| 1996 | 22.7% | 23.0% | Value | | | | |

figure 13.6

technical measurements (Figure 13.7). The dividends that mutual funds pay are measured by yield.

Figure 13.8 shows specific examples of large-company growth and value stocks and their P/Es and yields.

## Which Style Is Better?

Although the performance for growth and value stocks varies dramatically from year to year, over the long run value stocks have gained the edge.

A $10,000 investment in large-company growth stocks made in January 1980 grew to $335,241 by the end of 2012.[8] Similarly, a $10,000 investment made into large-company value stocks over the same period grew to $344,205.[9] The average compounded rate of return of *growth* stocks was

## Comparing Growth & Value
*Technical Measures of the Average Large-Cap Growth & Value Mutual Funds, December 31, 2012*

| | P/E Ratio | Price-to-Cash Flow Ratio | Price-to-Book Ratio | Yield | Volatility Standard Deviation | Total Return Best Year | Total Return Worst Year |
|---|---|---|---|---|---|---|---|
| Large-Cap Growth Fund | 18 | 12 | 3 | 0.45% | 17% | 39% | −40% |
| Large-Cap Value Fund | 13 | 8 | 2 | 1.64% | 16% | 29% | −37% |

figure 13.7

## Growth Stocks
*December 31, 2012*

## Value Stocks
*December 31, 2012*

| Company | 5-Year Avg P/E | Current Yield | Company | 5-Year Avg P/E | Current Yield |
|---|---|---|---|---|---|
| Amazon | 71 | 0.00% | AT&T | 14 | 5.20% |
| Apple | 18 | 1.00% | General Electric | 13 | 3.30% |
| Google | 24 | 0.00% | J.P. Morgan Chase | 12 | 2.60% |
| Qualcomm | 24 | 1.60% | Johnson & Johnson | 15 | 3.40% |
| Starbucks | 28 | 1.30% | MetLife | 12 | 2.30% |
| Visa | 30 | 0.70% | Pfizer | 13 | 3.50% |

figure 13.8

11.23 percent, while *value* stocks grew at 11.32 percent. For this period, growth stocks slightly won, but did so with more volatility.

There is no crystal ball to predict exactly when growth stocks will be in favor and value stocks out of favor. Rather than making futile attempts at guessing, it is better to have a portfolio balanced between both styles. This is referred to as "style neutral." A well-diversified stock portfolio will be balanced between growth and value stocks and include large-, mid-, and small-cap U.S. stocks, as well as international stocks.

Let's compare two hypothetical investors to examine how growth and value stocks can complement each other and reduce volatility.

On January 1, 1990, Gene Howard put all his eggs into one basket and

| Gene's Growth Portfolio | | |
|---|---|---|
| *100% Large-Cap U.S. Growth Stocks* | | |
| Annual Portfolio Performance | | |
| **Year** | **Annual Return** | **Growth of $100,000** |
| 1990 | 3.20% | $103,200 |
| 1991 | 41.37% | $145,894 |
| 1992 | 4.71% | $152,765 |
| 1993 | 4.30% | $159,334 |
| 1994 | 3.29% | $164,576 |
| 1995 | 38.26% | $227,543 |
| 1996 | 22.74% | $279,287 |
| 1997 | 34.70% | $376,199 |
| 1998 | 47.56% | $555,120 |
| 1999 | 29.87% | $720,934 |
| 2000 | −22.31% | $560,094 |
| 2001 | −19.68% | $449,867 |
| 2002 | −23.78% | $342,889 |
| 2003 | 24.77% | $427,822 |
| 2004 | 6.64% | $456,230 |
| 2005 | 1.98% | $465,263 |
| 2006 | 9.15% | $507,835 |
| 2007 | 10.97% | $563,544 |
| 2008 | −37.49% | $352,271 |
| 2009 | 37.40% | $484,021 |
| 2010 | 17.03% | $566,450 |
| 2011 | −0.56% | $563,278 |
| 2012 | 17.17% | $659,992 |
| Portfolio Performance 1990–2012 | | |
| Average Compounded Rate of Return | | 8.55% |
| Best Year | | 47.56% |
| Worst Year | | −37.49% |
| Years of Positive Return | | 18 |
| Years of Negative Return | | 5 |

figure 13.9

invested $100,000 into large-company growth stocks. By the end of 2012, twenty-three years later, Gene's $100,000 had grown in value to $659,992, an average compounded rate of return of 8.55 percent (Figure 13.9). Notice the extreme volatility Gene experienced when the markets fell in 2000–2002 and 2008. He watched his portfolio drop from a high mark of $720,934 at the end of 1999 to $342,889 at the end of 2002. That represents a loss of $378,045, or 52 percent. While large-company growth stocks were the single best-performing asset class from 1990 to 1999, they were the single worst investment from 2000 to 2002.[10] Not many investors could sustain such dramatic losses and stick to their long-term investment strategy. Many investors, shaken by market downturns, sell when the market is near the bottom, and they don't return until the market has bounced back. Sound familiar? It's called buying high and selling low.

Now let's look at our second hypothetical investor, Renee Williams, who followed a different strategy than Gene during the same time frame.

Renee invested 50 percent of her money into large-company growth stocks and 50 percent into large-company value stocks. Her portfolio performed a little better than Gene's, and she experienced less volatility (Figure 13.10). Her balanced growth and value portfolio dropped from its high water mark of $568,577 at the end of 1999 to $333,898 at the end of 2002—a loss of $234,679, or 41 percent, compared with the 52 percent drop in Gene's growth portfolio. Which investor is more likely to adhere to their investment strategy? Chances are it will be Renee, who had comparably more stability.

## International Investing

International stocks are also a key ingredient of a well-diversified portfolio, but investors too often overlook their benefits. Most portfolios should contain international exposure of between 5 and 20 percent. There are several important reasons not to overlook the international component of your portfolio.

### International Investing Adds More Diversification

An extra layer of diversification can reduce your portfolio's volatility and increase your returns. International stocks, like the different styles of U.S. stocks discussed earlier in this chapter, go through cycles of ups and downs. If international stocks are doing well and the U.S. market is struggling, the international portion of your portfolio will help offset the U.S. downturn and lower your portfolio's volatility. In other words, international stocks provide another potential "zigging" investment when other parts of your portfolio may be "zagging."

We've seen this principle played out over the past forty years. In the 1970s and 1980s, the foreign stock markets outperformed the U.S. market.

| Year | Annual Return | Growth of $100,000 |
|---|---|---|
| \multicolumn{3}{c}{**Renee's Blended Portfolio**} | | |

**Renee's Blended Portfolio**
*50% Large-Cap U.S. Growth Stocks & 50% Large-Cap U.S. Value Stocks, Rebalanced Annually*
Annual Portfolio Performance

| Year | Annual Return | Growth of $100,000 |
|---|---|---|
| 1990 | −2.58% | $97,420 |
| 1991 | 31.59% | $128,195 |
| 1992 | 7.43% | $137,720 |
| 1993 | 10.67% | $152,415 |
| 1994 | 1.22% | $154,274 |
| 1995 | 38.82% | $214,163 |
| 1996 | 22.89% | $263,185 |
| 1997 | 34.47% | $353,905 |
| 1998 | 32.12% | $467,579 |
| 1999 | 21.60% | $568,577 |
| 2000 | −12.36% | $498,301 |
| 2001 | −14.06% | $428,239 |
| 2002 | −22.03% | $333,898 |
| 2003 | 27.30% | $425,053 |
| 2004 | 10.03% | $467,685 |
| 2005 | 7.14% | $501,078 |
| 2006 | 15.51% | $578,795 |
| 2007 | 6.41% | $615,896 |
| 2008 | −37.06% | $387,645 |
| 2009 | 27.31% | $493,511 |
| 2010 | 16.10% | $572,966 |
| 2011 | 1.62% | $582,248 |
| 2012 | 16.19% | $676,514 |
| \multicolumn{3}{c}{Portfolio Performance 1990–2012} | | |
| Average Compounded Rate of Return | | 8.67% |
| Best Year | | 38.82% |
| Worst Year | | −37.06% |
| Years of Positive Return | | 18 |
| Years of Negative Return | | 5 |

figure 13.10

By owning international stocks during those two decades, you would have increased your portfolio returns. However, in the 1990s, the investment winds changed, as they often do, and the U.S. market dominated the global equities marketplace (Figure 13.11).

Again, because there is no way of knowing exactly when one market will

| U.S. vs. International Stocks | | |
|---|---|---|
| Cumulative Return, S&P 500 vs. EAFE | | |
| 1970–1979 | U.S. | 77% |
| | International | 162% |
| 1980–1989 | U.S. | 400% |
| | International | 678% |
| 1990–1999 | U.S. | 432% |
| | International | 103% |
| 2000–2009 | U.S. | –23% |
| | International | –11% |
| 2010–2012 | U.S. | 26% |
| | International | 1% |

figure 13.11

take off and another will falter, it is simply best to buy and hold both U.S.-based and foreign-based assets. You will enjoy more consistent long-term performance by diversifying rather than trying to supercharge your performance through attempts to be in the hottest market at just the right time.

## A Foreign Market *Will* Likely Outperform the U.S. Market

Virtually every year, the U.S. stock market is surpassed in performance by a foreign market. In fact, take a guess at how many times during the last thirty years the U.S. stock market was the best-performing market in the world. The answer, surprisingly, is zero. Figure 13.12 shows the top-performing markets each year from 1983 through 2012. The lesson is clear: by participating in international markets, you can potentially boost your portfolio returns.

## Overseas Companies Are Often Fueled by Our Consumer Purchases

Another reason to own international stocks is that we American consumers make foreign companies more profitable each day through our purchasing habits. If you examine your daily purchases, you will find that you buy many products produced by overseas companies. Even companies you may think are tried-and-true American may be foreign owned. Have you ever purchased any of the products listed in Figure 13.13? Are your daily spending habits making foreign companies more profitable? Why not own some of these companies (outright or through a mutual fund) and participate in that profitability?

## Foreign Equity Markets Are Expanding

In the past, most global stock market opportunities, as measured by total market capitalization, existed in the United States. For example, in 1970, 66 percent of the global equity opportunities were found in the United States, while only 34 percent were in foreign markets. The total global market cap in 1970 was

| The Best-Performing Global Stock Markets | | | |
|:---:|:---:|:---:|:---:|
| *MCSI Country Index* | | | |
| **Year** | **Market** | **Return** | **U.S. Return** |
| 1983 | Australia | 56% | 23% |
| 1984 | Hong Kong | 47% | 6% |
| 1985 | Germany | 137% | 32% |
| 1986 | Japan | 100% | 18% |
| 1987 | Japan | 43% | 5% |
| 1988 | France | 39% | 17% |
| 1989 | Germany | 47% | 31% |
| 1990 | United Kingdom | 10% | –3% |
| 1991 | Hong Kong | 50% | 31% |
| 1992 | Hong Kong | 32% | 8% |
| 1993 | Hong Kong | 117% | 10% |
| 1994 | Finland | 52% | 1% |
| 1995 | Switzerland | 44% | 37% |
| 1996 | Spain | 40% | 23% |
| 1997 | Portugal | 47% | 33% |
| 1998 | Finland | 122% | 29% |
| 1999 | Finland | 153% | 21% |
| 2000 | Switzerland | 6% | –9% |
| 2001 | New Zealand | 10% | –12% |
| 2002 | New Zealand | 26% | –22% |
| 2003 | Greece | 70% | 29% |
| 2004 | Austria | 72% | 11% |
| 2005 | Canada | 29% | 5% |
| 2006 | Spain | 50% | 16% |
| 2007 | Finland | 45% | 5% |
| 2008 | Japan | –31% | –37% |
| 2009 | Norway | 83% | 26% |
| 2010 | Sweden | 31% | 15% |
| 2011 | Ireland | 11% | 2% |
| 2012 | Belgium | 36% | 16% |

*figure 13.12*

$850 billion. This has changed dramatically. According to the World Bank, by the end of 2011, only 34 percent of the global opportunities were found in the United States and 66 percent were located overseas. The total market cap of the world equity markets in 2011 increased to more than $47 trillion.[11]

| Foreign Products | | | |
|---|---|---|---|
| **Brand** | **Product** | **Company** | **Country** |
| Blackberry | Smartphone | Research in Motion | Canada |
| Maybelline | Makeup | L'Oreal | France |
| Allegra | Allergy Medicine | Sanofi-Aventis | France |
| Bayer Aspirin | Pain Reliever | Bayer | Germany |
| Ray-Ban | Sunglasses | Luxottica | Italy |
| Bridgestone | Tires | Bridgestone | Japan |
| Nintendo | Game System | Nintendo | Japan |
| Panasonic | TV | Panasonic | Japan |
| PlayStation | Game System | Sony | Japan |
| Shell Gas Station | Gas | Royal Dutch Shell | Netherlands |
| Baby Ruth/Kit Kat | Candy Bars | Nestlé | Switzerland |
| Gerber | Baby Food | Nestlé | Switzerland |
| Nesquik | Chocolate Milk | Nestlé | Switzerland |
| Excedrin | Pain Reliever | Novartis | Switzerland |
| UBS | Brokerage | UBS | Switzerland |
| Aquafresh | Toothpaste | GlaxoSmithKline | United Kingdom |
| Dove | Soap | Unilever | United Kingdom |
| Lipton | Beverage | Unilever | United Kingdom |
| Slim Fast | Weight Loss | Unilever | United Kingdom |
| Vaseline | Personal Care | Unilever | United Kingdom |

figure 13.13

## Emerging Markets Have Room to Grow

International stocks are categorized by capitalization size (large and small) and style (growth and value), similar to domestic stocks. In addition, foreign stocks can be subcategorized by the maturity of the international market. Overseas stocks are located in either mature stable markets, such as Europe, or in developing emerging markets, such as South America. Our discussion about the international markets up to this point has revolved around the developed markets of the world. Some consideration, however, also must be given to the world's emerging markets.

There are many markets located in parts of the world such as Asia, Latin America, and Eastern Europe that are considered "emerging" because their economies are in the beginning stages of development. There is, of course, more risk when investing in these countries, but there is also more potential when an emerging market takes off. The room for growth in these economies is the attractive feature about investing in them. It may be hard to believe, but the United States was once considered an emerging country. There may well be future economic powers that have not yet popped up on the radar screen.

As the global standard of living improves, millions of people will have more money to spend. As spending increases, financial markets are driven upward. As more people in these emerging countries buy basic items like telephones, cell phones, and computers, the companies providing these services will likely do very well. Consider the statistics in Figure 13.14 outlining the number of telephone lines, cell phone subscribers, and computers per one hundred people in various countries. How much room is there for future growth?

| Room for Foreign Growth | | | | |
|---|---|---|---|---|
| Per 100 people (United Nations ESCAP, 2011) | | | | |
| Country | Home Telephone | Cell Phones Subscribers | Personal Computers | Internet Users |
| United States | 48 | 106 | 81 | 78 |
| China | 21 | 73 | 35 | 38 |
| India | 4 | 72 | 6 | 10 |
| Indonesia | 16 | 98 | 11 | 18 |
| Malaysia | 15 | 128 | 23 | 61 |
| Mongolia | 7 | 105 | 2.5 | 20 |
| Russia | 31 | 179 | 13 | 49 |
| Thailand | 10 | 113 | 27 | 24 |
| Tonga | 29 | 53 | 6 | 25 |
| Uzbekistan | 7 | 92 | 3 | 30 |

figure 13.14

# Bonds

Most investors, with the possible exception of very young people in their twenties and early thirties, should own some bonds. Bonds provide

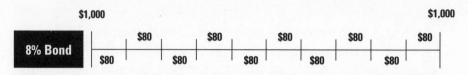

figure 13.15

diversification, income, and a cushion to soften the blow of a falling stock market. This is important particularly if you are a retiree, since you will not have as much time to make up for sharp market losses. During the 2000–2003 recession, the stock market fell 44.84 percent. During this same period, long-term government bonds gained 29 percent.[12] The same occurred in 2008 when stocks dropped 37 percent and long-term government bonds rose by almost 23 percent.[13] Investors with diversified portfolios consisting of stocks and bonds suffered much less than those invested in stocks alone.

While stocks represent a piece of ownership in a company, bonds simply represent the outstanding debt of a company or government. If you purchase a bond, you are loaning money to the issuer, which could be a corporation, a municipality, or a government entity. In return, the bond's issuer promises to pay you interest, called the coupon, and to repay your principal at a stated maturity date. For example, if you bought a ten-year bond with an 8 percent coupon, you would loan the issuer $1,000, and the issuer would promise to repay you the $1,000 at maturity while paying you $80 of interest each year along the way (Figure 13.15). The promise to repay your principal with interest is as sound as the institution that issued the bond.

Like stocks, bonds come in all shapes and sizes, based on such things as credit ratings, maturities, and yields. Some are taxable, others are tax-free. However, most bonds share some common characteristics. First, when interest rates go up, bond prices fall. Conversely, when rates fall, bond prices increase (Figure 13.16). Second, long-term bonds are more volatile than short-term bonds. Third, bonds issued by low-quality companies pay higher yields than those issued by high-quality companies.

## Interest Rates and Bond Prices

To understand the relationship between movements in interest rates and bond prices, let's look at the actual experience of a bond investor named Perry Langford. Perry purchased a ten-year General Electric corporate bond for $1,000 on January 1, 1976, with an 8 percent coupon. The bond

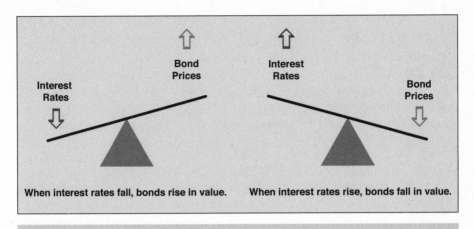

When interest rates fall, bonds rise in value.    When interest rates rise, bonds fall in value.

*figure 13.16*

paid him $80 of interest per year for ten years. At the end of ten years, he received his original investment of $1,000 back. The $80 of interest he received each year and his principal at maturity were guaranteed by the underlying bond issuer, General Electric.

Although General Electric guaranteed the interest and principal, the value of Perry's 10-year bond fluctuated between 1976 and 1985. Price movements in bonds are largely due to changes in interest rates. This ten-year period was marked by rising interest rates (Figure 13.17). After owning the bond for five years, Perry considered selling it. However, there was one problem. Because interest rates had increased, new bonds being issued in 1980 by similar companies were paying 10 percent interest

> Only 38 percent of investors understand that when interest rates go up, bond prices usually go down.[14]

($100 per year). Consequently, Perry's 8 percent bond wasn't very appealing to other investors. In 1980, why would an investor want to buy Perry's 8 percent bond when a newly issued bond paying 10 percent was available?

Perry asked his broker to put his 8 percent bond up for sale and see what investors would be willing to pay for it in this higher interest-rate environment. He received offers from investors to buy his bond for $924. (The open market told him that to make his bond attractive to bond buyers he'd have to discount the price of the bond by $76.) A bond purchased for $924 paying $80 of interest per year and maturing in five years at $1,000 would be equivalent to a new five-year bond paying $100 of interest each year (this assumes the bond type, maturity, and credit ratings are similar). Rather than selling the bond for less than he purchased it for, Perry decided to simply hold on to it until maturity and receive his original $1,000 investment back.

| Year | 3-Month T-Bill | 6-Month CD | Prime Rate | AAA LT Corp | Fed Funds | 30-Year Mortgage |
|------|------|------|------|------|------|------|
| 1956 | 2.46% | N/A | 3.77% | N/A | 2.73% | N/A |
| 1957 | 3.14% | N/A | 4.20% | N/A | 3.11% | N/A |
| 1958 | 1.54% | N/A | 3.83% | N/A | 1.57% | N/A |
| 1959 | 2.95% | N/A | 4.48% | N/A | 3.31% | N/A |
| 1960 | 2.66% | N/A | 4.82% | N/A | 3.21% | N/A |
| 1961 | 2.13% | N/A | 4.50% | N/A | 1.95% | N/A |
| 1962 | 2.73% | N/A | 4.50% | N/A | 2.71% | N/A |
| 1963 | 3.12% | N/A | 4.50% | N/A | 3.18% | N/A |
| 1964 | 3.54% | 4.03% | 4.50% | N/A | 3.50% | N/A |
| 1965 | 3.93% | 4.45% | 4.54% | N/A | 4.07% | N/A |
| 1966 | 4.76% | 5.60% | 5.63% | N/A | 5.11% | N/A |
| 1967 | 4.21% | 5.19% | 5.63% | N/A | 4.22% | N/A |
| 1968 | 5.21% | 5.97% | 6.31% | N/A | 5.66% | N/A |
| 1969 | 6.58% | 7.34% | 7.96% | N/A | 8.21% | N/A |
| 1970 | 6.52% | 7.64% | 7.91% | N/A | 7.17% | N/A |
| 1971 | 4.39% | 5.21% | 5.73% | N/A | 4.67% | N/A |
| 1972 | 3.84% | 5.01% | 5.25% | N/A | 4.44% | 7.38% |
| 1973 | 6.93% | 9.05% | 8.03% | N/A | 8.74% | 8.04% |
| 1974 | 8.00% | 10.02% | 10.81% | N/A | 10.51% | 9.19% |
| 1975 | 5.80% | 6.90% | 7.86% | N/A | 5.82% | 9.05% |
| 1976 | 5.08% | 5.63% | 6.84% | 8.43% | 5.05% | 8.87% |
| 1977 | 5.12% | 5.91% | 6.83% | 8.02% | 5.54% | 8.85% |
| 1978 | 7.18% | 8.60% | 9.06% | 8.73% | 7.94% | 9.64% |
| 1979 | 10.38% | 11.42% | 12.67% | 9.63% | 11.20% | 11.20% |
| 1980 | 11.24% | 12.94% | 15.26% | 11.94% | 13.35% | 13.74% |
| 1981 | 14.71% | 15.79% | 18.87% | 14.17% | 16.39% | 16.63% |
| 1982 | 10.54% | 12.57% | 14.85% | 13.79% | 12.24% | 16.04% |
| 1983 | 8.80% | 9.28% | 10.79% | 12.04% | 9.09% | 13.24% |
| 1984 | 9.85% | 10.71% | 12.04% | 12.71% | 10.23% | 13.88% |
| 1985 | 7.72% | 8.24% | 9.93% | 11.37% | 8.10% | 12.43% |
| 1986 | 6.16% | 6.50% | 8.33% | 9.02% | 6.80% | 10.19% |
| 1987 | 6.16% | 7.01% | 8.21% | 9.38% | 6.66% | 10.21% |
| 1988 | 5.47% | 7.91% | 9.32% | 9.71% | 7.57% | 10.34% |
| 1989 | 8.37% | 9.08% | 10.87% | 9.26% | 9.21% | 10.32% |
| 1990 | 7.81% | 8.17% | 10.01% | 9.32% | 8.10% | 10.13% |
| 1991 | 5.60% | 5.91% | 8.46% | 8.77% | 5.69% | 9.25% |
| 1992 | 3.51% | 3.76% | 6.25% | 8.14% | 3.52% | 8.39% |

**Continued**

| Year | 3-Month T-Bill | 6-Month CD | Prime Rate | AAA LT Corp | Fed Funds | 30-Year Mortgage |
|------|------|------|------|------|------|------|
| 1993 | 2.90% | 3.28% | 6.00% | 7.22% | 3.02% | 7.31% |
| 1994 | 3.90% | 4.96% | 7.15% | 7.97% | 4.21% | 8.38% |
| 1995 | 5.60% | 5.98% | 8.83% | 7.59% | 5.83% | 7.93% |
| 1996 | 5.21% | 5.47% | 8.27% | 7.37% | 5.30% | 7.81% |
| 1997 | 5.26% | 5.73% | 8.44% | 7.27% | 5.46% | 7.60% |
| 1998 | 4.86% | 5.44% | 8.35% | 6.53% | 5.35% | 6.94% |
| 1999 | 4.68% | 5.46% | 8.00% | 7.05% | 4.97% | 7.44% |
| 2000 | 5.89% | 6.59% | 9.23% | 7.62% | 6.24% | 8.05% |
| 2001 | 3.83% | 3.66% | 6.91% | 7.08% | 3.88% | 6.97% |
| 2002 | 1.65% | 1.81% | 4.67% | 6.49% | 1.67% | 6.54% |
| 2003 | 1.02% | 1.17% | 4.12% | 5.66% | 1.13% | 5.83% |
| 2004 | 1.20% | 1.74% | 4.29% | 5.60% | 1.29% | 5.84% |
| 2005 | 3.34% | 3.72% | 6.10% | 5.20% | 3.10% | 5.87% |
| 2006 | 5.07% | 5.23% | 7.94% | 5.70% | 4.94% | 6.41% |
| 2007 | 2.53% | 5.19% | 7.44% | 5.64% | 5.02% | 6.34% |
| 2008 | 1.80% | 3.68% | 5.21% | 5.63% | 2.21% | 6.03% |
| 2009 | 0.16% | 1.27% | 3.25% | 5.31% | 0.25% | 5.04% |
| 2010 | 0.14% | 0.73% | 3.25% | 4.94% | 0.25% | 4.69% |
| 2011 | 0.08% | 0.34% | 3.25% | 4.58% | 0.25% | 4.45% |
| 2012 | 0.07% | 0.47% | 3.25% | 3.65% | 0.25% | 3.66% |
| Average | 5.28% | 6.55% | 7.63% | 8.58% | 5.74% | 9.23% |

figure 13.17

Of course, the opposite is true also. When interest rates fall, the value of outstanding bonds will go up for the same reasons. So remember, when buying bonds, if interest rates are climbing, bond prices will fall, and if rates are falling, bond prices will climb. Where do you think bond prices are headed given the information in Figure 13.17?

Before buying his bond, Perry should have asked some "what if" questions. What if interest rates increase or decrease after buying the 8 percent General Electric bond? For example, what will the price of the bond be if rates increase or decrease 1, 2, or 3 percent? Figure 13.18 illustrates how rising and falling interest rates would affect the value of his ten-year bond if he decided to sell it after owning it for just five years. The first column outlines different interest-rate scenarios either up or down that could occur after purchasing his bond. The second column indicates the price Perry could sell his bond at as rates change. You will notice that the more interest rates either increase

| 10-Year Bond Sold in Year 5 | |
| --- | --- |
| $1,000 bond, 8% coupon | |
| Change in Interest Rate | Bond Value |
| up 1% | $961 |
| up 2% | $924 |
| up 3% | $889 |
| up 4% | $855 |
| up 5% | $824 |
| down 1% | $1,041 |
| down 2% | $1,084 |
| down 3% | $1,130 |
| down 4% | $1,178 |
| down 5% | $1,228 |

figure 13.18

or decrease, the more impact these rate fluctuations will have on the value of his bond. Before buying a bond, it is a good idea to ask similar questions so you understand how the value of your bonds will be affected by interest-rate changes.

It should be noted that if you buy a bond fund that comprises hundreds of bonds maturing at various times, the impact of rising interest rates can be reduced. For example, if you owned the Bond Fund of America-A Fund from 1977 to 1981, a period marked by a 187 percent increase in interest rates, you would have gained 22 percent (annualized 4 percent). While a 22 percent return over five years isn't off the charts, it is a decent return if interest rates are increasing like they were. Diversification through a bond fund can reduce the risk of rising interest rates.

## Maturities

Within each bond category, each type of bond can be classified based on when it matures: a bond can be short-term (zero to five years), intermediate-term (five to ten years), or long-term (ten years or more). Bonds of different maturities react differently when rates go up and down. For example, if interest rates fall, the prices of long-term bonds will go up to a greater degree than short-term bonds. If rates rise, the opposite is true. Thus, there is more risk in owning long-term bonds.

If you are planning to hold your bonds to maturity, the bond's issuer guarantees that you will receive back your principal, the face value of the bond. If you are not planning to sell, the price fluctuations between now and maturity are irrelevant even though they will be reported on your brokerage statement. The price movements only become important if you are going to sell your bond before maturity.

## Bond Ratings

Most bonds are rated. Bond ratings help investors determine the credit worthiness of the issuing company. Just as credit bureaus give you a credit score as an individual, bond-rating agencies give scores to companies. Those with little outstanding debt, a solid balance sheet, and the ability to repay their debt obligations are given the highest credit ratings. To attract investors and to offset the additional risk, bonds issued by low-quality companies must offer higher yields than those issued by high-quality companies. Changes in credit ratings will also cause the value of bonds to fluctuate. If a corporation's bond rating is downgraded, the value of the bond will generally fall. A rating upgrade will often increase the bond's value. There are two main bond-rating services: Standard & Poor's and Moody's. Standard & Poor's ratings are shown in Figure 13.19. Bonds rated BBB and above are referred to as investment grade bonds, while bonds rated BB or lower are considered junk bonds.

| Standard & Poor's Bond Ratings | |
|---|---|
| **Rating** | **Description** |
| AAA | Bonds of the highest quality |
| AA | High-quality debt obligations |
| A | Bonds that have a strong capacity to pay interest and principal but may be susceptible to adverse effects |
| BBB | Bonds that have an adequate capacity to pay interest and principal but are more vulnerable to adverse economic conditions or changing circumstances |
| BB | Bonds of lower medium grade with few desirable investment characteristics |
| B | Primarily speculative bonds with great uncertainties and major risk if exposed to adverse conditions |
| CCC | Extremely speculative bonds that are highly vulnerable to default |
| C | A bankruptcy petition has been filed but interest is still being paid |
| D | Bonds in default |

*figure 13.19*

## Taxable and Tax-Free Bonds

All the different types of bonds that we've discussed so far are either taxable or tax-free. Taxable bonds include corporate, government (with the exception of Treasury bonds), and international bonds. Tax-free bonds are issued by municipalities and offer interest that is not subject to federal income taxes. In some states, if you purchase a bond issued by the state, the interest is free from both state and federal taxes (double tax-free). Treasury bonds are exempt from state taxes.

To determine whether to buy taxable or tax-free bonds, compare the yields of each. To make an apples-to-apples comparison, yields must be compared after taxes are applied. Of course, tax-free bonds are not needed in a retirement account, where all interest is already tax-deferred.

James Gardner, a bond investor in the 40 percent tax bracket (state and federal combined), is considering buying a taxable bond yielding 4 percent or a tax-free bond yielding only 3 percent. Of course, there are more factors to consider than just yield, but we'll keep this example simple and stick strictly to yields.

Before applying taxes, it looks as if the taxable bond provides the greatest yield. However, the interest on the taxable bond will be taxed. James must factor in his tax rate and determine how much a taxable bond would have to yield to be equivalent to the 3 percent tax-free bond. In James's tax bracket, which bond offers the best after-tax yield? The formula in Figure 13.20 will provide the answer:

By inputting the tax-free yield and his tax rate, James can easily see that the tax-free bond would be the better investment. A taxable bond would have to yield 5 percent to be superior to the tax-free yield of 3 percent in James's high tax bracket. Based on yield alone, James would be better off owning the tax-free bond.

## Bond Diversification

The many types of bonds, with their varying issuers, credit ratings, maturities, and yields, all provide different rates of return from year to year. Like stocks, it is impossible to know exactly which types of bonds will be the best performing during the next twelve months. Because of this uncertainty, it is equally important to diversify your bond portfolio. Figure 13.21 highlights the performance of different types of bonds between 1991 and 2012.[15]

| Tax Equivalent Yield | | |
|---|---|---|
| $\dfrac{\text{Tax-Free Yield}}{1 - \text{Investor's Tax Bracket}}$ | = Equivalent Taxable Bond Yield | |
| $\dfrac{.03}{(1 - 0.40)}$ = 5% | | |

*figure 13.20*

# Cash

Cash equivalents are investments easily turned into cash without the risk of principal loss. This is called liquidity. Examples of cash equivalents include money market accounts, checking, savings, certificates of deposit, U.S. Treasury bills, and life insurance cash values. Cash investments can be an important component in a diversified portfolio due to their stability and consistent positive returns even during deep stock and bond market downturns. To locate the highest-yielding cash investments from around the country or to compare cash investments at financial institutions in your area, visit www.bankrate.com.

Some cash investments make sense for retirees. If you are a retiree and are living off your investments, consider maintaining one to two years of needed annual income in cash-type investments. This is your short-term money—money that you will use immediately to supplement your income. Because you will be spending this money over the next one to two years, you should not put this money at risk in the stock or bond markets. By keeping a cash cushion in your portfolio, you can avoid having to liquidate stock and bond investments during market downturns. This added stability will help you maintain a disciplined investment strategy and keep your intermediate- and long-term money invested in the stock and bond markets. Too much cash in a portfolio, however, can hamper long-term performance and may ultimately keep you from reaching retirement goals.

# Performance of Each Asset Class

Now that you know your team, Figure 13.22 lets you see at a glance how each asset class has performed annually for the past twenty-three years. The best investment of each year is distinguished with a dark box and the

| Year | High-Yield Junk Bonds | Investment-Grade Bonds | U.S. Gov't Bonds | Municipal Bonds | Money Markets |
|------|----------|----------|----------|----------|----------|
| 1991 | 40.22% | 16.18% | 12.04% | 14.63% | 5.82% |
| 1992 | 18.36% | 7.22% | 8.90% | 6.10% | 3.45% |
| 1993 | 19.84% | 10.00% | 12.43% | 8.32% | 2.72% |
| 1994 | –3.68% | –3.21% | –6.04% | –4.74% | 3.74% |
| 1995 | 17.38% | 17.12% | 17.31% | 16.94% | 5.53% |
| 1996 | 12.98% | 3.43% | 3.58% | 2.16% | 5.01% |
| 1997 | 13.17% | 8.79% | 9.39% | 9.12% | 5.14% |
| 1998 | –0.07% | 7.87% | 5.64% | 7.84% | 5.10% |
| 1999 | 4.78% | –0.98% | –4.07% | –2.66% | 4.63% |
| 2000 | –9.71% | 10.58% | 11.10% | 11.89% | 5.81% |
| 2001 | –1.04% | 8.22% | 4.15% | 6.67% | 3.70% |
| 2002 | –2.41% | 8.29% | 9.86% | 8.63% | 1.31% |
| 2003 | 26.36% | 5.41% | 1.30% | 5.34% | 0.69% |
| 2004 | 10.34% | 4.28% | 3.35% | 4.14% | 0.85% |
| 2005 | 3.00% | 2.28% | 2.51% | 3.70% | 2.67% |
| 2006 | 10.17% | 4.47% | 3.38% | 5.10% | 4.54% |
| 2007 | 2.13% | 5.43% | 6.44% | 1.38% | 4.74% |
| 2008 | –28.84% | –4.71% | 5.80% | –9.45% | 2.20% |
| 2009 | 49.49% | 14.30% | 3.30% | 18.50% | 0.25% |
| 2010 | 14.91% | 8.62% | 6.53% | 1.66% | 0.04% |
| 2011 | 2.85% | 6.28% | 8.57% | 10.96% | 0.02% |
| 2012 | 15.40% | 7.82% | 3.13% | 9.50% | 0.03% |
| Average | 9.80% | 6.71% | 5.85% | 6.17% | 3.09% |

Note: Performance numbers are based on the respective Lipper Index of each asset class.

figure 13.21

worst of each year with a light box. As you review the chart, notice that each year there are several asset classes with "zigzag" relationships. Trying to choose the asset class that you think will perform the strongest during the upcoming year is a natural temptation. Don't fool yourself. Moving in and out of asset classes trying to find the "hot" investment is a mistake, especially when you're gambling with your retirement savings. Attempting to time the market will hurt the performance of your portfolio. Decide on an appropriate asset allocation and diversification model and then adhere to it for the long term.

Now you can develop a diversified portfolio that meets your risk and return objectives. As we continue our discussion of Step 2 of the investment process in the next chapter, we will examine different diversified portfolios. After reviewing these portfolios, you'll be able to determine which portfolio best suits your needs. Once you decide how to diversify your portfolio, we can then start our search to identify the best investments in each asset class.

## Asset Class Performance 1990–2012

| Market Sectors | 1990 | 1991 | 1992 | 1993 | 1994 | 1995 | 1996 | 1997 | 1998 | 1999 |
|---|---|---|---|---|---|---|---|---|---|---|
| Large U.S. Company Growth Stocks<br>*DJ Large Company Growth Index* | 0.34% | 46.62% | 4.48% | 3.26% | 1.69% | 34.10% | 22.46% | 32.78% | 42.32% | 34.73% |
| Large U.S. Company Value Stocks<br>*DJ Large Company Value Index* | −7.59% | 25.64% | 11.14% | 16.95% | −0.80% | 41.19% | 21.92% | 33.26% | 14.94% | 8.27% |
| Mid–Cap U.S. Company Growth Stocks<br>*DJ Mid–Cap Growth Index* | −7.90% | 44.07% | 7.26% | 15.11% | −1.87% | 34.35% | 14.96% | 17.55% | 9.04% | 62.35% |
| Mid–Cap U.S. Company Value Stocks<br>*DJ Mid–Cap Value Index* | −15.97% | 39.68% | 21.05% | 15.93% | −1.65% | 34.67% | 20.95% | 32.88% | −2.26% | 3.69% |
| Small U.S. Company Growth Stocks<br>*DJ Small Company Growth Index* | −19.02% | 56.80% | 8.50% | 15.91% | −3.11% | 32.99% | 12.76% | 14.34% | 6.92% | 52.56% |
| Small U.S. Company Value Stocks<br>*DJ Small Company Value Index* | −19.39% | 49.00% | 29.95% | 22.10% | 0.38% | 27.33% | 21.16% | 33.90% | −6.99% | −1.41% |
| Large International Company Stocks<br>*Morgan Stanley EAFE Index NR USD* | −23.45% | 12.12% | 12.17% | 32.57% | 7.78% | 11.22% | 6.05% | 1.78% | 20.00% | 26.96% |
| Corporate Bonds<br>*Lehman Bros. Long Credit* | 6.48% | 20.98% | 9.34% | 13.64% | −5.76% | 27.94% | 2.20% | 13.46% | 9.16% | −5.76% |
| U.S. Government Bonds<br>*Lehman Bros. Long–Term Government Bond Index* | 6.29% | 18.68% | 8.09% | 17.18% | −7.59% | 30.90% | −0.83% | 15.12% | 13.32% | −8.26% |
| Municipal Bonds<br>*Lehman Bros. Municipal Bond Index* | 7.30% | 12.15% | 8.82% | 12.28% | −5.14% | 17.46% | 4.44% | 9.20% | 6.48% | −2.07% |
| International Bonds<br>*Citigroup Non-$ World Government Bond Index* | 15.29% | 16.24% | 4.77% | 15.12% | 5.99% | 19.55% | 4.08% | −4.26% | 17.79% | −5.07% |
| Cash<br>*3–Month Treasury Bill* | 7.52% | 5.68% | 3.59% | 3.12% | 4.45% | 5.79% | 5.26% | 5.31% | 5.02% | 4.87% |

figure 13.22

| Asset Class Performance 1990–2012 | | | | | | | | | | | | |
|---|---|---|---|---|---|---|---|---|---|---|---|---|
| **2000** | **2001** | **2002** | **2003** | **2004** | **2005** | **2006** | **2007** | **2008** | **2009** | **2010** | **2011** | **2012** |
| -24.99% | -20.36% | -24.98% | 25.35% | 6.46% | 1.98% | 9.15% | 10.97% | -37.49% | 37.40% | 17.03% | -0.56% | 17.17% |
| 1.09% | -8.17% | -17.99% | 31.68% | 15.43% | 12.30% | 21.87% | 1.84% | -36.62% | 17.21% | 15.16% | 3.79% | 15.21% |
| 15.38% | -12.72% | -23.71% | 39.15% | 17.34% | 11.15% | 11.57% | 11.24% | -41.64% | 55.55% | 28.22% | -0.56% | 16.68% |
| 24.91% | 7.10% | -12.34% | 48.28% | 20.50% | 14.76% | 15.71% | -1.29% | -34.80% | 32.04% | 21.88% | -0.98% | 18.57% |
| -24.74% | -14.31% | -28.90% | 43.91% | 16.12% | 9.84% | 13.79% | 8.05% | -41.26% | 47.38% | 31.97% | -2.09% | 16.96% |
| 23.21% | 10.06% | -13.90% | 51.15% | 20.26% | 10.71% | 20.04% | -4.13% | -33.92% | 36.83% | 24.98% | -3.97% | 19.75% |
| -14.17% | -21.44% | -15.94% | 38.59% | 20.25% | 20.99% | 26.34% | 11.17% | -43.38% | 31.78% | 7.75% | -12.14% | 17.32% |
| 9.18% | 12.16% | 11.95% | 10.45% | 9.38% | 3.76% | 3.47% | 3.60% | -3.92% | 16.80% | 10.69% | 17.13% | 12.73% |
| 20.28% | 4.34% | 16.99% | 2.59% | 7.94% | 6.61% | 2.06% | 9.65% | 22.69% | -12.97% | 9.43% | 29.15% | 3.79% |
| 11.69% | 5.08% | 9.60% | 5.32% | 4.48% | 3.51% | 4.84% | 3.36% | -2.47% | 12.91% | 2.38% | 10.70% | 6.78% |
| -2.63% | -3.54% | 21.99% | 18.52% | 12.14% | -9.20% | 6.94% | 11.45% | 10.11% | 4.39% | 5.21% | 5.17% | 1.51% |
| 6.32% | 3.67% | 1.68% | 1.05% | 1.43% | 3.34% | 5.07% | 4.77% | 1.51% | 0.16% | 0.14% | 0.06% | 0.09% |

# 14

# THE CHOICE

## RETIREMENT DECISION #11 (CONTINUED): HOW SHOULD I DIVERSIFY MY INVESTMENT PORTFOLIO?

N ow that we have thoroughly examined and understand each asset class composing a diversified portfolio (Figure 14.1), let's select a portfolio that fits your risk tolerance and return objectives. Review the portfolios showcased in Figures 14.2 through 14.12 and choose a portfolio that suits you.[1] As you do so, be sure to notice the performance of each portfolio during both good and bad markets.

Susan Callister, 63, chose the Balanced Growth and Income portfolio in Figure 14.7. She retired in December 2012 with a $650,000 nest egg. To determine how to diversify her money into the various asset classes, she first dedicated 50 percent of her money to stocks ($325,000), 40 percent to bonds ($260,000), and 10 percent to cash ($65,000). Then, she simply applied the percentages outlined in Figure 14.1 to each part of her portfolio to determine how much money to invest in each asset class. For example, using the percentages in Figure 14.1, she took $81,250 of the stock money (25 percent of $325,000) and invested it in large-company U.S. growth stocks. She invested $32,500 into mid-cap growth stocks (10 percent) and so on. Once you pick a portfolio, simply follow Susan's lead and diversify your money using Figure 14.1 as a guide.

Historically, this balanced portfolio has provided investors with a 9.96 percent annual return (Figure 14.7). Susan determined she could adhere to this investment strategy through the best and worst years. This portfolio achieved positive returns thirty-six out of the past forty-three years. During the worst year, 2008, the portfolio lost 15.34 percent; in its best year, 1985, it gained 31.46 percent. Although there is no guarantee that these returns will repeat themselves, it is reasonable to assume that the ups and downs will be at least similar in the future.

Each of the portfolios in Figures 14.2 through 14.12 is diversified as shown in Figure 14.1. In addition, each portfolio was rebalanced annually (this will be discussed in detail in Chapter 15).

Buying and holding a well-diversified portfolio of investments makes much more sense than trying to bounce in and out of each asset class based on your guess as to which will provide the best performance. Understanding the ups and downs of different investment portfolios and how they perform in particular

| Asset Class Distribution | |
|---|---|
| *Stocks* | |
| Large-Cap U.S. Growth Stocks | 25% |
| Large-Cap U.S. Value Stocks | 25% |
| Mid-Cap U.S. Growth Stocks | 10% |
| Mid-Cap U.S. Value Stocks | 10% |
| Small-Cap U.S. Growth Stocks | 5% |
| Small-Cap U.S. Value Stocks | 5% |
| International Growth & Value Stocks | 20% |
| | 100% |
| *Bonds* | |
| Corporate Bonds | 40% |
| Government Bonds | 40% |
| International Bonds | 20% |
| | 100% |
| *Cash* | |
| Cash Equivalents | 100% |

figure 14.1

economic environments can be invaluable in helping you build a portfolio to meet your retirement goals. Remember to pick a portfolio strategy that not only meets your return requirements, but also will allow you to maintain the strategy and not lose any sleep at night when things get tough. Invest with your eyes wide open by understanding the risks associated with your strategy. Then, if we have a drop in the market, you won't be surprised because you know what to expect from the outset.

## Ultra-Conservative Income

| | |
|---|---|
| Stocks | 0% |
| Bonds | 90% |
| Cash | 10% |

### Portfolio Performance 1970–2012

| | |
|---|---|
| Annual Rate of Return | 8.61% |
| Best Year | 38.37% |
| Worst Year | −6.35% |
| Years Positive | 38 |
| Years Negative | 5 |

### Annual Portfolio Performance

| Year | Annual Return | Growth of $10,000 | Year | Annual Return | Growth of $10,000 |
|------|--------|-----------|------|--------|-----------|
| 1970 | 14.37% | $11,437 | 1992 | 7.49% | $79,425 |
| 1971 | 11.35% | $12,735 | 1993 | 14.33% | $90,806 |
| 1972 | 6.21% | $13,526 | 1994 | −3.40% | $87,719 |
| 1973 | 0.71% | $13,622 | 1995 | 25.27% | $109,886 |
| 1974 | 1.38% | $13,810 | 1996 | 1.42% | $111,446 |
| 1975 | 11.31% | $15,372 | 1997 | 10.13% | $122,735 |
| 1976 | 16.44% | $17,899 | 1998 | 12.26% | $137,783 |
| 1977 | 0.97% | $18,073 | 1999 | −6.35% | $129,034 |
| 1978 | 0.16% | $18,102 | 2000 | 12.48% | $145,137 |
| 1979 | −1.40% | $17,848 | 2001 | 4.91% | $152,263 |
| 1980 | −1.90% | $17,509 | 2002 | 16.42% | $177,265 |
| 1981 | 1.75% | $17,815 | 2003 | 5.85% | $187,635 |
| 1982 | 38.37% | $24,651 | 2004 | 8.51% | $203,603 |
| 1983 | 3.99% | $25,635 | 2005 | 2.41% | $208,509 |
| 1984 | 15.54% | $29,618 | 2006 | 3.75% | $216,329 |
| 1985 | 28.25% | $37,986 | 2007 | 7.31% | $232,142 |
| 1986 | 20.69% | $45,845 | 2008 | 8.73% | $252,408 |
| 1987 | −0.79% | $45,483 | 2009 | 2.47% | $258,383 |
| 1988 | 9.80% | $49,940 | 2010 | 8.20% | $279,558 |
| 1989 | 16.29% | $58,075 | 2011 | 17.60% | $328,753 |
| 1990 | 8.20% | $62,837 | 2012 | 6.23% | $349,227 |
| 1991 | 17.59% | $73,890 | | | |

figure 14.2

## Conservative Income

| | |
|---|---|
| Stocks | 10% |
| Bonds | 80% |
| Cash | 10% |

### Portfolio Performance 1970–2012

| | |
|---|---|
| Annual Rate of Return | 8.95% |
| Best Year | 36.00% |
| Worst Year | −3.19% |
| Years Positive | 39 |
| Years Negative | 4 |

### Annual Portfolio Performance

| Year | Annual Return | Growth of $10,000 | Year | Annual Return | Growth of $10,000 |
|---|---|---|---|---|---|
| 1970 | 12.75% | $11,275 | 1992 | 7.33% | $86,494 |
| 1971 | 12.12% | $12,642 | 1993 | 14.47% | $99,010 |
| 1972 | 7.54% | $13,595 | 1994 | −2.81% | $96,228 |
| 1973 | −1.11% | $13,444 | 1995 | 25.63% | $120,891 |
| 1974 | −1.28% | $13,272 | 1996 | 3.14% | $124,687 |
| 1975 | 14.28% | $15,167 | 1997 | 11.53% | $139,063 |
| 1976 | 17.16% | $17,770 | 1998 | 13.03% | $157,183 |
| 1977 | 1.14% | $17,972 | 1999 | −3.19% | $152,169 |
| 1978 | 1.56% | $18,253 | 2000 | 10.40% | $167,995 |
| 1979 | 1.00% | $18,435 | 2001 | 3.33% | $173,589 |
| 1980 | 1.56% | $18,723 | 2002 | 12.65% | $195,548 |
| 1981 | 1.50% | $19,003 | 2003 | 8.69% | $212,541 |
| 1982 | 36.00% | $25,845 | 2004 | 9.04% | $231,755 |
| 1983 | 5.98% | $27,390 | 2005 | 3.17% | $239,101 |
| 1984 | 14.91% | $31,474 | 2006 | 5.13% | $251,367 |
| 1985 | 28.89% | $40,567 | 2007 | 7.21% | $269,491 |
| 1986 | 21.09% | $49,123 | 2008 | 3.91% | $280,028 |
| 1987 | 0.03% | $49,137 | 2009 | 5.49% | $295,486 |
| 1988 | 10.80% | $54,444 | 2010 | 9.03% | $322,173 |
| 1989 | 17.10% | $63,754 | 2011 | 15.44% | $371,900 |
| 1990 | 6.40% | $67,834 | 2012 | 7.23% | $398,785 |
| 1991 | 18.80% | $80,587 | | | |

figure 14.3

| Income | | |
|---|---|---|
| Stocks | 20% | |
| Bonds | 70% | |
| Cash | 10% | |
| Portfolio Performance 1970–2012 | | |
| Annual Rate of Return | 9.25% | |
| Best Year | 33.63% | |
| Worst Year | –3.93% | |
| Years Positive | 38 | |
| Years Negative | 5 | |

| Annual Portfolio Performance | | | | | |
|---|---|---|---|---|---|
| Year | Annual Return | Growth of $10,000 | Year | Annual Return | Growth of $10,000 |
| 1970 | 11.12% | $11,112 | 1992 | 7.17% | $93,813 |
| 1971 | 12.89% | $12,545 | 1993 | 14.62% | $107,523 |
| 1972 | 8.87% | $13,658 | 1994 | –2.22% | $105,137 |
| 1973 | –2.92% | $13,259 | 1995 | 25.99% | $132,465 |
| 1974 | –3.93% | $12,738 | 1996 | 4.85% | $138,887 |
| 1975 | 17.26% | $14,936 | 1997 | 12.94% | $156,852 |
| 1976 | 17.88% | $17,607 | 1998 | 13.79% | $178,488 |
| 1977 | 1.32% | $17,839 | 1999 | –0.03% | $178,441 |
| 1978 | 2.97% | $18,368 | 2000 | 8.32% | $193,292 |
| 1979 | 3.41% | $18,993 | 2001 | 1.75% | $196,684 |
| 1980 | 5.01% | $19,945 | 2002 | 8.88% | $214,154 |
| 1981 | 1.26% | $20,196 | 2003 | 11.52% | $238,819 |
| 1982 | 33.63% | $26,988 | 2004 | 9.57% | $261,666 |
| 1983 | 9.97% | $29,139 | 2005 | 3.93% | $271,947 |
| 1984 | 14.29% | $33,302 | 2006 | 6.52% | $289,666 |
| 1985 | 29.54% | $43,138 | 2007 | 7.12% | $310,277 |
| 1986 | 21.58% | $52,450 | 2008 | –0.90% | $307,487 |
| 1987 | 0.86% | $52,902 | 2009 | 8.52% | $333,675 |
| 1988 | 11.80% | $59,145 | 2010 | 9.87% | $366,602 |
| 1989 | 17.91% | $69,737 | 2011 | 13.27% | $415,260 |
| 1990 | 4.60% | $72,945 | 2012 | 8.23% | $449,436 |
| 1991 | 20.00% | $87,535 | | | |

figure 14.4

| Moderate Income | | |
|:---|:---|:---|
| Stocks | 30% | |
| Bonds | 60% | |
| Cash | 10% | |
| **Portfolio Performance 1970–2012** | | |
| Annual Rate of Return | 9.52% | |
| Best Year | 31.26% | |
| Worst Year | –6.59% | |
| Years Positive | 39 | |
| Years Negative | 4 | |

| Annual Portfolio Performance | | | | | |
|:---:|:---:|:---:|:---:|:---:|:---:|
| **Year** | **Annual Return** | **Growth of $10,000** | **Year** | **Annual Return** | **Growth of $10,000** |
| 1970 | 9.50% | $10,950 | 1992 | 7.01% | $101,193 |
| 1971 | 13.66% | $12,446 | 1993 | 14.76% | $116,129 |
| 1972 | 10.21% | $13,716 | 1994 | –1.63% | $114,236 |
| 1973 | –4.74% | $13,066 | 1995 | 26.35% | $144,337 |
| 1974 | –6.59% | $12,205 | 1996 | 6.56% | $153,806 |
| 1975 | 20.23% | $14,674 | 1997 | 14.34% | $175,861 |
| 1976 | 18.61% | $17,405 | 1998 | 14.56% | $201,467 |
| 1977 | 1.49% | $17,665 | 1999 | 3.14% | $207,793 |
| 1978 | 4.37% | $18,437 | 2000 | 6.24% | $220,759 |
| 1979 | 5.81% | $19,508 | 2001 | 0.18% | $221,156 |
| 1980 | 8.47% | $21,160 | 2002 | 5.11% | $232,458 |
| 1981 | 1.01% | $21,374 | 2003 | 14.35% | $265,815 |
| 1982 | 31.26% | $28,055 | 2004 | 10.10% | $292,663 |
| 1983 | 9.96% | $30,849 | 2005 | 4.69% | $306,388 |
| 1984 | 13.67% | $35,067 | 2006 | 7.90% | $330,593 |
| 1985 | 30.18% | $45,650 | 2007 | 7.02% | $353,801 |
| 1986 | 22.08% | $55,729 | 2008 | –5.71% | $333,599 |
| 1987 | 1.69% | $56,671 | 2009 | 11.54% | $372,047 |
| 1988 | 12.80% | $63,925 | 2010 | 10.70% | $411,873 |
| 1989 | 18.72% | $75,892 | 2011 | 11.11% | $457,633 |
| 1990 | 2.80% | $78,017 | 2012 | 9.23% | $499,877 |
| 1991 | 21.21% | $94,564 | | | |

figure 14.5

| Income & Growth | | |
|---|---|---|
| Stocks | 40% | |
| Bonds | 50% | |
| Cash | 10% | |
| Portfolio Performance 1970–2012 | | |
| Annual Rate of Return | 9.76% | |
| Best Year | 30.82% | |
| Worst Year | −10.53% | |
| Years Positive | 38 | |
| Years Negative | 5 | |

| Annual Portfolio Performance | | | | | |
|---|---|---|---|---|---|
| Year | Annual Return | Growth of $10,000 | Year | Annual Return | Growth of $10,000 |
| 1970 | 7.88% | $10,788 | 1992 | 6.86% | $108,579 |
| 1971 | 14.43% | $12,345 | 1993 | 14.90% | $124,757 |
| 1972 | 11.54% | $13,769 | 1994 | −1.04% | $123,460 |
| 1973 | −6.55% | $12,867 | 1995 | 26.72% | $156,448 |
| 1974 | −9.24% | $11,678 | 1996 | 8.27% | $169,386 |
| 1975 | 23.21% | $14,389 | 1997 | 15.74% | $196,048 |
| 1976 | 19.33% | $17,170 | 1998 | 15.32% | $226,082 |
| 1977 | 1.66% | $17,455 | 1999 | 6.30% | $240,326 |
| 1978 | 5.78% | $18,464 | 2000 | 4.16% | $250,323 |
| 1979 | 8.21% | $19,980 | 2001 | −1.40% | $246,819 |
| 1980 | 11.92% | $22,362 | 2002 | 1.34% | $250,126 |
| 1981 | 0.76% | $22,532 | 2003 | 17.18% | $293,098 |
| 1982 | 28.90% | $29,044 | 2004 | 10.63% | $324,254 |
| 1983 | 11.95% | $32,514 | 2005 | 5.45% | $341,926 |
| 1984 | 13.04% | $36,754 | 2006 | 9.28% | $373,656 |
| 1985 | 30.82% | $48,082 | 2007 | 6.92% | $399,513 |
| 1986 | 22.58% | $58,939 | 2008 | −10.53% | $357,445 |
| 1987 | 2.52% | $60,424 | 2009 | 14.57% | $409,541 |
| 1988 | 13.80% | $68,762 | 2010 | 11.54% | $456,806 |
| 1989 | 19.52% | $82,185 | 2011 | 8.95% | $497,681 |
| 1990 | 1.00% | $83,007 | 2012 | 10.23% | $548,602 |
| 1991 | 22.41% | $101,609 | | | |

figure 14.6

## Balanced Growth & Income

| | | |
|---|---|---|
| Stocks | 50% | |
| Bonds | 40% | |
| Cash | 10% | |

### Portfolio Performance 1970–2012

| | |
|---|---|
| Annual Rate of Return | 9.96% |
| Best Year | 31.46% |
| Worst Year | −15.34% |
| Years Positive | 36 |
| Years Negative | 7 |

### Annual Portfolio Performance

| Year | Annual Return | Growth of $10,000 | Year | Annual Return | Growth of $10,000 |
|---|---|---|---|---|---|
| 1970 | 6.25% | $10,625 | 1992 | 6.70% | $115,872 |
| 1971 | 15.20% | $12,240 | 1993 | 15.05% | $133,311 |
| 1972 | 12.87% | $13,815 | 1994 | −0.45% | $132,711 |
| 1973 | −8.36% | $12,660 | 1995 | 27.08% | $168,649 |
| 1974 | −11.90% | $11,154 | 1996 | 9.98% | $185,481 |
| 1975 | 26.19% | $14,075 | 1997 | 17.15% | $217,290 |
| 1976 | 20.05% | $16,897 | 1998 | 16.09% | $252,253 |
| 1977 | 1.83% | $17,206 | 1999 | 9.46% | $276,116 |
| 1978 | 7.18% | $18,442 | 2000 | 2.09% | $281,886 |
| 1979 | 10.61% | $20,398 | 2001 | −2.98% | $273,486 |
| 1980 | 15.37% | $23,533 | 2002 | −2.43% | $266,841 |
| 1981 | 0.51% | $23,653 | 2003 | 20.01% | $320,235 |
| 1982 | 26.53% | $29,929 | 2004 | 11.16% | $355,974 |
| 1983 | 13.94% | $34,101 | 2005 | 6.21% | $378,080 |
| 1984 | 12.42% | $38,336 | 2006 | 10.67% | $418,421 |
| 1985 | 31.46% | $50,397 | 2007 | 6.83% | $446,999 |
| 1986 | 23.08% | $62,028 | 2008 | −15.34% | $378,429 |
| 1987 | 3.35% | $64,106 | 2009 | 17.59% | $444,965 |
| 1988 | 14.80% | $73,594 | 2010 | 12.38% | $500,040 |
| 1989 | 20.33% | $88,555 | 2011 | 6.79% | $533,971 |
| 1990 | −0.80% | $87,847 | 2012 | 11.23% | $593,951 |
| 1991 | 23.62% | $108,596 | | | |

figure 14.7

| Growth & Income | | |
|---|---|---|
| Stocks | 60% | |
| Bonds | 30% | |
| Cash | 10% | |
| **Portfolio Performance 1970–2012** | | |
| Annual Rate of Return | 10.13% | |
| Best Year | 32.11% | |
| Worst Year | −20.15% | |
| Years Positive | 37 | |
| Years Negative | 6 | |

| **Annual Portfolio Performance** | | | | | |
|---|---|---|---|---|---|
| Year | Annual Return | Growth of $10,000 | Year | Annual Return | Growth of $10,000 |
| 1970 | 4.63% | $10,463 | 1992 | 6.54% | $123,034 |
| 1971 | 15.98% | $12,135 | 1993 | 15.19% | $141,723 |
| 1972 | 14.20% | $13,858 | 1994 | 0.15% | $141,936 |
| 1973 | −10.18% | $12,447 | 1995 | 27.44% | $180,883 |
| 1974 | −14.56% | $10,635 | 1996 | 11.69% | $202,028 |
| 1975 | 29.16% | $13,736 | 1997 | 18.55% | $239,504 |
| 1976 | 20.78% | $16,591 | 1998 | 16.85% | $279,861 |
| 1977 | 2.00% | $16,922 | 1999 | 12.62% | $315,179 |
| 1978 | 8.59% | $18,376 | 2000 | 0.01% | $315,211 |
| 1979 | 13.01% | $20,767 | 2001 | −4.56% | $300,837 |
| 1980 | 18.83% | $34,677 | 2002 | −6.20% | $282,185 |
| 1981 | 0.27% | $24,744 | 2003 | 22.84% | $346,636 |
| 1982 | 24.16% | $30,722 | 2004 | 11.69% | $387,158 |
| 1983 | 15.93% | $35,616 | 2005 | 6.96% | $414,104 |
| 1984 | 11.79% | $39,815 | 2006 | 12.05% | $464,004 |
| 1985 | 32.11% | $52,600 | 2007 | 6.73% | $495,231 |
| 1986 | 23.58% | $65,003 | 2008 | −20.15% | $395,442 |
| 1987 | 4.17% | $67,713 | 2009 | 20.62% | $477,032 |
| 1988 | 15.80% | $78,412 | 2010 | 13.21% | $540,067 |
| 1989 | 21.14% | $94,988 | 2011 | 4.62% | $565,036 |
| 1990 | −2.60% | $92,519 | 2012 | 12.23% | $634,160 |
| 1991 | 24.82% | $115,482 | | | |

figure 14.8

| Moderate Growth | | |
|---|---|---|
| Stocks | 70% | |
| Bonds | 20% | |
| Cash | 10% | |
| *Portfolio Performance 1970–2012* | | |
| Annual Rate of Return | | 10.26% |
| Best Year | | 32.75% |
| Worst Year | | −24.97% |
| Years Positive | | 36 |
| Years Negative | | 7 |

| *Annual Portfolio Performance* | | | | | |
|---|---|---|---|---|---|
| **Year** | **Annual Return** | **Growth of $10,000** | **Year** | **Annual Return** | **Growth of $10,000** |
| 1970 | 3.01% | $10,301 | 1992 | 6.38% | $129,996 |
| 1971 | 16.75% | $12,026 | 1993 | 15.34% | $149,938 |
| 1972 | 15.53% | $13,894 | 1994 | 0.74% | $151,047 |
| 1973 | −11.99% | $12,228 | 1995 | 27.80% | $193,038 |
| 1974 | −17.21% | $10,124 | 1996 | 13.41% | $218,925 |
| 1975 | 32.14% | $13,378 | 1997 | 19.96% | $262,622 |
| 1976 | 21.50% | $16,254 | 1998 | 17.62% | $308,896 |
| 1977 | 2.18% | $16,608 | 1999 | 15.79% | $357,671 |
| 1978 | 9.99% | $18,267 | 2000 | −2.07% | $350,267 |
| 1979 | 15.41% | $21,082 | 2001 | −6.14% | $328,761 |
| 1980 | 22.28% | $25,779 | 2002 | −9.97% | $295,983 |
| 1981 | 0.02% | $25,784 | 2003 | 25.67% | $371,962 |
| 1982 | 21.79% | $31,403 | 2004 | 12.21% | $417,379 |
| 1983 | 17.92% | $37,030 | 2005 | 7.72% | $449,600 |
| 1984 | 11.17% | $41,166 | 2006 | 13.44% | $510,026 |
| 1985 | 32.75% | $54,648 | 2007 | 6.63% | $543,841 |
| 1986 | 24.08% | $67,808 | 2008 | −24.97% | $408,044 |
| 1987 | 5.00% | $71,198 | 2009 | 23.65% | $504,407 |
| 1988 | 16.80% | $83,159 | 2010 | 14.05% | $575,279 |
| 1989 | 21.95% | $101,413 | 2011 | 2.46% | $589,436 |
| 1990 | −4.39% | $96,961 | 2012 | 13.23% | $667,446 |
| 1991 | 26.03% | $122,200 | | | |

figure 14.9

| Growth | | |
|---|---|---|
| Stocks | 80% | |
| Bonds | 10% | |
| Cash | 10% | |
| **Portfolio Performance 1970–2012** | | |
| Annual Rate of Return | 10.36% | |
| Best Year | 35.11% | |
| Worst Year | −29.78% | |
| Years Positive | 35 | |
| Years Negative | 8 | |

| Annual Portfolio Performance | | | | | |
|---|---|---|---|---|---|
| **Year** | **Annual Return** | **Growth of $10,000** | **Year** | **Annual Return** | **Growth of $10,000** |
| 1970 | 1.39% | $10,139 | 1992 | 6.22% | $136,573 |
| 1971 | 17.52% | $11,915 | 1993 | 15.48% | $157,715 |
| 1972 | 16.87% | $13,925 | 1994 | 1.33% | $159,812 |
| 1973 | −13.81% | $12,002 | 1995 | 28.16% | $204,815 |
| 1974 | −19.87% | $9,617 | 1996 | 15.12% | $235,783 |
| 1975 | 35.11% | $12,994 | 1997 | 21.36% | $286,147 |
| 1976 | 22.22% | $15,882 | 1998 | 18.39% | $338,769 |
| 1977 | 2.35% | $16,255 | 1999 | 18.95% | $402,966 |
| 1978 | 11.40% | $18,108 | 2000 | −4.15% | $386,243 |
| 1979 | 17.81% | $21,333 | 2001 | −7.72% | $356,425 |
| 1980 | 25.73% | $26,822 | 2002 | −13.74% | $307,452 |
| 1981 | −0.23% | $26,760 | 2003 | 28.50% | $395,076 |
| 1982 | 19.42% | $31,957 | 2004 | 12.74% | $445,409 |
| 1983 | 19.91% | $38,319 | 2005 | 8.48% | $483,179 |
| 1984 | 10.54% | $42,358 | 2006 | 14.82% | $554,787 |
| 1985 | 33.39% | $56,502 | 2007 | 6.54% | $591,070 |
| 1986 | 24.58% | $70,390 | 2008 | −29.78% | $415,049 |
| 1987 | 5.83% | $74,493 | 2009 | 26.67% | $525,767 |
| 1988 | 17.80% | $87,753 | 2010 | 14.89% | $604,038 |
| 1989 | 22.76% | $107,726 | 2011 | 0.30% | $605,841 |
| 1990 | −6.19% | $101,058 | 2012 | 14.24% | $692,086 |
| 1991 | 27.23% | $128,576 | | | |

figure 14.10

| Aggressive Growth | | |
|---|---|---|
| Stocks | 90% | |
| Bonds | 0% | |
| Cash | 10% | |

| Portfolio Performance 1970–2012 | |
|---|---|
| Annual Rate of Return | 10.41% |
| Best Year | 38.09% |
| Worst Year | −34.59% |
| Years Positive | 33 |
| Years Negative | 10 |

| Annual Portfolio Performance | | | | | |
|---|---|---|---|---|---|
| Year | Annual Return | Growth of $10,000 | Year | Annual Return | Growth of $10,000 |
| 1970 | −0.24% | $9,976 | 1992 | 6.06% | $142,808 |
| 1971 | 18.29% | $11,801 | 1993 | 15.63% | $165,128 |
| 1972 | 18.20% | $13,948 | 1994 | 1.92% | $168,299 |
| 1973 | −15.62% | $11,770 | 1995 | 28.52% | $216,298 |
| 1974 | −22.53% | $9,118 | 1996 | 16.83% | $252,701 |
| 1975 | 38.09% | $12,591 | 1997 | 22.76% | $310,215 |
| 1976 | 22.95% | $15,481 | 1998 | 19.15% | $369,621 |
| 1977 | 2.52% | $15,871 | 1999 | 22.11% | $451,345 |
| 1978 | 12.81% | $17,904 | 2000 | −6.23% | $423,226 |
| 1979 | 20.21% | $21,522 | 2001 | −9.29% | $383,908 |
| 1980 | 29.19% | $27,804 | 2002 | −17.52% | $316,647 |
| 1981 | −0.48% | $27,671 | 2003 | 31.34% | $415,885 |
| 1982 | 17.06% | $32,391 | 2004 | 13.27% | $471,073 |
| 1983 | 21.90% | $39,485 | 2005 | 9.24% | $514,600 |
| 1984 | 9.92% | $43,402 | 2006 | 16.21% | $598,016 |
| 1985 | 34.04% | $58,176 | 2007 | 6.44% | $636,529 |
| 1986 | 25.08% | $72,767 | 2008 | −34.59% | $416,353 |
| 1987 | 6.66% | $77,613 | 2009 | 29.70% | $539,864 |
| 1988 | 18.80% | $92,204 | 2010 | 15.72% | $624,749 |
| 1989 | 23.57% | $113,937 | 2011 | −1.86% | $613,105 |
| 1990 | −7.99% | $104,833 | 2012 | 15.24% | $706,521 |
| 1991 | 28.44% | $134,648 | | | |

figure 14.11

| Ultra-Aggressive Growth | | |
|---|---|---|
| Stocks | 100% | |
| Bonds | 0% | |
| Cash | 0% | |
| Portfolio Performance 1970–2012 | | |
| Annual Rate of Return | 10.80% | |
| Best Year | 41.68% | |
| Worst Year | −38.61% | |
| Years Positive | 33 | |
| Years Negative | 10 | |

| Annual Portfolio Performance | | | | | |
|---|---|---|---|---|---|
| Year | Annual Return | Growth of $10,000 | Year | Annual Return | Growth of $10,000 |
| 1970 | −0.99% | $9,901 | 1992 | 6.35% | $154,867 |
| 1971 | 19.83% | $11,864 | 1993 | 17.04% | $181,257 |
| 1972 | 19.79% | $14,212 | 1994 | 1.70% | $184,338 |
| 1973 | −18.13% | $11,636 | 1995 | 31.07% | $241,612 |
| 1974 | −25.92% | $8,620 | 1996 | 18.12% | $285,392 |
| 1975 | 41.68% | $12,212 | 1997 | 24.71% | $355,913 |
| 1976 | 24.93% | $15,257 | 1998 | 20.74% | $429,729 |
| 1977 | 2.23% | $15,597 | 1999 | 24.05% | $533,079 |
| 1978 | 13.43% | $17,692 | 2000 | −7.58% | $492,671 |
| 1979 | 21.30% | $21,460 | 2001 | −10.75% | $439,709 |
| 1980 | 31.18% | $28,151 | 2002 | −19.65% | $353,306 |
| 1981 | −2.16% | $27,543 | 2003 | 34.70% | $475,903 |
| 1982 | 17.78% | $32,441 | 2004 | 14.62% | $545,481 |
| 1983 | 23.36% | $40,019 | 2005 | 9.90% | $599,483 |
| 1984 | 9.93% | $43,993 | 2006 | 17.44% | $704,033 |
| 1985 | 36.96% | $60,252 | 2007 | 6.63% | $750,710 |
| 1986 | 27.18% | $76,629 | 2008 | −38.61% | $460,861 |
| 1987 | 6.79% | $81,832 | 2009 | 32.98% | $612,865 |
| 1988 | 20.19% | $98,354 | 2010 | 17.46% | $719,840 |
| 1989 | 25.26% | $123,198 | 2011 | −2.08% | $704,886 |
| 1990 | −9.75% | $111,186 | 2012 | 16.92% | $824,149 |
| 1991 | 30.97% | $145,620 | | | |

figure 14.12

# 15

# DIVORCE YOUR STOCK

RETIREMENT DECISION #12: WHAT SHOULD
I DO IF THE BULK OF MY PORTFOLIO IS
INVESTED IN ONE OR TWO STOCKS?

L inda Thompson, like many investors at retirement, did not have a complex investment portfolio. She invested her entire retirement plan in her
employer's stock, a large, successful Fortune 500 company. Her bet paid
off. The company stock outperformed the stock mutual funds offered in her
retirement plan. In fact, she became wealthy largely due to many years of sizable returns from her employer's stock.
In 1999, for example, her $250,000
portfolio went up 58 percent and her
balance climbed to $394,175. In 2000,
while the stock market fumbled, her
stock returned 87 percent, and her nest
egg almost doubled to $743,532. At the
end of 2000, she assumed she finally
had enough money to retire at age
62. Based on her calculations, she was
confident she could withdraw $35,000
per year from her nest egg to supplement the $15,000 of Social Security
she would receive. At retirement, she
rolled her company stock into her IRA.

Linda loved her company and was
confident its future prospects would
generate returns similar to those she'd

| Enron Corp. | | |
|---|---|---|
| Year | Stock Price* | Annual Price Change |
| 1994 | $15.25 | N/A |
| 1995 | $19.06 | 25% |
| 1996 | $21.56 | 13% |
| 1997 | $20.78 | –4% |
| 1998 | $28.53 | 37% |
| 1999 | $44.38 | 56% |
| 2000 | $83.13 | 87% |
| 2001 | $0.60 | –99% |
| 2002 | $0.06 | –90% |
| 2003 | $0.03 | –55% |

*Price on last trading day of each year
Source: www.bigcharts.com

figure 15.1

enjoyed in the past. At retirement, however, she faced a difficult decision. Should she reduce the amount of her company's stock she held, sell all of the stock, or just continue holding it in hopes of continued off-the-charts performance? Linda was married to her company stock and emotionally couldn't divorce an investment that had rewarded her so greatly. Divorce would simply be too devastating. How could she sell a stock that was the primary reason she could retire early? Think about it, with just one more year like 1999 or 2000, she would have more than $1 million. Greed got the best of her, and she decided to continue her single-stock strategy and simply hold on.

Tragedy struck in 2001, however, and the unimaginable happened as Linda's beloved company, Enron, dropped in value by more than 99 percent. As it began its descent from $90 per share to 5 cents, she was convinced it would rebound and continued her hold-at-all-costs strategy (Figure 15.1). The large nest egg that was ready and primed to support Linda for the next thirty years was worth a measly $7,435 when the dust cleared at the end of 2001, and Linda was forced to return to the workforce and attempt to rebuild an entire nest egg.

In hindsight you might ask, "Why didn't she sell her shares at retirement?" Usually the answer can be summarized in one word: greed. Most people want to squeeze every last drop of return from their stock before selling. No one wants to sell too soon and miss out on the next 20 percent run-up. Before you cast stones at Linda, are you certain you wouldn't have acted the same way?

Let's look at Linda's line of thinking at the end of 2000. Enron ended 2000 at $83 per share. Earlier in 2000, however, it had hit $90. Linda figured she'd just take a wait-and-see approach and see if it could climb back to $90. At $90, she told herself, she'd have almost $1 million, and she'd begin selling her shares. At the start of February 2001, the price was still hovering around $80. Over the next few months, though, the stock fell to $55. No big deal, Linda thought. She had experienced volatility like this several times over many years of owning Enron and was confident it would rebound. It always had in the past. By midyear, however, Linda began to get worried. The stock dropped into the $40s, trading at nearly half of its value at the beginning of the year. She couldn't possibly sell it now; surely it would rebound, she thought, and she didn't want to miss out on it. Over the second half of 2001, the stock made a quick descent to $4 per share. Linda's retirement savings was now down to $35,776. Selling at $4 wouldn't do much for her retirement. She had missed the boat.

Linda was not the only one affected by the Enron fiasco—62 percent of the money in Enron's 401(k) program was invested in the company's stock.[1]

## What Is the Maximum a Retiree Should Invest in Any One Company?

Retirement is not the time to gamble on the performance of one company, no matter how good its prospects may be. What is the maximum percentage of your portfolio that should be invested in a single stock position during retirement? At the bare minimum, you should follow the diversification laws required of mutual funds; diversified mutual funds cannot invest any more than 5 percent of their overall portfolios into any one company.[2] Experts agree that most retirees and pre-retirees, who have little time to make back big losses, should generally have no more than 5 percent of their portfolio invested in any one stock.

Where would Linda be now if she had followed this simple rule? Even if she had followed an aggressive strategy and invested in a portfolio composed entirely of stocks, putting 95 percent of her money into the Vanguard S&P 500 Index Fund and leaving 5 percent of her money in Enron, she would have ended 2001 with $622,000 and still been in a position to reach her retirement goals; $622,000 is a far cry from $7,435.

## What Are the Chances of Your Stock Dropping?

If you are thinking that the likelihood of an Enron situation occurring with your favorite company is impossible, consider the fate of shareholders of Citigroup, Bank of America, AIG, and Sprint Nextel. During the 2008–2009 stock market drop, stock owners of these companies watched their beloved stocks drop in a similar fashion to Enron. Each of these companies seemed invincible at one time. Okay, maybe you're right, maybe the chances of encountering a monstrous Enron drop are very low. However, even the largest, most solid companies experience dramatic stock price volatility at times. During the past five years, 235 stocks in the S&P 500, composed of our nation's biggest companies, have dropped more than 40 percent during a three-month period.[3] If history repeats and you own one of these "unshakable" stocks, you run a 47 percent chance of seeing a price drop of almost one-half at some point within a three-month period in the next five years. Any way you slice it, this is far too much risk to take with money that must support you for the next thirty to forty years.

If a large portion of your nest egg is tied up in one or two companies, ask yourself how a 25, 50, 75, or 100 percent price drop would impinge on your retirement plan. Run your retirement analysis with these assumptions and see what the outcome is. To make up these disastrous losses, you could be forced to go back to work for a few more years, or perhaps a few more decades. If you have the lion's share of your money tied up in one company's stock, you're taking huge risks with your future.

A single stock position can make you very wealthy indeed if your company does well. You must acknowledge, however, that your stock can also drop abruptly and destroy years of disciplined savings and accumulation—all in a shockingly short period of time. Recognize that individual stocks can easily swing up or down by 50 percent or more in a given year. You don't have to look any further than the daily newspaper to find examples of companies that have done a nosedive, leaving many retirees with nest eggs that will no longer see them through retirement.

Don't fool yourself into thinking that your big blue-chip stock can't fall. Consider the price drops of many well-known companies in Figure 15.2. This

### Even Big Blue-Chip Companies Can Fall

#### Returns from High to Low (2002–2012)

| Company | % |
| --- | --- |
| AIG | −99% |
| Citigroup | −95% |
| Sprint Nextel | −93% |
| Bank of America | −90% |
| Ford | −86% |
| Motorola | −83% |
| Alcoa | −82% |
| Sony | −79% |
| Morgan Stanley | −79% |
| Halliburton | −71% |
| Corning | −65% |
| Apple | −57% |
| Intel | −54% |
| Microsoft | −48% |
| AT&T | −43% |
| Procter & Gamble | −36% |

Source: www.bigcharts.com

figure 15.2

chart shows how far many solid U.S. companies have fallen from their ten-year highs to their subsequent ten-year lows. Consider this: Of the 13,700 stocks listed in the Morningstar database 7,151 of them fell by 40 percent or more at some point in the past five years. That means if you buy a stock, there is more than a 50 percent chance it will drop by 40 percent or more at some point in the next five years. It is clear to see why devoting a large portion of your retirement nest egg to just one or two stocks could be devastating. Of course, there is still potential for price drops if you diversify into a stock mutual fund, though most funds are composed of one hundred or more companies. If a few are falling, others will probably be climbing, and the impact of the troubled stocks is offset.

### What Are the Chances Your Stock Will Drop?

- 117 of the 273 (43 percent) largest U.S. stocks experienced a price drop of 40 percent or more over a three-month period at one point during the past five years.
- 305 of the 603 (51 percent) available U.S. mid-cap stocks experienced a price drop of 40 percent or more over a three-month period at one point during the past five years.
- 2,267 of the 3,462 (66 percent) available U.S. small-cap stocks experienced a price drop of 40 percent or more over a three-month period at one point during the past five years.
- 1,135 of the 3,340 (34 percent) available international stocks experienced a price drop of 40 percent or more over a three-month period at one point during the past five years.
- 7,151 of the 13,700 (52 percent) stocks listed in the Morningstar database experienced a price drop of 40 percent or more over a three-month period at one point during the past five years.[4]

## Why So Much Company Stock?

It's easy to understand the motivation of some investors who rely heavily on the success of one stock. If the stock has performed well in the past, and as an employee of the company you can see its prospects for continued growth are good, then why not ride that train all the way to prosperity? It does happen. There are many examples of companies that have brought riches to their stockholders. Apple is a great example. One thousand dollars invested in Apple on April 1, 2003, had grown to over $75,000 by the end of

2012 (average annual return of 56 percent). However, as we've seen, there are also many examples of once-successful companies going bust. If you can reach your retirement goals without taking the risk, then why make such a big gamble on a single stock when a steep decline could be so disastrous for you?

While you are employed, your company wants you to invest in its stock. If employees own company stock, they are more likely to work hard to help the company be profitable. Also, it is cost-effective for the company to provide matching contributions in company stock rather than in cash. What's good for the company, though, may not be good for you, the person who stands to be affected most adversely if the stock declines.

> Twenty percent of the money invested in 401(k) plans that offer company stock as an investment option is invested in company stock.[5]

Knowing these risks, what are other reasons some employees have virtually all of their retirement money invested in company stock? Some of it has simply to do with loyalty. Employees want to show support for their company and reinforce their emotional ties by buying stock. As long as those ties stay strong, the stock is seldom sold. Many of these loyal employees also believe "their" company will never go through a major downturn.

Many 401(k) plans offer company stock as one of the investment options available to plan participants. Not having a great deal of information on other investment choices leads employees to simply buy company stock as a default.

Yet another way for employees to accumulate company stock is the advent of stock options. Some companies may also offer stock purchase plans, which allow investors the ability to buy company stock at discounts as high as 20 percent. While this is often a pretty good deal, many employees end up with these discounted shares along with the shares in their 401(k) plan and more shares given to them through matching contributions. In the end, they find themselves with too much of their retirement portfolio tied up in their company. Fortunately, at retirement you can diversify the money invested in your employer's stock in most cases without restriction.

# Getting Out: Exit Strategies

If you have too much invested in one stock, it's time to develop an exit strategy. You can approach this in a couple of ways: sell all shares at once, or sell shares over a period of time. Before doing anything, though, get a feel for where the stock is trading in comparison to where it has been trading over the past ten years. Bigcharts.com is a good place to do this. Often, looking at a company's historic stock prices reveals that the current stock price, while maybe not at an all-time high, is trading at a reasonably high price level. This will help you with your decision to sell your shares. For example, if the price of your stock is $80 per share and it's only been above $80 for one of the past ten years, then it may not be a bad time to sell and diversify even if the stock's price is down from its recent high of $90/share. In this situation, too often people say, "I'll sell and diversify when it gets back to $90." If you need to diversify and you can sell at a reasonable price, I'd suggest you do so. In this example, if you do sell at $80 and diversify and your stock does go back up to $90, it's highly likely your diversified portfolio will also go up over the same period and you won't have entirely missed out on the gain. If you own a concentrated stock position in a non-retirement account, you will have to look beyond just the price and also examine the tax consequences of selling the stock.

## *Stop-Loss*

If you are unwilling to sell your large stock position now, consider a stop-loss strategy where you pick a price at which to sell your stock. First of all, run several different retirement projections to see what your retirement would look like if the value of your stock is reduced by 10, 20, 30, 40, and 50 percent. If you can still retire with the lifestyle you want if your stock falls 20 percent but not if it drops 30 percent, then you can set a stop-loss at the 20 percent mark. Let's return to Linda in our Enron example. At the end of 2000 with Enron trading at $83.13 per share, Linda was sitting on $743,532 of Enron stock. She could have projected her retirement assuming Enron lost 10 percent ($669,178), 20 percent ($594,825), 30 percent ($520,472), and so on. After reviewing these scenarios she could have determined the point at which she could no longer reach her retirement goals. If she determined that the breaking point was at $594,825 (a 20 percent drop), she could set a stop-loss at this level, which for her would have been

$66.50/share. When the stock hit $66.50, she would have sold, diversified, and never looked back. If Linda had owned Enron in a brokerage account instead of her 401(k), she could have entered a standing automatic stop-loss order at $66.50. This way her shares would automatically get sold when Enron hit $66.50. She wouldn't have had to make a call or sign into her brokerage account to place the order to sell. Using this stop-loss strategy, Linda would have walked away with $594,825 and salvaged her retirement.

## Shares in an IRA

If you own shares in a retirement account and your stock is trading at a reasonably high price relative to its historical price and relative to the price at which your shares were purchased, don't hesitate; sell it all at once and diversify. In hindsight, this is exactly what Linda should have done with her Enron shares. At the end of 2000, Enron was trading at $83 per share. In the prior ten years, the stock had only been priced that high for a few months earlier in 2000. Without hesitation, she should have sold all of her shares and diversified.

If you are preparing to retire and want to sell your company's shares in a 401(k) plan, sell the shares in the plan before you transfer the money to an IRA. This will allow you to avoid transaction costs. If you sell the shares after they have been rolled into your IRA, your brokerage firm will charge you a commission to sell your shares.

What if the stock is priced a lot lower than you'd like it to be? It still may make sense to sell it. Ask yourself the following questions:

- "If I hold on to the stock, how high could it realistically go over the next twelve months?"
- "If I hold on to the stock, how low could it drop over the next twelve months?"
- "If I sold the stock and reinvested the money into diversified investments, how much appreciation is reasonable to expect?"

If, for example, you think your stock has the potential to go up 10 percent over the next twelve months, and you think the diversified investments you could purchase would also climb 10 percent, then you might as well sell and diversify. In either case, the return potential is the same. The difference is the diversified portfolio can deliver the return with much less risk. In our example, although Enron delivered some off-the-chart returns in 1999 and 2000, it would have been reasonable to conclude that it might climb another 10 percent in 2001 (10 percent being approximately the average annual return of the stock market since 1925). However, had Linda asked herself the previous three questions, she would have sold her Enron shares and diversified.

The other alternative is to sell a portion of your holdings on a periodic basis over a period of months or years. How would Linda have made out using this strategy with her Enron stock? Let's say she held 8,944 shares of Enron at the end of 1999 and assume she decided to sell one-third of her stake each year for the next three years. She would have sold 2,981 shares the first year and diversified $247,795. She would have sold the next block of Enron one year later at 60 cents per share for $1,788 and the final block a year later at 3 cents for $92. These results still don't sound very appealing, but still with almost a quarter of a million dollars, Linda could salvage some kind of retirement. For most stocks, this may not be a bad approach. Enron simply showed us the worst-case scenario. She would have done much better had she sold out over a period of months, not years. The key to selling over a period of time is being disciplined, because in a year's time it is easy to get caught up in the excitement that may surround your stock. Greed could set in and your diversification plan put on hold.

## Shares in a Non-Retirement Account
In cases in which the stock is owned in a taxable account, selling may be a little trickier. The need for diversification is just as important, but you may have to pay capital gains taxes when you sell (Figure 15.3). In most cases, it still makes sense to sell your shares as previously discussed, pay the taxes, and diversify.

However, if you own a huge position of stock with extremely low-basis shares (the price was very low when shares were purchased), you should consider a few additional strategies before selling that can help you diversify while at the same time minimizing capital gains taxes. Following are explanations of some of these strategies.

### Charitable Remainder Trusts
You can contribute your company stock to a charitable remainder trust (CRT). The trustee (whom you can appoint as yourself) can sell the stock

| Capital Gains Tax Rates | | |
|---|---|---|
| **Long-Term Capital Gains** (Holding period longer than one year) | **2012** | **2013** |
| 10-15% tax brackets | 0% | 0% |
| 25-35% tax brackets | 15% | 15% |
| 39.6% tax bracket | 15% | 20% |
| **Short-Term Capital Gains** (Holding period less than one year) | **2012** | **2013** |
| All tax brackets | Income Tax Rates | Income Tax Rates |
| **Long-Term and Short-Term Capital Gains** | 2012 | 2013 |
| The medicare surtax on net investment income applies to those with AGI exceeding $200,000 for singles and $250,000 for married couples. | 0% | 3.8% |

figure 15.3

and reinvest it in a diversified portfolio of your choice. By making a contribution to a CRT, you will receive an immediate tax credit, avoid all capital gains taxes on the prior appreciation of the stock, and obtain tax-free growth on the investments in the portfolio in the future.

As an income beneficiary, you will receive a lifetime of income from the diversified portfolio. The downside of this strategy is that, outside of the lifetime income you receive, you give up the right to tap into assets held in the trust. Upon death (typically the death of both you and your spouse), the assets will revert to the charity you have chosen, not to your heirs. This strategy is usually used in conjunction with a second-to-die life insurance policy, which provides for your heirs upon the deaths of both you and your spouse.

## Margin or Hypothecation Loan

You can use your stock as collateral to secure a low-interest loan or to obtain margin to purchase other securities. Think of this like a home equity line; however, instead of using your home equity to obtain a loan, you are using your stock position as collateral to obtain a loan. The proceeds of the loan can be invested in a diversified portfolio of stocks and bonds, reducing the risk of being invested in just one company. For instance, if you owned $100,000 of IBM stock, you could obtain a loan against it for $100,000 and use the money to buy a diversified portfolio of securities. Now your overall portfolio will be composed of 50 percent diversified investments and 50 percent IBM stock. While you will be required to pay interest on the loan, you will avoid paying capital gains taxes and can reduce your portfolio risk considerably.

## Exchange Funds

In an exchange fund, a group of investors deposit their low-basis stock shares into a limited partnership in exchange for a partnership interest in the fund. This is done tax-free with no capital gains taxes.

As a limited partner, you will have a partnership interest in all the stocks held in the fund and, thus, obtain immediate diversification. Because exchange funds are managed passively, meaning not a lot of buying and selling occurs, the only companies accepted into the fund are those that meet specific requirements crucial to the fund's performance. Consequently, not all stocks are accepted. If you own an obscure company, it will be more difficult or even impossible to find an exchange fund that will accept your shares. When the limited partnership interest is redeemed, usually after at least seven years, the investor will receive a diversified portfolio of stocks without having to pay capital gains taxes in the process.

While this strategy works in certain situations, investors must be able to meet strict requirements to participate, such as an initial stock deposit of at least $1 million and a net worth of $5 million.

## Zero Premium Collars

There are several option strategies you can use to protect yourself from loss if your company stock nosedives. One strategy, referred to as a zero premium collar, uses "put" and "call" options to protect an investor from losing too much if the stock turns sour. This strategy is helpful to an investor who is not interested in selling the stock due to potential tax implications but is at too much risk if the stock drops.

To initiate this strategy, an investor sells a call option on his stock and uses the income to buy a put option. The put option protects the stock position on the downside, while the call option provides a source of income to pay for the put. However, protection strategies, like the "collar," are not available for all stocks.

•••

If your portfolio is heavily dependent on the success of one company, it's time to seriously rethink your strategy—if that company falters, it can jeopardize your ability to reach your retirement goals. Just ask those people holding Enron stock who once thought they would be wealthy in retirement and now are resigned to working far beyond age 65.

# 16

# READY...SET...BUY

## RETIREMENT DECISION #13: WHAT CRITERIA SHOULD I USE TO IDENTIFY THE BEST INVESTMENTS?

You've decided how to allocate your money among stocks, bonds, and cash (Step 1) and how to diversify your portfolio among the different segments of the stock and bond markets (Step 2). It's now time to buy the investments (Step 3). Most investors skip the first two steps and go right to Step 3. This is a big mistake. Determining which investments to purchase in each asset class is now your task at hand (see the sample portfolio in Figure 16.1).

| Sample Portfolio 60% Stocks, 35% Bonds, 5% Cash | | |
|---|---|---|
| **Asset Class** | **Target Allocation** | **Investment Choice** |
| Large-Cap U.S. Growth Stocks | 15% | _____ |
| Large-Cap U.S. Value Stocks | 15% | _____ |
| Mid-Cap U.S. Growth Stocks | 6% | _____ |
| Mid-Cap U.S. Value Stocks | 6% | _____ |
| Small-Cap U.S. Growth Stocks | 3% | _____ |
| Small-Cap U.S. Value Stocks | 3% | _____ |
| International Growth Stocks | 6% | _____ |
| International Value Stocks | 6% | _____ |
| Corporate Bonds | 14% | _____ |
| Government Bonds | 14% | _____ |
| International Bonds | 7% | _____ |
| Cash | 5% | _____ |

figure 16.1

You'll first need search criteria to help you screen the thousands of options available to identify the best ones for your portfolio. Think of this process as pouring thousands of investments into a big funnel (Figure 16.3) to narrow your choices down to a short list of finalists representing the best of the best. You can search for and buy investments on your own or you can hire a financial advisor to do it for you.

## Want a Million More? The 1 Percent Difference

You may ask, "What does it really matter if my investments aren't among the best?" Owning poor investments could mean having to endure unnecessary volatility, high expenses, poor or inconsistent performance, and even a reduction in retirement income. Owning better-than-average investments could put thousands or even hundreds of thousands of extra dollars in your pocket!

Let's oversimplify and assume at retirement you invested $500,000 into just one mutual fund that earned an 8 percent annual return. Your coworker, Dan, did a little extra legwork and found a good manager who squeezed out an extra percentage point every year and returned 9 percent annually. Big deal, you might say, what's one percentage point? Well, after thirty years in retirement, your buddy Dan is a whole lot richer than you. Your $500,000 investment grew to a little over $5 million. Not bad, until you compare that sum to Dan's kitty of $6.6 million. (That's 32 percent more than yours.) One percentage point of extra yearly return earned Dan an additional $1.6 million. Getting an extra percentage or two could have a big impact on the twenty-five to thirty years you spend in retirement.

How do the investments you own stack up? Are they above-average performers? If not, you may want to make some changes.

## Can You Make the Grade?

Imagine for a moment that you are a student in an investment class your company is offering. The instructor asks you to come to the front of the class and explain (1) the criteria you used to determine which investments to buy in your current investment portfolio, and (2) how you decide when it's time to sell an investment you own. Your grade on this assignment will depend on how persuasive your argument is that your strategy for identifying good investments will produce solid, above-average results. If you use a financial advisor, you can bring him or her up to the front of the class with you. (Surprisingly, many advisors themselves wouldn't do very well on this assignment.) Are you a little nervous, or are you confident in the strategy you are following?

As you can guess, most investors would get an F on this assignment. What would your grade be? The following are likely the most common strategies we would hear in class: "I buy the investments with the best returns last year." "I asked a coworker how to invest my 401(k) money." "My doctor and my brother-in-law give me hot stock tips." Your financial advisor might say, "I chose an investment for my client that paid me a high commission!" Unfortunately, these approaches don't often reveal the best investments available.

How well you choose your investments has a far greater impact on your life than getting an A or F on an assignment. It literally could mean the difference between being able to retire…and not!

## Do It Yourself or Delegate?

Before we start to examine the investment selection process, you need to make a couple of decisions.

First, are you a "do-it-yourselfer" or a "delegator"? Do-it-yourselfers can use the criteria outlined in this chapter to conduct an intense hands-on search to filter out the best investments. Delegators can take the search criteria to their financial advisors and request that their advisor identify the best investments available for them. In either case, screening for the best investments is a must.

Second, you must decide whether you want to build your portfolio using individual stocks and bonds or outsource the day-to-day money-management responsibilities to professional money managers, such as mutual fund managers. Building and managing a large, diversified portfolio of individual stocks is difficult. I recommend that you don't attempt it. You're not equipped to do it, and most financial advisors aren't equipped to do it either. The stakes are high. You want to entrust your retirement savings only to the best money managers available to you.

This chapter will focus on how to find the best money managers. By turning the daily management responsibilities over to professionals rather than picking stocks yourself or having your advisor do it, you will likely vastly improve your investment performance.

## Ways to Obtain Professional Money Management

There are several ways to hire a professional money manager. In fact, you've probably already hired many managers to manage your money without even knowing it. By investing in a mutual fund, variable annuity, variable life insurance policy, or a separately managed account (SMA) program, you are in reality hiring a money manager. If you have money in a 401(k) invested in mutual funds, you have hired several money managers. (For more detail on the different types of money-management vehicles, see "Understanding Your Money Management Choices" later in this chapter.)

> There are 29,176 mutual funds (all share classes) available to the public (December 31, 2012).[2]

Hiring a good manager may seem like a daunting task, considering the fact that there are so many from which to choose. For example, there are now 29,176 mutual funds available![1] Sound overwhelming? Be assured that with sound search criteria the process actually becomes quite easy.

Once we outline the search process, we will discuss some resources you can use to help you conduct your own money manager search, view a list of funds that have already been screened, and evaluate the funds you own. Regardless of the type of financial products you choose (i.e., mutual funds, variable annuities, variable life insurance, or SMAs), the process of evaluating money managers is the same.

## Forget Short-Term Results

Finding good money managers is easy, right? All we have to do is look at who's on the top-performing lists that dominate the financial media. Surely, last year's winners must be run by smart folks. These managers may know what they're doing, but chances are they won't continue to outperform. Remember, buying last year's winners is a loser's strategy. Often, if a fund is volatile enough to top a winners list one year, it's volatile enough to lead a losers list the next year. In a nutshell, short-term performance numbers are not effective predictors of future results.

Let's look at an example by considering Joan Gibson's investment portfolio results. On January 1, 2008, Joan decided to divide her $100,000 equally among the ten top-performing funds from the previous year (2007). How did she do in 2008? After investing for just one year, Joan's initial $100,000 investment was worth a meager $36,253, a loss of $63,747, or 64 percent. Figure 16.2 outlines her results.[3]

Although investors rarely go to the extreme of purchasing ten funds with last year's best returns, as Joan did, you would be surprised how often people use this method to choose their investments. You have likely seen a coworker handle his or her 401(k) fund selection this way. He or she goes down the list of the ten to twenty options available and chooses the funds with the best performance last year. Following this method of investment selection is perfect if you want to buy high and sell low, but that's a sure way to lose money. So remember, short-term returns should not be among your priority criterion for selecting a solid money manager.

| Hypothetical $100,000 Investment | | | |
|---|---|---|---|
| $10,000 investment in each fund January 2, 2008 | | | |
| Fund | 2007 Return | 2008 Return | Value 12/31/08 |
| Direxion Commodity Bull 2X Inv | 88% | –77% | $2,306 |
| iPath MSCI India Index ETN | 86% | –68% | $3,235 |
| Market Vectors Steel ETF | 84% | –64% | $3,613 |
| Direxion Latin America Bull 2X Inv | 84% | –86% | $1,421 |
| CGM Focus | 80% | –48% | $5,182 |
| iShares MSCI Brazil Index | 75% | –54% | $4,563 |
| AIM China C | 74% | –52% | $4,760 |
| Aberdeen China Opportunities R | 73% | –56% | $4,375 |
| Matthews China | 70% | –49% | $5,105 |
| ProFunds UltraEmerging Markets Svc | 68% | –83% | $1,693 |
| | | | $36,253 |

*figure 16.2*

# Finding the Best of the Best

I conducted a study and found that only 41 percent of mutual funds outperform their respective benchmark indexes (Figure 16.4).[4] Figure 16.4. If your fund can't beat its benchmark index, then the manager isn't providing any added value. In this case you might as well buy an index fund. The following search process will help you identify the top money managers in hopes of finding the managers that have the greatest chance of being in that 41 percent that provides outperformance. You can also use the same criteria to analyze the investments you currently own. If you find you own some below-average, poor-performing investments, you'll want to replace them. If your advisor has recommended below-average performers, it may be time to *fire* him or her and find a new advisor (see Chapter 3). At the very least, armed with the following search criteria, you will be able to hold your advisor accountable by providing a standard by which to measure his or her investment recommendations.

Let me walk you through the process of uncovering the best and most consistent money managers, as I did for Janet Reese, a recent retiree. She accumulated $350,000 in her employer's 401(k) plan and decided to roll the money into her IRA when she retired. We settled on the asset-allocation model outlined in Figure 16.1 and decided to use mutual funds. We then followed a simple process to find the best mutual fund money managers for each segment of her portfolio.

We started the search by looking for a fund that invests in large-cap U.S. growth companies. We wanted to allocate $52,500 (15 percent) to this part of the stock market. Janet wanted to find a money manager who consistently ranked at the top of this asset category.

To locate the top funds in this category, we dumped all 29,176 mutual funds into a "funnel" to narrow them down to just a handful that are among the best and most consistent (Figure 16.3). Following are the nine screens we used to create a short list of top-notch managers using the Morningstar Principia database (December 31, 2012).

# Conducting a Money Manager Search

## *Screen 1: Asset Category*

We began our investment manager search by identifying the asset category. The asset category is simply the part of the market you are searching, such as large-company growth funds or small-company growth funds. A fund's category is determined by the types of companies in which it invests. Categories are outlined in Chapter 13. For example, if we started a search looking for the best large-cap growth funds (category), we would immediately narrow the field from 29,176 funds to 1,802.

## Screen 2: Manager Tenure

When you buy a fund, make sure your money manager has some experience under his or her belt. You don't want a new manager cutting teeth and learning how to invest with your money. Your retirement money is your future, and you don't want someone "practicing" with it.

Preferably the manager you choose should have at least ten years' experience. This will ensure that he or she has been face-to-face with a couple of down markets and has gained experience handling adverse environments. Of the 1,802 large-company growth funds in Janet's search, only 540 of

> The average mutual fund manager today has only five years of experience.[5]

the funds have managers who have been with the fund for ten or more years. The average mutual fund manager today has only five years of experience managing a fund.[5]

## Screen 3: Performance vs. Peers (Over One, Three, Five, Ten, and Fifteen Years)

Performance vs. peers is an apples-to-apples comparison of returns for all funds in a respective investment category. It doesn't matter how a small-company stock fund compares with a fund that buys international stocks, but it does matter how it compares with all other small-company stock funds. What we want to know is how a fund ranks when stacked up against its peers during the past one, three, five, ten, and fifteen years. Is it above or below average? If your fund has been consistently below average, you may want to consider making a change. Often, funds that make our short list will rank in the top 10 percent of their asset class for all five periods. This isn't always possible but is preferable. Long-term performance comparisons will help you identify funds with the most consistent long-term returns.

Of the 540 large-company growth funds we identified for Janet with seasoned money managers, only seventy-one pass this one-, three-, five-, ten-, and fifteen-year performance screen.

## Screen 4: Performance in Bear Markets

How did the manager do when the market was falling? Checking the fund's performance versus its peers during *down* years will give you an indication of what to expect if the market heads south. If the fund ranks toward the top of its category in bear markets, the manager will likely narrow your losses during future negative years.

When you buy a fund, you should also know what the worst-case scenario is. Look for the fund's worst year in the past ten years. Could you have endured the manager's performance during the bad years? If not, don't buy the fund. For example, a fund that made the top of our list in a fund search we recently conducted had three years in which it lost money between 2002 and 2012, the worst being a return of –37 percent. Could you handle that?

Of the seventy-one large-company growth funds we identified with above-average one-, three-, five-, ten-, and fifteen-year performance, twenty-six pass this bear market performance test.

## Screen 5: Check Sales Charges and Management Expenses

Sales charges and management expenses need to be examined closely and can have a substantial impact on your performance. In a recent study I conducted, I discovered that low-cost funds produced returns 1 percent better per year than their high-cost counterparts. High built-in management expenses and sales charges can drag heavily on performance. Expenses should be, at the least, below the asset category average and preferably below 1 percent per year. Avoid funds with front- or back-end sales charges. In Chapter 18, we will examine the costs of different financial products in detail. No-load or load-waived investments could save you a lot of money. *Do not* purchase an investment until you've read Chapter 18 and see the expenses associated with the financial products you buy.

Of the twenty-six large-company growth funds that passed our bear market screen, only twenty-three have built-in expenses less than the 1.27 percent category average. And only eighteen are no-load funds. So, only eighteen of the 1,802 large-company growth funds we started out with have survived every filter to this point.

## Screen 6: Size and Style Discipline

It is important to buy a fund that is true to its investment size and style discipline. This means if you buy a large-company growth fund, you can be assured it will still be a large-company growth fund in five or ten years. If the manager begins buying small companies or international stocks or moves from growth to value stocks, it will change your overall allocation and throw your portfolio out of alignment. The manager is hired as a specialist and to manage money in only one part of the market. You should make sure your manager sticks to his or her guns. Only thirteen out of our eighteen funds have proven consistent to their size and style disciplines.

## Screen 7: Alpha

Alpha is a statistical number that measures a fund's actual return to its expected return. It's a reflection of the skill of the manager. A positive alpha indicates that the fund performed better than expected based on the risk it takes. A negative alpha means the fund underperformed its expected return. If a fund has an alpha of 1 percent, it means the manager provided one percentage point more yearly return than expected. The higher the alpha, the better.

Of the thirteen large-company growth funds that have made the cut to this point, only five have positive alphas.

## Screen 8: Performance Consistency vs. an Index

Once the long-term returns have been examined, you will need to do a quick check of the fund's year-to-year results versus its benchmark index. An index is a group of securities chosen to represent a portion of the stock or bond markets. Each manager of a fund or separate account is given a performance hurdle. This is a rate of return the manager is expected to provide investors. The rate is determined by a stock or bond index that comprises the types of stocks or bonds the manager buys based on the portfolio's objective. For example, large-company growth managers generally use the Russell 1000 Growth Index as their performance benchmark. As the name suggests, the index is made up of 1,000 large-company growth stocks.

Whether you are buying a mutual fund or a separate account, you should find out whether the manager has a record of consistently beating his or her benchmark index. At the very least, your manager should have beaten the index six of the past ten years. Only two of the five funds made this cut. Janet is now down to her short list.

## Screen 9: Tax Efficiency and Turnover

If you are investing taxable money (as opposed to tax-deferred money in a retirement account), you should find a fund with low turnover and a high tax-efficiency rating. Low turnover means that the fund isn't overactive in its buying and selling. A 100 percent turnover rate means that every position in the portfolio is sold at least once during the year. The average U.S. stock fund has a portfolio turnover rate of 78 percent. Lower turnover rates equate to lower taxable capital-gains distributions and often lower fund expenses. Turnover is not as much an issue in a retirement account

> The average U.S. stock mutual fund has turnover of 78 percent each year. Excessive trading within a fund can increase fund distributions and boost your tax burden.

in which there are no tax consequences for buying and selling. Index funds are tax efficient and should be considered in taxable investment accounts, especially if you are in a high tax bracket.

Figure 16.3 is a summary of the manager search at each stage using the criteria above to identify an above-average, large-company growth mutual fund for Joan Gibson.

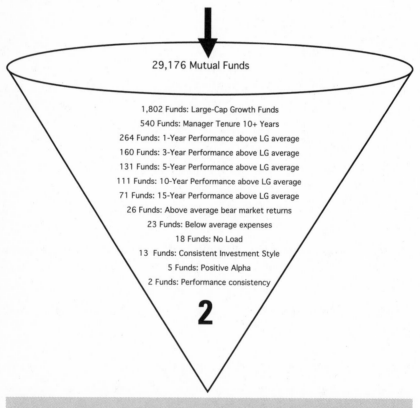

29,176 Mutual Funds

1,802 Funds: Large-Cap Growth Funds
540 Funds: Manager Tenure 10+ Years
264 Funds: 1-Year Performance above LG average
160 Funds: 3-Year Performance above LG average
131 Funds: 5-Year Performance above LG average
111 Funds: 10-Year Performance above LG average
71 Funds: 15-Year Performance above LG average
26 Funds: Above average bear market returns
23 Funds: Below average expenses
18 Funds: No Load
13 Funds: Consistent Investment Style
5 Funds: Positive Alpha
2 Funds: Performance consistency

2

figure 16.3

## *Screen 10: The Short List Compared*

Once we had a short list of fund finalists, we squared them off and let them battle head to head. This side-by-side comparison helped us identify our final choice.

The two funds that made our short list compared like this:

### Fund No. 1:

- Beat the Russell 1000 Growth Index seven out of ten years
- Manager with twenty-two years' tenure
- True to its size and style disciplines
- Has a –55 percent turnover rate
- Has expenses ½ percent lower than the category average (0.81 percent)
- Holds 373 stocks

### Fund No. 2:

- Beat the Russell 1000 Growth Index six out of ten years
- Manager with seventeen years' tenure
- True to its size and style disciplines
- Has a low turnover rate of 20 percent
- Has expenses ½ percent lower than the category average (0.81 percent)
- Holds 79 stocks

After using these ten screens, Janet and I made an educated decision. Fund No. 1 won the battle because of its consistent performance and manager tenure. Since we were buying the fund in her IRA, we weren't concerned about the portfolio turnover rate. We went ahead and purchased the fund in Janet's IRA.

After completing the search for a large-company growth fund, we repeated the same process for each of the other asset classes in her portfolio. Once completed, Janet and I had sifted through more than 29,000 funds and purchased twelve of the best funds available.

How far would the funds you own make it through this filtering process? If the answer is "not very," then you may need to make some changes to your portfolio (and maybe to your broker if the funds are a result of poor recommendations). Morningstar (www.morningstar.com) can help you see how the funds you own stack up. If you already own funds, use the criteria listed above to see how they rank. Chapter 19 will discuss at what point to sell a fund when it slips from the top of the pack. Managers can fall to the bottom of their asset category in one "off" year, but be well above average in the other nine and have fantastic track records. Don't make too much out of one bad year.

If you are working with a financial advisor, he or she can conduct an investment search for you using high-tech software. Your advisor should justify his or her recommendations and show you how the investments compare with all of the options available to you. *Make sure* your advisor is identifying above-average investments for your portfolio.

## Do Your Homework

By hiring professional money managers rather than managing a large portfolio of individual stocks and bonds on your own, you are more likely to enjoy better investment results. Using the information in this chapter, you should now be more prepared and equipped to identify the best money managers when you buy mutual funds, variable annuities, variable life insurance, or SMAs. Identifying a money manager who can deliver better-than-average returns over the long run could put hundreds of thousands of additional dollars in your pocket. Doing your homework will pay off.

There are a handful of sites on the Internet that make mutual fund searches relatively easy. These sites can be used to see if your current funds make the grade or to identify new funds for your portfolio.

### The Great Debate: Passive vs. Active Investing

An index mutual fund buys and holds every stock or bond in an index in hopes of mirroring the performance of that index. Index funds are "passively managed," meaning the manager of an index fund simply follows the actions of the index. The goal of an index fund is not to beat the index but to match it.

There are different indexes that measure each asset class in the market. Most people are familiar with at least two indexes, both of which measure the performance of U.S. large-company growth and value stocks: the S&P

500 (500 stocks) and the Dow Jones Industrial Average (thirty stocks). The Vanguard Index 500 Fund, for example, replicates the performance of the S&P 500 Index by owning all 500 stocks in the S&P 500 Index. If you want to own just large-company growth stocks or small-company value stocks, you could purchase an index fund made up of just those asset classes.

Why would you settle for the performance of a boring old index? Why accept mediocrity? After all, you can buy

> Fifty-nine percent of mutual funds are outperformed by their respective benchmark index.

a fund with a manager who actively buys and sells securities and whose stated goal is to earn returns better than an index's returns. You can look for a manager who has beat the index, but statistics are stacked against you finding one who can do this consistently.

As I mentioned earlier, 59 percent of stock fund managers are beaten by their benchmark indexes over the past ten years (ending December 31, 2012). By buying actively managed funds, you're essentially placing a bet that you can identify the 41 percent of money managers who can outperform their indexes (Figure 16.4). Some experts believe it is impossible to consistently identify these winning managers, no matter the level of your expertise. Oh, you might get lucky from time to time, they say, but in the long run, you won't beat the index.

Another advantage of index funds is expenses. Because index funds don't actively trade the securities they own, they are often much cheaper than actively managed funds. As we have seen, fees cut into returns, so a cheap index fund has a head start over an actively managed fund right out of the gate.

If you believe in index funds, then your life just became easier. No detailed fund search is necessary. Simply decide on your allocation (like the example in Figure 16.1) and buy the cheapest index funds available in each asset class. My favorite index fund companies are Vanguard (www.vanguard.com) and Barclays Global Investors (www.ishares.com).

## Understanding Your Money Management Choices

Read the following pages if you are still unclear on the differences between mutual funds, variable life or annuity subaccounts, and SMAs.

| Can You Pick Funds That Beat Their Index | |
|---|---|
| Asset Class/Benchmark Index | Funds that beat their benchmark index over the ten-year period ending 12/31/2012 |
| Large U.S. Company Growth Stocks<br>Russell 1000 Growth Index | 44.0% |
| Large U.S. Company Value Stocks<br>Russell 1000 Value Index | 38.0% |
| Mid-Cap U.S. Company Growth Stocks<br>Russell Mid Growth Index | 44.0% |
| Mid-Cap U.S. Company Value Stocks<br>Russell Mid Value Index | 21.0% |
| Small U.S. Company Growth Stocks<br>Russell 2000 Growth Index | 40.0% |
| Small U.S. Company Value Stocks<br>Russell 2000 Value Index | 55.0% |
| Large International Company Stocks<br>Morgan Stanley EAFE Ndtr Index | 41.0% |
| Out of the 5,586 funds measured, 2,305 beat their benchmark index | 41.3% |

figure 16.4

## Mutual Funds

The easiest and most popular way of hiring a professional money manager is by investing in mutual funds. Mutual funds have greatly increased in popularity over the past thirty years. In 1980, less than 6 percent of U.S. households (only 4.6 million households) owned a mutual fund. By the year 2011, that number had soared to more than 52 million, or 44 percent of households.[6] In 1980, there were only 450 mutual funds available to investors,[7] compared with the 29,176 available in 2012.

Forty-four percent of U.S. households own a mutual fund.

In a mutual fund, investors pool their money together in a common fund and hire a professional money manager to invest and manage the money. Investors become a fractional owner of each security held by the fund regardless of the size of their investment. If the underlying stocks or bonds held in the portfolio increase in value, the value of the fund shares, or net asset value (NAV), will appreciate also. Each fund has a specific investment objective that determines the types of stocks or bonds the manager can purchase (large-company stocks, small-company stocks, etc.). It's the money manager's responsibility to search for the best securities available, usually stocks or bonds, within the fund's objective and make the day-to-day decisions about what to buy and sell. A strict buy discipline is observed to determine which securities to add to the portfolio. Once purchased, each security is monitored and eventually sold based on a sell strategy.

Most managers diversify the money in the fund by owning one hundred to two hundred different securities. The average stock fund owns 179 securities, and the average bond fund owns 526 securities. Although you are a fractional owner of all the securities in the fund, you will not see a list of these securities and the shares of each you own on your statements. Your statements will simply report the number of shares and the value of the fund, not the individual stock and bond positions inside the fund. Therefore, it is not always apparent what you own. Professional money-management and diversification are the main reasons investors choose mutual funds.

## Separately Managed Accounts

Hiring a separate account manager (also referred to as private, independent, or institutional money manager) is another way to obtain professional money-management. As with mutual funds, the market for SMAs has grown rapidly. In the past, SMAs were exclusive to the ultrawealthy. In 1996 $244 billion was invested in SMAs.[8] By the end of 2011, that number had risen to $577 billion.[9] Today, there are nearly 6,300 SMAs from which to choose.[10]

When a separate account manager purchases a portfolio of stocks or bonds, the individual investor owns each security outright. This is different than a public mutual fund or a subaccount in a variable annuity or life insurance policy, in which investors own a fraction of each security held by the fund and essentially share what is owned.

In the past, these private money managers managed money only for the wealthy who could meet the high $1 million or more minimum initial investment. Now, through many SMA programs, investors can invest with as little as $100,000. Portfolios in the United States are getting larger and investment minimums have fallen as assets pour into SMAs. If you haven't yet heard about them, you will. However, even with lower minimums, it is difficult to obtain *proper diversification* without at least $1 million to invest. Hiring just two or three managers won't allow you to cover the many segments of the stock and bond markets.

Many mutual fund companies manage both mutual funds and SMAs. Often the managers and the holdings in portfolios using similar strategies are identical. They may offer a large-cap value stock strategy, for example, as a mutual fund and also an SMA, and each portfolio would include almost the exact same large companies. This is the case with the TCW Relative Value Large Cap Strategy and the TCW Relative Value Large Cap Mutual Fund (Figure 16.5). So what's the difference between owning the fund and the SMA if you own the same stocks in both cases? The answer is customization.

SMAs offer customization that mutual funds do not. For instance, if you own an SMA, you can request that certain stocks or an entire industry not be held in your portfolio. Perhaps someone close to you died of lung cancer due to smoking and you would prefer not to own tobacco stocks in your portfolio. In your SMA, tobacco companies will be excluded. In a mutual fund you share, with the funds' other investors, each position held in the fund. If the fund owns tobacco stocks then you own tobacco stocks. You have no say in the stocks the manager picks.

Tax efficiency is another feature of SMAs not available with a mutual fund. This may be important in your non-retirement accounts. At year's end you can request that your SMA manager tax harvest your portfolio. This means he/she will determine how much you've incurred in capital gains due to the buying and selling that occurred in the portfolio during the year. Then the manager will review the positions in the portfolio to see if any of the fifty to one hundred stocks you own are trading at a loss. If so, your manager can sell a position at a loss and you can use the loss to offset the gains. Let's assume the manager sold Microsoft earlier in the year and made you $1,000 (capital gain). If the manager sells Home Depot at a $1,000 loss, the loss cancels out the gain and no capital gains tax will be owed. In order for the loss to count, however, the manager can't buy back Home Depot for thirty days.

SMAs are often more concentrated than mutual funds. Many SMAs invest in just fifty to sixty different securities. By contrast, most mutual funds invest in closer to two hundred securities.

Figure 16.5 lists the holdings of the TCW Relative Value Large Cap SMA. Investors owning this portfolio would own only about fifty stocks. Contrary to mutual funds, each statement you receive from a separate account manager will itemize each position you own, including the number of shares, share price, purchase price (cost basis), profit and loss per position, and portfolio changes from the previous month.

If you can meet the higher minimums, want more customization in your portfolio composition, and want to own securities outright rather than sharing them with other investors, then you should consider SMAs.

| TCW Relative Value Large Cap Fund (Mutual Fund) | | TCW Relative Value Large Cap Strategy (SMA) | |
|---|---|---|---|
| Top Ten Holdings | % Net Assets | Top Ten Holdings | % Net Assets |
| Pfizer Inc. | 3.72% | Pfizer Inc. | 3.73% |
| JPMorgan Chase & Co. | 3.46% | Comcast Corp. | 3.59% |
| Comcast Corp. | 3.41% | JPMorgan Chase & Co. | 3.52% |
| Home Depot Inc. | 3.32% | Home Depot Inc. | 3.45% |
| Chevron Corp. | 3.28% | Chevron Corp. | 3.30% |
| General Electric Co. | 3.06% | General Electric Co. | 3.19% |
| State Street Corp. | 3.05% | Citigroup Inc. | 3.09% |
| The Travelers Companies Inc. | 3.03% | State Street Corp. | 3.06% |
| Textron Inc. | 2.86% | The Travelers Companies Inc. | 3.01% |
| Honeywell Intl. | 2.85% | Textron Inc. | 2.90% |

*figure 16.5*

## Variable Annuities

Would you like a tax-deferred mutual fund? Think of a variable annuity as a tax-deferred mutual fund account. You can buy variable annuities through brokerage firms, banks, insurance companies, and mutual fund companies. Ultimately, however, annuities are products of the insurance companies. Insurance companies administer the annuity contracts–providing tax deferral–while a mutual fund company is hired to perform the day-to-day money-management. The insurance company typically hires a number of portfolio managers from different fund companies to manage individual funds (called subaccounts) within the annuity contract.

Similar to the IRAs you own, money invested in variable annuities can't be withdrawn without penalty until you reach age 59½. The average annuity offers fifty-five different subaccount investment choices, covering a wide spectrum of asset classes including large-company stocks, small-company stocks, international stocks, bonds, and more. Today, there are 2,618 variable annuities available. These annuities combined offer more than 145,058 subaccounts.[11]

It is not a good idea to buy annuities with your IRA money, because IRA dollars are already tax-deferred. There is no sense paying an insurance company an extra fee for tax deferral—you already have it. The primary attraction of variable annuities, as you can see, is tax deferral.

## Variable Life Insurance

Variable life insurance combines mutual funds with life insurance. When you pay a premium to buy variable life insurance, part of your premium covers the cost of the insurance, and the balance is deposited into an investment account within the policy (cash value). Much like a variable annuity, the insurance company will generally hire forty to fifty money managers to manage each subaccount (like mutual funds). Using these investment choices, you can develop a strategy for investing your policy's cash value. There are 551 variable life insurance policies available.[12]

The nice thing about variable life insurance is that your cash value (the money you invest in stock and bond subaccounts) grows tax-deferred and can be withdrawn tax-free. A tax-free growth or income mutual fund doesn't sound too bad, does it? Unfortunately, to obtain this tax-free benefit you must buy life insurance, which comes with additional costs. If you need the insurance and can find a low-cost, *no-load policy,* adding an investment component to your life coverage may be worth considering.

## Mutual Funds Win!

In most cases, people who are looking for professional money management should stick with mutual funds. While the other money management options do have their place in the right situation, as you'll see in Chapter 18, good no-load funds often come with lower expenses and fewer restrictions. Variable annuities, for instance, are more expensive than mutual funds, often have surrender charges that last for seven or more years, and in most cases shouldn't be purchased with IRA money. Variable life insurance, in addition to higher built-in investment expenses, also carries an annual premium. Investors shouldn't pay the additional insurance expenses and agree to lengthy surrender charges unless they need the insurance. And finally, while SMAs provide some customization that funds don't, the higher minimum investment requirements often make proper diversification hard to obtain. Be sure to compare all of your options before investing any money.

# 17

# SAFER WAYS TO OWN STOCKS

D id your stock investments cause you to lose any sleep from 2000 to 2002 while the U.S. stock market suffered a 45 percent drop or from 2007 to 2009 when the market plunged 51 percent?[1] If so, you likely invested too aggressively. As we've discussed, a properly diversified investment portfolio could have dramatically softened the blow of both of these monstrous declines (see sample portfolios in Chapter 14). However, if you're still a little skittish about investing in stocks in the wake of these market plunges, diversification alone simply may not be enough for you. Many investors need the higher returns offered by stocks over the long term to reach their retirement goals, but they are scared away by the volatility and uncertainty of the equity markets.

This raises an interesting question: Is there a way to participate in the stock market while at the same time protecting investment principal? The answer may surprise you. Here are four strategies that will allow you to reap much of the gains the stock market offers without exposing your fragile nest egg to the wild west of the open market. Finally, you'll be able to get a good night's sleep.

## Strategy #1: Buy Index-Linked CDs

Index-linked certificates of deposit (CDs) pay interest based on the performance of the stock market, rather than a fixed interest rate with which most CD investors are familiar. Index-linked CDs are tied to major stock *indexes* like the S&P 500, NASDAQ, the Dow Jones Industrial Average, or an international stock index. However, unlike buying a stock or stock mutual fund, the investment principal is FDIC insured.

## During the Bad Times

To illustrate how index-linked CDs work, let's consider the fate of two separate investors, Peter Chung and Catherine Swenson, each with $100,000 to invest. In January 2004, Peter deposited $100,000 into a five-year index-linked CD tied to the S&P 500. That same month, Catherine used her $100,000 to buy the Vanguard 500 Index Fund (VFINX), an S&P 500 index mutual fund.

How did each investor fair from 2004 to 2008, a period marked by the *largest one-year loss* in the stock market since the Depression? Peter got his principal back at maturity without losing a cent; Catherine was left with $89,033. The difference in ending values doesn't seem too dramatic. However, at one point in October 2007, the fund balance reached $148,588 and then dropped to a low of $88,119. That's a high-to-low swing of $60,469.[2] Think of the difference in stress and anxiety Peter and Catherine must have been feeling during this time. While Catherine was losing sleep, Peter knew that he would at least get his principal back at maturity regardless of what happened in the stock market. Imagine the peace of mind this guarantee may have provided from 2004 to 2008. Determining which investment to buy is easy now, in hindsight, after experiencing a year like 2008; however, consider how Peter was feeling in October 2007 when Catherine mentioned that, since 2004, she had made 49.58 percent ($49,580) on her $100,000 investment. He wondered whether he made the right decision going with the index CD since his account value was sitting at $138,870. He felt like he had just left $10,710 of easy money on the table.

However, like many investors, Catherine was wondering at her low point, $88,119, if she would ever recover. She was tempted to sell her fund and give up entirely on investing in stocks. Though she nearly recovered her original investment by patiently holding on and riding out the stormy markets, many investors fared much worse. Thousands of people in 2008 simply could not handle the continued stress of a plummeting stock market and incurred big losses as they sold their stock positions to get out of the market. Unlike Catherine, these impatient investors weren't invested when the stock market quickly began to rebound in 2009.

## During the Good Times

The results are dramatically opposite during times when the market is strong. For example, if Peter had invested his $100,000 into a five-year S&P 500 index-linked CD in January 2003 (80 percent participation rate), he would have received $153,234 at maturity in January 2008 (annual rate of return 8.9 percent). This doesn't sound too bad; however, Peter would have settled for less profit than what Catherine's mutual fund generated. Catherine's investment into an S&P 500 *mutual fund* over the same period would have provided $28,454 more, finishing at $181,688, which equates to a 12.7 percent annual compounded rate of return (dividends reinvested).

## So, What's the Catch?

The trade-off for principal protection is restrictions. Index-linked CDs often have caps, limited participation rates, and call provisions that can limit upside potential.

*Caps* limit the maximum gain you can receive. An investment into an index-linked CD with a 100 percent cap, for example, would limit your gain to 100 percent. A $100,000 investment in a CD with a 100 percent cap would return a maximum of $100,000, plus the $100,000 principal, even if the market went up 200 percent during the CD's term.

*Participation rates* are another way returns are curbed. Some index-linked CDs will allow investors to participate in only 80 to 90 percent of the stock market index increase. *Call provisions* give the bank the option of redeeming the CD prematurely to avoid having to pay huge sums of interest in the event of a big stock market run-up.

In addition to these drawbacks, money invested in index-linked CDs is normally tied up for at least five years, and any early withdrawals by investors are penalized. Also, index-linked CDs are tied to the absolute performance of a stock index and don't take into account dividends, which can compound growth if reinvested in an index mutual fund.

Even with all the restrictions, index-linked CDs make sense for investors looking for stock market participation *and* peace of mind.

## Where to Buy?

Banks issue index-linked CDs. They are FDIC insured up to $250,000 per depositor (2013). To obtain FDIC insurance for portfolios over $250,000, investors can purchase CDs from multiple banks. If you plan to manage a large portfolio of index-linked CDs, use a single brokerage account to buy and hold CDs from multiple banks.

If you like the idea of being ultrasafe even if it means having to endure some restrictions and limited access to your money, index-linked CDs may be the perfect investment for you. You could buy a diversified portfolio of CDs and essentially guarantee your entire equity portfolio. Add to that a portfolio of insured municipal bonds or U.S. Treasury bonds and a money market account or traditional certificate of deposit, and you could participate in the stock, bond, and cash markets without risking principal at all. See the sample principal protection portfolio in Figure 17.1.

| Sample Principal Protection Portfolio |
|---|
| **Stocks** |
| S&P 500 Index-Linked CD |
| Dow Jones Ind. Index-Linked CD |
| NASDAQ Index-Linked CD |
| EAFE Index-Linked CD |
| **Bonds** |
| U.S. Treasury Bond |
| Insured Municipal Bond |
| **Cash** |
| Money Market Interest Account |
| Traditional Certificates of Deposit |

figure 17.1

## Strategy #2: Zeros and Stocks

Keith and Rose Young retired in 2004 with a savings of $100,000. They needed this sum to grow at a fairly good rate during their retirement but were afraid to invest money in stocks. Investing in stocks had always caused them too much anxiety. It stressed them out to think about their life savings being exposed to the illogical ups and downs of the market, and they vowed not to live their retirement in a panic. So they decided to employ the "zero strategy." As you will see, using an instrument called U.S. Treasury zero coupon bonds, Keith and Rose were able to participate in the stock market without risking their $100,000 savings.

### The Zero Strategy

Here's how the zero strategy works. First, because Keith and Rose wanted to protect their $100,000 foremost, they purchased a ten-year zero coupon bond yielding 5 percent from the U.S. Treasury for $61,391. In return, the Treasury promised to give them $100,000 in ten years. Zero coupon bonds are purchased at a discount ($61,391 in our example), pay no interest during the life of the bond, and mature at face value ($100,000 in our example). The difference between the purchase price and the face value represents the investment return on the bond. Because the zero coupon bond will mature at $100,000, Keith and Rose have guaranteed their initial principal if they hold on to the bond until maturity in 2012. Knowing they'll receive $100,000 at maturity gives them the peace of mind to place the rest of their money in more volatile investments.

Next, they invested the remaining $38,609 in a diversified portfolio of stock mutual funds. They are hoping their stock funds will produce a 10 percent average annual return over the next ten years. If this occurs, note their results in 2012. The original $61,391 they invested in the zero coupon bond will mature at $100,000, and their $38,609 stock fund investments will be worth $100,141, giving them an ending balance of $200,141 and a 7 percent annual return. Not bad. If everything goes as planned, Keith and Rose will double their investment in ten years without risking their initial principal.

## Worst-Case Scenario

If Keith and Rose's stock portfolio produces an 8 annual percent return, they would end up with $219,913. A 6 percent annual stock return will bring their total to $183,353.

In the unlikely event that, after ten years, their stock funds are only worth half their original amount ($19,304), they would end the ten-year period with a total of $119,304 (2 percent annual return). A 2 percent return isn't too exciting in this extreme scenario, but it's not disastrous. Remember, their objective would still be met—they would not lose any of their original principal. They are willing to trade big returns in the stock market for modest returns and no principal risk.

Another benefit of this strategy is its liquidity. If something unforeseen occurs and they need cash quickly, they can sell their zero coupon bond and stock mutual funds at the going rate at any time without penalty.

## Adopting the Zero Strategy for Your Situation

If you, like Keith and Rose Young, are willing to accept modest returns to avoid risking principal and have the patience to stay the course for a long period of time, the zero coupon bond strategy may work for you. To employ the zero strategy, you must first determine what percentage of your portfolio you would need to invest in a zero coupon bond to insure your portfolio principal. The answer depends on the yield on your zero coupon bond and the years until the bond matures. Figure 17.2 shows that if you obtain a zero coupon bond yielding 5 percent and want to protect your portfolio over a ten-year period, you would need to invest 61 percent of your portfolio into the bond. A 7 percent zero coupon bond would require a smaller investment into the bond.

You might ask yourself, "How good is the bond's guarantee?" That depends on the strength of the bond's issuer. If the U.S. Treasury issues the zero, then it's backed by the full faith and credit of the U.S. government. This is the strongest guarantee in the world today.

| Amount to Invest in a Zero-Coupon Bond to Insure $100,000 Principal | | | |
|---|---|---|---|
| Yield | Years to Maturity | % of Portfolio | Amount of Portfolio |
| 5% | 15 | 48% | $48,000 |
| 5% | 14 | 51% | $51,000 |
| 5% | 13 | 53% | $53,000 |
| 5% | 12 | 56% | $56,000 |
| 5% | 11 | 58% | $58,000 |
| 5% | 10 | 61% | $61,000 |
| 5% | 9 | 64% | $64,000 |
| 5% | 8 | 68% | $68,000 |
| 7% | 15 | 24% | $24,000 |
| 7% | 14 | 26% | $26,000 |
| 7% | 13 | 29% | $29,000 |
| 7% | 12 | 32% | $32,000 |
| 7% | 11 | 35% | $35,000 |
| 7% | 10 | 39% | $39,000 |
| 7% | 9 | 42% | $42,000 |
| 7% | 8 | 47% | $47,000 |

figure 17.2

If you are willing to accept modest returns to avoid risking your principal, and you have the patience, the zero strategy may work for you.

## Strategy #3: Equity-Indexed Annuities

Another way to participate in stock market gains without risking principal is through an insurance-company instrument called an equity-indexed annuity (EIA). An EIA is a fixed annuity. Traditional fixed annuities pay low interest rates but guarantee principal. EIAs offer a minimum guaranteed interest rate combined with an interest rate linked to a stock market index. Like our first two strategies, you'll need to accept some big trade-offs to employ this strategy.

### The Story of Edward and Van

Edward Baxter's experience investing in EIAs provides a helpful example of how they work. Edward invested $250,000 into his first EIA in 1989. In

1999, he invested $250,000 in a second EIA at another firm. Both annuities were pegged to the S&P 500 Index with a 10 percent annual cap. With a 10 percent cap, Edward couldn't make more than 10 percent per year, even when the market returned more than 10 percent. However, when the stock market dropped as it did from 2000–2002 and again in 2008, his account value didn't fall. You can examine his year-to-year experience (Figure 17.3). As you can see, by 1998 his $250,000 had grown to $531,369 and his second $250,000 investment finished 2008 with a balance of $405,078.

| Index vs. Index Annuity 1989–2008 | | | | |
|---|---|---|---|---|
| $250,000 Initial Investment | | | | |
| Year | Vanguard 500 Return | Year-End Balance | EIA Return | Year-End Balance |
| 1989 | 31.33% | $328,325 | 10.00% | $275,000 |
| 1990 | –3.35% | $317,326 | 0.00% | $275,000 |
| 1991 | 30.17% | $413,063 | 10.00% | $302,500 |
| 1992 | 7.43% | $443,754 | 7.67% | $325,702 |
| 1993 | 9.88% | $487,597 | 9.99% | $358,239 |
| 1994 | 1.18% | $493,351 | 1.31% | $362,932 |
| 1995 | 37.58% | $678,752 | 10.00% | $399,226 |
| 1996 | 22.80% | $833,507 | 10.00% | $439,148 |
| 1997 | 33.16% | $1,109,898 | 10.00% | $483,063 |
| 1998 | 28.60% | $1,427,329 | 10.00% | $531,369 |
| Year | Vanguard 500 Return | Year-End Balance | EIA Return | Year-End Balance |
| 1999 | 21.04% | $302,600 | 10.00% | $275,000 |
| 2000 | –9.06% | $275,184 | 0.00% | $275,000 |
| 2001 | –12.04% | $242,052 | 0.00% | $275,000 |
| 2002 | –22.14% | $188,462 | 0.00% | $275,000 |
| 2003 | 28.51% | $242,192 | 10.00% | $302,500 |
| 2004 | 10.73% | $268,180 | 10.00% | $332,750 |
| 2005 | 4.77% | $280,972 | 4.91% | $349,088 |
| 2006 | 15.27% | $323,876 | 10.00% | $383,997 |
| 2007 | 5.72% | $342,402 | 5.49% | $405,078 |
| 2008 | –37.03% | $215,610 | 0.00% | $405,078 |

figure 17.3

Edward's brother Van invested $250,000 in the Vanguard 500 Index Fund at the same time. At the end of 1998, Van had $1,427,329 in his fund. For comparison, you can see what Van would have experienced had he invested $250,000 into the Vanguard 500 Index Fund in 1999 when Edward purchased his second EIA. While the Vanguard fund provided an amazing 19 percent annual return from 1989–1999, it was a roller-coaster ride from 1999–2008 and ultimately produced a negative return (annual return of –1.5 percent). It plunged from a high of $302,600 in 1999 to $188,462 at the end of 2002 (a loss of $114,138). It also experienced a monstrous drop in 2008, falling from $342,402 to $215,610 (a loss of $126,792).

While Edward was kicking himself at the end of 1998 when comparing his portfolio to his brother's (a difference of $895,960), he enjoyed tremendous peace of mind during the 2000–2002 and 2008 bear markets.

## *The Trade-Off*

For further comparison, let's look at a longer period of time. Suppose in 1979 Edward and Van invested their respective $250,000 into the same investments and let them ride until 2012. Van's investment in the Vanguard fund would have finished this period with a massive $9,178,139 balance (annual return of 11.18 percent). Edward's annuity was a dismal investment when viewed side by side (Figure 17.4). His original $250,000 would have ended the period at $2,550,003 (annual return of 7.07 percent). The mutual fund won by a whopping $6,628,136. During big bull markets, EIA investors trade huge returns for peace of mind. The title of an article that appeared in *Forbes* magazine sums up Edward's experience: "Equity-Indexed Annuities: A Costly Way To Limit Your Losses."[3]

If you carve up the time frame in Figure 17.4 into three-year periods, you'll find that the Vanguard 500 Index fund provided better returns in twenty-six of the thirty-two periods measured. With an EIA, the odds of obtaining returns closely tracking the stock market seem pretty low.

## *Beware of Commissions and Complexities*

EIAs are only available from insurance companies. Beware that insurance agents have tremendous incentive to push investors into EIAs whether they are a good fit for them or not. Some annuities pay commissions as

| Index vs. Index Annuity 1979–2012 | | | | |
| --- | --- | --- | --- | --- |
| $250,000 Initial Investment | | | | |
| Year | Vanguard 500 Return | Year-End Balance | EIA Return | Year-End Balance |
| 1979 | 18.05% | 295,125 | 10.00% | $275,000 |
| 1980 | 31.90% | 389,270 | 10.00% | $302,500 |
| 1981 | −5.25% | 368,833 | 0.00% | $302,500 |
| 1982 | 21.02% | 446,362 | 10.00% | $332,750 |
| 1983 | 21.29% | 541,392 | 10.00% | $366,025 |
| 1984 | 6.19% | 574,905 | 6.27% | $388,975 |
| 1985 | 31.14% | 753,930 | 10.00% | $427,872 |
| 1986 | 18.28% | 891,748 | 10.00% | $470,659 |
| 1987 | 4.71% | 933,750 | 5.23% | $495,275 |
| 1988 | 16.23% | 1,085,297 | 10.00% | $544,802 |
| 1989 | 31.33% | 1,425,321 | 10.00% | $599,283 |
| 1990 | −3.35% | $1,377,573 | 0.00% | $599,283 |
| 1991 | 30.17% | $1,793,186 | 10.00% | $659,211 |
| 1992 | 7.43% | $1,926,420 | 7.67% | $709,772 |
| 1993 | 9.88% | $2,116,750 | 9.99% | $780,679 |
| 1994 | 1.18% | $2,141,728 | 1.31% | $790,906 |
| 1995 | 37.58% | $2,946,589 | 10.00% | $869,996 |
| 1996 | 22.80% | $3,618,411 | 10.00% | $956,996 |
| 1997 | 33.16% | $4,818,277 | 10.00% | $1,052,695 |
| 1998 | 28.60% | $6,196,304 | 10.00% | $1,157,965 |
| 1999 | 21.04% | $7,500,006 | 10.00% | $1,273,761 |
| 2000 | −9.06% | $6,820,506 | 0.00% | $1,273,761 |
| 2001 | −12.04% | $5,999,317 | 0.00% | $1,273,761 |
| 2002 | −22.14% | $4,671,068 | 0.00% | $1,273,761 |
| 2003 | 28.51% | $6,002,790 | 10.00% | $1,401,138 |
| 2004 | 10.73% | $6,646,889 | 10.00% | $1,541,251 |
| 2005 | 4.77% | $6,963,945 | 4.91% | $1,616,927 |
| 2006 | 15.27% | $8,027,340 | 10.00% | $1,778,619 |
| 2007 | 5.72% | $8,486,504 | 5.49% | $1,876,266 |
| 2008 | −37.03% | $5,343,951 | 0.00% | $1,876,266 |
| 2009 | 26.49% | $6,763,569 | 10.00% | $2,063,892 |
| 2010 | 14.91% | $7,773,435 | 10.00% | $2,270,281 |
| 2011 | 1.97% | $7,924,604 | 2.11% | $2,318,184 |
| 2012 | 15.83% | $9,178,139 | 10.00% | $2,550,003 |

figure 17.4

much as 10 percent. This means Edward's $250,000 investment would have generated a $25,000 commission for his agent. That's a lot of money considering there are no further investment decisions to make once the initial paperwork is completed and the contract is issued.

Another trade-off is the complexity of EIAs. Buying them can be difficult and confusing. Virtually every major insurance company offers them with dramatically different features. The differences between annuity policies make shopping for them a time-consuming process.

When shopping for an EIA, I strongly urge you to use the checklist below.

1. Index: Determine which stock index you would like your returns to be tied to: S&P 500, NASDAQ, Dow, or Russell 2000.

2. Participation Rate: Seek out an annuity with a 100 percent guaranteed participation rate for the life of the contract. A contract with a 90 percent participation rate, for example, will provide investors with only a 9 percent return if the market goes up 10 percent.

3. Cap Rate: Look for a contract with a high cap rate. The highest caps are generally 10 to 11 percent. If a contract has a 100 percent participation rate up to a 10 percent cap, investors will make a maximum of 10 percent even if the market went up 20 percent.

4. Surrender Charges: Surrender charges range from five to fifteen years. Only consider annuities with five- to six-year surrender charges. Agents make more commissions on an annuity with a long surrender period, so they may push you in this direction. Some annuities have surrender charges that last as long as fifteen years. Do not buy a contract with a term this long. The surrender charge is essentially a penalty charged to investors who cash out of the annuity early. For example, let's say you buy a contract carrying a ten-year surrender charge. You will pay a 10 percent penalty for surrendering the contract in the first year, 9 percent in the second year, 8 percent in the third year, and so on until the tenth year. So find an annuity with a short surrender charge period. If you want to change your investment plan, you don't want to have to wait ten to fifteen years to do so. Also, ask how much commission is being paid to your agent.

5.  Minimum Guarantee: This feature guarantees a minimum annual interest to be credited to the policy. Guarantees generally range from 0 to 3.5 percent.

6.  Interest Crediting Method: Insurance companies use three methods to determine how much interest EIAs are credited: point-to-point, annual reset, and high water mark. Point-to-point annuities are straightforward and simply take the difference between the starting and ending value of the underlying index during the term of the annuity to calculate the interest to be credited. Annual reset annuities credit interest based on the change in the index annually (the disadvantage being that participation rates may change annually). High water mark annuities look at different points during the term of the contract, and they credit interest between the starting point and high point of the index (the disadvantage being typically lower participation rates).

7.  Asset Fees (Spreads): Some contracts charge investors an annual fee. Look for an equity index annuity with no spreads.

8.  Bonus: To attract clients, some insurance companies offer an up-front bonus to investors when they buy the contract. Essentially, the insurance company will pay you for buying the annuity. This might amount to an additional 3 to 10 percent credited to your contract value. Some contracts pay this up-front while others spread it out, paying it over the life of the contract. Beware: The bigger the bonus, the longer you will be locked into surrender charges. Think about it: If they pay you a big sum up-front, they need to make sure you stay invested in the contract for the long term so they can recoup the bonus they pay you. In my opinion, a short surrender charge period is more important than a bonus. Too many people lock into long surrender charge periods only to change their plan midstream and are forced to pay large penalties for early withdrawals. This is a mistake.

With all these trade-offs, make sure you understand the features of the EIA you choose. Because you are going to own your annuity for a long time, you don't want to be surprised five years down the road and find out the features and guarantees were not what you thought.

It is helpful to visit a website like www.annuityadvantage.com to compare equity index annuities side by side.

WARNING: Many people buy EIAs only to discover later that they really didn't understand what they bought and are stuck in an underperforming investment for many more years. All you have to do is Google for "EIA complaints" to see the disgust many people have toward their EIA and those who sell them. In fact, after gathering data from sixteen states, *Money Magazine* reported that in 2009 EIAs accounted for 30 percent of annuity-related complaints (55 percent in senior-heavy Florida) but represented just 13 percent of annuity sales.[4]

## Strategy 4: Use Variable Annuities with Principal Protection Riders

Insurance companies are continually adding features to their variable annuity contracts to make them more attractive. One of the most popular features is called a "living benefit." This rider can be added to a variable annuity to provide another way of protecting your portfolio.

What's a variable annuity? Think of it as a tax-deferred mutual fund account. You can buy variable annuities through brokerage firms, banks, insurance companies, and mutual fund companies. Ultimately, however, they are products of insurance companies that administer the annuity contract–providing tax deferral–while a mutual fund company is hired to perform the day-to-day money-management. The insurance company typically hires a number of portfolio managers from different fund companies to manage individual funds (called subaccounts) within the annuity contract. Most contracts offer between fifty to sixty different investment choices, covering a wide spectrum of asset classes, including large-company stocks, small-company stocks, international stocks, bonds, and more.

### Living Benefit

When you invest your money into some variable annuities, you can opt to have a living benefit rider added to the contract. Here's how the living benefit works: Regardless of the performance of the investments you choose, you are guaranteed that your principal will grow at a fixed rate, usually 3 to 4 percent per year, which varies by contract. While you can cash in on this guarantee typically any time after the seventh year, many investors falsely believe this means they can take a complete withdrawal and walk away. It's a little trickier than that.

For example, Ruth White invested $100,000 into a variable annuity with a 6 percent living benefit in 2002. She invested the entire amount into an aggressive stock subaccount.[5] The subaccount grew to $133,402 by 2007. During 2008, however, Ruth's portfolio balance dropped to just $61,856. Under most circumstances, an investor like Ruth would have been deeply concerned. But because of her annuity's living benefit feature, however, Ruth had two options to handle this loss: (1) Ride out the market downturn in hopes of a future rebound, or (2) exercise her living benefit option.

Ruth elected to exercise her living benefit option. She decided to hand her money over to the annuity company in return for a stream of income for the rest of her life. To calculate how much income to pay Ruth, the insurance company took her original investment of $100,000 and added 6 percent per year for the previous seven years. This gave Ruth an additional $50,363, making the living benefit value $150,363. The living benefit option allowed Ruth to *annuitize* this $150,363. Ruth liked the fact that she could start receiving payments from the annuity that would provide her with income for life. It felt much like receiving a traditional corporate pension payout. (Payments are based on age, life expectancy, and an interest-rate assumption.)

Ruth had many annuity payout options from which to choose. She chose the life-only annuity option and is receiving $13,000 per year for the rest of her life.

So, even though the living benefit does not exactly guarantee the return of your principal investment, it does guarantee the stream of income your principal can provide. This makes good sense. The reason you have a retirement portfolio is not to admire the dollars it contains but to provide you with income. Why not guarantee your future income?

## *The Downside*

This strategy does have a downside, however. Once you annuitize, you cannot touch your principal from that time forward. Ruth can make no additional withdrawals from the $150,363 portfolio, except for the $13,000 that is being paid out annually. Keep in mind, however, that annuitization is optional and typically would be used only if the markets performed very poorly for a long period of time. In addition, when you add a living benefit to your variable annuity, it will increase the built-in internal expenses that you pay but never see. Most people never cash in on their living benefit and consequently wind up paying higher annual fees for a benefit they'll never use.

Although this principal protection feature seems somewhat restrictive, it may make sense for two main reasons. First, if the markets perform as they have historically and provide good, solid returns, you will probably never annuitize your contract by exercising the living benefit option. However, having this option may provide you peace of mind during times of market turmoil and will help you stay invested. You can be confident that no matter what happens in the market, your future retirement income will not be at risk if there is a severe market downturn. Second, the annuity provides tax deferral, which can help your money grow more rapidly.

## Know Their Features

You should be familiar with other annuity features available whenever purchasing variable annuity contracts. Again, the features offered by each annuity contract will vary. Here are some examples:

- Many variable annuities will pay you a bonus when you invest. In some cases, this can amount to 4 to 6 percent of the amount you initially deposit. If you invest $100,000, the annuity company will add an extra $4,000 to $6,000 to your account.
- Variable annuities provide a death benefit. Many guarantee a benefit that is equal either to your initial investment or to the highest annual market value of the annuity, whichever is greater. This feature protects the portfolio for your heirs in the event of a market drop.
- Some contracts provide an additional payout at death to cover taxes that may be owed from portfolio gains.
- At one time, virtually all annuities had to be held for five to seven years before they could be liquidated without surrender charges. Now, many contracts offer zero to one-year holding periods, providing tax deferral with liquidity.

## Before You Buy

Before you buy a variable annuity, consider the following important factors. First, the money cannot be withdrawn before age 59½ without a 10 percent IRS early-withdrawal penalty, much like the penalties that kick in when you withdraw money early from an IRA. Second, while variable annuities offer additional features, they also carry additional expenses. In addition to the cost of the underlying mutual fund management (usually about 1 percent annually), there are additional insurance company fees. These fees typically range between 1 and 1.5 percent. Furthermore, if you purchase an annuity and opt for the living benefit, you may pay an additional 0.50 percent per year for this additional rider. You could easily be paying 3 percent per year in built-in expenses. You will not see any of these expenses because they are all built into the price of each subaccount. Higher expenses drag returns down.

Therefore, when you purchase an annuity, an important consideration is whether the additional benefits are worth the extra expense. Regarding the living benefit feature, if it gives you the peace of mind to stay invested in stocks for the long run instead of pulling your money out of the market, then it is definitely worth the extra cost. Remember, as you consider adding a living benefit to your annuity, that the guarantees are only as solid as the insurance company making them. Only buy annuities from the highest-rated companies.

• • •

These four strategies are certainly not for everyone. But as we've seen, it is possible to participate in the gains of the stock market while protecting your principal. Each strategy is worth considering if the volatility of the stock market is too much for you. Most retirees need some exposure to the stock market to keep their retirement portfolio growing to stave off the impact of inflation. Being too conservative could keep you from attaining your goals. So if you need peace of mind to stay in the stock market, consider what we've detailed in this chapter.

But remember, if an investment product seems too good to be true, it probably is. Be informed. Each of the above strategies has considerable trade-offs that you must weigh before investing. Only you can decide what your peace of mind is worth.

# 18

# "NO-LOAD" MEANS LOWER COSTS

## RETIREMENT DECISION #14: SHOULD I BUY LOAD OR NO-LOAD MUTUAL FUNDS, ANNUITIES, AND LIFE INSURANCE?

Would you buy a blue BMW for $100,000 when you could buy an identical BMW for only $50,000 at another dealership? To make it even easier to decide, what if the $100,000 BMW had a condition attached requiring you to pay a penalty of up to $5,000 if you decide to sell the car during the next five years? The answer is obvious, right? Well, millions of investors are choosing the equivalent of the $100,000 BMW when they purchase mutual funds, variable annuities, or life insurance policies that come with "loads" and pay twice as much in expenses.

Loads are sales charges. They can occur when an investment or insurance product is bought or sold. The money from loads, in the form of commissions, ends up in the pockets of advisors and brokers who sell these products. And that's on top of the built-in expenses an investment product charges for the day-to-day management of the fund or policy. As you can see, loaded investment products can be quite expensive. Fortunately

> According to an NASD survey, 78 percent of Americans can name a character on *Friends,* but only 12 percent know the difference between "load" and "no-load" funds.[1]

for you and me, there are thousands of mutual funds, annuities, and life insurance products available that have no loads. You can often save thousands of dollars per year in investment and insurance expenses by using no-load products. Why pay more if you don't have to?

Let's compare the cost differences between load and no-load financial products. During the past year, Thomas Rockwell changed jobs, sold some land, and decided to update his life insurance plan. He is 55 years old and needs to make some big financial decisions. After careful consideration, he decides on the following strategy:

- Roll over the $100,000 in his former employer's 401(k) to his IRA and buy a large-company U.S. stock mutual fund.
- Take the $100,000 he received from the land sale and buy a variable annuity to build up his retirement assets.
- Buy a $1,000,000 cash value life insurance policy.

After doing his homework, he's narrowed his choices to two mutual funds, two annuities, and two life insurance policies: one carries a load; the other is no-load. He now must decide between the two. My advice to Thomas: Proceed with caution! The wrong decision will increase his expenses by more than $9,000 per year.

## Mutual Funds: Load vs. No-Load

Thomas decided to roll his $100,000 401(k) balance into a U.S. stock mutual fund in an IRA. After evaluating the performance and management of many funds, he narrowed the choices to two funds with similar management, performance, and investment strategies: a load fund recommended by a commissioned advisor and a no-load fund he found on his own. Which should he choose? A quick price check will help answer the question.

First of all, with load funds there's no such thing as a *quick* price check. There are a myriad of expenses and fees, and they are complicated. In a nutshell, there are two things to look at when you're trying to figure out how much a load fund will cost you: the expense ratio and the sales charge (load).

The expense ratio is straightforward. It's the percentage the fund charges you annually to manage and operate the fund. The fund automatically deducts the expense ratio from your total return. If the fund returns 7 percent and its expense ratio is 2 percent, you take home a total return of 5 percent.

Loads are more complicated. Load funds are often divided into three different share classes, each with different charges and expenses, depending on how they are sold to investors. "A" shares typically carry a front-end sales charge, meaning that investors pay the charge when they buy shares. "B" shares are back-loaded; investors pay a sales charge if they sell the fund within a certain period of time. "C" shares are "level-loaded," meaning they carry a small load on the back end but have a sky-high expense ratio (Figure 18.1). In our example, Thomas is considering the B share of the load fund.[2]

| Front- & Back-End Sales Charges (Loads) | | |
|---|---|---|
| Fund Type | Front-End Sales Charge | Back-End Sales Charge |
| No-Load Mutual Funds | 0% | 0% |
| Load Mutual Funds | | |
|    Class A Shares | 4–5% | 0% |
|    Class B Shares | 0% | 5% in year 1<br>4% in year 2<br>3% in year 3<br>2% in year 4<br>1% in year 5<br>0% in year 6 |
|    Class C Shares | 0% | 1% in year 1<br>0% in year 2 |

figure 18.1

No-load funds are a bit easier to evaluate since there are no sales charges when you buy or sell them.

The B share load fund Thomas is considering has an expense ratio of 2.06 percent per year, which is average for this type of load fund.[3] On a $100,000 investment, the fund will cost him $2,060 per year in unseen expenses. Keep in mind that these high expenses are what pay the fund manager's salary and the advisor a commission. When Thomas invests $100,000 into a B share, the fund company will typically pay his advisor a 4 percent up-front commission, or $4,000, and a commission of $250 each year that Thomas stays invested in the fund. If he buys the class B share fund, he won't write a check to the advisor for $4,000 to cover the commission. The commission is built into the higher annual expenses the fund charges. This is problematic for three reasons. First, the fees aren't transparent and it is rare that a commissioned advisor will disclose how much he/she will make when the fund is sold. Second, because Thomas doesn't know his advisor will receive $4,000 in commission, he likely won't demand $4,000 in service (i.e., a financial plan, consistent reviews, etc.). If he paid his attorney or CPA $4,000, you can bet he would expect $4,000 worth of service. He should expect the same from his advisor. And third, since the advisor is receiving the $4,000 commission up-front right when the transaction is complete and will receive very little each year thereafter, his advisor will have very little incentive to provide ongoing service. Since his advisor gets paid up-front, he can't make any more money off Thomas unless he sells him something else. Once Thomas has more money to invest, he will catch his advisor's interest again. Since his advisor isn't going to be compensated much going forward (just $250 per year), he will likely just move on and look for someone else to sell his products to. You can't altogether blame Thomas's advisor for all these problems. His advisor works for a company utilizing a flawed business model. He is likely doing the best he can with the products he is able to offer. There are some lessons to learn from Thomas's experience. If you do buy a loaded/commission product from an advisor, make sure you know how much your advisor will make in commission so you can make sure you receive an equal level of service. When possible, make sure you buy a product that pays the advisor a little at a time over time and not all up-front so he/she has incentive to provide ongoing service. If your advisor gets paid up-front, you run the risk of him/her forgetting all about you.

Also remember that the expense ratios of load funds tend to be higher than those of no-load funds. The funds' expenses are taken directly from its returns; the higher the funds' expenses, the lower your returns. For example, when I measured the performance of load versus no-load U.S. stock funds, I discovered that no-load funds provided 1 percent better returns for the past one, three, five, ten, and fifteen years (ending December 31, 2012).[4]

The B share fund Thomas is contemplating also has a five-year back-end sales charge. If Thomas sells the fund during the first five years, he will pay a sales charge that starts at 5 percent of the balance in the first year and declines to 0 percent at the six-year mark. If he wants to make changes with his investment during the next five years, it will cost him.

By contrast, the cost of the no-load fund is just 1.13 percent.[5] That's just $1,130 annually for a $100,000 portfolio. (You could easily find even cheaper no-load funds; some no-load index funds have expense ratios as low as 0.15 percent.) In addition to the lower annual expense, the no-load fund doesn't lock Thomas into owning it for five years. He can sell anytime if the fund isn't performing or he needs his money back.

Which would you choose if you were Thomas: the load fund or the no-load fund?

If all other variables are equal, why would Thomas choose to pay $2,060 per year, plus a back-end sales charge, when he can pay just $1,130 (a savings of $930)? Multiply that difference over ten, twenty, and thirty years, and he'll really see that costs do matter. We're not even taking into account the missed returns he would have earned if the money he saved with the cheaper fund was invested back into the fund. The funny thing about this scenario is that all the other variables can be exactly equal because some fund companies offer loaded share classes and no-load share classes of the very same fund.

Figure 18.2 outlines the annual expenses of the average mutual fund, according to Morningstar (December 31, 2012), broken down by load and no-load funds.

| Annual Built-In Mutual Fund Expenses | | | | | |
|---|---|---|---|---|---|
| Fund Type | Load Fund Class A | Load Fund Class B | Load Fund Class C | No-Load Fund | Difference between Load & No-Load |
| U.S. Equity | 1.40% | 2.06% | 2.04% | **1.13%** | 0.93% |
| U.S. Equity $100,000 | $1,400 | $2,060 | $2,040 | **$1,130** | $930 |
| U.S. Bond | 1.02% | 1.73% | 1.70% | **0.79%** | 0.94% |
| U.S. Bond $100,000 | $1,020 | $1,730 | $1,700 | **$790** | $940 |

*figure 18.2*

All mutual funds charge fees that are built in to the pricing of your shares. Because you will never receive a bill for these fees, however, most people have no idea what they are paying to have their money managed. By understanding the fees your funds are charging, you can often find ways to dramatically reduce your costs and increase your liquidity. One of the easiest ways to accomplish this is by owning no-load funds. Why pay more?

# Variable Annuities: Load vs. No-Load

After selling the land, Thomas decided to sock another $100,000 away for his retirement by purchasing a variable annuity. He's evaluated the performance and management of many annuities and narrowed his choices: a popular load annuity or a low-cost no-load annuity. As you'll see, buying a no-load annuity is an even bigger no-brainer than buying a no-load mutual fund.

Putting $100,000 into the load annuity will cost Thomas about $2,550 (2.55 percent) per year in insurance and fund-management expenses.[6] His insurance agent will receive a $5,000 up-front commission. By contrast, the no-load annuity will only cost him $570 (0.57 percent).[7] If all other variables are equal, why would he choose to pay $1,980 more each year to go with the more expensive annuity (Figure 18.3)? To make matters worse, the load annuity has a seven-year deferred sales charge. If he decides to move his money to an annuity at another company or surrender it during the first seven years, he will pay a surrender charge of 8 percent in year one, declining to 0 percent in year eight. In contrast, no-load annuities, like no-load mutual funds, do not tack on deferred sales charges, so his money is available anytime without penalty.

| Annual Built-In Variable Annuity Expenses | | |
|---|---|---|
| | Expense % | $100,000 Investment |
| **No-Load Variable Annuity** | | |
| *Vanguard Variable Annuity* | | |
| Insurance Expense | 0.30% | $300 |
| Fund Expense (Average) | 0.27% | $270 |
| **Total Expenses** | **0.57%** | **$570** |
| **Load Variable Annuity** | | |
| *John Hancock Venture Variable Annuity* | | |
| Insurance Expense | 1.40% | $1,400 |
| Fund Expense (Average) | 1.15% | $1,150 |
| **Total Expenses** | **2.55%** | **$2,550** |

figure 18.3

With the choice of 1,925 variable annuities, there is no reason to purchase one with high expenses and surrender charges. Vanguard, Fidelity, and TIAA-CREF are among the most well-known companies offering no-load annuities. Like Thomas, you would be wise to consider your no-load options before buying a variable annuity. Why pay more?

## Life Insurance: Load vs. No-Load

As you can see in Figure 18.4, no-load life insurance can also save you thousands of dollars each year. Let's assume Thomas now decides to purchase a $1 million variable universal life insurance policy. His commissioned advisor quoted him a minimum premium of $10,032 per year.[8] This policy has a ten-year surrender period, meaning he will incur a penalty if he withdraws any of his cash value during this time. Thomas's agent will make a commission of about 90 percent of the premium he'll pay in the first year, or $9,028! (Commission amounts vary company to company.) Thomas also obtained a comparable quote from a no-load life insurance company with a minimum premium of only $3,595 per year.[9] The no-load policy has no surrender charges, so his cash value is always available to him without penalty. With all assumptions being equal, why would he pay $6,437 more per year for the same amount of insurance and also agree to restrictions when he has a need to access cash value?

| Life Insurance Comparison | | |
|---|---|---|
| **$1 Million Universal Life** | **Load Policy** | **No-Load Policy** |
| *(Male, Non-Smoker, Age 55)* | *ING Reliastar Select\* Life III VUL* | *ING Security Life of Denver, Strategic Investor VUL* |
| Minimum 1st Year Premium | $10,032 | $3,595 |
| Cash Value (End of 1st Year) | $0 | $910 |
| Maximum Premium | $26,000 | $26,000 |
| Cash Value (End of 1st Year) | $7,298 | $24,777 |

figure 18.4

Never heard of no-load life insurance? You are not alone. Insurance agents are unwilling to discuss these policies with their clients because "no-load" means "no commission." What happens to insurance when you remove the agent and strip out the commissions? Often premiums for cash-value policies are slashed by 50 to 70 percent, and surrender charges are completely eliminated. If you need help finding a no-load insurance policy, pay an hourly fee to a fee-only planner.

Insurance companies incur expenses during the first year of a load policy of about 150 to 250 percent of the first-year premium payment. Because of these high costs, premiums are high. No-load insurance costs insurance companies only about 28 percent of the first year's premium.[10] These lower expenses translate into lower premiums for you.

How long is the surrender period on your cash-value policies? In order to recoup the high up-front expenses of load policies, insurance companies must charge consumers high premiums and strap on long surrender periods to policies in order to recover their high up-front costs. For example, if your policy has a fifteen-year surrender period, you will not be able to withdraw your cash value without paying a surrender charge (penalty) until the period is over. If you cancel your policy during the first few years, the surrender charge will likely equal 100 percent, meaning you will not receive any of your cash value if you pull your money out.

> Investors pay more than $6 billion each year in unnecessary surrender charges.[11]

It's outrageous what investors pay each year in surrender charges ($6 billion). Some policies even carry twenty-year surrender periods! Would you believe that more than 55 percent of traditional life insurance policies are canceled within the first five years and more than 90 percent are canceled by the twelfth year?[12] Considering your odds of canceling your policy during the first twelve years, it seems ludicrous to purchase insurance with a ten- to twenty-year surrender penalty period. Remember these statistics when your agent tries to convince you that you need to buy a whole life insurance policy to fund your retirement. According to these statistics, you have only a 10 percent chance of holding on to your policy for twelve years.

With no-load life insurance, however, you won't be penalized with surrender charges if you need to make a change in your insurance strategy. Because no-load policies have no surrender charges, cash values are immediately available. Lower premiums and no-surrender charges make a pretty good case for the purchase of no-load life insurance. Ameritas Life Insurance Co., Fidelity, ING Security Life of Denver, and TIAA-CREF each offer solid no-load policies (Figure 18.5). Finally, a life insurance policy without buyer's remorse! Why pay more if you don't have to?

## Buying No-Load Funds, Annuities, and Life Insurance

Before buying a no-load investment or insurance product, you must decide whether you want to do it yourself or retain the expertise of a financial advisor. If you're a "do-it-yourselfer," you can simply call the no-load companies and deal with them directly.

If you would like an investment professional to work with you face-to-face and help you evaluate and sift through all of the no-load products, hire a "fee-only" financial advisor. As opposed to commissioned brokers and agents, fee-only advisors do not accept commissions for recommending specific products—consequently, they can be totally objective. Fee-only advisors are compensated only by a previously agreed upon, fully disclosed fee with you, either paid hourly, by project, or as a percentage of assets managed. Fee-only advisors can help investors:

- Compare costs of load and no-load products.
- Identify and purchase cost-effective financial products.
- Sort through all the features and benefits each product offers.
- Develop an investment strategy and financial plan.
- Manage your portfolio and financial plan on an ongoing basis.

## What to Do If You Own Expensive Funds, Annuities, and Life Insurance

It's easy to make the move from load to no-load products.

First, have your investments and insurance analyzed to determine what you are actually paying and determine if a no-load solution could reduce your costs and increase your liquidity.

Second, check to see what you would be charged (if anything) to transfer your money from your loaded product. This is the biggest issue you'll face when making the switch from load to no-load. Beware of back-end and surrender charges and redemption fees. If these charges are substantial, you may have to wait it out until the back-end charges cease.

Third, determine if any tax consequences will result from the move to no-load. Selling your loaded mutual funds in a non-retirement account, for example, may result in a capital gain.

With mutual funds, you can directly transfer money from your load company to a no-load fund company or a discount brokerage firm. If you directly transfer an IRA, there are no taxes or penalties. With annuities and life insurance, you can transfer your cash surrender value tax-free to another annuity or life-insurance product (known as a 1035 exchange). Making the jump from load to no-load is simple, and it could save you a lot of money and increase your liquidity.

$$\bullet\ \bullet\ \bullet$$

Remember, "load" is synonymous with "commission." Loaded financial products are sold by commissioned financial advisors. To pay your advisor a commission, companies simply increase built-in expenses. They also strap on front- and back-end sales and surrender charges that restrict your ability to sell or withdraw your money without penalty. These restrictions are intended to keep you invested, so the load companies can recoup the money they must pay to your advisor. No-load products, by contrast, don't pay commissions to advisors and consequently don't have to build in high internal expenses and restrictive charges.

By choosing the no-load mutual fund, annuity, and life insurance policy in our example, Thomas would reduce his investment and insurance expenses by $9,347 per year (annual savings: mutual fund $930, variable annuity $1,980, and life insurance $6,437). If these savings continued for ten years, it would amount to more than $93,470. If we could account for his increased returns as a result of not having to pay these extra costs, and compound the savings over ten years, his savings would be considerably more.

Let's add up what Thomas's commissioned advisor would miss out on if he chooses the no-load route. On the $100,000 investment made into the mutual fund, the advisor would make 4 percent, or $4,000, and 5 percent, or $5,000, on the variable annuity. The life insurance policy would pay a $9,028 commission. That totals $18,028 that his advisor would receive immediately, all for filling out a few applications. The advisor would receive an ongoing commission of about $1,000 per year. This ongoing commission doesn't provide his advisor with much incentive to provide ongoing planning and investment management. Why would he want to spend time working with an existing client who is generating only $1,000 in commission for him each year when he could make another $18,028 in commission by finding another person like Thomas? If, for some reason, he does choose the load products, Thomas should insist that his advisor disclose the commissions he will receive and demand years of investment help and financial planning equal to this compensation.

| No-Load Companies | |
| --- | --- |
| **Mutual Funds** | |
| Vanguard | 1-800-662-7447 |
| Fidelity | 1-800-343-3548 |
| American Century | 1-800-345-2021 |
| Janus | 1-800-525-8983 |
| T. Rowe Price | 1-800-638-5660 |
| **Variable Annuities** | |
| Vanguard | 1-800-523-9954 |
| Fidelity | 1-800-544-2442 |
| TIAA/CREF | 1-800-842-2776 |
| Ameritas | 1-800-552-3553 |
| **Life Insurance** | |
| Fidelity | 1-888-343-8376 |
| Ameritas | 1-800-552-3553 |
| TIAA/CREF | 1-866-966-5623 |

figure 18.5

Although cost is only one variable to consider when choosing investments and insurance, it must not be overlooked. Carefully evaluate the investment and insurance expenses you pay. By making some minor adjustments, you may save thousands of dollars.

# 19

# A MISSION STATEMENT FOR YOUR MONEY

## RETIREMENT DECISION #15: HOW WILL I MANAGE MY PORTFOLIO ON AN ONGOING BASIS?

Have you ever found yourself in the same position as Calvin Morton? Calvin invested $350,000 a few years ago at retirement into a balanced portfolio of several stock and bond mutual funds. He grew increasingly frustrated with the performance of his portfolio after listening to friends tout their investment successes. He decided it was time to make some changes. He diligently read the most popular investment magazines and surfed financial websites for several months looking for investment ideas. At last, he found an article, "The 10 Best Funds." It highlighted ten funds that beat the pants off his diversified portfolio over the past year. He sold each of his funds and bought the top five funds listed in the magazine article, all of which happened to be small-company growth stock funds. Mistake? Probably. The funds he purchased racked up big numbers during the previous year but lacked long-term performance consistency, had high expenses, and were invested entirely in just one part of the stock market. By adjusting his portfolio, Calvin reduced his diversification and increased his level of risk, two things he shouldn't be doing during retirement.

Although Calvin started out with a well-balanced, diversified portfolio, greed set in and his strategy was quickly abandoned and forgotten. You, like Calvin, may have already found that the first three steps of the investment process are easy; the hard part is sticking to your investment strategy over time. Adhering to an investment discipline is extremely difficult without a predetermined set of written rules to govern your future investment decisions.

Calvin would likely have made better decisions if he had prepared a mission statement for his money, a statement answering the following questions:

- What is your target investment return?
- How will you diversify your portfolio?
- What amount of risk is acceptable?
- How are you going to measure performance?
- When will you sell an investment?
- What criteria will you use to choose new investments?

## Mission Statement for Your Money: Investment Policy Statement

Now that you have determined your asset allocation (Step 1) and diversification mix (Step 2), and you have selected the best investments available (Step 3), it's time to formalize your investment strategy by developing a written mission statement for your money. This mission statement is more commonly called an investment policy statement. Your investment policy statement will establish a clear set of rules you will use to govern your future investment decisions and will be an integral part of Step 4: Ongoing Portfolio Management. This will take the guesswork out of your future decisions and help you discipline your own actions. This step is imperative; in fact, if you fully understood its importance, you wouldn't invest a penny without first developing a mission statement for your money.

The purpose of an investment policy statement is to:

1. Establish a clear understanding of your investment objectives.
2. Outline your investment time horizon.
3. State income needs.
4. Establish reasonable risk and return expectations.
5. Outline a portfolio framework and structure, including permissible ranges of exposure into different asset classes.
6. Outline the investment philosophy to which you are adhering (buy and hold, rebalancing, etc.).
7. State the selection process used to identify your investments and the types of investments that will be used in the portfolio.

8.  Establish a sell discipline and determine at what point you will sell.
9.  Provide an outline of duties and responsibilities of your financial advisor, if you're working with one.

## Investment Policy Statements Made Simple

An investment policy statement does not have to be extravagant like those used by money managers to govern the investment decisions of 401(k)s, pensions, and endowment funds. The important thing is that it is in writing, so you can refer back to it when you review your portfolio or get a little anxious about the direction your portfolio is taking at the moment. By going through this process, you'll eliminate the guesswork of investing.

To make this easy, I have created a fill-in-the-blank investment policy statement for you to use or copy as you develop your own investment policy (see next page).

If Calvin had an investment policy statement in place before he evaluated his portfolio and made changes, do you think he would have acted so impulsively? I believe he would have handled the pressure much better. First, he would not have compared his investments to those of his friends who have different investment objectives than his own. He would have instead compared his performance to the performance expectations outlined in his investment policy statement. If a few of his investments were in fact underperforming, he would have followed his plan of attack for identifying new investments to take their place. Ultimately, he would have fared much better.

It is not important whether you type up a formal statement, scribble some notes on a yellow pad, or fill in the blanks in the above sample investment policy statement. The important thing is that you establish a clear set of rules in writing to govern your investment decisions. By having prepared your mission statement ahead of time, you will avoid making impulsive decisions when your portfolio goes through difficult times. When you set your objectives in advance, it becomes easy to stick to them. It is easy to adhere to an investment strategy if you've done your homework ahead of time and know what to expect from your portfolio.

# My Investment Policy Statement

Name _____

Date  _____

Age   _____

## OBJECTIVE

My investment objective is to:

_____

_____

_____

_____

## TIME HORIZON

My investment time horizon is _____ (years).

## INCOME NEEDS & TAXES

I will need to withdraw $ _____ from my portfolio each year.

The money I am investing is _____ (taxable/nontaxable/both).

## TARGET RETURN & ASSETS

My target average rate of return is _____%. This was determined when I developed my financial plan.

To obtain this rate of return, I am investing _____% of my portfolio in stocks, _____% in bonds, and _____% in cash.

## RISK

To set my risk and return expectations, I am using historical data to measure risk. Long-Term 1926–2012: A portfolio allocated similar to mine from 1926 to 2012 averaged _____% per year. The worst year this portfolio experienced was _____%, while in the best year it produced a _____% return (Figure 11.6 in Chapter 11). Short-Term 1970–2012: A portfolio allocated similar to mine from 1970 to 2012 averaged _____% per year. The worst year this portfolio experienced was a return of _____%, while in the best year it produced a _____% return. My model portfolio experienced _____ (how many) positive years and _____ negative years from 1970 through 2012 (Figures 14.2 through 14.12 in Chapter 14). I can accept this amount of risk in the future _____ (initial).

I understand that using past performance to determine my risk and return requirements will give me a rough idea of what to expect from the mix of investments I have chosen. However, I do realize that there is no guarantee of these results repeating.

## DIVERSIFICATION

I am adhering to the following diversification strategy:

| | |
|---|---|
| *Stocks* | _____% |
| Large-Cap Growth | _____% |
| Large-Cap Value | _____% |
| Mid-Cap Growth | _____% |
| Mid-Cap Value | _____% |
| Small-Cap Growth | _____% |
| Small-Cap Value | _____% |
| International Growth & Value | _____% |
| *Bonds* | _____% |
| Government Bonds | _____% |
| Corporate Bonds | _____% |
| Municipal Bonds | _____% |
| International Bonds | _____% |
| *Cash* | _____% |
| Money Market/CDs/T-Bills | _____% |
| *Other* | _____% |
| Total: | _____% |

## INVESTMENT SELECTION

I will identify the best investments for my portfolio by screening the investments I buy and applying the following criteria:

_____

_____

_____

_____

_____

_____

_____

(For example, you might state, "I will start with the whole universe of mutual funds within a specific asset class. I will narrow my search by looking for funds that have above-average performance for the past one, three, five, and ten years versus their peers. I will only buy funds with managers who have more than ten years' experience managing money. I will only buy funds that have beaten their respective benchmark index for at least six out of the past ten years. I will buy funds with managers who have been true to their size [i.e., large-cap, small-cap, etc.] and style [growth/value] objectives. I will buy no-load funds with expense ratios below 1 percent. I will review my investments every six months and will sell only if there is a manager change or if the fund is no longer meeting my performance criteria. Of course, I will evaluate each possible sell on a case-by-case basis and take taxes into consideration.")

## TYPES OF SECURITIES

I will purchase _____ (individual stocks, stock mutual funds, or separately managed stock accounts) for my stock portfolio.

I will purchase _____ (individual bonds, bond mutual funds, or separately managed bond accounts) for my bond portfolio.

I will purchase _____ (certificates of deposits, money market mutual funds, Treasury bills, or other) for my cash portfolio.

I will follow a "buy and hold" investment strategy.

I will rebalance my portfolio _____ (quarterly, semiannually, or annually). (See Chapter 20.)

## FINANCIAL ADVISOR EXPECTATIONS

I am working with an investment advisor. He/she has agreed to meet with me every _____ months to review my financial plan and investment portfolio. My financial advisor is charging me _____% each year to manage my portfolio. (Note: If you are buying loaded funds and don't know what fees you are being charged, refer to Chapter 18 to see how to determine what your built-in fees are and Chapter 3, Figure 3.2, to calculate how much money your advisor and his/her firm will be making on your investment.) In dollars, I am paying my advisor (and his/her firm) $ _____ per year. I expect my financial advisor to provide advice and service equal to what I am paying in fees; if not, I will fire him/her. We have outlined this in a contract signed on _____ (date).

Signature _____ Date _____

# 20

# ROUTINE CHECKUPS

## RETIREMENT DECISION #15 (CONTINUED): HOW WILL I MANAGE MY PORTFOLIO ON AN ONGOING BASIS?

C ongratulations! By following the steps outlined in the previous nine chapters, you are light-years ahead of most investors. You have properly allocated your money, diversified it, and purchased good, consistent investments using the help of professional money managers. Surprisingly, however, the first three steps are the easiest in the investment process. Would you believe that the real work begins after you purchase your investments?

It's not easy to adhere to a disciplined investment strategy. You should review your investment portfolio twice a year and update your overall financial plan at least once a year. Following the steps outlined in this chapter will help you regularly evaluate and make adjustments to your portfolio to keep it on track to meet your goals.

If you want to make money investing, you should buy good investments with the intent of holding them for the long term, while making only occasional adjustments. That may sound easy, but it's not. Compared to the hypertrading habits of many investors, making only minor, infrequent changes may feel like you're doing nothing to increase your wealth. Buying and holding good investments requires a tremendous amount of self-discipline. For example, if a portion of your portfolio is underperforming, your natural instincts will tell you to take immediate action and make changes. The more it lags, the more changes you'll want to make. This is where your self-discipline needs to kick in. The investment decisions you make at these points will greatly determine your investment success or failure.

Taking too much action often leads to poor investment results. However, by avoiding excessive adjustments to your portfolio and keeping your eye focused on long-term investment results, you're far more likely to enjoy success. Remember, it is not important how your portfolio performs during a one-month stretch or even over the course of a year, but rather how it does during the next five, ten, fifteen, and twenty years.

Although this is a buy-and-hold strategy for investing, I'm not suggesting that you invest your money and then completely forget about it. You should monitor your portfolio every six months and make adjustments when necessary. Most of the time you will be better off simply being patient with the investments you own. However, as you will learn in this chapter, there are times when you'll have valid reasons to sell investments and replace them with others.

Investors who remain patient with their investments and stay disciplined through the market's ups and downs will be rewarded for their ability to stay the course.

## Portfolio Reviews

Every six months, you should review your investment portfolio. There is no reason to do this more frequently if you have hired good professional money managers and are properly diversified. It's your money manager's job to watch your individual stocks and bonds daily, so there is absolutely no reason to spend hours each day on the Internet looking at your money. Constant monitoring will only increase the temptation to start tinkering.

The purpose of a semiannual review is not to change your asset allocation or dramatically alter your investments, but rather to give your portfolio a routine checkup and do whatever fine-tuning is needed. Often semiannual reviews can be completed in just ten to fifteen minutes.

If you are working with a financial advisor, request that he or she review your portfolio with you at least every six months. Don't be afraid to ask for a review if your advisor hasn't taken the initiative to set up a schedule for review meetings. Semiannual reviews can often be conducted informally over the phone, particularly if nothing alarming is occurring in the market. Financial advisors have tools that make such reviews an easy task.

Your investment checkup will help you determine if your portfolio is performing within the parameters you established in your investment policy statement (Chapter 19). Conducted properly, a review will bring to the surface any problems that exist in the portfolio. Start by evaluating your portfolio as a whole before breaking it down into its individual pieces. Once a problem is identified, changes can be made. However, as a general rule, if you can make a case for keeping an investment, you should probably do so. If you can't, then you should sell it and seek a better alternative.

There are a number of questions you should ask when conducting a portfolio review. Use these questions when you meet with your advisor or conduct your own portfolio review. Your answers to these questions will determine if your portfolio is meeting expectations or if modifications should be made.

## Portfolio Allocation

- Is my portfolio out of alignment? Does it need to be rebalanced?
- Will there be tax consequences and other costs if I rebalance?

Note: Your target stock, bond, and cash allocations need to be adjusted only every three to five years if your investment objectives change. For example, an investor with 70 percent of his portfolio invested in stocks may want to reduce his stock weighting as he transitions into retirement and his tolerance for risk changes. You should never alter your allocation strategy due to short-term market gyrations.

## Overall Portfolio Performance

- Is my portfolio meeting performance and risk expectations as outlined in my investment policy statement?

## Individual Investments

- Are my money managers meeting performance expectations?
- How are they performing versus their peers and benchmarks over the short and long term?
- Has any size or style drift occurred with any of my funds?
- Have there been any money manager changes?

- Are any of the managers causing unwanted tax consequences due to excessive trading? (This question is not applicable for money in retirement accounts.)

Let's take a closer look at each of these questions and why you need to get good answers to each of them.

## *Is My Portfolio Out of Alignment?*

Your portfolio allocation—how your money is divided among different asset classes—will change over time as a result of individual investments growing at different rates of return. Rebalancing is the process of realigning the portfolio back to its original allocation targets. By rebalancing your portfolio annually, it will grow more consistently, maintain the level of risk you initially outlined as acceptable, and often enhance your portfolio returns.

To better understand the need for rebalancing, let's assume you invested in an aggressive diversified portfolio consisting of 80 percent stocks, 15 percent bonds, and 5 percent cash beginning in 2009. Left unchecked and never rebalanced, this portfolio was significantly out of alignment by 2012 (Figure 20.1). As you can see, the portfolio shifted from 80 percent stocks in 2009 to 85 percent stocks by the end of 2012 due to strong stock market returns. This increase in the amount invested in stocks put your money more at risk than you originally determined was acceptable. In addition, the portfolio shifted more heavily to growth stocks. This portfolio by 2012 was sitting at 38 percent large-, mid-, and small-cap growth stocks, up from the 32 percent in 2009. This shift to growth stocks occurred in many investors' portfolios from 2009 to 2012. This also occurred in the years leading up to the bursting of the tech bubble in 2000.

Once you start banking heavily on one sector of the market, one style of investing, or one asset class, you run the increased risk of experiencing heavy losses if your overweighted investments underperform. And for growth stocks, that's exactly what occurred in 2000. Growth stocks took a beating in 2000 and continued to get hammered in 2001 and 2002. In 2000, large-cap growth stocks fell 25 percent, while large-cap value stocks rose 1 percent; mid-cap growth stocks dropped 15 percent, while their mid-cap value competitors jumped 25 percent; and small-cap growth stocks dropped 25 percent, while small-cap value stocks gained 23 percent. Would

| Aggressive Portfolio Over Time | | |
|---|---|---|
| Asset Class | Jan. 1, 2009 | Dec. 31, 2012 |
| Large-Cap Growth Stocks | 20% | 22% |
| Large-Cap Value Stocks | 20% | 19% |
| Mid-Cap Growth Stocks | 8% | 11% |
| Mid-Cap Value Stocks | 8% | 9% |
| Small-Cap Growth Stocks | 4% | 5% |
| Small-Cap Value Stocks | 4% | 5% |
| International Growth & Value Stocks | 16% | 14% |
| Corporate Bonds | 5% | 5% |
| Government Bonds | 5% | 4% |
| International Bonds | 5% | 3% |
| Cash | 5% | 3% |
| Allocation | | |
| Stocks | 80% | 85% |
| Bonds | 15% | 12% |
| Cash | 5% | 3% |

figure 20.1

you really have wanted to be that overexposed to growth stocks during the 2000–2002 recession? In hindsight, the answer is no. Annual rebalancing will protect you from the possibility of becoming overexposed to one or two asset classes or investment styles.

The same aggressive portfolio (80 percent stocks, 15 percent bonds, and 5 percent cash) would have been knocked dramatically out of alignment in 2008. Because of the stock market plunge, the stock portion of the portfolio would represent only 68 percent of the total portfolio at year's end. Bonds represented 25 percent of the portfolio and cash 7 percent. Rebalancing would require an investor with this portfolio to sell bonds and cash investments and add money to stocks to bring them back to 80 percent of the portfolio. This was not easy to do. But was it a good idea? By having more money in stocks during the market's giant 110 percent rebound that began in the second quarter of 2009, portfolio losses were made back more quickly. So yes, it was a good idea.

Rebalancing is difficult because it requires you to do the opposite of what you think you should do: sell some of your winning investments and buy more of your losing investments. This will go against your natural instincts. Who is excited to sell a recent winner to buy a recent loser? By following this course of action, however, you will be forcing yourself to *sell* some of your investments *high* that have recently done well and *buy low* as you add to underperforming asset classes in your portfolio. This disciplined process of selling high and buying low to rebalance will help you enhance your investment returns.

Rebalancing also allows you to control your portfolio risk and sustain growth at a more consistent rate. If your portfolio consists of stocks and bonds and is not checked regularly, stocks, because of their higher expected growth, will likely outperform bonds, causing your stock weighting to become a larger piece of your portfolio, while your bond weighting shrinks. This imbalance will make your portfolio more aggressive than you initially planned and put you in a risky position. By rebalancing your portfolio, risk is controlled.

## Will I Face Tax Consequences and Other Costs if I Rebalance?

Once you make the decision to rebalance, there are two additional factors to consider. First, will there be any tax consequences? If so, do your rebalancing in a retirement account where taxes can be avoided. Second, will there be any cost to rebalance? In many cases, you may be required to pay a small transaction fee to move from one fund to another.

## Is My Portfolio Meeting Performance and Risk Expectations as Outlined in My Investment Policy Statement?

During your semiannual portfolio evaluation, take another look at your investment policy statement. It will outline realistic short- and long-term expectations and acceptable levels of risk and volatility. Is your overall portfolio meeting the performance and risk expectations as outlined in your investment policy statement?

For example, your portfolio may be built to provide annual returns between –10 percent and positive 20 percent annually, with a target long-term average of 10 percent. If your portfolio drops 8 percent or gains 18 percent, you're operating within the range of your expectations. If in a given year the portfolio drops 25 percent, however, you may want to take a closer look. Some of your money managers may be investing too aggressively or dramatically underperforming their benchmarks. Further examination of each manager is recommended if this occurs.

## Are My Money Managers Meeting Performance Expectations?

To answer this question, you need the correct performance yardstick. For example, you can't compare the performance of a small-company stock mutual fund to the Dow Jones Industrial Average or the S&P 500 (both large-company stock indicators). It's not an apples-to-apples comparison. The correct performance yardstick for small-company stock funds is the performance of other small-company stock funds or a small-company index like the Russell 2000.

Now let's suppose your money manager, who once had performance numbers in the top of an investment category, slides below average for a year or two. What should you do? This is likely to happen to even the best managers at one time or another. Yes, it's frustrating to see a fund slip from among the best in its category to below average, but your best course of action is still to stay put. A quick study of any of today's top mutual funds will reveal that they don't stay at the very top of their respective categories year in and year out. This would be virtually impossible. Money managers' investment styles will naturally go in and out of favor with the market, outperforming in some years and underperforming in others.

We buy funds when there is consistent above-average performance, and we sell when the performance falls consistently below average. When extended poor performance occurs, put the money manager on trial and see if you can build a case for continued ownership; if not, make a change. Below are several items to consider as you attempt to make a case for your investment.

## How Are My Managers Performing Versus Their Peers and Benchmarks over the Short and Long Term?

### Short-Term Performance

Let's suppose you owned a large-cap international stock fund that was down 8 percent in 2011. You can't help but notice that the S&P 500 climbed 2.11 percent for the same period. It would be easy to get down on your large-cap international fund, wouldn't it?

Actually, this comparison doesn't provide you with enough information to make a decision with your investment. Remember, it doesn't really matter how your international fund did against the S&P 500. A far more useful and accurate comparison would be to match your fund's performance versus all of the other large-cap international funds. In this example, you would find that the average large-cap international fund posted only a –13.77 percent return in 2011. If your fund provided you with a –8 percent return, then you should be quite pleased. This performance would have placed your fund in the top 6 percent of all large-cap international funds in 2011.[1] As a general rule, if your fund posts performance numbers that are above the average when compared with its respective category, then you should hold on to it.

The same comparison can be made against a market index. An index measures a representative group of stocks to provide information about how certain sectors of the market are performing. Each money manager uses an index as a benchmark to evaluate their performance. For example, our large-cap international fund provided a –8 percent return in 2011 while the MSCI EAFE Index (international stocks) posted a –14.82 percent return. This is another indication that your fund did a nice job.

## Long-Term Performance

Let's change the scenario and assume that your fund isn't doing well and its performance is below the average of its peer group and respective tracking index. What do you do then? The smart thing is to turn to its performance over longer time periods, such as three, five, and ten years. By looking at the long-term numbers, you can see how your fund did through complete business cycles. Although future performance will not be identical to past years, studying historical returns should provide an indication of the fund's potential. For example, what would you do with the Ivy Mid Cap Growth fund if you owned it when you conducted your 2012 year-end review? You may be concerned because for the previous twelve months, 60 percent of the mid-cap growth funds had better one-year performance numbers. During this same period its respective index, the Russell Mid Cap Growth Index, was up 15.81 percent while the Ivy fund was only up 13.11 percent.[2]

During 2012 it underperformed its peer group, mid-cap growth stock funds, and its respective index. Research tells us that before 2012, the fund was considered one of the best-performing mid-cap growth funds available. Should it be held or sold? Further examination is required.

How did the fund perform over the longer term? The performance column in Figure 20.2 outlines the average annual returns for the fund for various periods of time through December 31, 2012. Although performance was poor in the short term, Ivy Mid Cap Growth fund was one of the leading mid-cap growth stock funds for longer time periods. Its rank was in the top of its category for the past three-, five-, and ten-year periods. It has also outperformed the Russell Mid Growth Index, beating it six out of the previous ten years. A $10,000 investment made at the beginning of 2002 would have grown to $21,065 through 2012, while the Russell Mid Growth Index increased to $19,385.[3]

| Ivy Mid Cap Growth Fund (WMGAX) December 31, 2012 | | | |
|---|---|---|---|
| | Fund Performance | % Rank vs. Category | Index Performance* |
| Last Year | 13.11% | 60 | 15.81% |
| Last 3 Years | 13.40% | 19 | 12.91% |
| Last 5 Years | 6.00% | 7 | 3.23% |
| Last 10 Years | 11.01% | 15 | 10.32% |
| Last 15 Years | 9.50% | 4 | 5.98% |

* Russell Mid Growth Index

figure 20.2

What should we do with this fund? Watch it more closely in upcoming reviews to see if the manager can turn the performance around. Hold it for now; it's been a good, solid long-term fund. But check it in your next review.

If a manager has done a good job over the long term but just recently stumbled, you should hold on. Every manager is going to have a rough year occasionally. Flag the fund, however, and watch its performance for another year. If the fund continues to underperform, it will be a sell candidate next year.

## Manager Tenure and Performance Figures

When reviewing long-term performance numbers, remember to check the length of time the manager has been handling the portfolio. If the term is, say, just two or three years, then the five- and ten-year performance numbers are irrelevant because they were achieved by a different manager. In the case of Ivy Mid Cap Growth fund, Kimberly Scott has been managing the fund for twelve years.

## *Has Any Size or Style Drift Occurred with Any of My Funds?*

Is your fund manager staying true to the fund's size and style objectives? If not, it often means the manager is chasing returns and not adhering to the fund's stated investment discipline.

This frequently happened in 1999. Value managers, after enduring several years of poor performance relative to growth managers, began buying growth stocks to get in on the action. Growth stocks were leading the market at the time. Unfortunately for their shareholders, when value stocks came back into favor in 2000, many value funds didn't do as well as they should have because of this shift in strategy. Many of their portfolios were overloaded with technology growth stocks, and this hurt performance in 2000.

If you have developed a well-diversified portfolio, a manager who suddenly changes the fund's size or style objectives could dramatically throw your portfolio diversification out of balance. For example, if you had allocated your portfolio as outlined in the Target Allocation column in Figure 20.3, what effect would it have on your portfolio if your large-cap value manager began buying growth-oriented stocks and your small-cap value fund began buying mid-cap value stocks? Your allocation would entirely change and your portfolio would no longer be covering all of the desired bases (see the last column in Figure 20.3).

The portfolio in the previous example is no longer as diversified as it should be. If this style drift had occurred sometime in 1999, this portfolio would have suffered much worse than it should have in 2000 and 2001 when growth stocks fell out of favor.

How do you avoid this problem? During each review, check your fund's size and investment style to make sure the manager is handling your money as you intended. If the manager is not adhering to his or her size and style mandates, consider another fund.

| Ultra Aggressive Growth Portfolio | | |
|---|---|---|
| Asset Class | Target Allocation | Actual Allocation |
| Large-Cap Growth Stocks | 22.5% | 35.0% |
| Large-Cap Value Stocks | 22.5% | 10.0% |
| Mid-Cap Growth Stocks | 12.5% | 12.5% |
| Mid-Cap Value Stocks | 12.5% | 15.5% |
| Small-Cap Growth Stocks | 5.0% | 5.0% |
| Small-Cap Value Stocks | 5.0% | 2.0% |
| International Growth Stocks | 10.0% | 10.0% |
| International Value Stocks | 10.0% | 10.0% |
| Bonds | 0.0% | 0.0% |

figure 20.3

## Have There Been Any Money Manager Changes?

What do you do if one of your fund managers leaves a fund? This is often a signal to sell, but don't do so hastily without diligently collecting and reviewing all of the essential information.

Find out how successful the newly hired money manager was in his or her previous fund-management experience. If the manager has successfully handled a similar fund, you may want to hold tight and take a "wait-and-see" approach. Give the manager some time to prove him- or herself before deciding to sell the fund. However, if the manager does not have much management experience or has not managed successfully in the past, consider selling the fund immediately. In many cases, the new fund manager will dramatically alter the portfolio and management discipline. This is typically not a good thing for investors.

## Are Any of My Managers Causing Unwanted Tax Consequences Due to Excessive Trading?

If you are investing in a non-retirement account, taxes are most likely a concern. Although you should have a rough idea of what taxes to expect from a fund before you purchase it, it is still a good idea to check the fund during reviews to see that its turnover rate hasn't ramped up recently. Increasing turnover rates in funds drive up the chances you will get hit with higher-than-expected capital gains distributions.

If no manager changes have taken place, your managers are staying true to their size and style mandates, the funds are performing in line with their respective indexes, and the overall portfolio performance is within expectations, there is no reason to make any adjustments.

## Selling a Fund

If you do sell a fund, don't repeat the big mistake made by so many investors–taking your proceeds and reinvesting them in a fund from whichever asset class has recently enjoyed the most success during the past twelve months! This is a classic way to sell low and buy high. Replace a large-growth fund, for example, with a better, more consistent large-growth fund. By approaching changes this way, you will be able to maintain your asset allocation and diversification targets.

Morningstar.com is an excellent source when conducting a portfolio review. In addition, Morningstar offers other services that will help you monitor your portfolio, including e-mail bulletins to alert you to any fund-manager changes, performance problems, style drift, and much more.

Most financial advisors have computer programs that allow them to save your investment criteria on their systems when you initially invest. They can call them up easily for you during each semiannual review.

Remember, reviewing your portfolio is important, but don't confuse regular reviewing with excessive trading. The latter will do little to aid your success as an investor.

## Adhere to Your Strategy

If you have followed the first three steps for developing a successful investment strategy as outlined in the past nine chapters, you have properly allocated your money, diversified it, and purchased good investments using the help of professional money managers. As was noted at the beginning of this chapter, however, the first three steps are actually the easiest in the investment process. The real work begins after you purchase your investments. By following the guidelines outlined in this chapter on how to best manage your portfolio, you will greatly increase your chances of adhering to a solid investment strategy and obtaining good long-term returns.

# SECTION 4

## INSURANCE AND RETIREMENT

Health Insurance
Long-Term-Care Insurance
Life Insurance

# 21

# HEART SURGERY ISN'T CHEAP

## RETIREMENT DECISION #16: HOW WILL I COVER MY MEDICAL EXPENSES DURING RETIREMENT?

Walter Sheller, a production manager at a large manufacturing firm, and his wife, Margaret, a nurse, would like to retire next year at age 62 but are worried that their $500,000 nest egg is not large enough to sustain them once they factor in the cost of health care. Their concern is a result of the large medical bills Walter accrued a few years ago. At age 59, Walter had a heart attack that eventually required heart valve surgery. Heart problems are one of the most costly medical conditions (Figure 21.1).[1] The procedure came with a $36,418 price tag. Fortunately, Walter's group health insurance covered most of the expense at the time, so he had very little out-of-pocket costs. They are worried that if similar expenses are incurred after they retire it could put them on the path of depleting their nest egg prematurely. Let's break it down for the Shellers and see what the same procedure would cost before and after reaching the Medicare age of 65.

| The 10 Most Costly Medical Conditions | |
|---|---|
| 1 | Heart Conditions |
| 2 | Trauma |
| 3 | Cancer |
| 4 | Mental Disorders |
| 5 | Arthritis |
| 6 | Pulmonary Conditions |
| 7 | Hypertension |
| 8 | Diabetes |
| 9 | High Cholesterol |
| 10 | Back Problems |

figure 21.1

Most retirees receive health insurance from either Medicare, private insurance, or a continuation of their employer-provided coverage (Figure 21.2).[2] As of 2014, another option, Obamacare, was added to the list of options. This chapter will discuss these health insurance options, and how understanding each of them will help protect your nest egg and ensure that you are able to make the most of your retirement years.

## Private Insurance

If you're planning on early retirement and your employer doesn't provide health insurance to its retirees, you have some major health insurance decisions ahead of you. Medicare coverage doesn't kick in until age 65. That means most people retiring early will either need private insurance or will need to pick up a policy via their state health insurance exchange. This is the boat the Shellers find themselves in right now.

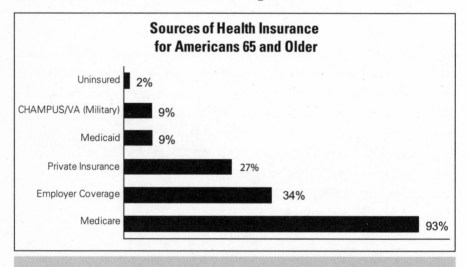

**Sources of Health Insurance for Americans 65 and Older**

Uninsured — 2%
CHAMPUS/VA (Military) — 9%
Medicaid — 9%
Private Insurance — 27%
Employer Coverage — 34%
Medicare — 93%

figure 21.2

For people ages 62 to 64, private health insurance premiums range between $500 and $1,000 per month. If you are planning to retire before age 65, start evaluating your health insurance options as soon as possible. To see what your coverage will cost visit www.ehealthinsurance.com or one of the many websites that provide instant online health insurance quotes, or contact a local health insurance agent.

### The Shellers–Private Insurance

The Shellers will pay a $668 premium per month if they opt for a private policy with a $2,500 deductible and a 70/30 copay. The Shellers will pay 30 percent of medical expenses out-of-pocket after paying their $2,500 deductible. So, back to the question, if they incurred a $36,418 health bill under this scenario, what would it cost them total out-of-pocket? The answer is $7,500. Their policy has an annual out-of-pocket limit of $5,000 (plus their deductible of $2,500).

On average, older Americans spend $4,769 per year on out-of-pocket health-care expenses. By contrast, the total population spends only $3,313.[3]

## Strategies for Keeping Premiums Down

You can keep your premium costs down by purchasing a comprehensive medical policy with a high deductible. This will mean you'll cover a sizable portion of the routine medical costs out of your own pocket, like doctor visits and prescriptions. The purpose of the policy is to help cover the cost of major, nonroutine health problems. Purchasing a high-deductible policy could save you $4,000 to $5,000 in premiums each year. Figure 21.3 compares the same policy at different deductibles. The policy with a $500 deductible is 300 percent more expensive than the policy with a $10,000 deductible.

| Premium Comparison for a 62-Year-Old Couple | | |
| --- | --- | --- |
| **Annual Deductible** | **Monthly Premium** | **Annual Premium** |
| $500 | $982 | $11,784 |
| $1,000 | $923 | $11,076 |
| $3,000 | $673 | $8,076 |
| $5,000 | $569 | $6,828 |
| $10,000 | $322 | $3,864 |

figure 21.3

### The Shellers–Private High-Deductible Insurance

The Shellers are toying with the idea of buying a policy with a $10,000 deductible and a 70/30 copay. It'll only cost them $293 per month, instead of the $668 each month for the private policy with the $2,500 deductible. They'll save $4,500 each year in premiums with a high-deductible policy. If they go with this option, the maximum they'll pay if they incurred a $36,418 medical bill would be $20,000 (maximum out-of-pocket $10,000 plus their deductible $10,000). While saving $4,500 in premiums each year sounds nice, with Walt's health problems, they anticipate they could have some sizable ongoing expenses and don't want to risk paying so much out-of-pocket. They will likely decide against a high-deductible policy. For very healthy retirees who can afford it, a high-deductible policy often makes lots of sense.

## Health Savings Accounts (HSAs)

If you are going to buy a high-deductible health insurance plan, you may as well buy one that will provide you with some tax advantages, too. Through the Health Savings Account (HSA), you can receive a tax deduction for money you spend on health care. To qualify for the tax deduction, you must purchase a *qualified* high-deductible health insurance policy. Annual insurance deductibles must be between $1,250 and $6,250 for an individual and $2,500 and $12,500 for a family (2013). You will also need to open a health savings account. An HSA is similar to opening an IRA. You simply deposit money into an HSA at a financial institution of your choice. The money you contribute to your HSA is tax-deductible up to the HSA contribution limits. You can contribute up to $3,250 for individual coverage and up to $6,450 for family coverage. Individuals over age 55 can also contribute an additional $1,000 each year (2013). From your HSA, you pay your medical expenses.

Any money you don't use this year can be used in subsequent years or can be invested. HSA money not used to cover medical expenses grows tax-deferred and can be withdrawn after age 65 without penalty and used as an additional source of retirement income. A 15 percent penalty will apply to money withdrawn prior to age 65 that is not used to cover qualified medical expenses.

Some people buy HSA coverage, contribute the maximum, and then pay for all of their medical expenses out-of-pocket rather than dipping into their HSA. So, they receive the tax deduction for their contribution and then invest the HSA money toward retirement. In this way the HSA works like an IRA with a tax-deductible contribution and ongoing tax deferral on growth.

### The Shellers–Qualified HSA Policy

The Shellers are also looking at a qualified HSA policy. They can purchase a policy with a $6,450 deductible, with no copay and a $430 monthly premium. Since they are over age 55, they can contribute $7,450 to their HSA and receive a $7,450 tax deduction. The maximum they'll pay if they incurred a $36,418 medical bill would be $11,900 (maximum out-of-pocket $5,450 plus their deductible $7,450).

Private health insurance can be expensive, but when you consider that it protects your well-being and your nest egg, it's worth every penny. If you retire before age 65, you must consider your health insurance needs and your available insurance options. If you don't have insurance, you will be jeopardizing the assets you've built up over many years of hard work. A serious illness can deplete your resources in the blink of an eye.

## Obamacare

The Patient Protection and Affordable Care Act (Obamacare) goes into effect in 2014. The three biggest provisions of the Act are: (1) the creation of state health insurance exchanges, (2) that you can't be denied coverage due to preexisting conditions, and (3) that you are required to carry health insurance coverage or pay a penalty ($95 or 1 percent of income, whichever is greater).

Does it make more sense to purchase a private policy or obtain coverage through your state's health insurance exchange? This decision will largely depend on your income level and the policy benefits you want. If you want a policy with lots of extras and more flexibility, you may want to buy a private policy. You may be able to find a private policy that actually costs less than those offered on the exchange.

If you are married with annual gross income of less than $60,520 or $44,680 if you are single (2014), your insurance premium is subsidized by the government and can't be more than 9.5 percent of your income (Figure 21.4). For example, if your income is $50,000 per year, your premium will be $396 per month ($4,750 per year).[4]

| Obamacare for a Retired Couple (not yet 65) | | | | |
|---|---|---|---|---|
| 2014 Silver Level Plan (you pay 30% of costs after deductible | | | | |
| Income | $20,000 | $30,000 | $40,000 | $50,000 | $60,000 |
| Annual Premium | $1,900 | $2,850 | $3,800 | $4,750 | $5,700 |
| Monthly Premium | $158 | $238 | $317 | $396 | $475 |

figure 21.4

Through the insurance exchanges you can choose between four different coverage plans: Platinum, Gold, Silver, and Bronze. The main difference between each plan is the amount
of co-insurance you'll have to pay once
your deductible is met. The copay for
the Platinum plan is 10 percent, Gold
plan 20 percent, Silver plan 30 percent,
and Bronze plan 40 percent (Figure 21.5).
The less co-insurance you pay, the higher
the annual premium will be.

## Obamacare: Out-of-Pocket

| Coverage Level | Amount you'll pay after your deductible is met (coinsurance) |
|---|---|
| Platinum | 10% |
| Gold | 20% |
| Silver | 30% |
| Bronze | 40% |

figure 21.5

### The Shellers–Obamacare
In our example, the Shellers will pay $396
per month if they buy a Silver-level policy
with a $2,000 deductible through their state insurance exchange since their
retirement gross income will be $50,000. This is $272 less per month than
the private policy they are considering. Since their income will be less than
$60,520, their premiums will be subsidized by taxpayers. Assuming they are
okay with the features of the policy, this route may make the most sense
for them until they qualify for Medicare at age 65. The maximum they'll
pay if they incurred a $36,418 medical bill would be $12,325 (maximum
out-of-pocket $10,325 plus their deductible $2,000).

# Continued Employee Coverage (COBRA): Group Health Insurance
In the cost-cutting corporate world, fewer and fewer companies provide free or
low-cost health insurance to their retirees. For most, employer-provided health
insurance terminates at retirement. You are fortunate if you have continued
employer coverage. If you
don't, there are legal requirements that prevent employers
from completely eliminating
health coverage for a period of time after an employee is off the payroll.

Group health insurance provides 34
percent of retirees with coverage.[5]

Under COBRA, which stands for Consolidated Omnibus Budget
Reconciliation Act of 1985, employers with twenty or more employees are
required to provide continued health insurance coverage to former workers

for up to eighteen months (twenty-nine months if the worker is disabled). COBRA only guarantees you access to coverage, however; it doesn't help pay your premiums. Under COBRA, your employer will no longer subsidize your monthly premiums, and you will be responsible for paying the entire amount, plus an administrative fee of up to 2 percent.

Thomas Caldwell, 59, a recent retiree, was shocked by how expensive his COBRA premium was. While he had been working, his employer had paid $912 per month of his insurance premiums, and Thomas was only required to pay $344 per month for his group health insurance coverage. When he retired and enrolled in COBRA, the same coverage cost $1,256 per month—a jump of more than 300 percent.[6] Because COBRA coverage must be identical to the coverage he had while working, he was unable to choose a less-expensive plan to save money, although his employer did allow him to drop certain "noncore" benefits like dental and vision care.

Although COBRA's costs may seem substantial (Figure 21.6), it may be your best route if you can't obtain less-expensive private health insurance.[7] COBRA can also buy you some time while you are searching for a private health insurance plan.

| Sample COBRA Premiums | |
| --- | --- |
| Single | $513 |
| Enrollee + Child | $768 |
| Enrollee + Spouse | $1,262 |
| Family | $1,664 |

figure 21.6

To initiate COBRA, you and your employer must follow proper procedures. If you don't, you could forfeit your coverage rights. First, the employer must notify the health-plan administrator within thirty days of your "qualifying event" (job termination, reduced hours of employment, or eligibility for Medicare). Once notified, the health-plan administrator has fourteen days to alert you and your family members of your right to elect COBRA coverage. The IRS is tough on this point. If the plan administrator fails to act, he or she can be held personally liable for this breach of duty.

You, your spouse, and your children have sixty days to decide whether to buy COBRA insurance. The sixty-day clock starts running on the date your eligibility notification is sent to you, or the date you lost your health coverage, whichever is later. As long as you pay the premium, your COBRA coverage will be retroactive to the date you lost your benefits.

If you elect COBRA, you have forty-five days to pay your first premium.

The first premium is likely to be high because it covers the period retroactive to the date your employer ended your coverage. Successive payments are due according to health plan requirements, but COBRA rules allow for a thirty-day grace period after each payment due date.

If you have questions about COBRA, or self-insured employer plans (both governed by the U.S. Department of Labor), contact your regional or district office of the Pension and Welfare Benefits Administration of the U.S. Department of Labor (www.dol.gov).

Not every company discontinues its insurance for employees who retire. Some firms will not only continue to offer coverage, but will also subsidize all or part of the premiums. Be sure to check with your company's personnel department regarding its policy on health coverage. The number of companies that are generous in this respect will likely continue to diminish as health-care costs continue to soar.

## Medicare

Medicare provides more than forty million Americans with basic health coverage. For many people, Medicare is their only source of health insurance during retirement. Because this program is such an integral part of retirement health-care planning for so many, it's important that we cover it here in detail.

Eligibility for Medicare is similar to that for Social Security. You or your spouse must have worked forty quarters (ten years) in Medicare-covered employment to receive Medicare coverage. Additionally, you must be 65 years old and a citizen or permanent resident of the United States. The Social Security Administration recommends applying for Medicare benefits when you turn 65, whether or not you begin collecting Social Security at that time.

> Ninety-three percent of all retirees obtain coverage from Medicare. For those with private coverage or a continued group plan, Medicare becomes a secondary coverage.[8]

Contact the Social Security Administration toll-free at (800) 772-1213 or visit www.ssa.gov if you have questions about your eligibility or want to apply for Medicare.

Medicare consists of two main parts: Part A and Part B. Medicare Part A helps pay for inpatient hospital care, skilled nursing facilities, hospice care, and some home health care. Part B helps pay for doctors' services, outpatient hospital care, and some other medical services such as blood work, medical equipment, lab tests, and physical and occupational therapy. Part B may also cover preventive services such as mammograms and flu shots.

## Medicare Part A: Hospital Insurance

For most retirees, no premiums are required for Medicare Part A because premiums were taken from each of your paychecks (1.45 percent) while you were employed. Even if you or your spouse did not work the required forty quarters of Medicare-covered employment, you may still be eligible, but you will be required to pay a monthly premium. In 2013, the premium was $441 per month if you worked less than thirty quarters, and $243 per month for those with thirty to thirty-nine quarters.

Although the majority of people do not have to pay a premium, there are still expenses involved. For every benefit period, a $1,184 deductible must be met (2013 rates). Also, if you stay over sixty days in the hospital, you will have to pay up to the following co-insurance rates:

- $296 per day, between the 61st and 90th day in the hospital
- $592 per day, between the 91st and 150th day in the hospital
- All costs for hospitalization beyond 150 days

## Medicare Part B: Medical Insurance

Medicare Part B helps pay for doctors' services and outpatient hospital care. Part B, however, will not pay for routine physical exams, eyeglasses, custodial care, dental care, dentures, routine foot care, hearing aids, orthopedic shoes, or cosmetic surgery. It does not cover most prescription drugs or any health care you receive while traveling outside the United States.

Part B coverage requires a premium of $105 per month (2013 rates). If you did not sign up for Part B at age 65 when you first became eligible, the premium may go up 10 percent for each year you wait. You will have to pay this extra amount for the rest of your life. Also, as in Part A, you are required to pay a deductible. However, the deductible is significantly less, amounting to only $147 per year. Medicare generally pays 80 percent of Medicare-approved medical costs after you meet your deductible. You will be required to pay the other 20 percent.

## *Applying for Benefits*

If you receive Social Security benefits before age 65, you will be automatically enrolled in both Medicare Part A and Part B, effective the month you turn 65. Your Medicare card will be mailed to you about three months before your 65th birthday. The enrollment package contains information on how to "unenroll" yourself from Part B coverage if you don't want it.

If you decide to delay receiving Social Security benefits until age 65 or later, you will not be automatically enrolled in Medicare. However, you should still apply for Medicare three months before you turn 65, so your coverage start date will not be delayed.

You can apply using any one of the following three options:

- Visit your local Social Security office.
- Call Social Security at (800) 772-1213.
- Apply online at www.ssa.gov.

You may want to delay signing up for Medicare Part B if you are receiving medical coverage through either your employer or your spouse's employer. There's no need to pay that $105 per month if you already have adequate coverage.

The Social Security Administration advises that you should sign up for Medicare Part A even if you keep working past age 65. The Part A coverage carries no premium costs and may help pay some of your health costs not covered through your employer or union group health plan.

Also remember, if you plan to join a Medicare managed-care plan or a Medicare private fee-for-service plan (more on this later), you will need to be a Medicare Part B participant.

If you didn't sign up for Medicare Part B when you were first eligible because you were still enrolled in a group plan, you can sign up for Medicare Part B during a "special enrollment period," thus avoiding the 10 percent penalty for late enrollees. Special enrollment allows you to sign up within eight months of when your employer health plan coverage ends, or when your employment ends, whichever comes first.

## The Shellers–Medicare

Once the Shellers reach age 65, they can apply for Medicare. What will they pay out-of-pocket if they incur a $36,418 medical bill like they did at age 59? For a similar hospital stay of nine days ($28,840), they'll pay only the $1,184 Part A deductible. Under Part B their $7,578 of physician services will only cost them $1,486 after paying the Part B $147 deductible. Figure 21.7 summarizes each of the Shellers' insurance options.

| Walter & Margaret Sheller, Age 62 | | | | | |
|---|---|---|---|---|---|
| **Before Age 65** | **Deductible** | **Co-Pay** | **Monthly Premium** | **Annual Premium** | **Max Out-of-Pocket Deductible** |
| Private Policy | $2,500 | 30% | $668 | $8,016 | $5,000 |
| Private Policy (High Deductible) | $5,000 | 30% | $480 | $5,760 | $5,000 |
| Private Policy (High Deductible) | $10,000 | 30% | $293 | $3,516 | $10,000 |
| Private Policy (HSA) | $6,450 | 0% | $430 | $5,160 | $5,450 |
| Health Insurance Exchage (Silver @ $50,000 Income) | $2,000 | 30% | $396 | $4,752 | $8,000 |
| COBRA (18-Months) | $2,000 | 30% | $1,262 | $15,144 | $5,000 |
| **After Age 65** | | | | | |
| Medicare Part A (Hospital for 150 days) | $1,184 | 0% | $0 | $0 | $44,400 |
| Medicare Part B (Doctor's Services) | $147 | 20% | $105 | $1,260 | No Max |
| Medicare Advantage Part C | $0 | $0-$100 | $49 | $588 | $5,000 |

figure 21.7

## *Medicare Part C: Medicare Advantage Plans*

Medicare Advantage Plans are a type of Medicare coverage offered by a private company that contracts with Medicare to provide you with all of your Part A and Part B benefits. These plans include Medicare Health Maintenance Organizations (HMOs), Preferred Provider Organizations (PPOs), Private Fee-for-Service Plans, Medicare Special Needs Plans, and Medicare Medical Savings Account plans. Coverage can also include prescription drugs. The average monthly premium for a Medicare Advantage Plan is $60.09, and $68.05 for a plan with drug benefits.[9] You can obtain Medicare Part A, B, and D through Medicare Advantage plans. Be aware that there are an enormous number of plans to sift through (would you believe 43,306?). However, you can narrow down your choices and compare plans and costs using the Medicare Plan Finder at Medicare.com.

### Medicare Part D: Prescription Drugs

You must join a Medicare Prescription Drug Plan to obtain prescription drug coverage through Medicare. The coverage is offered through private health insurance companies. There are four costs associated with Part D plans: premiums, deductibles, copayments, and a gap in coverage when you are required to pay the full amount. Monthly premiums typically range between $10 and $50 per month. The beneficiary pays the first $325 of prescription expenses (tax-deductible). From $325 to $2,970 the beneficiary pays 25 percent of the costs and 100 percent of the costs between $2,970 and $4,750. For prescription expenses above $4,750, Medicare Part D generally pays 95 percent of the costs.

## Filling in the Gaps: Medicare Supplemental Coverage

Medicare enrollees must use a doctor, specialist, or hospital that accepts Medicare. Medicare pays the fee charged for each visit or service after you have met the annual deductible and paid the monthly Part B premium of $105.

You might think that Medicare doesn't provide you with the sufficient coverage you desire. Who could blame you? With a whole array of services not covered by Medicare, you could still be looking at a substantial sum of out-of-pocket health costs if you wind up needing one of these uncovered services. To pay for medical costs not covered by Medicare Part A and B, you can purchase supplemental Medicare coverage.

### Medigap (Medicare Supplemental Insurance)

Medigap plans are private health insurance policies that cover some of the costs and services Medicare Part A and Part B do not cover. Medigap plans are different than Medicare Advantage plans. Medicare Advantage plans are a way to obtain Medicare coverage, while Medigap plans provide additional benefits beyond Advantage plans.

In 1992, Congress mandated that Medigap plans be categorized into twelve types (lettered A through L; M and N were added later, bringing the total to fourteen) to make it easier for consumers to shop for coverage and avoid scams. The fourteen plans differ in areas such as deductibles, coverage for eyeglasses, prescription drugs, or medical care received while in foreign countries. To buy a Medigap policy you must have both Medicare Part A and B. Premiums can vary by hundreds of dollars, so it pays to shop around. You can use the Medicare Plan Finder at www.medicare.com to see Medicare health insurance options in your area and compare plans.

Insurance companies may charge a fixed level premium for all participants, based on your age at the time of purchase. Other companies charge a variable premium based on how old you are each time you renew the policy, which means that your premiums will increase as you get older. It is necessary to shop around. I recommend you find an insurance agent who specializes in health coverage, and works for an insurance broker who can represent multiple companies, to help you sift through the intricacies of all of the options.

## Medicaid
Medicaid helps pay medical costs for people with low incomes. Because state governments, rather than the federal government, administer these programs, benefits can vary depending on the state in which you live. Medicaid can help pay for nursing home care and outpatient prescription drugs not covered by Medicare. Some states also have programs that help subsidize Medicare's premiums, deductibles, and co-insurance.

## The Inflation of Health-Care Costs
With the pace of rising health-care costs increasing, all people nearing retirement must give considerable thought to their health insurance plans. If you retire early, be sure you qualify for some type of health insurance to bridge the gap between your retirement and age 65. Even when Medicare kicks in, you may decide you need additional coverage. The number of Americans over age 65 will reach fifty-five million in 2020. By 2030 it is estimated that the population age 65 and older will grow to seventy-two million

(Figure 21.8).[10] Retiring baby boomers are going to put an enormous strain on the Medicare program. It's unlikely that Medicare will continue operating without reducing benefits, increasing retirees' out-of-pocket costs, or cutting payments to doctors and hospitals. By the time you retire, or sometime during your retirement, Medicare's health-plan options will likely be more limited and more expensive than they are now. You should count on it.

| Growth of Elderly Population Age 65+ | |
| --- | --- |
| 1920 | 5 million |
| 1940 | 9 million |
| 1960 | 17 million |
| 1980 | 26 million |
| 1990 | 31 million |
| 2000 | 35 million |
| 2010 | 40 million |
| 2020 | 55 million |
| 2030 | 72 million |

figure 21.8

Already, health insurance is too expensive for forty-six million Americans who live without coverage (2013).[11] The Health Care Financing Administration predicts that the amount of money America spends on health care will double every ten years (Figure 21.9). Health costs will continue to increase rapidly for individuals, employers, and the government.

Although there is no way to protect yourself from rising health-care expenses, it's not all doom and gloom. You're not powerless. You can fight back. Here are my suggestions: First, stay active, eat healthy, and eliminate stress. A healthy body and mind can better fight off sickness and disease. Second, plan properly. Make sure you're covered. As you age, you are more susceptible to disease, and if you get sick, it will be expensive to treat. Retirement is not the time to roll the dice and risk all that you have saved. Before you retire, you must examine all of your health insurance options for retirement and obtain the coverage that best protects your nest egg. Don't let health-care costs ruin the retirement you've worked so hard your entire life to achieve.

| Projected National Health Expenses | |
| --- | --- |
| 2015 | $3.97 trillion |
| 2025 | $7.95 trillion |
| 2035 | $15.9 trillion |

figure 21.9

# 22

# TOILETING AND RETIREMENT

## RETIREMENT DECISION #17: SHOULD I PURCHASE LONG-TERM-CARE INSURANCE?

"Toileting" is not a term you'd expect to find in a retirement-planning book like this. However, it is a term that describes what many retirees, their families, and caregivers must face every day. The definition of *toileting* is "getting to and from, and on and off, the toilet and performing associated personal hygiene." As you age and your health deteriorates, you may need help with many of the things you take for granted today. If you

> Forty-five percent of people over age 65 will spend some time in a nursing home.[1]

do need assistance performing the basic activities of everyday living, who is going to provide it for you? Not being prepared for this possibility carries some devastating consequences, such as prematurely depleting your assets, receiving substandard long-term care, or becoming a burden to your family.

How interested do you think your children would be in applying for the following job listed in your local paper's Help Wanted section?

*Home Health-Care Aide: Home health-care aide needed to provide twenty-four-hour, seven-day-a-week care for a poor, 85-year-old, bedridden patient suffering from Alzheimer's disease. The elderly patient requires room and board and must move in with you and your family. The patient requires constant supervision and will need a babysitter when you leave your home. Must be able to administer eight to ten medications daily and make frequent trips to the doctor's office. Applicant should enjoy cooking and cleaning and be proficient at toileting. Diaper changing skills are also a plus. The job will likely last one to two years but may last ten or more. This is a volunteer (unpaid) position. No experience necessary.*

Now ask your children how they would feel about accepting this health-care aide position if you were the patient needing the care. Would you like to heap this burden upon your children and their families? If you don't want to take the risk of becoming a burden to your family, you need to do some planning. You can either purchase a long-term-care insurance policy or acquire sufficient assets to provide for both you and your spouse if you should enter a nursing home during retirement.

## Becoming a Burden to Your Family

The above scenario is one Howard and Karen Everett know all too well. Three years ago, while visiting Karen's 84-year-old parents, Glenn and Shirley Kramer, they discovered that the Kramers were no longer able to take care of themselves. For example, Karen noticed that her parents weren't washing their clothes regularly, and when they did wash them, they did it by hand because they couldn't remember how to use the washer and dryer. Karen also noticed that her parents left the stove on frequently and were eating spoiled food. Cleanliness was becoming an issue.

It looked as if Shirley and Glenn had forgotten how to live. It was clear that Glenn was beginning to exhibit some early signs of dementia, and Shirley was diagnosed soon after with Alzheimer's disease. Allowing them to continue to live alone would be dangerous. They clearly needed help.

Because of her parents' limited assets and lack of planning, Karen believed that she and Howard had only two options: they could place her parents in a nursing home and let Medicaid pick up the bill, or they could move Glenn and Shirley into their own home and take on the daunting task of twenty-four-hour care.

They started to explore nursing-home options and visited several inexpensive homes. Unfortunately, the facilities were run-down, often smelled bad, lacked cleanliness, and were understaffed. The Everetts concluded that their parents deserved better and immediately made arrangements to move them into their own home. Little did they know what they were getting themselves into.

Most of us wouldn't have the stomach and stamina required to take care of one elderly parent, let alone two. Watching up close as both parents completely lost their dignity and were reduced to the equivalent of 1-year-olds took its toll emotionally and physically. Would you like your children to do for you what Karen and Howard did for their parents? Consider for a moment their daily routine.

Karen worked around the clock: cooking, cleaning, bathing, toileting, dressing, feeding, blowing noses, administering medicines, clipping toenails, changing bedsheets when wet or soiled, cleaning up when accidents occurred due to incontinence, changing diapers, answering the same questions over and over, and helping them find their beds when they wandered the house at night. Around-the-clock care was utterly exhausting.

Although less costly than a nursing home facility, home care carries its own financial drain. Adult diapers and specialty dietary items are not cheap. Utility costs also increased since neither parent could sleep with the lights off. Home maintenance costs rose due to accidents, like the basement flooding when Shirley left the water running in the bathroom. Also, many modifications were made to the home to assist with deteriorating physical health.

Twenty-three million adult children in the United States are taking care of their aging parents.[2]

The Everetts' lifestyle changed completely. Three years ago, with their kids grown, they were looking forward to winding down Howard's career by traveling and enjoying their increased freedom. This is not exactly what happened. All travel was completely out of the question. In fact, it was difficult just to go to the store. Somebody always had to be home. This meant that the Everetts rarely, if ever, went out together or even visited other relatives. If they did leave the house, they had to find a babysitter. Their married and college-age children helped out when they could but weren't always excited about having to change Grandma's diaper.

Besides not being able to leave the house, Karen and Howard found that they couldn't have friends over, either. Shirley had difficulty getting dressed by herself, but she had mastered the skill of taking her clothes off (and often did), making stark-naked appearances at the least expected times. Most dinner guests would prefer not to see an 84-year-old in her birthday suit. Their only social outings, it seemed, were occasional visits with support groups to cope with the pressures of taking care of elderly parents.

The worst component, however, was the realization that their *relationship* with their parents had changed. Adoration grew into aversion, and respect decayed to resentment. While they still loved their parents and would continue to provide the needed care, they privately wished their parents would have been wiser by preparing for this stage of life.

Most people put the burden of long-term care on their families. While about 12.8 million Americans require long-term care, only 2.4 million live in nursing homes.[3]

So what advice would the Everetts give you? "Buy long-term-care insurance. You will maintain your relationship with your children and grandchildren, and they won't have to experience with you the loss of your dignity." The Everetts felt so strongly about this that they bought themselves a long-term-care policy.

## Leaving Your Spouse with Nothing—Spousal Impoverishment

Let's fast-forward to the day you reach age 80 and assume you enter a nursing home and stay for five years before dying. Let's also assume your spouse is healthier and younger than you. Could the assets you've accumulated cover the additional expense of a nursing-home stay? A nursing-home stay could double your annual retirement expenses. Of course, in addition to covering the cost of a nursing home, your spouse, who will likely continue to live in your family home, will still need money to meet the expenses of everyday life. And who knows, your spouse may need a continued stream of income for another twenty years.

If your assets aren't sufficient to cover the costs incurred by your going to a nursing home and also the continued cost of retirement for your spouse, then you are a candidate for long-term-care insurance. If your nursing-home stay completely drains your nest egg, your spouse could be literally left with nothing but your home and a monthly Social Security check. No one wants to be forced to live on Social Security alone.

## $500,000 to Spare or $0 and Destitute

David Sanders, a 62-year-old office manager, plans to retire this year and begin enjoying the good life with his wife, Mary, age 60. According to his retirement calculations, he has accumulated enough money to enjoy a $50,000 annual retirement income (after taxes and inflation). In fact, using modest rates of return, his projections show that thirty years from now they will still have a nest egg of more than $500,000. A modern-day success story, right? Well, maybe. (See Chapter 1 on how to estimate how much money you'll need in retirement.)

One thing David did not plan on is the possibility that some of their assets may be needed to cover long-term-care expenses. What would happen if either David or Mary requires nursing-home care sometime during retirement? Could their nest egg withstand the additional expense? To answer this question, David needs to take a few extra steps in his retirement calculations.

What if, at age 70, David enters a nursing home that costs $60,000 per year and stays for five years before he dies? Of course, $60,000 per year will have to be withdrawn from the Sanders' nest egg for five years to take care of David in the nursing home, while Mary will continue to need $50,000 of income each year to cover the originally planned retirement expenses. The additional nursing-home expense will more than double the amount they must withdraw from their investments during these years. Should this occur, their investment assets would be completely depleted by the time Mary is age 80. She would have to live out her remaining life on Social Security alone.

If David does not require this nursing-home care until he reaches 75 or 80, their assets would last a little longer. Mary would run out of assets at age 81 and 83, respectively (Figure 22.1). Needless to say, an extended long-term-care stay by David would leave Mary penniless.

| Retirement Nest Egg with and without Long-Term Care (LTC) Expenses *Retirement: David and Mary Sanders* *Starting Portfolio: $1,025,000* | | | | | |
|---|---|---|---|---|---|
| David's Age | Mary's Age | No LTC Needed | LTC at Age 70 | LTC at Age 75 | LTC at Age 80 |
| 62 | 60 | $1,042,491 | $1,042,491 | $1,042,491 | $1,042,491 |
| 63 | 61 | $1,060,012 | $1,060,012 | $1,060,012 | $1,060,012 |
| 64 | 62 | $1,082,612 | $1,082,612 | $1,082,612 | $1,082,612 |
| 65 | 63 | $1,105,618 | $1,105,618 | $1,105,618 | $1,105,618 |
| 66 | 64 | $1,129,060 | $1,129,060 | $1,129,060 | $1,129,060 |
| 67 | 65 | $1,152,971 | $1,152,971 | $1,152,971 | $1,152,971 |
| 68 | 66 | $1,177,391 | $1,177,391 | $1,177,391 | $1,177,391 |
| 69 | 67 | $1,202,364 | $1,202,364 | $1,202,364 | $1,202,364 |
| 70 | 68 | $1,217,542 | $1,133,272 | $1,217,542 | $1,217,542 |
| 71 | 69 | $1,231,423 | $1,024,867 | $1,231,423 | $1,231,423 |
| 72 | 70 | $1,243,825 | $892,821 | $1,243,825 | $1,243,825 |
| 73 | 71 | $1,254,547 | $743,768 | $1,254,547 | $1,254,547 |

**Continued**

| David's Age | Mary's Age | No LTC Needed | LTC at Age 70 | LTC at Age 75 | LTC at Age 80 |
|---|---|---|---|---|---|
| 74 | 72 | $1,263,369 | $576,230 | $1,263,369 | $1,263,369 |
| 75 | 73 | $1,269,211 | $526,485 | $1,131,343 | $1,269,211 |
| 76 | 74 | $1,264,833 | $470,116 | $973,931 | $1,264,833 |
| 77 | 75 | $1,256,907 | $406,560 | $796,524 | $1,256,907 |
| 78 | 76 | $1,245,083 | $335,212 | $597,391 | $1,245,083 |
| 79 | 77 | $1,228,983 | $255,421 | $374,667 | $1,228,983 |
| 80 | 78 | $1,208,198 | $166,487 | $294,080 | $1,040,461 |
| 81 | 79 | $1,182,289 | $67,658 | $204,183 | $828,363 |
| 82 | 80 | $1,150,781 | $0 | $104,208 | $590,655 |
| 83 | 81 | $1,113,162 | $0 | $0 | $325,146 |
| 84 | 82 | $1,068,881 | $0 | $0 | $29,475 |
| 85 | 83 | $1,017,346 | $0 | $0 | $0 |
| 86 | 84 | $957,919 | $0 | $0 | $0 |
| 87 | 85 | $901,900 | $0 | $0 | $0 |
| 88 | 86 | $838,053 | $0 | $0 | $0 |
| 89 | 87 | $765,709 | $0 | $0 | $0 |
| 90 | 88 | $684,148 | $0 | $0 | $0 |
| 91 | 89 | $592,595 | $0 | $0 | $0 |
| 92 | 90 | $490,219 | $0 | $0 | $0 |

figure 22.1

The Sanderses have two basic options: accept the risk of depleting their assets and do nothing in hopes that neither one of them requires care *or* purchase a long-term-care insurance policy to cover the cost of long-term-care expenses should they arise.

> Ninety percent of "private-pay" nursing home patients are impoverished within one year of entering a nursing home.[4]

What would you do? Have you considered long-term-care expenses in your retirement projections?

## Playing the Odds

What are the chances you could be afflicted with a chronic illness or disability that would leave you unable to care for yourself for an extended period of time during retirement? The answer might surprise you.

The vast majority of Americans don't believe they will ever enter a nursing home or need any long-term-care services. If you're age 65, you have a 45 percent chance of entering a nursing home.[5] Fifty-three percent of those who enter nursing homes stay for more than one year.[6] Those odds, of course, increase with age. Women, because they live longer than men, have a greater likelihood of needing long-term care at some point. Sixty-five percent of nursing home residents are women.[7]

## The High Cost of Aging

Long-term care is not just a health issue, but also a financial concern that can throw a wrench into your retirement planning (Figure 22.2). Currently

| 2012 Annual Nursing Home Costs* | | | |
|---|---|---|---|
| Alabama | $63,875 | Montana | $70,263 |
| Alaska | $273,750 | Nebraska | $64,145 |
| Arizona | $67,708 | Nevada | $80,300 |
| Arkansas | $53,593 | New Hampshire | $98,550 |
| California | $81,760 | New Jersey | $106,489 |
| Colorado | $75,190 | New Mexico | $67,645 |
| Connecticut | $135,050 | New York | $118,625 |
| Delaware | $91,250 | North Carolina | $69,350 |
| Florida | $78,475 | North Dakota | $75,132 |
| Georgia | $59,495 | Ohio | $73,000 |
| Hawaii | $116,800 | Oklahoma | $49,447 |
| Idaho | $73,000 | Oregon | $82,125 |
| Illinois | $59,678 | Pennsylvania | $91,652 |
| Indiana | $68,255 | Rhode Island | $91,250 |
| Iowa | $55,480 | South Carolina | $65,700 |
| Kansas | $54,750 | South Dakota | $65,700 |
| Kentucky | $69,003 | Tennessee | $65,700 |
| Louisiana | $51,512 | Texas | $47,450 |
| Maine | $96,360 | Utah | $58,400 |
| Maryland | $89,060 | Vermont | $92,108 |
| Massachusetts | $117,530 | Virginia | $72,088 |
| Michigan | $80,300 | Washington | $87,600 |
| Minnesota | $76,716 | West Virginia | $83,950 |
| Mississippi | $71,750 | Wisconsin | $83,585 |
| Missouri | $50,735 | Wyoming | $72,270 |

*Median cost of a semiprivate room

figure 22.2

the average cost for a one-year stay in a private room in a nursing home is $90,520 ($248 per day); semiprivate rooms run $81,030 ($222); assisted-living facilities average $42,600 per year ($117 per day); and the average home health-care rate runs $21 per hour. Two hours of home health care each day would cost $15,330 per year.[8]

Today, the average nursing home stay is two and a half years[9] (Figure 22.3) at a total cost of $226,300 for a private room.[10] The same stay will cost $495,851 in twenty years assuming nursing-home costs continue to rise 4 percent per year.[11] What will it cost for a two-and-a-half-year stay when you reach age 80? You can see the impact these costs can have on reaching your retirement goals. Large long-term-care expenses could deplete your assets prematurely and impoverish your spouse. The strain on your nest egg is compounded in the event of Alzheimer's. The average nursing home stay for Alzheimer's victims is seven years.[12]

| Average Length of a Nursing Home Stay | |
|---|---|
| Less than 3 months | 13% |
| 3 months to 1 year | 23% |
| 1 to 3 years | 32% |
| 3 to 5 years | 14% |
| 5 years or longer | 18% |

figure 22.3

## Who Pays for Long-Term Care?

Long-term care leads to poverty for a disturbing number of retired Americans. Of those receiving long-term care, 32 percent pay for it out-of-pocket. Within a year of admission, more than 90 percent of these private-pay residents are impoverished.[13] Medicare and health insurance coverage typically pay little for long-term-care nursing home facilities. Medicaid, a government welfare program, will pay but only after you have depleted all other financial resources. The government currently pays about 56 percent of all

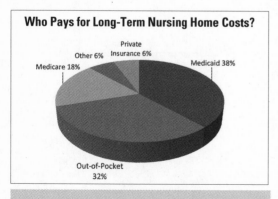

**Who Pays for Long-Term Nursing Home Costs?**

Private Insurance 6%
Other 6%
Medicare 18%
Medicaid 38%
Out-of-Pocket 32%

figure 22.4

long-term-care expenses. Although long-term-care coverage is affordable, only 6 percent of long-term-care expenditures are paid for through the utilization of private insurance coverage.[14]

According to these statistics, if you don't own a long-term-care policy, the odds are very high that a lengthy nursing-home stay will completely eat away your assets and leave you dependent upon Medicaid. Figure 22.4 summarizes who gets stuck with the long-term-care bill.[15]

## Cost of Coverage

Long-term-care coverage, like life insurance, is cheaper if you purchase it when you are younger and healthier. A policy purchased at age 65 will generally cost twice as much as a policy bought when you're 55. For example, a 55-year-old can plan on paying a premium between $500 and $1,300 per year for five years of coverage. That same policy would cost a 65-year-old between $1,000 and $2,500. Those in their late 70s may be required to pay as much as $4,000 to $8,000 for similar coverage, depending on the policy's features. Premiums will almost double for coverage purchased for a married couple.

Buying coverage when you are younger will reduce your premiums, though you will likely pay them for a longer period of time. To obtain a quick, free quote to get an idea of how much a long-term-care policy will cost, spend five minutes at www.ltcq.net or www.insure.com.

## Who Should Purchase Long-Term Health-Care Coverage?

Long-term-care insurance is not for everyone but very essential for some. Figure 22.5 will help you decide if you should buy a long-term-care policy.

# How Much Coverage Do You Need?

You can purchase coverage that will provide a daily benefit of anywhere from $50 to $400. To determine how much long-term coverage you need, first decide how much long-term care you can afford to cover out of your own pocket. For example, if the average nursing home cost is $150 per day in your area, and you can afford to pay $50 per day, then you would need a policy to cover the $100 difference. You should plan on needing this benefit for at least two and a half years, which is the average nursing home stay.

Estimating what you can pay out-of-pocket can be a difficult process.

| LTC is for you if... | LTC is not as important for you if... |
|---|---|
| • You would like to insure your independence and not become a burden to your family.<br>• Your family has a history of ailments requiring long-term care (e.g., Alzheimer's, diabetes, strokes).<br>• You have sufficient money to pay premiums every year.<br>• You want to preserve assets for family members.<br>• Paying for long-term care for one spouse would seriously hamper your ability to accomplish retirement goals.<br>• You are in good health and qualify for lower premiums.<br>• You are between age 45 and 60 and can lock in lower premiums for life. | • You have health conditions making the cost of LTC coverage too expensive compared to the benefit you may receive.<br>• You are likely to cancel the policy because your fixed income won't keep up with increasing premium payments.<br>• Your only source of income is Social Security.<br>• You're self-insured because of the size of your financial portfolio.<br>• Buying an LTC policy stretches your budget to the point of having to forego other financial needs (e.g., paying for utilities, buying food or medicine).<br>• You are age 79 or older (although you may need coverage, premiums will likely be too high). |

figure 22.5

You must attempt to predict your future financial status and the future cost of long-term care. The best method for doing this is to revisit the retirement section of your financial plan and enter some additional hypothetical situations (see Chapter 1). For example, how would it affect your retirement assets if you or your spouse entered a nursing home at age 75, 80, or 85, and you had to pay $81,000 per year, adjusted for inflation? Would this eat up all of your assets? Would the spouse living outside the nursing home have enough money to meet living expenses? Your retirement plan can help you answer all these questions. Be more exact in your planning by contacting nursing homes in your area and base your estimates on local costs (Figure 22.2).

## Nursing Home, Assisted Living, and Home Health Care

Nursing-home coverage is just one of several types of long-term care. Most policies also include coverage for assisted-living facilities and home health care. Figure 22.6 lists the different types of long-term care and their definitions.

Assisted living is the step between living in your own home and living in a nursing home. If your health won't allow you to continue living at home, but you don't require round-the-clock nursing-home care, an assisted-living facility will suit you nicely. The goal of assisted living is to help you continue living as independently as possible. Assisted-living facilities provide the privacy and feel of living in your own apartment, condominium, or small home. However, assistance is available to help you with the basic activities of daily living. Assisted-living facilities average $42,600 per year.[16]

> Seventy percent of seniors reaching age 65 will need home health care.[17]

| Types of Long-Term Care | |
|---|---|
| Nursing Home Care | Nursing homes serve as permanent residences for people who are too frail or sick to live at home or as a temporary facility during a recovery period. |
| Home Health Care | Home health care can cover a broad range of needs, both temporary and permanent. Oftentimes people require only minimal assistance: a couple of hours each day or a visit in the morning and the evening. Some people require a few brief visits each week; others need round-the-clock assistance because of physical or mental disability. Services can include help with meals, home maintenance, supervision, and/or medication administration. |
| Assisted-Living Facility | Assisted-living facilities provide meals, social activities, and on-call assistance with bathing and dressing. The goal is to help people continue living as independently as possible. |
| Adult Day Care | A planned program that includes a variety of health, social, and supportive services in a safe environment during daytime hours. Adult day care is a community-based service. |
| Respite Care | Short-term care provided to people with disabilities in order to provide families a break from the daily routine of caregiving. |

*figure 22.6*

No one wants to leave his or her home any sooner than necessary, even when health conditions begin to deteriorate. The best way to ensure you can remain in your home as long as possible is to hire a home health care agency to provide you with the level of help you need. Nonskilled help, which can assist with dressing, bathing, preparing meals, and other household duties, can cost $1,000 per month. Skilled help provided by a physical therapist or health-care professional can cost much more. Home health care averages $21 per hour.[18]

## *What Is Not Covered by Long-Term-Care Insurance?*

If you purchase a policy, make sure you understand exactly what is covered and what is not. Long-term-care policies do not cover a number of items, and the exclusions in each policy differ. Treatment that was under way or recommended before obtaining long-term coverage is usually not. In addition, the following ailments are often excluded:

- Mental disorders (other than Alzheimer's disease or other dementia)
- Nervous disorders
- Alcoholism
- Drug abuse
- Care necessitated by an act of war
- Intentional self-inflicted injury

## *Focus on the Benefits*

The most serious blunder people make when purchasing a long-term-care policy is that they focus on the premium more than the benefits they may need. Here are some benefits to focus on:

### Coverage Amount

Long-term-care policies generally pay benefits on a daily, weekly, or monthly basis. Check the costs of nursing homes in your area to determine the amount of coverage you need. For example, if nursing homes in your area run $150 per day, you can buy a policy that will pay $150 per day, $1,050 per week, or $4,500 per month. Usually, assisted-living and home health care benefits will be paid as a percentage of the nursing-home coverage amounts.

## Inflation

Many people save a lot of money on premiums by purchasing a policy that doesn't adjust for inflation. They'll save money in the short run, but it's not likely that their policy will provide them with nearly enough benefits if they enter a nursing home. If nursing-home costs continue to increase at 4 percent per year, a nursing home that costs $150 per day today could cost $328 per day in twenty years. If costs continue to soar at this pace,

> The cost of long-term care is increasing at a rate of 4 percent per year.[19]

wouldn't it be wise to add a feature to your policy that adjusts your benefits by 4 percent per year to combat this inflation?

Choosing a policy that adjusts for inflation will increase your premium. For example, one plan that pays a $150-per-day benefit for four years of nursing-home coverage would cost a 65-year-old about $1,500 annually without an inflation feature. With 4 percent compound inflation protection, the same policy would cost $2,700 yearly. However, the additional cost is worth it if it protects you and your spouse from bankrupting your life savings.

## Elimination Periods

An "elimination period" represents the number of days you must be in a nursing home before your policy kicks in and begins paying benefits. Most policies offer a range between zero and one hundred days. Not surprisingly, the longer the elimination period you select, the lower your premium will be. You can determine your optimum elimination period by looking again at your retirement plan to estimate whether your investment resources are sufficient. If you have plenty of assets, you may want to opt for a policy with a longer elimination period.

## How Long Will Benefits Be Paid?

Most policies provide a maximum dollar amount, or ceiling, on the number of covered days. Often, benefits will last two to six years or a lifetime. In addition, some policies have various limits for different types of coverage–nursing homes, assisted-living facilities, home health care, etc.

## When Will the Policy Pay?

Most policies will begin paying benefits when you need substantial assistance with at least two of six activities of daily living. These activities include bathing, continence, dressing, eating, toileting, and transferring (moving in or out of bed or a wheelchair). Incidentally, the ability to bathe is typically the first daily living skill to go.

# Getting a Quote

When you begin shopping for a long-term-care policy, you may want to follow the example of Alan Rucker, a recently retired 62-year-old. To get the ball rolling, Alan requested premium quotes from three top-rated companies using the following key parameters:

• Coverage for both Alan and his wife, Margaret, age 60, who both enjoy excellent health
• Three-year benefit period
• $100 per day of coverage
• Ninety-day elimination period
• 4 percent compound inflation protection
• Nursing-home, assisted-living, and home health-care coverage

For this coverage, premiums ranged from $2,100 to $2,400 per year. Alan then used the following questionnaire to compare the policies and narrow his choices down to the policy that best fits his needs.[20]

## Long-Term-Care Questionnaire

1. What services are covered?
   A. Nursing-home care
   B. Home health care
   C. Assisted-living facility
   D. Adult day care
   E. Alternate care
   F. Respite care
   G. Other

2. How much does the policy pay, per day, for nursing-home care? For home health care? For an assisted-living facility? For adult day care? For alternate care? For respite care? Other?

3. How long will benefits last in a nursing home? At home? In an assisted-living facility? Other?

4. Does the policy have a maximum lifetime benefit? If so, what is it for nursing-home care? For home health care? For an assisted-living facility? Other?

5. How long must I wait before preexisting conditions are covered?

6. How many days must I wait before benefits begin for nursing-home care? For home health care? For an assisted-living facility? Other?

7. Are Alzheimer's disease and other organic, mental, and nervous disorders covered?

8. Does the policy require an assessment of activities of daily living? An assessment of cognitive impairment? Physician certification of need? A prior hospital stay for nursing-home care? Home health care?

9. Is the policy guaranteed renewable?

10. What is the age range for enrollment?

11. Is there a waiver-of-premium provision for nursing-home care? For home health care?

12. How long must I be confined before premiums are waived?

13. Does the policy have a nonforfeiture provision? (This feature returns part of your premium if you cancel or lapse your policy.)

14. Does the policy offer an inflation adjustment feature? If so, what is the rate of increase? How often is it applied? For how long? Is there an additional cost?

15. What does the policy cost per year?
    A. With the inflation feature?
    B. Without the inflation feature?

16. Is there a thirty-day free look?

17. What is the insurance company rated?

18. Is the policy tax qualified or nontax qualified?

19. Has the insurance company ever raised its long-term-care insurance rates?

# Is Long-Term-Care Coverage Worth the Cost?

The answer depends, of course, on whether you wind up needing long-term care. Let's assume you purchase a policy at age 65 to cover the average cost of a five-year stay in a nursing home. The premium is $2,500 per year. Let's also assume your policy has an inflation feature, so your benefits will increase as long-term-care costs escalate.

At age 80, you incur a chronic illness that requires your admission into a nursing home for the average stay of two and a half years. Was this a good investment? For fifteen years, you paid $2,500 per year in premiums for a total of $37,500. The total cost of your two-and-a-half-year nursing home stay, adjusted for inflation, is $364,826. By having the coverage in place, you avoid having to withdraw $364,826 from your investment accounts to pay for your stay. The ability to keep this money invested may prove vital if your spouse is using it as a source of retirement income.

In this scenario, buying a long-term-care policy was a very wise investment decision. If you never used the coverage, you would have spent $37,500 on a policy you didn't need. But would it be worth the risk of financial ruin to bet that you and your spouse will never require long-term care? Looked at in that light, $37,500 may seem like a small sum for peace of mind.

Understandably, "toileting" is not a term most people want to think about when they're dreaming about their happy retirement. It's not enjoyable to consider a future where you might need others to care for you, either in your own home, in an assisted-living facility, or in a nursing home. But by thinking about it now and planning for its eventuality, you'll save your spouse and children the burden of caring for you later on. By taking the simple steps outlined in this chapter, you'll have enough money to cover your long-term-care needs, leaving your spouse a healthy nest egg. After all, no one wants their kids to be forced to take the job of home health-care aide.

# 23

# PLEASE! NO MORE LIFE INSURANCE PREMIUMS

## RETIREMENT DECISION #18: SHOULD I CANCEL MY LIFE INSURANCE POLICY SINCE I NO LONGER NEED THE COVERAGE?

R eid and Sylvia Jeppson, ages 60 and 59, respectively, have decided to retire in three months. For the past fifteen years, Reid has been paying $1,500 per year on a $150,000 life insurance policy. He is tired of paying premiums and would like to avoid this expense during retirement. He initially purchased the insurance coverage for two main reasons: to pay off the remaining $100,000 balance owed on the couple's home and to provide Sylvia with income upon his premature death. The policy was to supplement the insurance his employer provided him.

Since the time he purchased the life insurance, however, his situation has changed dramatically. First, the Jeppsons now own their home free and clear and carry no other debt. And second, their retirement nest egg is large enough to provide them both with a comfortable income for the next thirty-five years. Sylvia would not need any of the $150,000 insurance to maintain her standard of living upon Reid's death. With no debt and no need to replace income, does Reid really need this policy? Why should he pay a $1,500 premium each year for coverage that is not needed? What should he do with his policy?

Many retirees find themselves in a position similar to that of Reid and Sylvia. They want to eliminate unneeded expenditures. Does it make sense to continue paying premiums on a policy that is not needed? Probably not, in most cases, but let's answer the following questions and look at your options.

# Why Did I Purchase Life Insurance?

First, ask yourself *why* you purchased your life insurance coverage in the first place. Most people purchase coverage for the following reasons: to cover final expenses, to replace income to a surviving spouse and family, to pay off debts, to cover college education expenses, and for very large estates, to pay estate taxes.

Look at Alex Jackson, a married 35-year-old with several young children and a large mortgage. He absolutely needs life insurance coverage. If Alex died, his income would be lost. Life insurance can provide his wife, Janice, with a lump sum of money that she can use to support the family. If Alex wants to make sure the home and other debts are paid off and also be ensured the children will have the opportunity to obtain college educations, this too could be built into the amount of coverage needed. In Alex's situation, to cover all of these needs, he would need to buy a $2 million policy.

But if you, unlike Alex, are retired, you no longer need to replace income to support a surviving spouse upon your death. Whatever income you were planning to use to support both you and your spouse during retirement will continue to support one of you if the other dies. If you have no debt, then you don't need life insurance to pay off debt upon death. If your kids are grown and through college, there is no need for life insurance to ensure that there is money available to accomplish this.

# Do I Still Need Coverage?

Next, update your financial plan and ask yourself an important question: "If I die right now, would my spouse be left with enough money to support him or her throughout the remaining years of his or her life?" Both the retirement and life insurance segments of a financial plan should address this question for you. If you determine coverage is no longer needed, read "Canceling Coverage" (Option 1 or 2) to help you decide what to do next. If your analysis indicates that you still need coverage, continue making premium payments or "pay-up" your policy (Option 3).

# Canceling Coverage

If you determine that you no longer need coverage and want to stop paying premiums, you have several options.

This is really easy if you own a term life insurance policy; just stop paying your premiums and cancel the policy.

If you own a cash-value policy (whole life, universal life, or variable life), you have several choices and more things to consider. These policies are a little trickier because of the cash value (the savings component within the policy). Insurance companies often impose penalties for withdrawing cash value, so before considering any of the options below, call your insurance company and ask if there will be any surrender charges if you surrender your policy. Most cash-value policies penalize people who take withdrawals within the first ten to fifteen years of owning a policy. These penalties or surrender charges may be as much as 100 percent of the cash-value balance in year one and not decline to zero until the tenth or fifteenth year. Avoiding big surrender charges for making changes to your insurance strategy may be reason enough to keep paying on the policy.

## Option 1: Send Me Cash

Your first option is to simply cancel the coverage and ask that a check be sent to you for the balance of your cash value. Be careful, however; this can have tax ramifications. If the policy's cash value is greater than the total premiums you've paid over the life of the policy, then you will pay taxes on the difference. For example, Reid and Sylvia have paid a total of $22,500 in premiums and have $40,000 of cash value. Because their cash value is higher than the premiums they've paid, they will be required to pay income taxes on the difference, or $17,500. This is treated as ordinary income.

## Option 2: Tax-Free Exchange

If your goal is to eliminate the premium and also to keep the money invested on a tax-deferred basis, your best bet is to move the cash value via a "1035 tax-free exchange" from your life insurance policy directly to an annuity (fixed or variable). Your annuity carrier can provide you with the forms necessary to accomplish this. Once the money is in the annuity, you can stop making premium payments and cancel your policy. Reid and Sylvia decided to do this and moved their $40,000 cash value to a *no-load* variable annuity (see Chapter 15). They used the money to buy mutual funds (called subaccounts in a variable annuity).

## Option 3: Pay It Up

Another way of eliminating unwanted premiums is to "pay up" your policy. In simple terms, this means using the cash value you've accumulated to make the premium payments each year for you. Although you are still paying a premium, it's not coming directly out of your pocket. Consider this option if you decide to keep your coverage but want to stop writing checks to pay premium payments. Call your insurance company and ask how long the premiums could be paid from your cash value before the cash value would run completely out and the policy lapses. If your cash value is large enough, there may be enough money to pay the premiums for the rest of your life. If you own an expensive commission policy, you may want to consider transferring your cash value via a 1035 exchange to a similar, but cheaper, no-load life insurance policy. Your cash value can then be stretched further to "pay up" the policy. With lower premium costs, your cash value may cover premiums for many more years. If you go this route, don't cancel your old policy until your health has been reviewed and the new policy is issued. If you have health problems, this strategy of moving to another policy likely won't work.

## Do the Math

Do you think Reid and Sylvia made a good investment decision by moving the cash value of their life insurance policy to an annuity? Of course, it depends entirely on when Reid will die. Let's do the math.

If the Jeppsons would have kept the policy, and Reid died this year, Sylvia would receive the $150,000 tax-free. But because they canceled their life insurance and moved their $40,000 cash value into a variable annuity, Sylvia will receive the market value of the annuity. If no growth occurs in such a short span of time, Sylvia will simply receive $40,000. If we knew Reid was going to die this year, the best investment decision would have been to keep the life insurance policy and receive the full $150,000.

How many years will it take before the annuity is a better investment than the life insurance? Or, in other words, how long will it take for the $40,000 in the annuity (after-tax) to be equal to $150,000 of life insurance proceeds that would have been paid out to Sylvia at Reid's death? At 8 percent interest, the answer is twenty years, or when Reid is 80 years old. This is the break-even point, assuming the Jeppsons' policy is paid up and

## Life Insurance vs. Annuity Payout

| Reid's Age at Death | Life Insurance Payout (Tax-Free) | Annuity Payout* | Reid's Age at Death | Life Insurance Payout (Tax-Free) | Annuity Payout* |
|---|---|---|---|---|---|
| 60 | $150,000 | $38,025 | 81 | $150,000 | $168,721 |
| 61 | $150,000 | $40,617 | 82 | $150,000 | $181,769 |
| 62 | $150,000 | $43,416 | 83 | $150,000 | $195,860 |
| 63 | $150,000 | $46,440 | 84 | $150,000 | $211,079 |
| 64 | $150,000 | $49,705 | 85 | $150,000 | $227,516 |
| 65 | $150,000 | $53,231 | 86 | $150,000 | $245,267 |
| 66 | $150,000 | $57,040 | 87 | $150,000 | $264,438 |
| 67 | $150,000 | $61,153 | 88 | $150,000 | $285,143 |
| 68 | $150,000 | $65,595 | 89 | $150,000 | $307,505 |
| 69 | $150,000 | $70,393 | 90 | $150,000 | $331,655 |
| 70 | $150,000 | $75,574 | 91 | $150,000 | $357,737 |
| 71 | $150,000 | $81,170 | 92 | $150,000 | $385,906 |
| 72 | $150,000 | $87,214 | 93 | $150,000 | $416,329 |
| 73 | $150,000 | $93,741 | 94 | $150,000 | $449,185 |
| 74 | $150,000 | $100,790 | 95 | $150,000 | $484,670 |
| 75 | $150,000 | $108,403 | 96 | $150,000 | $522,994 |
| 76 | $150,000 | $116,626 | 97 | $150,000 | $564,383 |
| 77 | $150,000 | $125,506 | 98 | $150,000 | $609,084 |
| 78 | $150,000 | $135,096 | 99 | $150,000 | $657,361 |
| 79 | $150,000 | $145,454 | 100 | $150,000 | $709,499 |
| 80 | $150,000 | $156,640 | | | |

* assumes a tax rate of 25% upon withdrawal and an 8% rate of return

figure 23.1

no more premiums remain. If Reid lives past age 80, the annuity will yield him more money; if he dies sooner than 80, the insurance policy would have been the better investment. (Figure 23.1.)

If Reid dies in twenty-five years at age 85, the annuity will be worth $227,516 after taxes (8 percent growth) as opposed to the life insurance death benefit at $150,000, thus yielding $77,515 more for Sylvia. On the other hand, if Reid dies after just fifteen years, Sylvia would receive $150,000 from the insurance policy and only $100,790 from the annuity, $49,210 less than the life insurance.

The break-even point drops to sixteen years if the Jeppsons can earn 10 percent on their annuity. Further, if Reid has to continue making premium payments throughout retirement, the break-even drops to eighteen years at 8 percent and fifteen years at 10 percent.

Again, whether the Jeppsons made a good investment decision to drop their coverage and move their cash value to an annuity depends entirely on how long Reid lives. Reid and Sylvia are betting, by using this strategy, that Reid will live past age 80 and that they will maintain an 8 percent growth rate on their annuity throughout retirement.

If Reid had any life-shortening health conditions or a family history of such conditions, obviously it wouldn't make sense to cancel the policy.

## Other Considerations

There is more to making the decision to drop your policy than just the math, however. There are many legitimate reasons to keep your coverage and continue making premium payments during retirement.

First, you may own life insurance so you can maximize your company pension plan (see Chapter 7). This insurance strategy allows you to choose the pension payout option with the highest payment, *single life with no survivor benefits*, and still provide for your spouse upon your death.

Also, some retirees may actually use cash value via a tax-free policy loan to supplement their retirement income. In addition, you may need life insurance for estate-planning purposes, especially if your overall estate is worth more than $10.5 million (in 2013). Life insurance can provide liquid assets to pay estate taxes upon your death.

The decision to cancel a policy can largely be made by answering one question: "Why do I own this coverage?" If your answer is, "To replace income or pay off debt when I no longer have an income or debt to repay," then canceling your policy may make sense for you.

Don't be too quick to act, and be sure to carefully evaluate each option before making any decisions. Whether you decide to keep your policy, cash it out, or exchange it, there is likely a strategy that will help you reduce your retirement expenses by eliminating future premium payments.

# SECTION 5

## OTHER RETIREMENT CONSIDERATIONS

Mortgages
Estate Planning

# 24

# TO PAY OR NOT TO PAY

Monty Van Wagner, like many Americans, had the admirable goal of paying off his mortgage by the time he hit retirement at age 65. Unfortunately, things didn't go as he planned. He reached retirement with a $100,000 outstanding mortgage and seven more years of $1,500 monthly payments. Now at the tail end of his mortgage, he is faced with a difficult question. Should he use some of his

> Twenty-two percent of retirees over age 65 carry a home mortgage.[1]

$400,000 retirement nest-egg money to pay off the mortgage, or should he keep the money invested and continue making mortgage payments?

Like many decisions retirees must make at retirement, the answer largely boils down to risk and return. Which do you think is the greatest priority at this stage in life–higher investment returns *or* peace of mind? Let's look at both sides of the equation and help Monty make a decision.

## Simple Math Says "Don't Pay It Off"

Many financial professionals look at paying off a mortgage strictly from a financial perspective, a "just do the math" approach. This conventional wisdom suggests that if you believe you can obtain investment returns greater than the interest rate you are paying on your mortgage, you shouldn't pay off the mortgage. In Monty's case, he has a 6 percent mortgage. If he believes his nest egg will earn 8 percent, logic suggests it would be advantageous for him to stay invested rather than paying off his mortgage. Let's do the math.

With a $100,000 mortgage balance, he will pay almost $6,000 in interest this year. If he keeps his $100,000 invested and it returns 8 percent this year, he will make $8,000 and pocket the $2,000 difference. If the growth of his investments continues at that rate for the remaining seven years of his mortgage, he will accumulate an additional $18,000 by not paying off the mortgage. That's $18,000 worth of profits he would have left on the table if he had taken a $100,000 withdrawal from his portfolio to pay off the mortgage.

Of course, the deal is sweetened if he can still itemize his mortgage interest when he files his taxes. Itemizing his mortgage interest will give him a $6,000 tax deduction, which will save him $1,800 in taxes. When the tax savings are added into the calculation, Monty's after-tax mortgage interest rate is only 4.2 percent.

Although there is no guarantee, it is reasonable to expect even a conservative investment portfolio will achieve a higher average rate of return than the interest rate most homeowners are paying on their mortgages. For example, since 1926 a moderate income and growth portfolio made up of 40 percent stocks, 50 percent bonds, and 10 percent cash has *averaged* 8 percent annually.[2]

Although you still must make a mortgage payment, choosing not to pay off your mortgage will likely put more money in your pocket, if you experience good long-term rates of return on your investment money. However, beware! During years when your investments don't perform as expected, you will actually be worse off by using

Fifty-nine percent of homeowners over age 65 own their homes free and clear.[3]

this strategy. For instance, if your portfolio loses 10 percent in a given year, then you're faced with a double whammy: investment losses and paying mortgage interest. If your investments experience a period of multiple years with losses, you could actually end up with negative compounding on your money. Ultimately, the investment markets will determine whether the *don't-pay-it-off* approach is effective.

## Peace of Mind
On the other hand, people who pay off their mortgage and rid themselves of the burden of a monthly mortgage payment can live on much less

income and are often better equipped to survive economic storms. This means peace of mind. In Monty's case, by paying off his $100,000 mortgage, he would eliminate his mortgage payments and reduce his annual expenditures by $18,000. Essentially, he would be guaranteed to make a 6 percent return by getting rid of the mortgage (not having to pay 6 percent interest on his mortgage is essentially the same as making 6 percent). A guaranteed 6 percent return sounds pretty good in periods when the stock and bond markets are declining in value.

In addition, Monty would own his home and save having to pay $26,000 of interest over the next seven years. No matter what the financial markets do during his retirement, he would have the security of knowing that his home is paid for and he has a place to live. If the economy encounters serious problems during his retirement, Monty can always tighten his belt and survive, a luxury he may not have if his investments are down and he must make a large mortgage payment each month.

Owning your home free and clear might boost your sense of security. To many, this financial security takes precedence over making a little extra return when comparing the two options.

## Where's Your Money Stashed?

Monty must consider the tax implications of withdrawing money from his various investment accounts before deciding to pay off his mortgage. If Monty has all of his money invested in tax-deferred retirement accounts, any money he withdraws will be taxed as income. Taking a large withdrawal will put him in a higher tax bracket. If he taps into a taxable account that has experienced a lot of growth, he'll have to pay capital gains taxes. Let's take a closer look at Monty's situation.

Monty is fortunate enough to have a taxable brokerage account with a $150,000 balance and an IRA with $250,000–giving him more than enough money to pay off his $100,000 mortgage balance. But which money should he use to pay it off? His decision will boil down to the tax consequences of each choice. Let's look at his IRA first, then his taxable brokerage account.

As you know, an IRA withdrawal will trigger state and federal income taxes and penalties for those not yet 59½. Monty will not face an early-withdrawal penalty, but any money he takes out of his IRA will be added to his taxable income for the year. A $100,000 withdrawal would propel him into the 25 percent federal tax bracket and a 5 percent state tax bracket. That's a 30 percent combined tax rate. To cover these taxes and still have enough money to pay off his $100,000 mortgage, he would need to take a $142,857 withdrawal from his IRA. And if that weren't bad enough, the IRA distribution would boost his income over the $44,000 threshold (for joint filers), causing 85 percent of his Social Security income to be taxed also. Does it make sense for Monty to deplete his IRA by more than 50 percent and pay all of this extra tax just to avoid $26,000 of mortgage interest? The answer is no. It's apparent that if he dipped into his retirement funds to pay off his mortgage, the effects on his retirement would prove devastating. He would likely run out of assets prematurely.

What about his taxable account? If Monty decides to use the money in his taxable brokerage account to pay off his mortgage, he would have to sell some investments first before taking the $100,000 withdrawal. He would need to be careful here. Selling investments that have appreciated a lot will trigger capital gains taxes. To combat the taxman, Monty should look to sell investments where the tax consequences would be the smallest. Monty was smart when he assembled his portfolio in his taxable account. He purchased tax-friendly investments, such as municipal-bond mutual funds and index mutual funds. Although many of his investments have increased in value, he could offset most of those gains by selling his losers. Monty found that he could take $100,000 out of his taxable portfolio and pay hardly any capital gains taxes.

## It's Time to Be Conservative

Monty has determined that he will need $36,000 each year during retirement after paying taxes and mortgage payments to meet his spending needs. His pension and Social Security will provide him with $28,500 of after-tax income. Without a mortgage, he will only need to withdraw $7,500 from his investment portfolio to meet his annual spending needs. On the other hand, with a mortgage he would have to pull out an extra $18,000 each year for the next seven years to make mortgage payments.

Monty needs to ask himself this question: "If the economy turns sour and my investments are losing money, do I want to be in a position where I have to sell investments at lows to meet my $1,500-a-month mortgage obligation?" His answer is no. Therefore, paying off the mortgage now will eliminate the monthly burden and not put him in a position where he is forced to sell investments when they are down in value.

"But wait a minute," you might say. "If Monty pays off his mortgage, isn't he giving up the last great tax break Uncle Sam offers?" Being able to deduct mortgage interest is often cited as a reason to keep paying on a mortgage. Of course this tax deduction will be lost when Monty pays off his mortgage. Is this a big deal? For many retirees, as in Monty's case, it's not. He does not have enough tax deductions to itemize and will instead claim the standard deduction when he files his taxes ($12,200 in 2013 for married filing jointly). Consequently, he wouldn't receive a tax deduction at all for the $6,000 of mortgage interest he would pay this year if he chooses not to pay off his mortgage.

At this stage in his life, Monty decides that peace of mind is more important to him than a little extra investment return. Plus, Monty has the resources in a taxable account that will allow him to pay off his mortgage with minimal tax consequences. Monty decides it's time to settle his mortgage debt. It's better to be safe than sorry.

## Other Ways to Get Rid of Your Mortgage

From Monty's example, we can see that there are advantages to using a taxable account to pay off a mortgage. There are major drawbacks to taking large distributions from a tax-deferred retirement account to do the job. However, what if that's all you own? What if, for peace of mind, you want to retire your mortgage but all of your savings are in retirement accounts? Is there a way to use your IRA or 401(k) without getting hammered by taxes? Absolutely. I have three solutions.

First, you don't have to pay off your mortgage all at once. Rather than pulling the entire amount out of your retirement account all at once, you could take out $10,000 or $20,000 chunks each year until you pay down your mortgage. This strategy shouldn't dramatically affect your income tax bracket or taxation of your Social Security. Still, be cautious so that you don't deplete your retirement savings too quickly.

Second, you could refinance your mortgage to a shorter term. This will, of course, increase your monthly payments, but it will also get you closer to being "free and clear" from debt and save you a lot of interest in the process. For example, a $100,000 thirty-year mortgage at 4.5 percent requires a monthly payment of $506. The interest alone over the thirty years would equal $82,407, making the total outlay for a $100,000 loan $182,407. In contrast, a shorter fifteen-year $100,000 mortgage at 4.5 percent requires a slightly higher $764 monthly payment, but the total interest paid over the life of the mortgage would equal only $37,699 for a total outlay of $137,699. The fifteen-year mortgage is $44,708 cheaper than the thirty-year.

Third, you could simply begin making half a payment every two weeks rather than a whole payment once per month. With this strategy, instead of making the standard twelve payments per year, you would make twenty-six half payments. This translates into making one extra monthly payment every year, which would also reduce your total interest. For example, a traditional thirty-year $100,000 mortgage at 4.5 percent requires a regular monthly payment of $506. Over the course of thirty years, the total interest paid would equal $82,407. By making just one extra monthly payment per year, the total interest would drop substantially to $69,058, and the home would be paid off four years earlier. For a fee, your mortgage company will set up a biweekly payment plan. You can obtain the same result for free by simply saving up an extra payment and sending it in each year.

## The Hard Realities

You, like many retirees, may have to face some hard realities. If your mortgage payment is too large and you are forced to withdraw too much from your portfolio to meet expenses, you may run the risk of running out of money prematurely during retirement. If, after completing a retirement analysis, you find this is the case, you need to seriously consider cutting your expenses. Often the easiest way is to downsize. Trading down to a smaller home or condo will not only lower your mortgage payments, but it will also lower many other costs associated with living in a larger home. It's never easy to move, especially from a home you planned to live in throughout retirement; however, moving is much better than running out of money before you run out of life.

> Eight out of ten baby boomers are planning to stay in their home during retirement.[4]

## A Last Resort: Reverse Mortgage

Most retirement projection calculators assume you will stay in your home throughout retirement and never use your home equity to supplement your living expenses. This, of course, is the ideal but is not always possible. If worse comes to worst, you can obtain a reverse mortgage and pull money out of your home to supplement your income. If your retirement projections show you running out of money prematurely, add in the equity in your home as an additional source of income during retirement.

Reverse mortgages allow homeowners age 62 and over to borrow money against the value of their home. As long as you don't move, the loan doesn't have to be repaid until after death.

With a reverse mortgage, you can take out a lump sum or choose to have fixed monthly payments sent to you for the rest of your life. The amount you can borrow depends on several factors, including your age, the value of your home, current interest rates, and where you live (Figure 24.1). The maximum loan amount is $625,500 (2013). To determine how much you can borrow and to examine your options, simply plug your home value into the reverse mortgage calculator at www.reversemortgage.org. For example, if you are age 85 and own a $250,000 home, you could pull out a lump sum of $131,585 or begin receiving monthly payments of $1,461 for life through a reverse mortgage.[5]

Reverse mortgages are fairly expensive. Origination fees and insurance premiums can run from $5,000 to $10,000. Paying these up-front costs doesn't make much sense if you plan to move during the next few years. Your home is likely one of your largest assets and can be your safety net if it looks like you are going to deplete your nest egg too soon.

Choosing to pay off your mortgage or to keep your money invested is a decision that should be incorporated into your planning as you assemble your retirement strategy. Once again, some professional advice and a retirement analysis are needed to truly examine the viability of each option. Plugging multiple scenarios into a retirement calculator (including both paying off your mortgage and continuing to make mortgage payments) will help you view the hard facts before making your decision.

| Reverse Mortgage Home Value $250,000 | | |
|---|---|---|
| Age | Lump Sum | Monthly Income |
| 65 | $110,085 | $824 |
| 70 | $115,085 | $906 |
| 75 | $120,085 | $1,023 |
| 80 | $125,335 | $1,185 |
| 85 | $131,585 | $1,461 |

figure 24.1

Remember, the goal at retirement is no longer to obtain off-the-chart returns; the goal is to meet your retirement objectives with as little risk as possible. Don't take more risk than is necessary and get caught shortchanging your retirement. It's time to be conservative.

# 25

# YOU CAN'T TAKE IT WITH YOU

RETIREMENT DECISION #20: WHAT STRATEGIES
SHOULD I USE TO ENSURE THAT MY ESTATE
PASSES TO MY HEIRS AND NOT TO UNCLE SAM?

Just two years after retirement, Wade and Cheryl McGrath were involved in a car accident and died. Their estate was valued at $1.3 million (Figure 25.1). They had intended to update their estate plan but never got around to it; going to see an attorney just seemed too costly and too painful for them. Besides, who wants to talk about death? As it turned out, their ten-year-old will was contested in probate court as their four children squabbled over the estate. The probate, which oversees the distribution of one's estate to heirs, resulted in a two-year delay and cost the estate 10 percent, or $130,000, in fees. An additional $210,000 was due for income taxes. The McGraths sure hadn't planned on such a mess. They hadn't planned, period.

Could these expenses and delays have been avoided? The answer is, unequivocally, "Yes!" In fact, there are many things they could have done without ever seeing an attorney, or in other words, free estate planning. They could have avoided probate by just implementing some simple strategies.

Don't follow the McGraths' lead and let your good intentions slip away. Retirement is a good time to update your estate plan; double-check the titling of your assets and the beneficiaries you've named. To help you

| McGraths' Estate | |
|---|---|
| IRA (Wade) | $600,000 |
| Home (Jointly Owned) | $400,000 |
| Brokerage Account (Jointly Owned) | $200,000 |
| Bank Account (Jointly Owned) | $100,000 |
| Total | $1,300,000 |

figure 25.1

with your planning, let's examine some of the strategies the McGraths could have adopted.

First, if you are married you should know that estate taxes are due upon the death of the second spouse, not the first. Probate, too, with a little planning, can also be avoided until the second death. Estate taxes, whether you are married or not, only apply to estates that are larger than $5,250,000 (2013).

There are many mechanisms for transferring your assets to your heirs. The question is which are the most efficient and cost-effective.

## Joint Tenants

Setting up accounts titled as "joint tenants with rights of survivorship" is the most common estate-planning strategy. Very simply put, if one joint owner dies, the assets pass to the other joint owner. There are no probate proceedings required. The McGraths did take this step. They had titled their $400,000 home, a $200,000 brokerage account, and a $100,000 bank account as "Wade and Cheryl McGrath, joint tenants with rights of survivorship" (JTWROS). Had Cheryl not died in the car accident, all of these assets would have transferred directly to her without going through probate. Joint tenancy alone works well as long as both joint tenants don't pass away at the same time.

## Wills

Many people have the misconception that by having a will their assets will somehow pass to their heirs without probate court proceedings. This is simply not true. In fact, it is kind of a funny notion. A will is largely nothing more than a list of instructions to a probate judge about how to divide up an estate among heirs. Passing assets through the use of a will actually guarantees probate. Probate costs will usually run between 5 and 10 percent of the value of an estate.

It is important to note that any assets with a beneficiary designated avoid these proceedings, and beneficiary designations trump wills. For example, if your will says, "My wife gets everything I own at my death," but your IRA or life insurance policy lists your ex-wife as the beneficiary, then guess who gets the money? You got it, your ex-wife. Remembering this little gem of knowledge about beneficiaries can save you and your heirs a lot of confusion, time, and money.

If you have a will, make sure it is up to date and is drafted properly. If it is more than a few years old or your life situation has changed, you should have it updated. If there are legal holes in your will, you are leaving it open to being contested. While I am sure you have perfect kids who would never fight over your money, it has been known to happen.

If you don't have a will, guess what? Your state, with the help of your state legislature, has been so kind as to draft one for you. So even if you've never written out your final wishes, the probate judge has a will to work with. It may just not be a will that is in line with your express desires. Most state wills pass assets to "next of kin." If you are in your retirement, the distribution of your assets would generally start with your children, then your parents, then your siblings, in that order. If your desires are the same as those outlined in the will the state has drawn up for you, you can save the money you set aside to pay an attorney to draft you a will. However, this is seldom the case.

The McGraths' will was outdated, having been drafted over ten years ago when they lived in another state. Their will referenced assets they no longer owned and made bequests the children felt didn't reflect their parents' intentions at their deaths. Consequently, the will was challenged; the children hired attorneys, and the battle over their parents' assets began.

## Pay-on-Death/Transfer-on-Death

In which type of accounts can you name beneficiaries? Many people believe this can only be done with retirement accounts like IRAs, 401(k)s, and life insurance; this is not the case. You can, and should, name beneficiaries for as many of your non-retirement accounts as you can. For instance, you can establish beneficiaries via Pay-on-Death (POD) instructions on all of your bank accounts. POD simply provides the bank with instructions regarding whom you would like to receive the bank assets when you die. Most people forget to do this, especially if the account is set up in joint name. It is true that a joint account doesn't need a beneficiary if only one of the joint owners passes away. The money will simply flow to the surviving account owner. However, the problem arises if both owners die at the same time or if the surviving owner forgets to add a beneficiary to the account then passes away. For example, the McGraths had $100,000 in a joint bank checking and savings account at their local bank. Had they spent an extra couple of minutes in the bank one day signing a POD form, this $100,000 could have passed directly to their four children in whatever proportions they decided upon, with no probate proceedings. Upon Wade and Cheryl's deaths, the bank would have read the POD instructions and paid the money directly to their children without argument.

The McGraths also had $200,000 invested in stocks and bonds in a joint brokerage account. Once again, had they filled out another simple, one-page form, this money could have also passed to their heirs without probate. You can name beneficiaries to your brokerage accounts by completing a form to provide Transfer-on-Death (TOD) instructions. Ask your brokerage firm or mutual fund company to provide you with a TOD form.

## Stretch IRA

At retirement, Wade had rolled his 401(k) money into an IRA. When he died, the account was worth $600,000. Unfortunately, Wade made a big mistake when setting up his IRA account. He listed Cheryl as the primary beneficiary but didn't name any secondary beneficiaries. Had Cheryl not died at the same time as Wade, she could have taken Wade's IRA money and transferred it into her IRA and avoided all taxes and penalties in the process. With no secondary beneficiaries listed, the IRA money was paid to the McGraths' estate and divided up via probate proceedings.

Remember, most IRA money has never been taxed. Uncle Sam allowed Wade to accumulate this money before taxes and didn't tax the investment earnings each year. As you can imagine, Uncle Sam is eager to tax this money. At death, the $600,000 IRA was assumed to be income paid to Wade in the year of his death. A $600,000 income put Wade in the highest federal income tax bracket and created a $185,000 income tax bill. If he had lived in a state with a state income tax, this would have been levied at the highest state tax rate, too. In addition, since this money went through probate, probate costs were also levied against this account. The huge tax bill and probate expenses could have been totally avoided.

Wade should have named his children as secondary beneficiaries on his IRA account. The children would then have had the option to stretch the taxes owed on this IRA over their lifetimes. This is how it works. Let's assume Wade's son Chris, age 35, was named as a 25 percent secondary beneficiary. At the death of his parents, Chris could take his 25 percent in one of two ways:

1.  Take the $150,000 in cash now or over the next five years, and pay the income taxes owed.
2.  Transfer the money into a beneficiary IRA (also called an inherited IRA) in his name. Moving the money to his own beneficiary IRA would allow the money to continue to grow on a tax-deferred basis and avoid having to pay a big income tax bill at his parents' final tax rates.

Even in this second option, Uncle Sam wants to get his hands on this money and will require that Chris begin taking withdrawals so the money can be taxed. But Uncle Sam will allow Chris to pay income taxes on this money over his life expectancy of another forty-eight years, according to IRS tables, rather than all at once. That means the income taxes will be imposed at Chris's tax rate of 15 percent, rather than his parents' final tax rate of 39.6 percent, and Chris will only have to pay a little in taxes each year. Because Chris is expected to live another forty-eight years, he will need to withdraw approximately 1/48th of the balance this year, 1/47th next year, 1/46th the next, and so on. This equates to only a little over 2 percent annually, or about $3,000, which will be added to his income and taxed. This would have been a nice gift for Wade to give his son; $150,000 growing tax-deferred until Chris's retirement could easily be worth more than $1 million when he reaches age 65, even after taking mandatory withdrawals each and every year.

So the big question is this: Would you like to give your children the option of transferring your IRA to an IRA in their name, pay income taxes at their tax brackets over their own lifetimes, and allow them to create their own retirement nest egg?

If Mr. McGrath had the chance to do it all over again, he would have made sure to list secondary beneficiaries to his IRA. You should do the same.

## Living Trusts and Portability

With the strategies we've discussed so far, the McGraths could have kept their bank account, brokerage account, and IRA account out of probate and had an ironclad will in place to distribute the only asset left, their $400,000

| 2013 Federal Estate Tax Rates | | | |
|---|---|---|---|
| Column A | Column B | Column C | Column D |
| Taxable amount over— | Taxable amount not over— | Tax on amount in Column A | Rate of tax on excess over amount in Column A |
| - 0 - | $10,000 | - - - - | 18% |
| $10,000 | $20,000 | $1,800 | 20% |
| $20,000 | $40,000 | $3,800 | 22% |
| $40,000 | $60,000 | $8,200 | 24% |
| $60,000 | $80,000 | $13,000 | 26% |
| $80,000 | $100,000 | $18,200 | 28% |
| $100,000 | $150,000 | $23,800 | 30% |
| $150,000 | $250,000 | $38,800 | 32% |
| $250,000 | $500,000 | $70,800 | 34% |
| $500,000 | - - - - | $155,800 | 40% |
| | | | |
| Applicable exclusion amount | | $5,250,000 | |
| Applicable Credit Amount | | $2,055,800 | |

figure 25.2

home. The probate for the home and some personal property alone would be fairly quick and easy and would require very little expense. Furthermore, the McGraths could have taken things even a step further by having their attorney set up a living trust.

Living trusts serve two purposes. First, they can keep your assets out of probate court, and second, they can reduce your estate-tax bill. What would have happened if, years earlier, Wade and Cheryl had drawn up The McGrath Family Living Trust, named themselves as trustees, and named their children as beneficiaries? They could have placed their home in the trust and as trustees would have continued to control the home and any other trust property just as they did as joint owners. In their case, a trust would have acted like a beneficiary designation for their home. Upon their death, the home would have been transferred to the beneficiaries named in the trust. This strategy would have allowed the home to change hands without probate.

You may be wondering why we haven't talked about the McGraths having to pay estate taxes. While $475,800 of estate taxes were levied against the McGraths' estate (see estate-tax rates in Figure 25.2), Uncle Sam has given everybody a tax credit to use toward paying these estate taxes. The tax credit, called the unified credit, which is a maximum of $2,055,800 (2013), covers all of the taxes owed on an estate valued up to $5.25 million (Figure 25.3). Because the McGraths' estate was valued at $1.3 million, their unified credit ($2,055,800) easily satisfied their entire estate tax bill ($475,800).

Let's assume the McGraths' estate was valued at $10.5 million instead of $1.3 million and Wade passed away one year before Cheryl. Upon Wade's passing, the entire estate would pass to Cheryl tax free via the unlimited marital deduction and no estate taxes would be due. Estate taxes are due upon the second death. At Cheryl's death, the size of McGrath estate would place it in the 40 percent estate tax bracket. They would owe $4,155,800 in estate taxes. The maximum tax rate was 40 percent in 2013 (Figure 25.2). However, they could apply *one* of their unified credits of $2,055,800 toward this tax bill. Their estate would be left owing $2,100,000 in estate taxes. This is where a living trust or portability provisions would come to the rescue.

| Estate Tax Credit and Exemption | | |
|---|---|---|
| Year | Unified Tax Credit | Exemption Equivalent |
| 2002 | $345,800 | $1,000,000 |
| 2003 | $345,800 | $1,000,000 |
| 2004 | $555,800 | $1,500,000 |
| 2005 | $555,800 | $1,500,000 |
| 2006 | $780,800 | $2,000,000 |
| 2007 | $780,800 | $2,000,000 |
| 2008 | $780,800 | $2,000,000 |
| 2009 | $1,455,800 | $3,500,000 |
| 2010 | No Estate Tax | No Estate Tax |
| 2011 | $1,730,800 | $1,000,000 |
| 2012 | $1,772,800 | $1,000,000 |
| 2013 | $2,055,800 | $5,250,000 |

figure 25.3

While everyone has a unified credit, not everyone can use their credit without doing some additional planning. One way to utilize both unified credits is through the use of a trust with a unified credit provision. With a trust, both Wade's and Cheryl's credits could be used. If they use both unified tax credits, totaling $4,111,600, they can protect $10.5 million from estate taxes. In this scenario, a trust could have saved their estate $2,100,000 in taxes. Not a bad savings, considering most trusts only cost $500 to $5,000 to create.

The other way to utilize both tax credits is to use the portability provisions in the estate tax law. Here is how it works. Upon Wade's death, Cheryl would need to file an estate tax return for him and select all the appropriate provisions. By filing the return, Wade's unified credit would have passed on to Cheryl. Like the trust, by utilizing both tax credits, $10,500,000 can be exempted from estate tax. The key here is that the estate tax return must be filed upon the death of the first spouse.

## Other Estate Planning Documents

While you're getting your estate plan updated, consider having the following documents created as well:

- Durable Health Care Power of Attorney: This document gives someone you designate the right to make health decisions on your behalf at the point you are no longer able to make them yourself.
- Durable Power of Attorney: This document gives someone else the legal right to manage your affairs in the event that you no longer can. Whomever you designate as power of attorney can sign on your behalf as if it were you signing.
- Living Will (also called a health-care directive): This document states your desire to be allowed to die if terminally ill and incapable to make such decisions on your own.

There are some additional strategies you may want to explore if you have an estate worth more than $10.5 million, such as family limited partnerships (FLP), family limited liability companies (LLC), irrevocable life insurance trusts (ILIT), and charitable trusts (CRT).

# Estate-Planning Costs

What will it cost to develop a sound estate-planning strategy? Figure 25.4 outlines the estimated costs of various estate-planning strategies.

Most attorneys will charge an hourly fee to prepare your estate-planning documents. This fee could range from $100 to $500 an hour. To keep your costs as low as possible, go to your attorney's office prepared. Compile a list of all of your assets, including who owns the asset, the value of the asset, beneficiaries named, and where it is held. Also, prepare a list of your family members and their dates of birth. Give some thought as to whom you want your assets transferred. If you do this beforehand, it will reduce the hours you'll be charged. If your attorney is doing your estate planning for a flat fee, obviously this isn't as crucial.

| Estate Planning Costs | |
|---|---|
| Joint Tenancy with Rights of Survivorship | $0 |
| Transfer on Death (TOD) | $0 |
| Pay on Death (POD) | $0 |
| Simple Will | $300–$1,000 |
| Living Trust | $500–$5,000 |

figure 25.4

Estate planning is one aspect of financial planning that most often gets pushed to the back burner. Because there are many steps you can take without the additional expense and time associated with seeing an attorney, there is no excuse not to get your strategy in motion. It literally only takes minutes and costs nothing to establish beneficiaries on your IRA, annuity, and life insurance and to establish POD and TOD instructions on your bank and brokerage accounts. There are plenty of people who have put off their estate planning for years and ultimately leave a mess for their heirs to clean up. Don't be one of them. You can't take it with you, but you can, with just a little planning, make sure your heirs, not Uncle Sam and the probate court, get your estate.

# A PARTING THOUGHT

The biggest reward you'll receive from addressing all twenty of the financial decisions addressed in this book isn't necessarily making more money, although the strategies we discussed will definitely help you improve your investment performance. The biggest reward for all your planning and effort is peace of mind. Once you've built and implemented a well-structured financial plan, you can relax. Routine checkups will keep you on track. In between checkups, go visit your kids and grandkids, travel the world, enjoy your hobbies and develop new ones, do some charity work, or do whatever it is that you've been waiting until now to do. Whatever you do, if you have a solid plan in place, you shouldn't have to worry about your money.

Retirement means every day is Saturday. It's time to enjoy life. Good luck! And remember, the best is yet to come.

# NOTES

## Chapter 1

1. Employee Benefit Research Institute, "The 2012 Retirement Confidence Survey," Issue Brief, no. 369 (2012): 6.
2. Ibid., 17.
3. MetLife Mature Market Institute, "MetLife Retirement Income IQ Study," (2011): 2.
4. "The 2012 Retirement Confidence Survey," 24.
5. U.S. Bureau of Labor Statistics, Consumer Expenditures in 2009, News, USDL-10-1390, October 2010.
6. "The 2012 Retirement Confidence Survey," 5.
7. AARP, "Aging, Migration, and Local Communities: The Views of 60+ Residents and Community Leaders–An Executive Summary," (2006): 2.
8. Sharon E. Epperson, "Death and the Maven," *Time*, 18 (1995): 61.
9. "The 2012 Retirement Confidence Survey," 26.
10. U.S. Department of Labor, Past Annual Inflation (CPI) Rates, "All Urban Consumers–(CPI-U) 1913–2012."
11. "Personal Savings Rate," U.S. Department of Commerce (August 2, 2013), http://research.stlouisfed.org/fred2/data/PSAVERT.txt.
12. "The 2012 Retirement Confidence Survey," 14.
13. Ibid., 19.

# Chapter 2

1. HSBC, "The Future of Retirement, The Power of Planning" (2011): 40.
2. Certified Financial Planning Board of Standards, Inc. & The Consumer Federation of America, "2012 Household Financial Planning Survey" (July 23, 2012): 3.
3. HSBC, "The Future of Retirement, The Power of Planning" (2011): 40.
4. Annamarie Lusardi and Olivia S. Mitchell, *Financial Literacy. Implications for Retirement Security and the Financial Marketplace*, Oxford University Press, (2011): 30.
5. Certified Financial Planning Board of Standards, Inc. & The Consumer Federation of America, "2012 Household Financial Planning Survey," (July 23, 2012): 29.
6. Certified Financial Planning Board of Standards, Inc., "2004 General Market Consumer Survey" (2004): 12.
7. Ibid.
8. Certified Financial Planning Board of Standards, Inc. & The Consumer Federation of America, "2012 Household Financial Planning Survey," (July 23, 2012): 6.

# Chapter 3

1. Financial Engines & AON Hewitt, "Help in Defined Contribution Plans: 2006 Through 2010," (September 2011): 3.
2. Ibid., 9.
3. HSBC, "The Future of Retirement, The Power of Planning" (2011): 40.
4. Susan Konig, "Can FA Training Programs Redeem Themselves?," Wealthmanagement.com (August 13, 2012).
5. LIMRA, "Agent Production and Retention," 2010.
6. Joseph Lisanti, "The Second (or Third) Time Around: How Financial Advisors Got to Where They Are from Other Fields," Financial -Planning.com (October 1, 2012).

7. Bureau of Labor Statistics, U.S. Department of Labor, Occupational Outlook Handbook, 2012–13 Edition.
8. NAPFA, "Pursuit of a Financial Advisor, Field Guide," (2011): 6.
9. Diana Briton, "IBD Broker Report Card 2012," *Registered Representative Magazine* (February 1, 2012).
10. *Senior Magazine*, "Finding a Financial Advisor" (April 2009). www.seniormag.com/legal/financial-advisor.htm
11. Ibid.
12. *The Intelligent Investor*, Fourth Revised Edition, Collins Business; Revised edition (July 8, 2003): 15.
13. DALBAR, "2012 QAIB, Quantitative Analysis of Investor Behavior Study," (April 2012): 9.
14. Ibid., 5.
15. Financial Engines & AON Hewitt, "Help in Defined Contribution Plans: 2006 Through 2010," (September 2011): 9.
16. Eric Garland, *Financial Planning* magazine (April 2004): 25.
17. Morningstar Principia. (September 30, 2012).
18. Morningstar Principia, September 30, 2012, Screen: All fifty-two distinct funds proprietary mutual funds managed by Morgan Stanley, above average performance versus asset category for the past one, three, five, and ten years, and manager tenure ten or more years.
19. Morningstar Principia, September 30, 2012, Screen: All 29,176 distinct mutual funds, above average performance versus asset category for the past one, three, five, and ten years, alpha greater than 1, and manager tenure ten or more years.

# Chapter 4

1. SSA, Relative Importance of Social Security for Beneficiary Aged Units, Table 9.A1, Percentage distribution of beneficiary units, by age, 2010.
2. Transamerica Center for Retirement Studies, "The New Retirement: Working," (May 2011): 16.
3. Philip L. Cooley, Ph.D.; Carl M. Hubbard, Ph.D.; and Daniel T. Walz, Ph.D., "Portfolio Success Rates: Where to Draw the Line," *Journal of Financial Planning*, FPAnet.org (January 2013).

4.    The Retire Early Home Page, "What's the 'Safe' Withdrawal Rate in Retirement?" www.retireearly.com (March 4, 1998).
5.    Harvard University Fact Book 2010–2011, 43.

## Chapter 5

1.    The Society of Actuaries, "2011 Risks and Process of Retirement Survey Report Findings," (March 2012): 51.
2.    IRC, Section 72(T).
3.    Ibid.
4.    Jim Blankenship, CFP®, EA, "Did you know you can access your 401(k) penalty-free at age 55?" Forbes.com (May 9, 2012).

## Chapter 6

1.    www.ssa.gov/policy/docs/chartbooks/income_aged/2010/iac10.html.
2.    U.S. Census Bureau, 2010 American Community Survey, "Population 65 Years and Over in the United States."

## Chapter 7

1.    Jerry Geisel, "Fewer Employers Offering Defined Benefit," Workforce.com (October 3, 2012).
2.    Josh Gotbaum, "Providing Service in Troubled Times," PBGC 2012 Annual Report, (November 14, 2012): 3.
3.    U.S. Social Security Administration, Office of Retirement and Disability Policy, "Income of the Aged Chartbook, 2010."
4.    Pension Benefit Guaranty Corporation, www.pbgc.gov (February 2013).
5.    This calculation assumes the portfolio is depleted in the thirtieth year.
6.    Morningstar Principia, December 31, 2012, Dodge & Cox Balanced Fund. Hypothetical illustration: $500,000 hypothetical investment made from January 1, 1983, to December 31, 2012. Assumes all

interest and dividends are reinvested and $25,000 withdrawn from the portfolio annually.

# Chapter 8

1.  Investment Company Institute, "Frequently Asked Questions," www .ici.org (September 30, 2012).
2.  EBRI, "Employment-Based Retirement Plan Participation: Geographic Differences and Trends, 2011," EBRI Issue Brief #378 (November 2012): 9.
3.  Charles Schwab, "Charles Schwab Finds Many Workers Who Have Left Their Jobs Have Also Left Their 401(k) Savings Behind," www .schwab.com (May 21, 2009).
4.  Ibid.
5.  Plan Sponsor Council of America (PSCA), "PSCA's Annual Survey Shows Company Contributions are Bouncing Back," www.psca.org (October 11, 2012).
6.  IRA Rollover Trends, Financial Research Corporation (2003).

# Chapter 9

1.  Jack VanDerhei, EBRI; Sarah Holden, ICI; Luis Alonso, EBRI; and Steven Bass, ICI, "401(k) Plan Asset Allocation, Account Balances, and Loan Activity in 2011," EBRI Issue Brief #380 (December 2012): 26.
2.  Ibid.
3.  IRC § 402 (e) (4) (A) and (B).
4.  IRC § 402 (e) (4) (D).

# Chapter 10

1.  U.S. Social Security Administration, Office of Retirement and Disability Policy, "Income of the Aged Chartbook, 2010," www.ssa .gov/policy/docs/chartbooks/income_aged/2010/iac10.html.

2.   DALBAR Inc., "2012 QAIB Quantitative Analysis of Investor Behavior," Advisor Edition (April 2012): 10.

3.   Brad M. Barber and Terrance Odean, "Trading is Hazardous to Your Wealth: The Common Stock Investment Performance of Individual Investors," *The Quarterly Journal of Economics* (April 2000): 792.

4.   Brad M. Barber and Terrance Odean, "Boys Will Be Boys," *The Quarterly Journal of Economics* (February 2001): 261.

5.   DALBAR Inc., "2012 QAIB Quantitative Analysis of Investor Behavior," Advisor Edition (April 2012): 5.

6.   Morningstar Principia (December 31, 2012). Stock mutual funds with 90 percent of their assets invested in the United States were split into five groups based on turnover rate. The average turnover rate for all of the funds was 77 percent. The low turnover group had turnover of 26 percent or less, while the high turnover group experienced performance of 106 percent or more. Index funds, enhanced index funds, and exchange traded funds were excluded. Only distinct funds were measured.

7.   Richard H. Thaler, "Boys Will Be Boys," *The Quarterly Journal of Economics* (May 1997): 133.

8.   Brian O'Reilly, "Why Johnny Can't Invest," *Fortune Magazine* (November 9, 1998): www.business2.0.com.

9.   Putnam Investments, "Don't Miss the Market's Best Days," *Investor Education* (Q4 2011): 2.

10.   Hulbert Interactive, Stock, Fund, and Newsletter Screener, www.marketwatch.com/hulbertinteractive/newsletter; all performance measured was as of December 31, 2012.

11.   Stan Luxenberg, "Beating the Bear," *Registered Rep Magazine* (April 2008).

12.   Morningstar Principia Pro (June 30, 2009).

13.   Morningstar Principia for mutual funds (December 31, 2002). The Nicholas-Applegate Global Tech I fund closed on February 14, 2003. Assets were merged into the Nicholas-Applegate Global Sel I fund.

14.   Ameritrade, www.youtube.com/watch?v=uK0ziaFHMFM.

15.   Jason Zweig, "Wall Street Lays Egg with Its Nest Eggs," *Wall Street Journal* (September 27, 2008): B1.

16.   Morningstar Principia (June 30, 2009), 151 technology funds measured.

17. Stocks: 40 percent large-cap, 16 percent mid-cap, 8 percent small-cap, and 16 percent international stocks with equal exposure to both growth and value in each market segment. Bonds: 8 percent long-term governments, 9 percent long-term corporate bonds, and 3 percent international bonds.
18. Michael Pretzer, "Men Behaving Badly," *Investment Advisor* (October 1999), www.djfpc.com.
19. LPL, "Market Insight Quarterly Chart Book," (Third Quarterly 2012): 42.
20. Morningstar Principia (December 31, 2012).
21. Sharon E. Epperson, "Death and the Maven," *Time* (December 18, 1995): 61.

# Chapter 12

1. Morningstar Mid Value TR Index.
2. Morningstar Small Value TR Index.
3. Citigroup Non-$ World Government Bond Index.
4. Morningstar Long-Term U.S. Government TR Index.
5. Ibid.
6. Citigroup Non-$ World Government Bond Index.
7. Morningstar Principia Pro for Mutual Funds (June 30, 2009).
8. Ibid.

# Chapter 13

1. Morningstar Principia (June 30, 2009).
2. Ibid.
3. Ibid.
4. Ibbotson SBBI, "Stocks, Bonds, Bills, and Inflation, 1926–2012," (December 31, 2012).
5. U.S. Census Bureau, Statistical Abstract of the United States: 2009, Banking, Finance, and Insurance, 734.
6. "The Facts on Savings and Investing," Securities and Exchange Commission, Office of Investor Education and Assistance (April 1999).

7.   Morningstar Principia (December 31, 2012).
8.   DJ Wilshire Large Company Growth Index.
9.   DJ Wilshire Large Company Value Index.
10.   DJ Wilshire Large Company Growth Index.
11.   World Bank, "Market capitalization of listed companies," http://data
.worldbank.org/indicator/CM.MKT.LCAP.CD/countries?display
=default, (2011).
12.   Vanguard S&P 500 Index Fund and the Vanguard Long-Term
Treasury Fund.
13.   S&P 500 and the Barclays Long-Term Government Bond Index.
14.   "The Facts on Savings and Investing."
15.   Money Markets are measured by the Lipper Money Market Index
until 2008, after which the average performance numbers of the
sixty-two taxable money market funds included in Morningstar
Principia were used.

# Chapter 14

1.   Indexes used to measure each portfolio's performance: DJ U.S. Large-
Cap Growth, DJ U.S. Large-Cap Value, DJ U.S. Mid-Cap Growth,
DJ U.S. Mid-Cap Value, DJ U.S. Small-Cap Growth, DJ U.S. Small-
Cap Value, MSCI EAFE, Barcap Long-Term U.S. Corporate, Barcap
Long-Term Government, Citigroup Non-$ World Government
Bond Index, 3-Month Treasury Bill.

# Chapter 15

1.   EBRI Special Report, "Company Stock in 401(k) Plans: Results of
a Survey of ISCEBS Members," Information compiled at year-end
2000, 2.
2.   Investment Company Act of 1940.
3.   Morningstar Principia (December 31, 2012).
4.   Ibid.
5.   EBRI Issue Brief, no. 380 (December 2012): 26.

# Chapter 16

1. Morningstar Principia (December 31, 2012).
2. Ibid.
3. Ibid.
4. Ibid., compared the ten-year returns of all large-cap U.S. growth, large-cap U.S. value, mid-cap U.S. growth, mid-cap U.S. value, small-cap U.S. growth, small-cap U.S. value, and large-cap international funds to their respective benchmark indexes. Two thousand three hundred and five out of 5,586 beat their benchmark indexes (41 percent) for the ten years ending December 31, 2012.
5. Morningstar Principia (December 31, 2012).
6. Investment Company Institute, "2012 Investment Company Factbook," (2012): 86.
7. Investment Company Institute, "2009 Investment Company Factbook," (2009): Section 6.
8. John Churchill, "Morphing SMAs," *Registered Rep Magazine* (October 2008).
9. www.lifehealthpro.com/2012/03/23/cerulli-report-managed-account-assets-hit-2428-bil
10. Number of separately managed accounts tracked in the Morningstar database, December 31, 2012.
11. Morningstar Principia (December 31, 2012).
12. Ibid.

# Chapter 17

1. As measured by the S&P 500. Morningstar Principia for mutual funds (December 31, 2012).
2. Performance of Vanguard Index Investor fund using month-end balances.
3. Scott Woolley, "Equity-Indexed Annuities: A Costly Way To Limit Your Losses," Forbes.com (June 5, 2009).
4. Lisa Gibbs, "Index annuities are a safety trap," *Money Magazine* (January 17, 2011).

5.   Jackson National Perspective Variable Annuity, American Funds Blue Chip Income and Growth A Sub-Account, Morningstar Principia, December 31, 2012.

# Chapter 18

1.   National Association of Securities Dealers (NASD), "NASD Launches Major Public Disclosure, Investor Education Initiative," Press Release (February 19, 1997).
2.   Class B share mutual funds usually convert to Class A shares in year seven or eight and qualify for a lower expense ratio at that time.
3.   Expense ratio of the average Class B domestic stock fund is 2.06 percent according to Morningstar Principia (December 31, 2012).
4.   Morningstar Principia (December 31, 2012).
5.   Expense ratio of the average no-load domestic stock fund according to Morningstar Principia (December 31, 2012).
6.   John Hancock Venture Variable annuity, annual insurance expense equals 1.40 percent, average annual fund management expenses equal 1.15 percent, Morningstar Principia (December 31, 2012).
7.   Vanguard Variable Annuity, annual insurance expense equals 0.30 percent, average annual fund management expenses equal 0.27 percent, Morningstar Principia (December 31, 2012).
8.   ING Reliastar Select* Life III VUL.
9.   ING Security Life of Denver, Strategic Investor VUL.
10.   www.ulivi.com.
11.   Low Load Insurance Services, Inc. News (November/December 2006): 2.
12.   "Who Needs Whole Life," *Consumer Reports*, Vol. 63, Issue 7 (July 1998): 42.

# Chapter 20

1.   Morningstar Principia for mutual funds (December 31, 2012).
2.   Ibid.

3.   Ibid.


# Chapter 21

1.   Felicia Vance, "The Most Expensive Medical Conditions," cncdws
     .com, (August 5, 2012).
2.   U.S. Dept. of Commerce, U.S. Census, "Income, Poverty, and Health
     Insurance Coverage in the United States: 2011," (September 2012): 73.
3.   Consumer Expenditure Survey, U.S. Bureau of Labor Statistics,
     Table 3. Age of reference person: Average annual expenditures and
     characteristics, (2011).
4.   Chuck Saletta, "How Obamacare Could Help You Retire Earlier (or
     Destroy Itself Trying)," DailyFinance.com, (June 29, 2012).
5.   U.S. Department of Commerce, U.S. Census, "Income, Poverty, and
     Health Insurance Coverage in the United States: 2011," (September
     2012): 73.
6.   Denise Trowbridge, "COBRA health insurance: Beware its bite!",
     Bankrate.com, (June 5, 2012).
7.   Oklahoma State and Education Employees Group Insurance Board,
     Monthly Premiums for COBRA Participants and Dependents, 2012.
8.   U.S. Department of Commerce, U.S. Census, "Income, Poverty, and Health
     Insurance Coverage in the United States: 2011," (September 2012): 73.
9.   How Much Does Medicare Advantage Cost?–eHealth Publishes
     Analysis of 2013 Medicare Advantage Plan Costs and Benefits,
     http://finance.yahoo.com/news/much-does-medicare-advantage
     -cost-190000029.html (October 15, 2012).
10.  Administration on Aging, "A Profile of Older Americans: 2011," www
     .aoa.gov/Aging_Statistics/Profile/2011/4.aspx (February 10, 2012).
11.  Jeffrey Young, "Uninsured Americans 2012: More Than 45 Million
     Lacked Health Insurance Last Year, CDC Reports," *Huffington Post*,
     (March 21, 2013).

# Chapter 22

1.  Money Tree Software, Silver Financial Planner 4.0 (2009): 40.
2.  Ibid.
3.  National Association of Insurance Commissioners (NAIC), "A Shopper's Guide to Long-Term-Care Insurance" (2006): 7.
4.  Harry R. Moody, *Aging: Concepts and Controversies*, Pine Forge Press; 5th edition (January 13, 2006): 333.
5.  Money Tree, 4.
6.  "A Shopper's Guide to Long-Term Care Insurance," 7.
7.  MetLife, "The MetLife Market Survey of Nursing Homes and Assisted Living Costs," (2008): 5.
8.  MetLife, "Market Survey of Long-Term Care Costs," (November 2012): 4.
9.  National Center for Health Statistics.
10. MetLife, "Market Survey of Long-Term Care Costs," (November 2012): 4.
11. U.S. Bureau of Labor Statistics, "U.S. Inflation Rate for Nursing Homes and Adult Day Services," (December 13, 2012).
12. Money Tree, Silver Financial Planner 4.0 (2013).
13. *Aging: Concepts and Controversies*, 333.
14. U.S. Senate Special Session on Aging Hearing (June 3, 2009): 10.
15. U.S. Department of Health and Human Services, National Clearing House for Long-Term Care Information, "National Spending on Long-Term Care," www.longtermcare.gov (2009).
16. "The MetLife Market Survey of Nursing Homes and Assisted Living Costs," 5.
17. Money Tree, Silver Financial Planner 4.0 (2013).
18. MetLife, "The MetLife Market Survey of Adult Day Care and Home Care Costs, 2007" (2007): 4.
19. U.S. Bureau of Labor Statistics, "U.S. Inflation Rate for Nursing Homes and Adult Day Services," (December 13, 2012).
20. www.ltcq.net premium price quote; quotes from The State Life Insurance Co., Metropolitan Life Insurance Co., Prudential Insurance Co. of America (May 26, 2004).

# Chapter 24

1.  Consumer Expenditure Survey, U.S. Bureau of Labor Statistics, (March 2013): Table 1300.
2.  The compounded rate of return from 1926 to 2012 for a 40 percent stock (large-cap stocks), 50 percent bond (long-term government bonds), and 10 percent cash portfolio (Treasury bills) was 7.72 percent.
3.  Consumer Expenditure Survey, U.S. Bureau of Labor Statistics, (March 2013): Table 1300.
4.  MetLife, "Transitioning into Retirement," (April 2012): 4.
5.  www.reversemortgage.org.

# ABOUT THE AUTHOR

R ay E. LeVitre is a fee-only CERTIFIED FINANCIAL PLANNER™ who specializes in helping people develop and manage their financial plans at and through retirement. Ray has seen all sides of the financial services industry. Early in his career he spent time at Fidelity Investments, Citicorp, and Mutual of New York and later went on to build a career at Merrill Lynch working as a financial consultant and branch manager. Ray now runs an independent fee-only financial planning practice he founded in 2003. He has been retained by many Fortune 500 companies to teach financial management seminars to their employees and has been quoted by *Newsweek*, *Business Week*, *Money Magazine*, *Kiplinger's*, *New Yorker*, and many newspapers and financial industry magazines. He has also appeared as a guest on TV programs on CBS, NBC, and Fox.

Ray can be contacted to answer questions or arrange speaking engagements.

Net Worth Advisory Group (Fee-Only)
9980 South 300 West, Suite 110
Sandy, Utah 84070
801-56MONEY (801-566-6639)
ray@networthadvice.com
www.networthadvice.com